xMas '91

To Ben & Claire

love from

Lin and Patrick

X

CHILDREN'S ILLUSTRATED ENCYCLOPEDIA

BRIAN WILLIAMS

Editor Rachel Pilcher
Designer Ralph Pitchford
Picture Research Elaine Willis

Published in 1990 by
Grisewood & Dempsey Ltd
Elsley House
24–30 Great Titchfield Street
London W1P 7AD

Printed in Italy

ISBN 0-906279-82-8

CHILDREN'S ILLUSTRATED ENCYCLOPEDIA

BRIAN WILLIAMS

WHSMITH
EXCLUSIVE
· BOOKS ·

CONTENTS

THE UNIVERSE

THE STARS

The Universe is teeming with stars. There are too many to count. Stars generate their own heat and light. How were they made? How do stars change? (See page 8.)

THE SOLAR SYSTEM

The Solar System is the Sun's family of planets. Nine planets orbit our Sun. What are these worlds like? What are comets and asteroids? (See page 10.)

THE MOON

The Moon is the Earth's only natural satellite. Why is the Moon so different to Earth? The Moon is a dead world. (See page 14.)

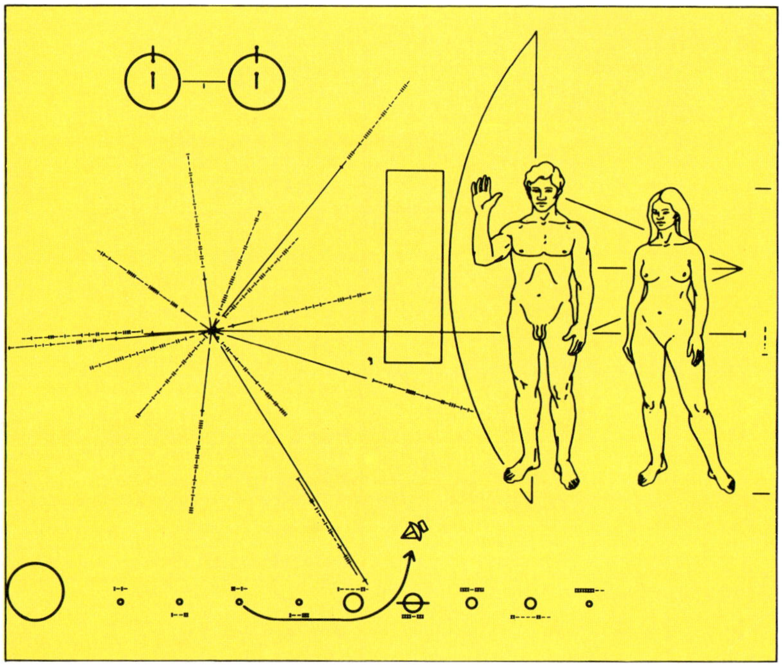

SPACE TRAVEL

Before the invention of space rockets, people could not explore beyond the Earth. Now probes are sent out of the Solar System. (See page 16.)

ASTRONOMERS

Early astronomers made discoveries without telescopes. Today, scientists explore the limits of the Universe. (See page 20.)

THE GALAXIES

Right: From the Earth astronomers have seen millions and millions of galaxies. Within these galaxies are old stars and young stars being born within nebulae. Light from these far-distant stars began its journey through space long before the first human beings walked on the Earth. Galaxies more than a few hundred million light-years away appear as faint smudges in the night sky. Even through big telescopes they appear only as tiny specks.

Many scientists think the Universe began about 17,000 million years ago with an incredible explosion. They call this the Big Bang (*top*). The force of the explosion sent matter hurtling through space. The galaxies developed and the first stars were born inside them. The galaxies are still spreading farther and farther apart. This is how the Universe looks today (*right*). Millions of star clusters are moving away from one another at incredible speeds.

The Stars

The Universe began about 17,000 million years ago. The first stars were born inside galaxies after 500 million years. Our Sun is a medium-sized star, born out of a gas cloud over 4600 million years ago. There are many millions of stars, made mainly of hydrogen and helium gas.

The colour of a star is linked to its surface temperature. A blue-white star may be shining at about 20,000 degrees, or three times as hot as our yellowish-white Sun. A reddish star may be only half as hot as the Sun.

Some stars are far larger than the Sun, others are much smaller. Some spin on their axes in just a few hours. Some have other companion stars nearby, and they orbit around each other as twins. Some are still very young and belong to a cluster of other young stars born at the same time. Some stars are dying away gently at the end of their long life, while others are pulled apart in a massive explosion.

Above: All the stars visible in the sky were born, like the Sun, out of clouds of gas and dust. But some are much hotter, and others are cooler, than our Sun. The Sun is an average star.

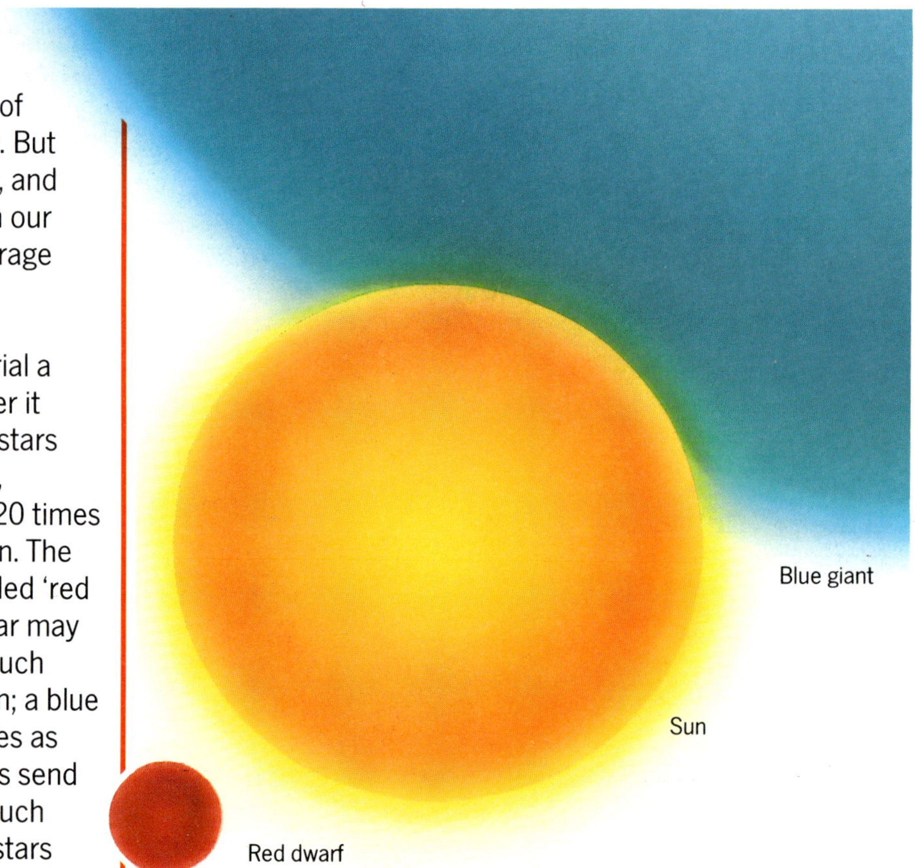

Right: The more material a star contains, the hotter it becomes. The hottest stars are called 'blue giants', because they may be 20 times the diameter of the Sun. The small dim ones are called 'red dwarfs'. A red dwarf star may have only a tenth as much material in it as the Sun; a blue giant may have 20 times as much. Some giant stars send out 50,000 times as much light as the Sun. Such stars are incredibly huge 'nuclear furnaces'.

Left: Nebulae are enormous clouds of hydrogen and tiny solid particles of dust. Some of these clouds are dark while others are bright. A single nebula can be a thousand light-years across – big enough to hold a million million Solar Systems.

This photograph of the Horsehead Nebula in Orion shows just a small part of the famous Orion Nebula. This is a fairly small nebula, only 15 light-years across. Because it is near to Earth, it can be seen with the naked eye.

The bright part is shining because of newborn stars in the centre of the nebula.

One of the stars nearest to our Sun is called Sirius. It is 82 million million kilometres away, or half a million times the distance from the Earth to the Sun. Astronomers measure the huge distances between stars in light-years. A ray of light travels at a speed of 300,000 kilometres in one second, or 9.5 million million kilometres in one year. Sirius is about 8.7 light-years away. The light that we are now seeing from Sirius left the star 8.7 years ago and has taken all that time to travel through space as far as the Earth. Sirius is the brightest star in the sky.

Below: How our Milky Way Galaxy would appear to an approaching spacecraft. Edge-on, the Galaxy looks like a flat disc with a swollen middle – the nucleus. From above, it looks like a whirlpool of stars. The position of our Solar System is marked in both views by the red arrow.

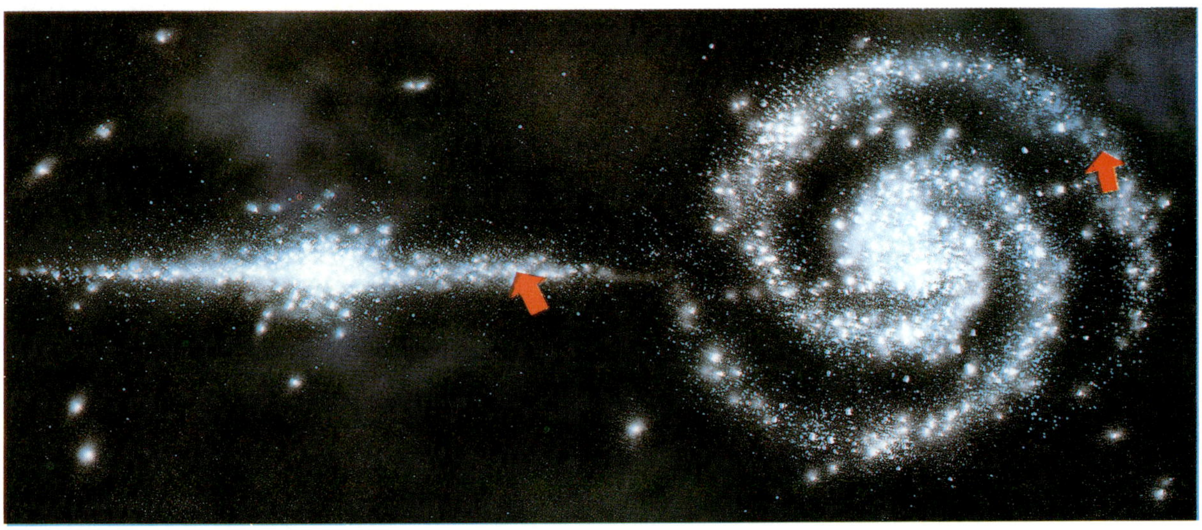

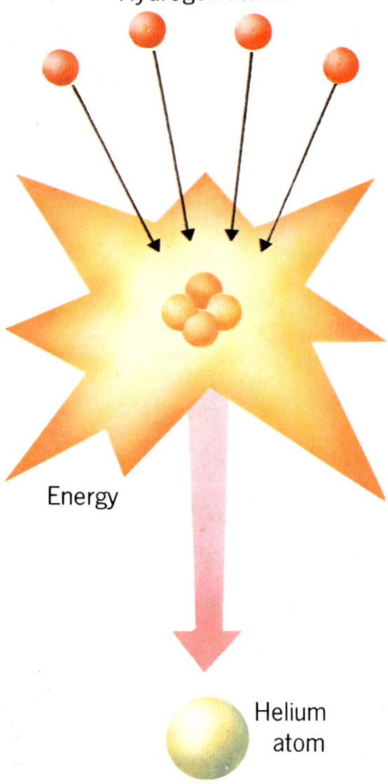

Above: The Sun shines brightly because it is very hot – about 6000 degrees. Every second, the Sun turns about four million tonnes of hydrogen into helium, releasing enormous energy.

Key: 1 Mercury **2** Venus **3** Earth **4** Mars **5** Jupiter **6** Saturn **7** Uranus **8** Neptune **9** Pluto

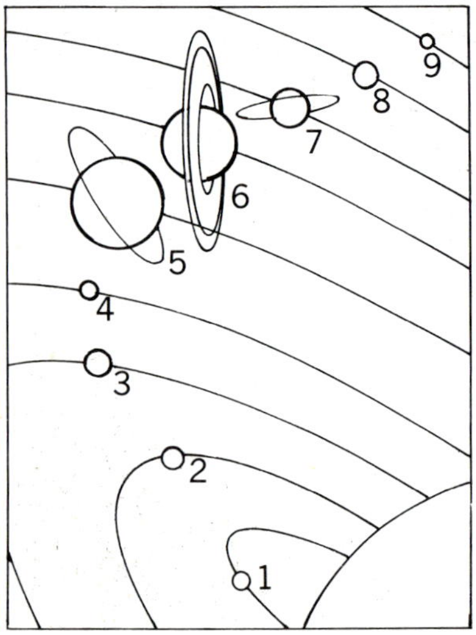

Solar System

After our Sun was formed, leftover material around it formed a ring whirling at high speed. This ring formed a system of nine planets, which we call the Solar System.

The four planets nearest the Sun are much smaller than the four outer giant planets. They are made up differently, being rocky globes instead of masses of liquid gas and ice. The giant planets spin faster than the inner planets. This has made them bulge out at the equator. Another feature of the giant planets is the rings circling them. Beyond the giant planets lies the smallest and most distant planet, Pluto.

There is a very large 'gap' between the orbits of Mars and Jupiter, as though there should be another planet there. In place of the 'missing planet' are 30,000 or so minor planets or asteroids.

PLANET PROFILE
The planets (see key) are pictured, *right*, in order of their orbits around the Sun.

1 Mercury
58 million km from Sun
Diameter: 4878 km
Moons: None
Length of year: 88 Earth days

2 Venus
108 million km from Sun
Diameter: 12,104 km
Moons: None
Length of year: 225 Earth days

3 Earth
150 million km from Sun
Diameter: 12,756 km
Moons: 1
Length of year: 365$^1/_4$ days

4 Mars
228 million km from the Sun
Diameter: 6790 km
Moons: 2
Length of year: 687 Earth days

5 Jupiter
778 million km from Sun
Diameter: 142,700 km
Moons: 16
Length of year: 11.9 Earth years

6 Saturn
1427 million km from Sun
Diameter: 120,000 km
Moons: 24
Length of year: 29.5 Earth years

7 Uranus
Distance from Sun: 2870 million km
Diameter: 50,000 km
Moons: 15
Length of year: 84 Earth years

8 Neptune
Distance from Sun: 4497 million km
Diameter: 50,000 km
Moons: 8
Length of year: 165 Earth years

9 Pluto
Distance from Sun: 5900 million km
Diameter: 3000 km
Moons: 1 known
Length of year: 248 Earth years

Left: This cutaway shows what the inside of the Earth is thought to be like.

At the centre is a very hot inner core of solid iron and other materials, with a molten metal layer surrounding it. Around the core is the hot rocky mantle. On top of the mantle is a surface skin, known as the crust.

THE EARTH
Age: About 4600 million years
Area: Land 148,800,00 sq. km (= 29 per cent)
Water 361,300,000 sq. km (= 71 per cent)
Weight: About 600 million million million tonnes
Volume: 1,084,000 million cubic km
Average land height: 840 metres above sea level
Average ocean depth: 3795 metres below sea level
Crust thickness: 40 km beneath mountains, 6 km beneath oceans
Mantle: About 2900 km thick, made of partly melted rocks
Outer core: about 2400 km thick, made of hot, melted metals
Inner core: about 2500 km across, thought to be made of iron and nickel at a pressure of 3800 tonnes per sq. cm

The Earth, our own planet, is special in many ways. It is rocky, but it also has plenty of water; it has clouds, but it also has clear sky. All the other planets of the Solar System are either rock or ice, cloudy or airless. The Earth is in a delicate balance, and this balance has allowed life to develop here in many forms.

The Earth turned out like this because it happens to be the right distance away from the Sun. Without the Sun, the Earth's surface would be dark and frozen. The Sun's light and warmth help plants and animals grow. Just a little bit closer, and the Earth would have turned into a choking, scorching Venus; a little bit farther away, and it would have been a barren, frozen Mars.

The inside of the Earth seems to be special, too. A hard surface crust, up to 40 kilometres thick, 'floats' on hot molten rock beneath. Earthquakes and volcanic eruptions prove that there is plenty of heat and activity below the surface. The other inner planets seem to be much 'quieter' in comparison. The Earth also has a stronger magnetic field than the other rocky planets.

Most importantly, Earth (alone of all the planets) teems with life. If you tested a spoonful of almost any part of our planet – air, water, earth, or rock – with a microscope, it would show you tiny living organisms by the million. No other planet in the Solar System supports such life.

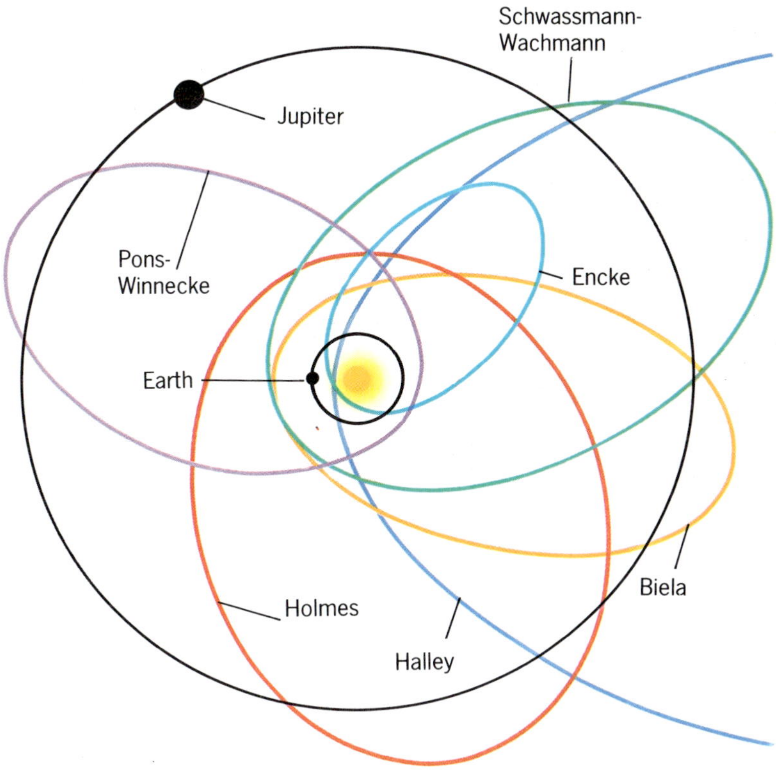

Unusual space objects include comets, meteors and asteroids. A comet orbits the Sun, its glowing tail streaming for tens of thousands of kilometres behind its small solid nucleus. Meteors or 'shooting stars' burn up as they hit the Earth's atmosphere. They are very small. Asteroids are mini-planets. Most are less than 95 km in diameter. Ceres, the largest, is 687 km across.

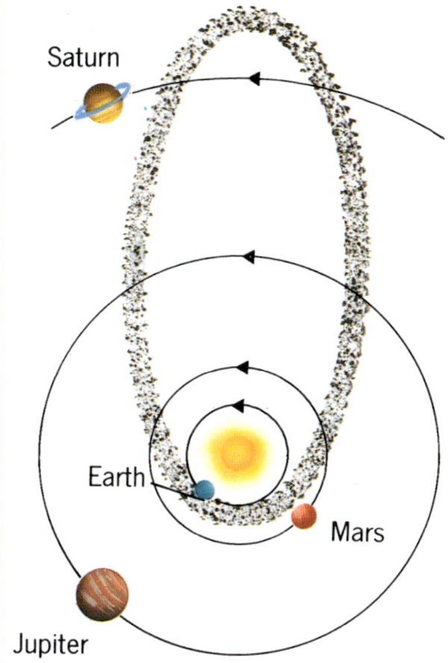

Above: Meteor 'showers' may occur when the Earth passes through the orbit of a swarm of tiny meteoroid particles.

Above left: Comets travel around the Sun. Halley's Comet returns close to the Earth every 76 years.

Below: A large meteorite crater on Earth.

Right: The Earth's gravity keeps the Moon in orbit.

Below: The Moon's gravity causes the tides in the ocean **(1)**. The Sun also raises tides **(2)**. At New Moon and Full Moon, both Sun and Moon pull together on the oceans and we get high spring tides **(3)**. When the Sun and Moon are at right angles, at First Quarter and Last Quarter, we get weak neap tides **(4)**.

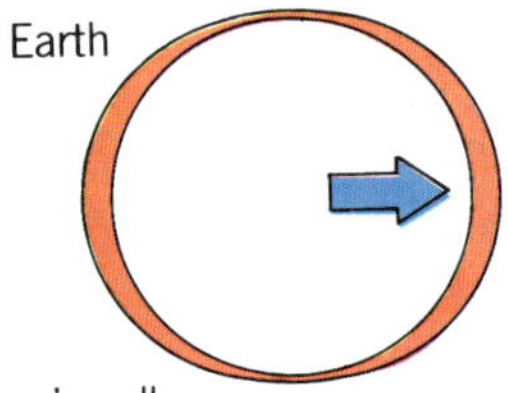

1 Moon's pull

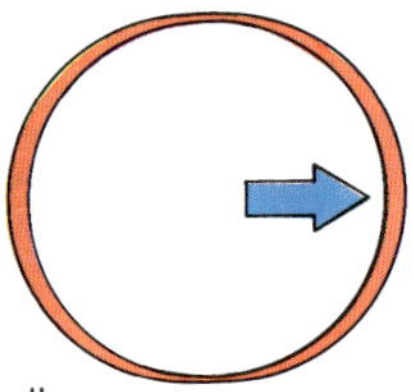

2 Sun's pull

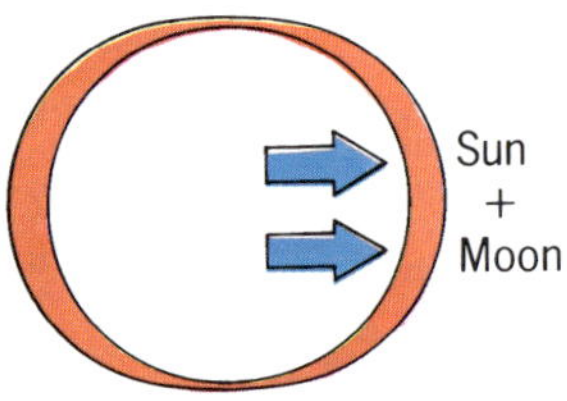

3 Spring tide

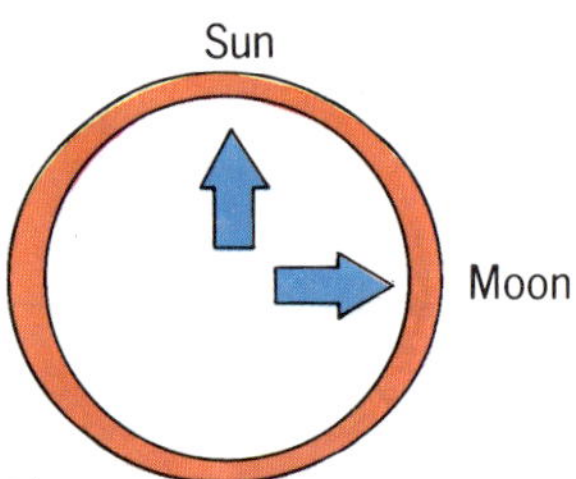

4 Neap tide

The Moon

The cratered Moon is a dead world. The Moon is only a quarter of the Earth's diameter, and its gravity is only one-sixth as strong. As it formed, its crust set solid much more quickly than the Earth's, since a small body cools faster than a large one. The gases in its atmosphere were too light for its weak gravity to hold down, and they floated off into space. So there is no air on the Moon.

Many of the craters on the Moon were made by collisions with stray pieces of rock. Some of these craters are

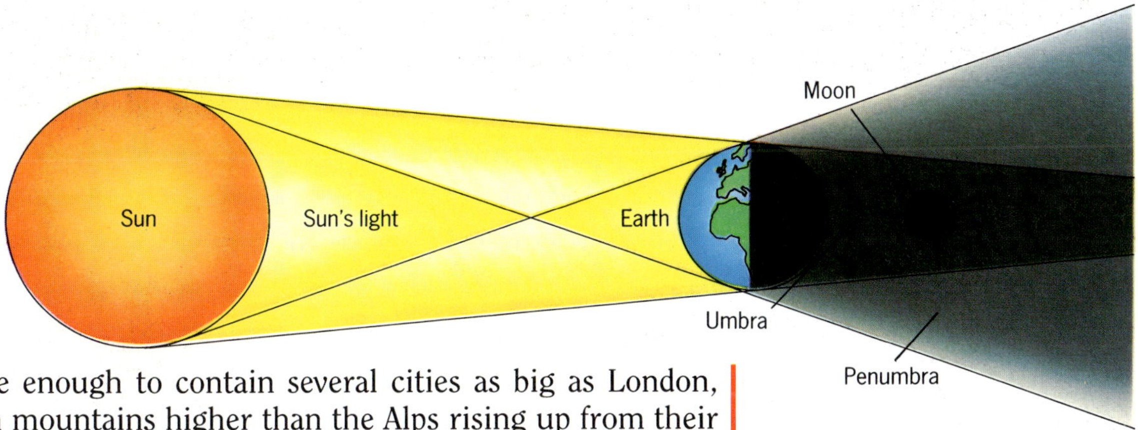

large enough to contain several cities as big as London, with mountains higher than the Alps rising up from their floors. Astronomers have made maps of the Moon's surface, giving names to most of the larger craters and to the smooth, dark patches on the Moon known as 'seas' (although there is no water on the Moon).

Rock samples collected from the Moon by the Apollo astronauts were found to be 4000 million years old. This proves that most of the Moon's surface has not changed much since that time.

Above: This diagram shows how the Moon is eclipsed, or darkened, through the Earth's long central shadow or umbra. If it passes through the outer shadow or penumbra, the effect on the Moon is not likely to be noticed.

PHASES OF THE MOON

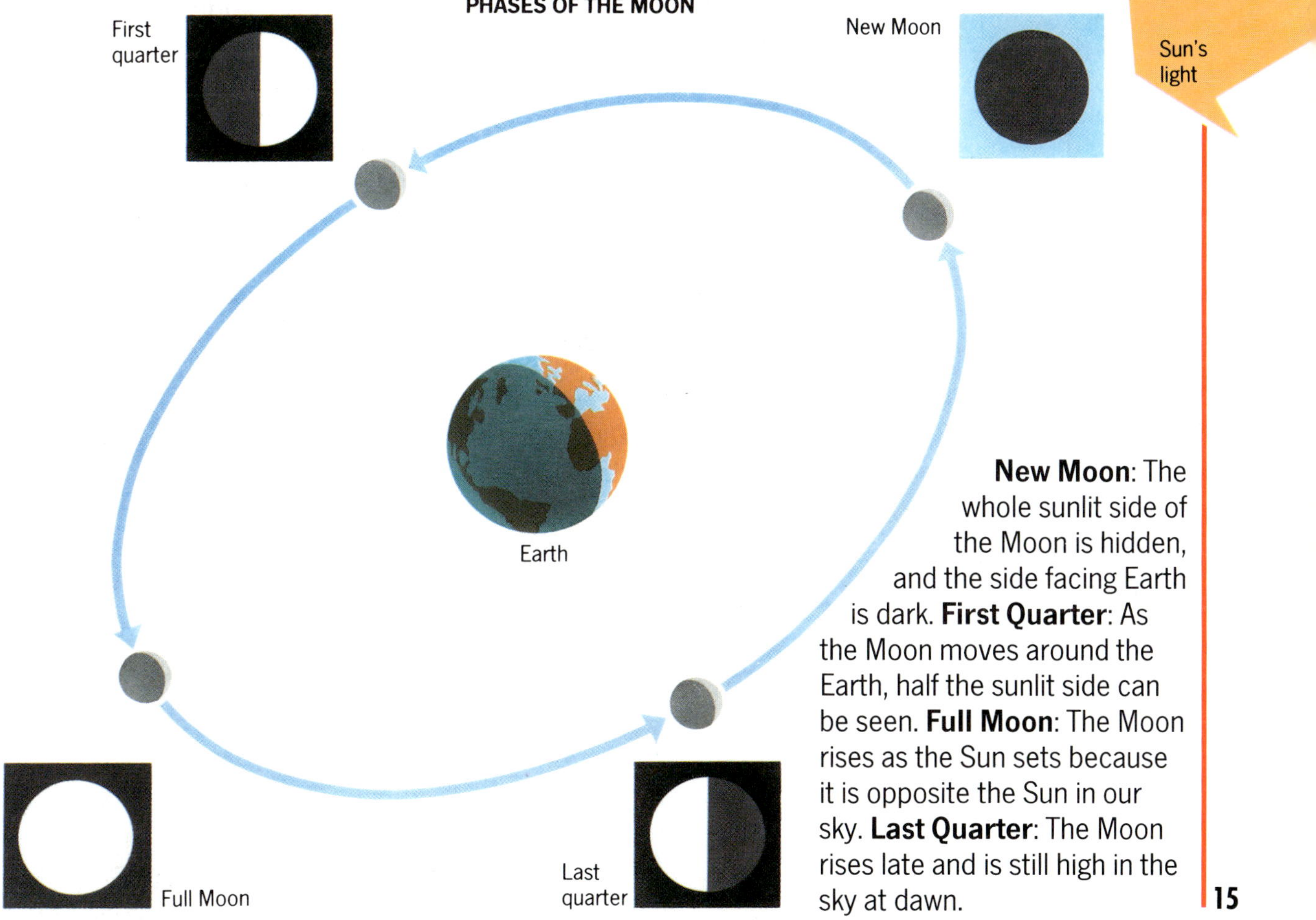

New Moon: The whole sunlit side of the Moon is hidden, and the side facing Earth is dark. **First Quarter**: As the Moon moves around the Earth, half the sunlit side can be seen. **Full Moon**: The Moon rises as the Sun sets because it is opposite the Sun in our sky. **Last Quarter**: The Moon rises late and is still high in the sky at dawn.

Above: The Landing Module from Apollo 11 (called Eagle) begins its descent to the lunar surface. In the distance, the Earth shines blue and white in the black sky.

Above: The Apollo Moon flights began with the launch of a huge Saturn 5 rocket.

Space Travel

Space travel has been a fantastic dream for so long that the world was taken completely by surprise when the USSR launched the first artificial satellite, Sputnik 1, on 4 October 1957. Two years later, a Soviet rocket hit the Moon, and in 1961 a Russian became the first person in space. At the same time, the United States announced its plans to send astronauts to the Moon, and this feat was achieved in 1969.

Between 1969 and the end of 1972, the Americans sent seven Apollo spacecraft to the Moon. One, Apollo 13, had a malfunction on the way out and had to loop round the Moon and return to Earth. The other six each landed two astronauts safely on the Moon.

The Apollo spacecraft was built in two parts – the Command Module and the Landing Module. The Command Module stayed in orbit around the Moon, two of its three crew members flying down to the Moon in the Landing Module. After returning to orbit again, the Landing module was left behind. Only a part of the Command

Module, just large enough for the three astronauts, returned to Earth, floating down into the Atlantic Ocean supported by three parachutes.

The astronauts making the first three Apollo landings had to explore the Moon on foot. The last three spacecraft carried a Lunar Rover, a battery-powered car. Their most important task was to collect samples of rock and dust to bring back to Earth.

Nowadays, space travel is taken so much for granted that successful satellite or space-probe launches do not attract much attention. It took the explosion of the Space Shuttle *Challenger* in January 1986 to remind the public that risks are still involved, and that to be an astronaut a man or woman must be brave as well as fit.

Above: Sputnik 1, the world's first artificial satellite.

Above left: Exploring the Moon. An Apollo 17 astronaut and his Lunar Rover.

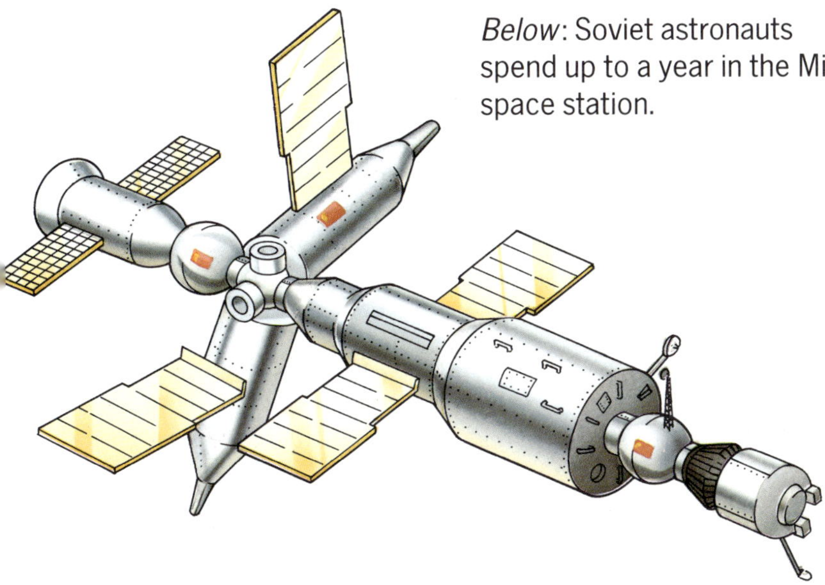

Below: Soviet astronauts spend up to a year in the Mir space station.

SPACE FIRSTS

1957	First artificial satellite, Sputnik 1 (USSR)
1959	Soviet Luna 2 craft crash-lands on Moon
1961	Yuri Gagarin (USSR) is world's first astronaut
1962	First communications satellite (USA)
1965	First space 'walk' or EVA by Aleksei Leonov (USSR)
1968	Apollo 8 astronauts (USA) fly round Moon
1969	First Moon landing by Apollo 11 astronauts Neil Armstrong and Edwin Aldrin
1971	First space station, Salyut 1 (USSR)
1976	First landing on Mars, by unmanned Viking craft (USA)
1981	First space shuttle (USA)
1983	Pioneer (USA) is first craft to leave the solar system
1989	First close look at Neptune, by Voyager 2 (USA)

Are there other planets like the Earth? We may never know for certain, because even the nearest star is so far away that our biggest telescopes would have no hope of showing us a planet like the Earth, or even a giant planet like Jupiter, at such a distance.

In 1974, Mariner 10 flew near Mercury for the first close-up look. The Viking Spacecraft took their life-hunting experiments to Mars in 1976, where they made chemical tests on the Martian soil to see if the results were

Above: The Voyager 2 probe, launched in 1977, has sent back amazing close-up shots of the planets Jupiter, Saturn, Uranus and Neptune.

Right and below: Two Viking probes visited Mars in 1976. Each one sent down a lander to the 'Red Planet'. The lander's robot arm took samples of Martian soil to test for life-forms, but found none.

Above: Travel to distant galaxies at near light-speed remains a futuristic dream. This is how twin galaxies, eight and a half million light-years away, might look from such a spacecraft.

the same as the ones obtained using soil from the Earth, which contains living things. They were not, but this could just mean that living forms on Mars are completely different from ours.

Whether or not there is life elsewhere in the Solar System, few people deny that intelligent life may well exist elsewhere in the Universe. But can we ever hope to communicate with it? So far, no one has picked up radio signals from intelligent beings in space. However, the space probes Pioneer 10 and Voyager 1 and 2 are carrying messages into space – just in case they are ever found by an unknown, far-distant civilization.

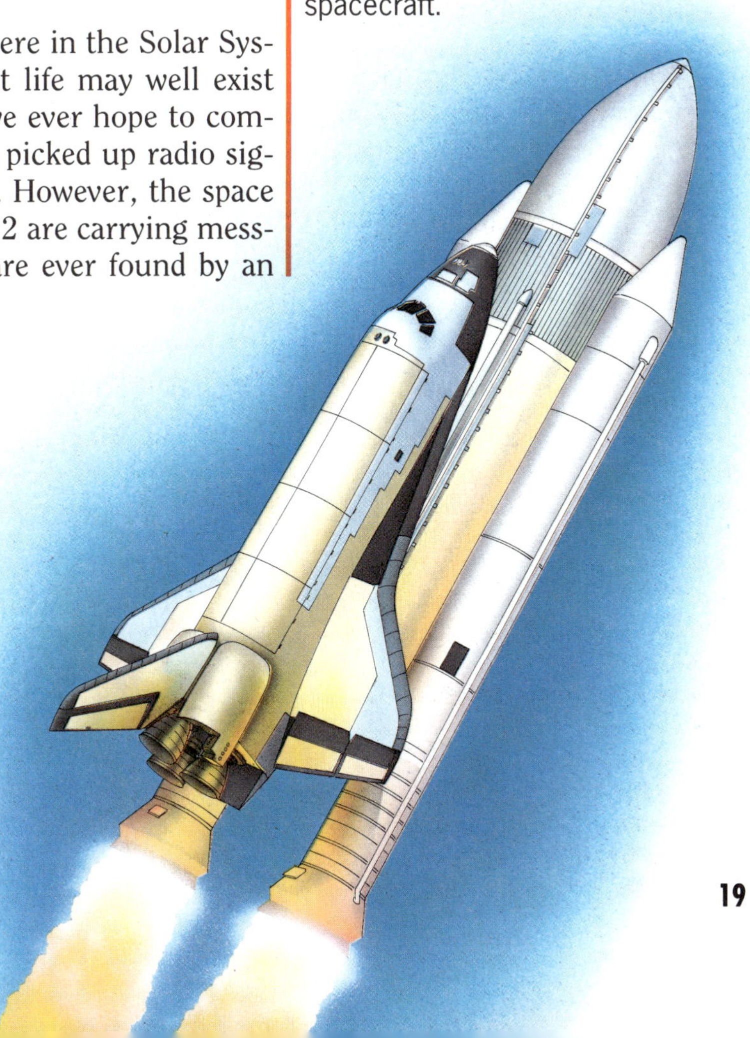

Right: The American Space Shuttle was first launched in 1981. It was the world's first reusable space launch system. The winged Shuttle is boosted into orbit by rockets which fall away when their fuel is used up. After its mission in Earth's orbit, the Shuttle glides back to land like an aeroplane. The Shuttle *Challenger*, with seven astronauts on board, blew up in 1986. A redesigned Shuttle returned to space in 1988. The Russians also have a Shuttle.

Astronomers

Above: Astronomers of the ancient world drew star maps.

Below: How Ptolemy and Copernicus saw the Universe.

In ancient times, anyone looking up at the sky probably thought that the Sun, the Moon, and the stars were controlled by the gods. The first people who thought they might be able to find out anything else about these heavenly bodies were the Ancient Greeks. The most famous Greek astronomer was Ptolemy. Like most people in those days, he thought the Earth was the centre of the Universe, with the Sun, Moon, planets and stars all circling around it in their different paths or orbits.

No one found a better method of calculating the way the planets move until 1543. This was when the Polish astronomer Nicolas Copernicus published a book showing that the puzzling movements of the planets could be more easily explained if they moved in circles around the Sun, not the Earth.

The telescope allowed astronomers to uncover far more of the secrets of the Universe. The radio telescope, invented in the 1930s, can detect far distant galaxies that

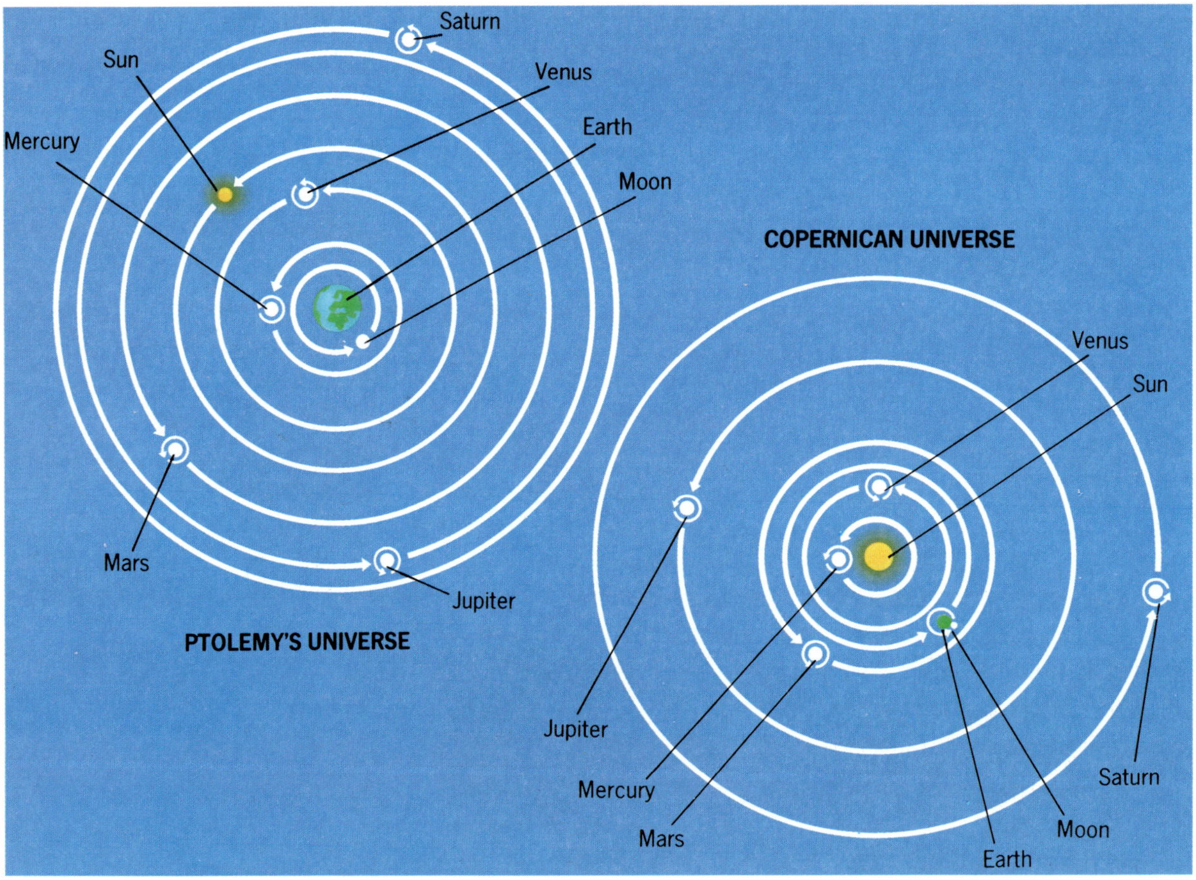

send out strong radio waves, even though they are too far away to be seen properly. The 'mirror' used in a radio telescope is usually a dish of metal or wire mesh. Some radio telescopes are nothing more than a collection of wire aerials spread over a field. The signals they receive from space are analyzed by computers.

Above: The telescope was invented in 1608. The Italian scientist Galileo built this telescope and in 1610 he discovered four of Jupiter's moons.

Above left: William Herschel (born 1738) built the largest telescope of his day.

Above: The 2.5-m reflecting telescope on Mount Wilson in California, USA.

Left: The 100-m dish of the Effelsberg radio telescope in West Germany.

THE LIVING WORLD

PLANTS
Plants include the largest living things on the Earth. Algae, mosses and trees are all plants. (See page 24.)

ANIMALS
There are over two million animal species on Earth. Each one is a miracle of evolution. (See page 32.)

INSECTS
Of all forms of life, the most varied and numerous are insects. Species are found each year. (See page 36.)

MOLLUSCS
Molluscs are soft-bodied invertebrates. They include snails, octopuses and oysters. (See page 40.)

FISH
There are about 13,000 species of fish. Fishes are the largest group of back-boned animals or vertebrates. (See page 41.)

AMPHIBIANS AND REPTILES
Once reptiles ruled the Earth. Today there are 5000 species of reptile, and 3000 species of amphibian. (See page 44.)

BIRDS
There are nearly 11,000 species of bird and almost all can fly. Birds are descended from reptiles. (See page 46.)

MAMMALS
Mammals are the most advanced animals. All mammals are warm-blooded creatures. (See page 50.)

PREHISTORIC LIFE
Animal life began in the sea. Millions of years ago reptiles and amphibians lived on land before mammals had developed. (See page 54.)

FIRST HUMANS
Human beings evolved from primitive ape-like creatures. We belong to the species *Homo sapiens* or 'wise man'. (See page 58.)

Animals and plants live together in communities. Each species has its own food, and way of life. Some are hunters, others are hunted. Each exists within a balanced ecological system that has taken millions of years to evolve. Nature's systems are delicate, and can easily be upset by human interference. Animals, like those shown here, may become endangered. Some have died out, or become extinct.

California condor

SPECIES IN DANGER

Mississippi alligator

Pampas deer

Monk seal

Humans are mostly responsible for the dying out of species. Hunting, whether for food or sport, has taken its toll on animals such as the dodo, the moa and the American bison. Others have suffered through the destruction of their habitats for farming or timber.

Bare-headed rock fowl

Thylacine

Monkey-eating eagle

Pygmy hog

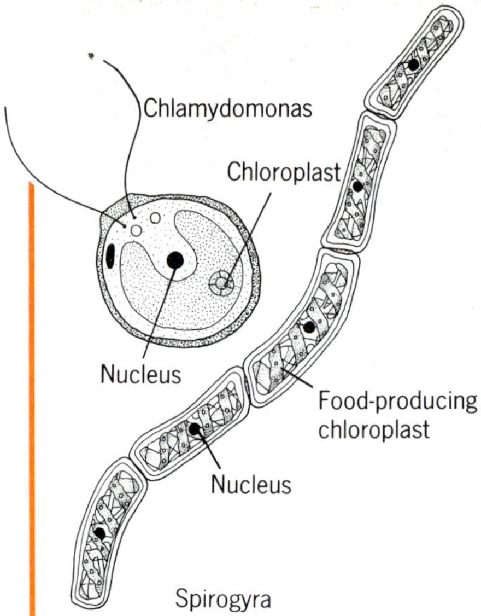

Above: Algae (plural of alga) are the simplest of all plants on Earth. They have no roots, no flowers or seeds. They reproduce by dividing, or by producing separate male and female cells which join to make a new plant.

Plants

More than 375,000 different plant species have so far been studied and officially named by scientists. But these are just the ones we know about. In the world's unexplored jungles and remote mountain regions there could be almost as many again – still waiting to be discovered, studied and named.

Plants are without any doubt the great record-breakers of the natural world. Firstly, they are by far the largest living things the world has ever seen. Many specimens of Douglas fir and giant redwood in the west coast mountain forests of the United States tower more than 100 metres into the sky, and the heaviest specimen of all has been estimated to weigh more than 6000 tonnes – 32 times as heavy as the biggest blue whale ever recorded.

Secondly, plants are the longest-living things on Earth. Some of the lichens found in Antarctica are more than 10,000 years old. They started growing when the people of northern Europe were primitive hunters, dressed in ani-

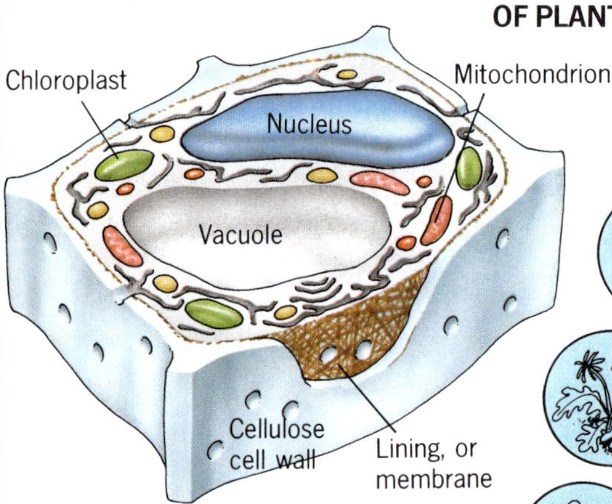

Above: A typical plant cell. Inside the cell is a weak solution of salts and sugars. The nucleus is the cell's control centre, the chloroplasts manufacture sugars and starches, and the mitochondria are chemical powerhouses that enable the plant to use its stored food.

THE CLASSIFICATION OF PLANTS

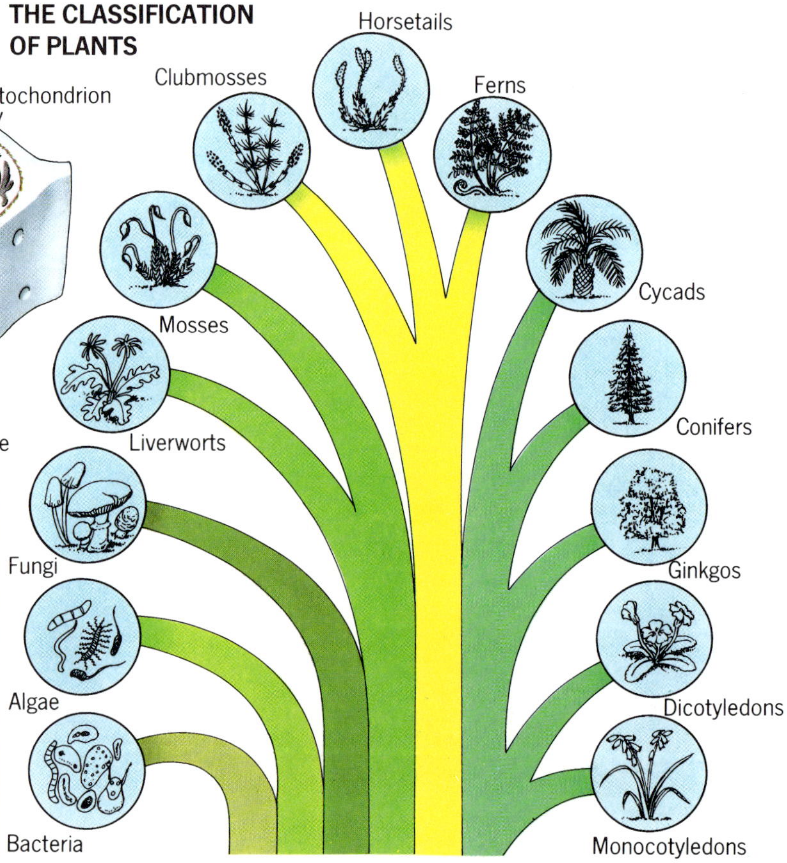

mal skins and armed with spears and bows. One of the gnarled and twisted bristlecone pines in the desert of Arizona, U.S.A., has been dated at 4600 years old, a mere youngster by comparison with Antarctica's lichens, yet it sprouted from seed at about the time the Great Pyramid of

Above: The sundew is a plant that feeds on insects. Flies are trapped by the sticky stalks and are digested.

Below: Plants have colonized sea and land. Seaweeds belong to the alga family. Some cling to rocks, others grow in deep water but rely on sunlight reaching them.

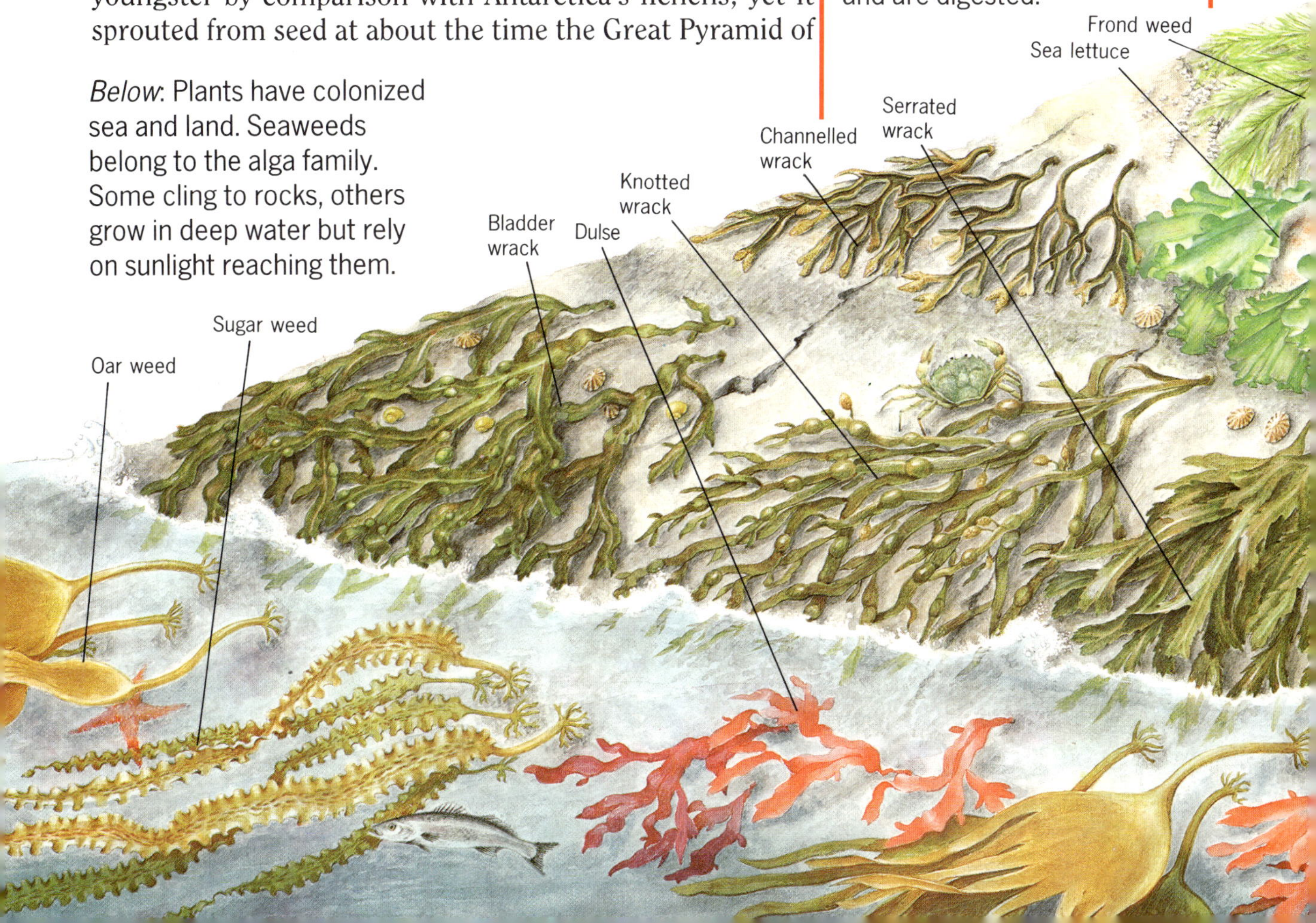

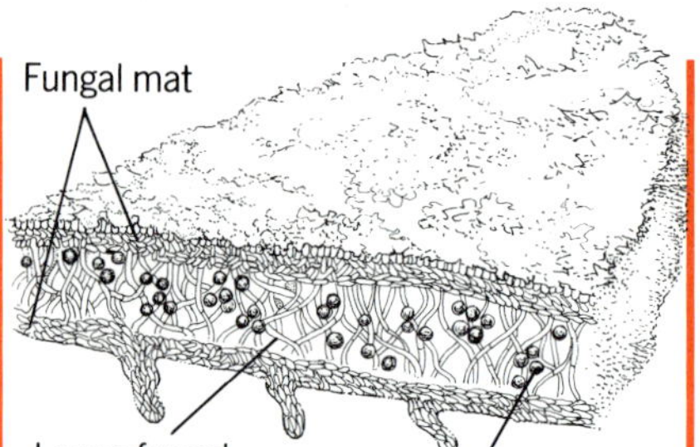

Above: A cross-section through a crusty lichen. The fungal mat is made of tightly packed cells. Inside, the lichen consists of much looser threads, and large, green, algal food cells.

Below: Mushrooms and toadstools are fungi. They come in a variety of shapes and sizes. Some are good to eat; others are deadly! Penicillin used in combatting disease is a fungus, as is yeast. In contrast some species harm plants and animals.

King Cheops was built in Ancient Egypt in about 2600 BC.

Mosses were amongst the earliest land plants. They thrive in damp conditions because they need moisture to reproduce. They have no roots, but have special cells that hold water like a sponge. Larger land plants need a proper stem to support them and to hold their leaves up to the light so that photosynthesis (making food using sunlight) can take place efficiently. They also need roots – to anchor them in the ground and to collect water and minerals from the soil – and special liquid-carrying cells.

The ferns are by far the most successful surviving members of the ancient plant families. There are now over 7000 species. Some are small water plants. Others, such as bracken, grow in woodlands and on hillsides. Largest of all are the tropical tree-ferns, some of which grow up to 25 metres tall. Ferns reproduce by spores which are released from spore-cases under the leaf fronds.

The fungi (plural of fungus) do not really qualify to be called plants at all. They contain none of the green chemical chlorophyll and therefore cannot make their own food. Instead, they produce chemicals called enzymes which break down cellulose – and this enables the fungi to feed on the cells and cell contents of other plants and animals or on decaying matter such as rotting leaves or wood. There are over 50,000 types of fungi. Moulds and mildews are examples of simple fungi. They have no specific shape but grow over and through their 'host' or food source. Larger fungi grow into a toadstool to reproduce.

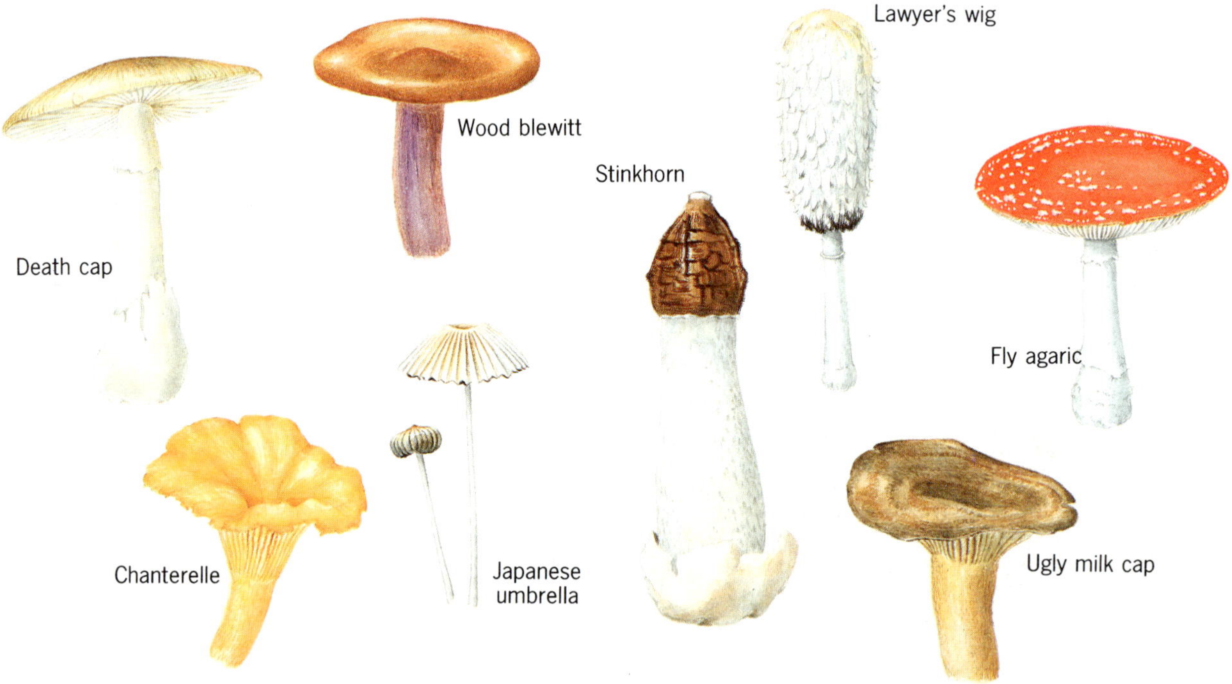

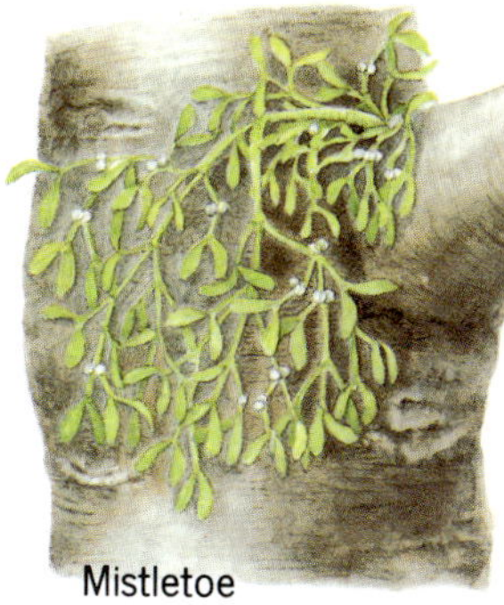

Fungi (*far left*) cannot make their own food, so they take it from other plants. Mistletoe (*left*) is a partial parasite. It feeds on the host tree, but also makes its own food.

trees of forests, woods and orchards. It includes peas and beans, potatoes and cabbages, climbing vines, and spices and herbs. And last but not least it includes the hundreds of plants we value for their beauty alone – such as roses, daffodils, orchids and lilies.

The bright colours, conspicuous shapes and sweet scents of many flowers are designed to make the flowers attractive to insects, birds and other small animals. As it forces its head inside the flower to get at the sweet nectar inside (the nectar is always right at the bottom, of course) the animal food-collector is forced to push past the pollen-coated anthers. The result is that its hairs, fur or feathers soon become dusted with the yellow grains. When the animal visits another flower, some of this pollen is carried with it to fertilize other flowers. In this way, many flowering plants reproduce.

There are two main sub-groups of the flowering plants – the monocotyledons and the dicotyledons. Cotyledons are the very first leaves to appear when a seed germinates – that is, when it splits open and starts to grow. In the monocotyledons there is just one of these seed-leaves. The dicotyledons have two seed-leaves.

Right: Tendrils and hooks may attach some plants to others.

Left: Tropical epiphytes live high in trees, absorbing moisture through aerial roots.

Animals

More than two million different animal species are known to science, but they are very unevenly spread amongst the main animal groups. There are about 4000 species in the human family, the mammals, compared with about 11,000 different bird species and 13,000 different kinds of fish. These animal groups contain some of the most complex and highly specialized creatures on Earth, but in sheer numbers they cannot compete with the flies and beetles, butterflies and bugs of the most successful animal group of all. With over one million species studied so far, the insects easily outnumber all other animal and plant species added together! The simplest animals are microscopic dots of floating jelly-like material.

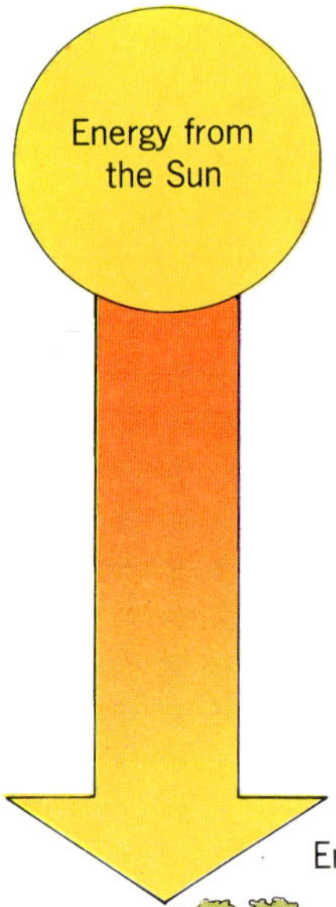

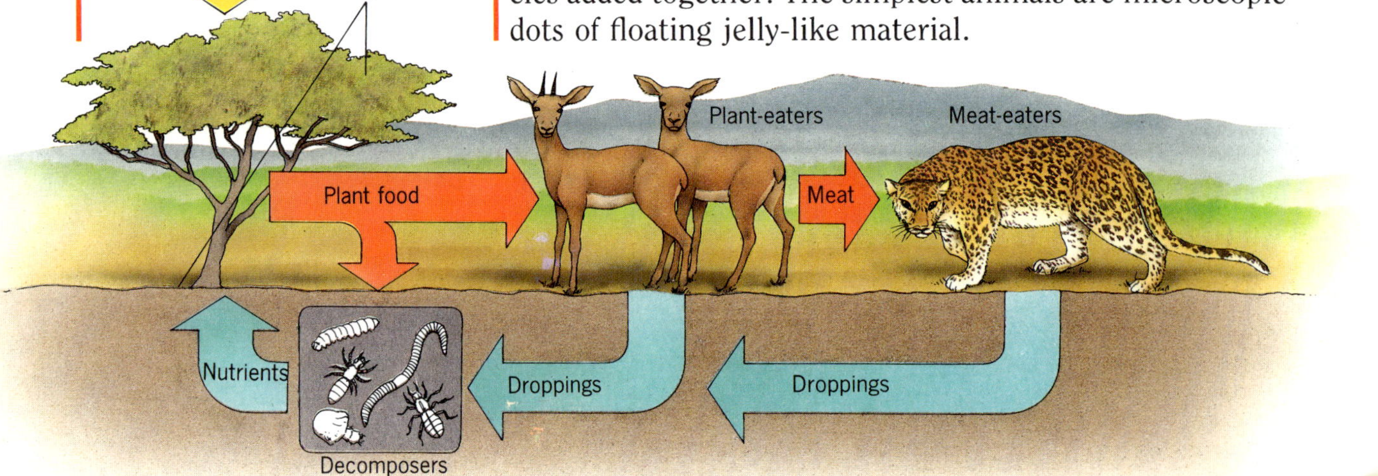

Above: All living things are part of the Earth's energy cycle. Green plants are the energy 'fixers'. They store the Sun's energy in the form of food, which is used by animals.

Dead leaves are recycled straight away to make nutrients by millions of decomposers in the soil. Living vegetation is eaten by herbivores (plant-eaters). Carnivores (meat-eaters) feed on the plant-eaters. Nothing is wasted. Even the body of the meat-eater is recycled when it dies.

Right: The main group in the animal kingdom. Mammals, birds and reptiles are the most advanced animals.

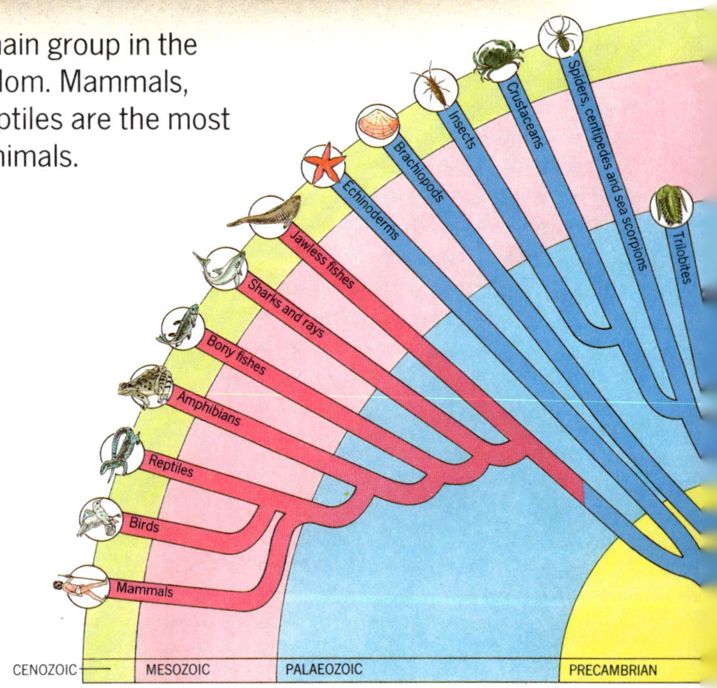

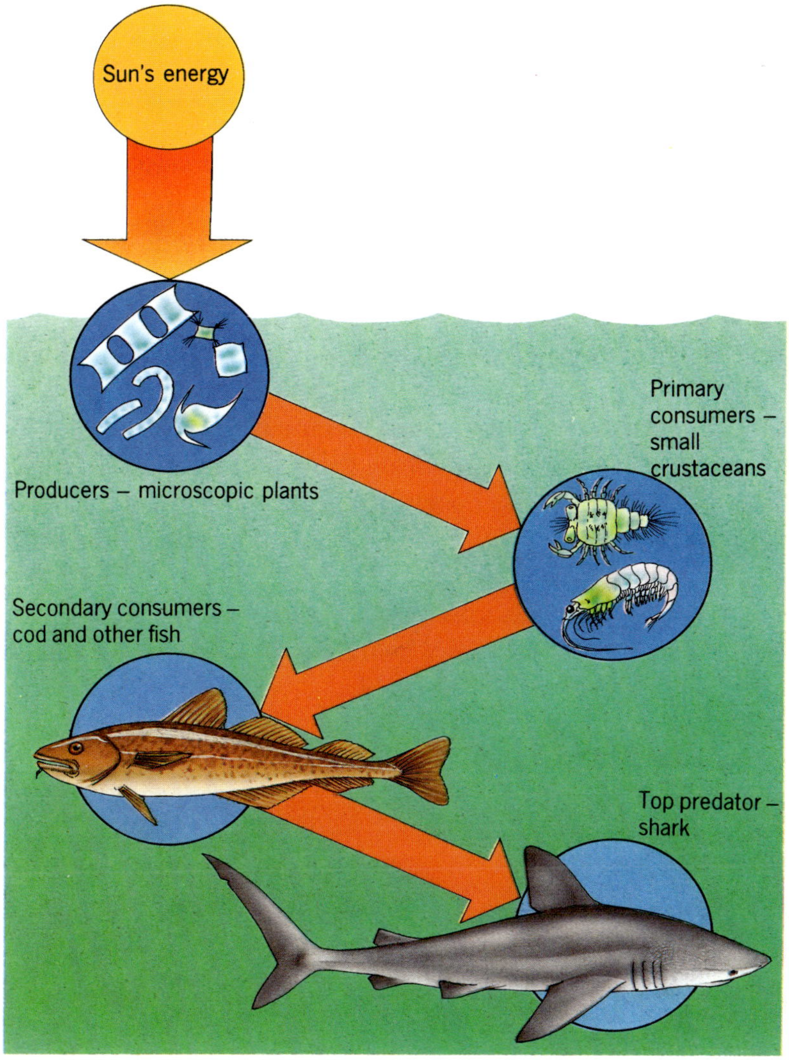

Left: An underwater *food chain*. This is a way of describing how animals and plants depend on one another. The Sun's energy is 'fixed' or captured by tiny floating plants in the oceans. They are eaten by small sea animals. This is the first link in the food chain. The plants are the producers. The small sea animals are primary consumers. Next comes a secondary consumer, a large fish like cod which feeds on the smaller animals. It in turn is prey for the hunter at the end of the chain, in this case a shark. The shark is a top predator. However, even the top predator could be caught by a fisherman. Since most animals eat many different foods they play a part in many different food chains. These chains are linked to form a 'food web'.

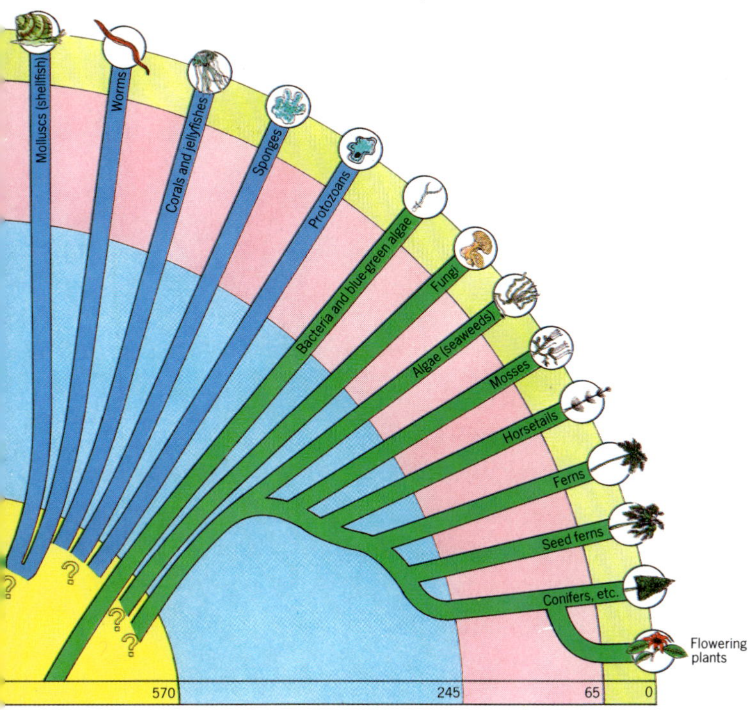

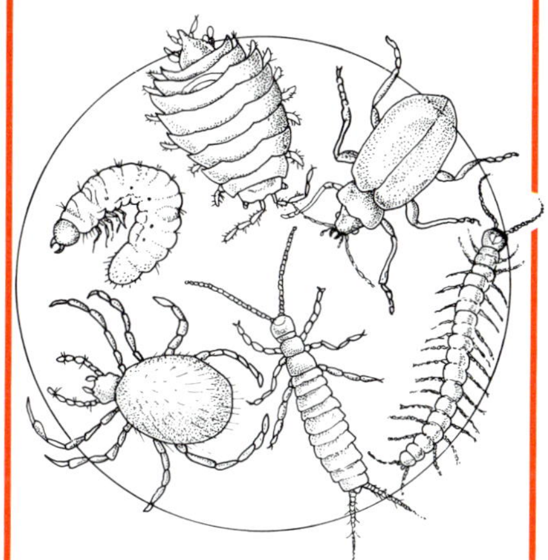

Above: Without the 'decomposers' the Earth would soon be covered in a thick layer of dead plants and animals. Decomposers include insects, fungi and bacteria.

The marsupials have been on the Earth for over 100 million years. As the Earth's ancient land-masses broke up, Australia became isolated, along with its native marsupials such as the koala and the kangaroo. The koala (*below*) eats only the leaves of some eucalyptus trees and carries its young in a rear pouch.

Koala

Right: Desert animals have special adaptations for life in hot, dry areas. Desert foxes have large ears to help lose body heat. Desert rats hop with long back legs, keeping off the hot sand.

Below: The Coelacanth fish was thought to have died out 70 million years ago. But it was found alive and unchanged in 1938.

Coelacanth

Evolution and Adaptation

Over millions of years of evolution, some animal designs have been more successful than others. Many animals and plants have become extinct. The mighty dinosaurs died out. So did mammals such as the giant ground sloth and the woolly mammoth. But other designs worked so well that they lasted for many millions of years.

Australia has lots of marsupials (pouched mammals) but not many ordinary mammals (placentals) and so the marsupials have taken over many of the niches normally filled by placentals. The job of anteater, for example, is filled by the numbat, a marsupial, while the job of grassland grazer is filled by kangaroos. Zebras and antelopes fill this particular niche in Africa while the llamas do the same job in the highland grasslands of South America. In South America some hummingbirds and giant moths seem 'designed' for the same niches. Both feed by hovering and sipping nectar from the flowers of forest trees.

ANIMAL ADAPTATIONS TO CLIMATE

In order to survive extreme climatic conditions, some animals have gradually developed special characteristics. The Arabian camel has splayed feet which do not sink into the desert sand. It stores food in its hump so it can travel for days without eating. Some mountain and Arctic animals have grown large hearts and lungs to cope with the thin air. Others have dense fur and thick layers of insulating fat to combat the cold.

JUNGLE LIFE

Habitats

The different vegetation zones encircle the Earth in broad bands. A traveller moving north from the tropical rainforest near the Equator would pass through grasslands and desert regions, then mixed woodlands and dark pine forests, before finally emerging into the cold, barren, treeless plains of the tundra. These vegetation zones make up the major habitats of the Earth. Each one is home to a group of often highly specialized animals.

Take the rainforest, for example. The rainforest is a curiously upside-down world. Trees rise straight up for 30 metres or more and then spread out so that their crowns become interwoven to form an almost continuous green 'roof' – the canopy – high above the ground. The result is that very little light reaches the ground.

In the heart of the forest, most animal life is to be found in the canopy. Here live monkeys and sloths, leaf-eating insects and countless seed- and fruit-eating birds. The hunters, too, have taken to the trees. There are eagles, lizards, snakes, tree-climbing anteaters and hunting cats.

European hedgehog

Nine-banded armadillo

Above: For protection against enemies, some animals have evolved 'body armour'. The hedgehog (top) has prickles, while the armadillo has an armoured skin.

Beetles form the largest of the insect groups. Most beetles can fly. The ladybird (*above*) folds its hind wings under its tough front wings or *elytra* after flying. Ladybirds have hard, biting jaws (smaller picture). Both larval and adult ladybirds feed on aphids.

Below: Some common beetles and aphids.

Insects

There are more insects than any other kind of animal on Earth. In fact, there are at least one million known different kinds of insects. Insects are *arthropods* (animals with jointed legs). Only a few live in the sea, but you can find insects everywhere else. Some, such as butterflies and moths, are beautiful to look at. Others, such as ants and bees, amaze us with their complicated colonies, in which each insect has a special job to do. Many insects are helpful, but others eat our crops or carry dangerous diseases.

Insects are many shapes and sizes, but it is easy to recognize one. Its body is divided into three parts: the head, the thorax and the abdomen. On the head are two antennae, or feelers. On the thorax are three pairs of legs. Most adult insects also have wings. The shape of the wings helps us to identify the insect. Flies have only two wings, but most other insects have four.

Many young insects look very different from the adults. They go through several different stages as they grow up. The change that takes place is called *metamorphosis*.

Insects inhabit every part of the Earth. Tiny primitive springtails are found in the soils of the polar regions, while huge beetles, bugs, butterflies and other insects abound in the warm food-rich tropical forests. One reason for the insects' success is that they have evolved ways of using every kind of food imaginable. Some, like the mosquito and greenfly, have hollow needle-like mouth-parts for sucking blood or sap. Others, like locusts, are specialized for cutting and chewing. Butterflies carry long, coiled-up

CICADAS

Cicadas are insects that suck the juices, or sap, from plants. The males are very noisy. The male cicada uses a muscle to make a membrane on each side of its body vibrate at high speed like a miniature drum-skin. This produces a shrill, whistle-like sound which attracts females. Grass-hoppers also use sound-signals.

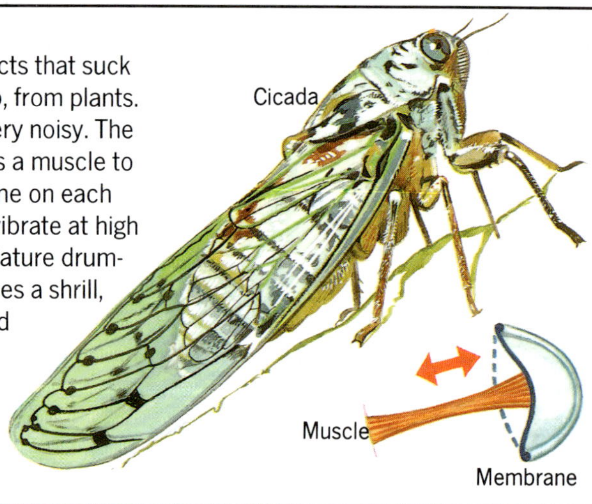

BUTTERFLIES

All these butterflies live in the fields of Britain and Europe. Butterflies are among the most beautiful insects. If you have a garden, you can attract many kinds of butterfly by planting flowers that are rich in nectar for them to feed on. You can watch them plunging their long tongues into the flowers to suck up the nectar. When they are not feeding, their tongues are coiled up. Butterflies can judge the sweetness of the nectar which lies deep down in the flower using 'taste' sensors in their feet!

The patterns on a butterfly's wings are made from thousands of tiny scales too small to see without the help of a microscope.

Butterflies fly by day. The bright colours of many butterflies' wings allow members of the same species to recognize one another during the short mating period. But bright wings also make a resting butterfly tempting prey for birds. So butterflies camouflage themselves by resting with wings folded upright, showing only the dull, 'dead leaf' colours on the underside of the wings.

drinking tubes, while many flies have a spongy pad with which they mop up their semi-liquid food.

Butterflies, like many other insects, develop by *metamorphosis*. The female butterfly lays her eggs on a leaf. The eggs hatch into tiny *larvae*, called caterpillars. Each caterpillar feeds on leaves and grows steadily. When it is ready, it spins a silken cocoon around itself with a special, thread-like material from its body. The caterpillar enters

Below: The week-long life cycle of the housefly shows how metamorphosis works. The fly's mouth (circled) is a tube with a sponge-like tip to mop up liquid food.

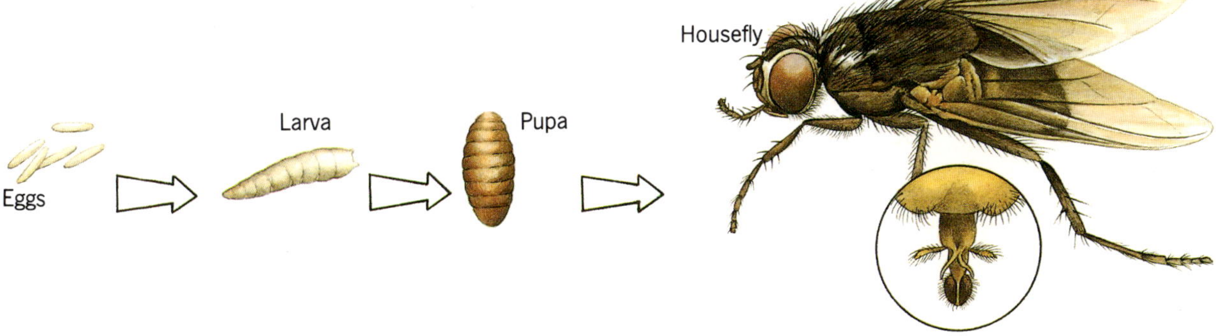

Above: The larva of the caddis fly has a soft body with no natural protection, so it spins a cocoon of silk and covers it with stones and bits of shell.

Right: Bees are social insects. They live in colonies in hives. In each hive there are many workers that build the wax cells of the comb and gather nectar for honey. Males or drones mate with the large queen, who lays the eggs.

FIREFLIES

Firefly beetles, also known as glow-worms, may be seen as tiny flashes of bright light at night as they can emit a light from their bodies for short periods. These on/off signals are used to send messages between males and females. The drab-coloured female attracts males with this strong greenish light as she sits in the grass at night.

Below: There may be as many as one million ants inside an ants' nest. The queen ant lays all the eggs. Female workers collect food and look after the young. Some ants 'milk' aphids for a sweet, sticky food called honeydew.

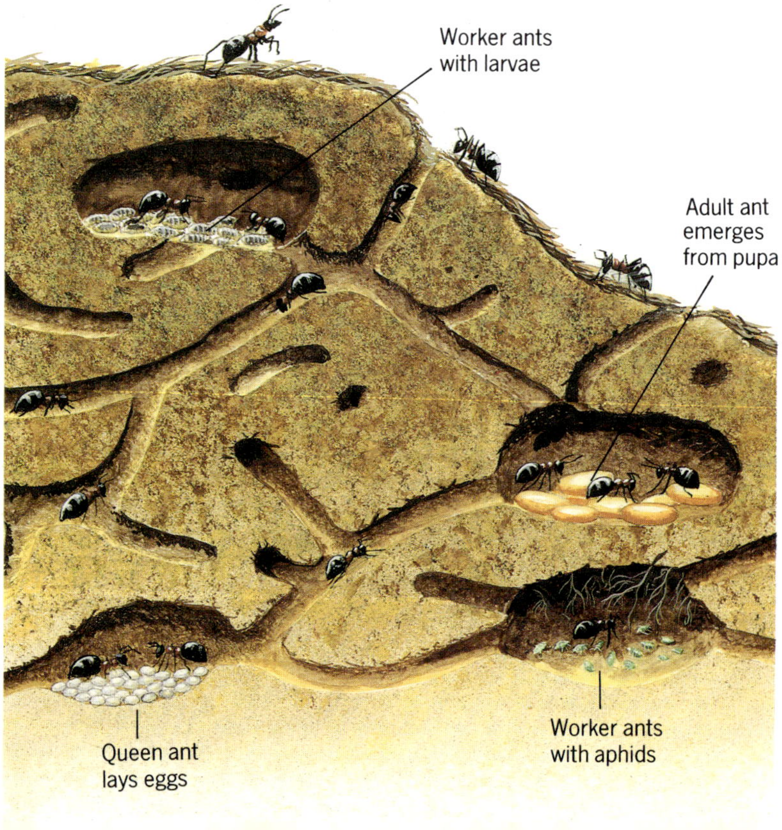

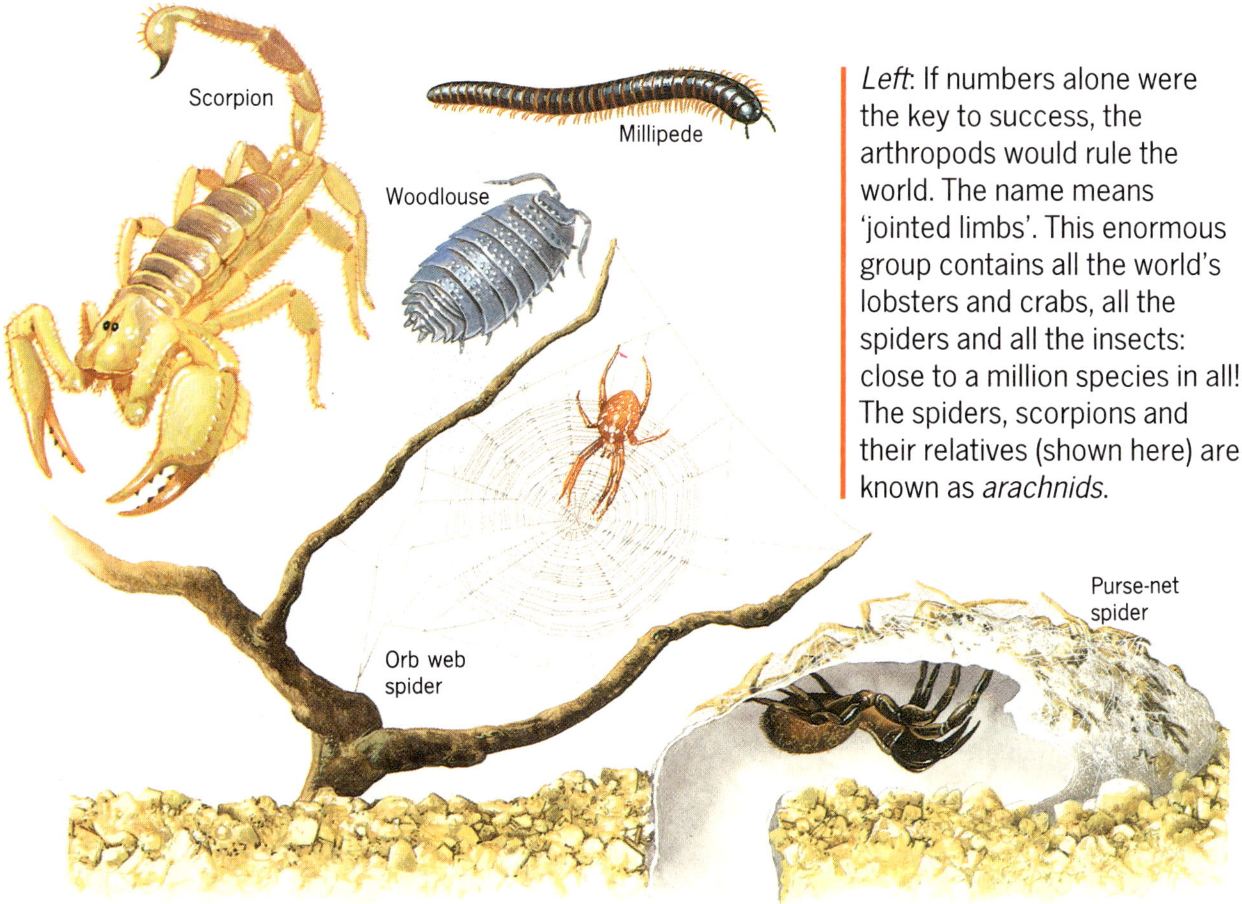

Left: If numbers alone were the key to success, the arthropods would rule the world. The name means 'jointed limbs'. This enormous group contains all the world's lobsters and crabs, all the spiders and all the insects: close to a million species in all! The spiders, scorpions and their relatives (shown here) are known as *arachnids*.

the resting stage known as the *pupa* or *chrysalis*. Here metamorphosis takes place. The adult butterfly eats its way out of the cocoon, spreads its wings and flies away. Soon it will find a mate, lay its own eggs, and the cycle will begin again.

Some insects are prickly, poisonous or taste nasty. This protects them from hungry birds and other predators. Other insects that mimic, or imitate, these defences are also left alone.

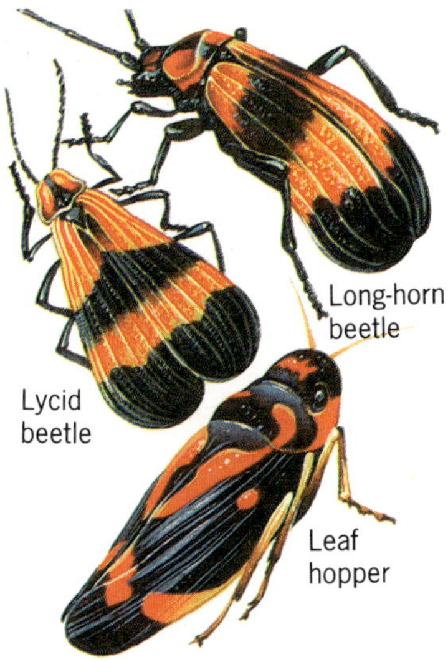

Above: In this group only the orange-banded lycid beetle (middle) is poisonous. The others are 'mimics'.

Left: Insects are masters of disguise. Some imitate twigs or leaves to escape detection.

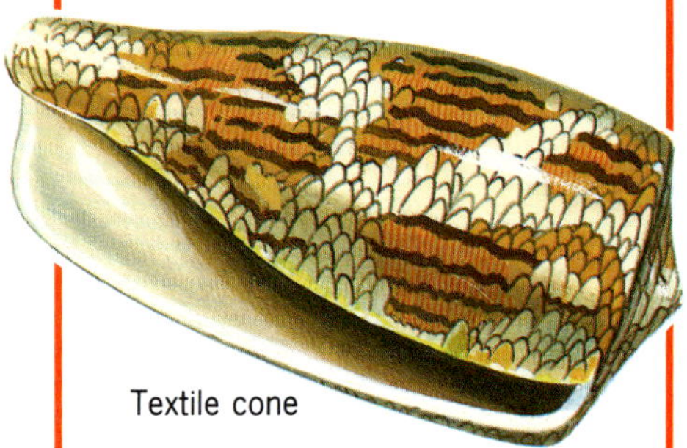

Above: Molluscs are plentiful in the warm waters of the Pacific and Indian oceans. The pearly Nautilus, a relative of the octopus and squid, swims in tropical waters.

Below: Gastropods, such as snails and whelks, have spiral-shaped one-piece shells.

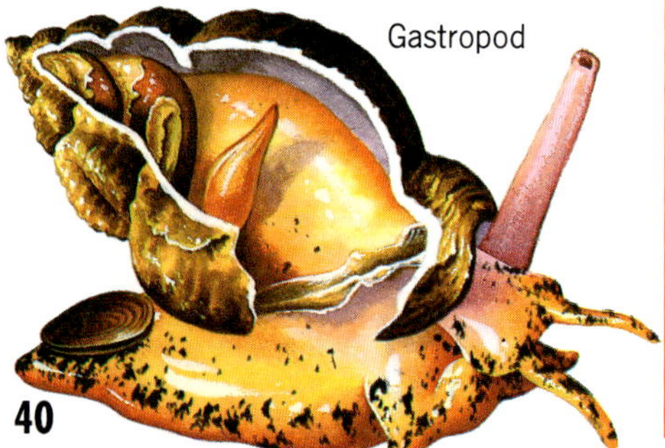

Molluscs

The 120,000 members of the huge mollusc family are soft-bodied animals, usually (like a snail) with a large muscular foot and a protective shell of some kind. This may be coiled like a snail shell or in two parts like a clam or oyster. But there are few other similarities between the different molluscs, for the variety of shapes in the family ranges from garden snails to giant clams and from gaudily-coloured sea slugs to the streamlined octopus and squid.

Most of the molluscs feed by means of a rasp-like tongue called a 'radula'. It can be used to scrape algae off rocks, or even to drill through the shell of another mollusc. The two-shelled molluscs have no radula. They feed by filtering tiny particles of food from the water.

A snail-like mollusc moves around slowly on its muscular foot. Some two-shelled molluscs swim along by 'clapping' their shells together, while others use the muscular foot to pull them down into a sandy burrow when danger threatens. By far the fastest movers are the octopus and its relatives the squid and cuttlefish. They propel themselves through the water at great speed by squirting water through a nozzle called a siphon.

Most land molluscs are tiny, and even the giants amongst them are small compared with their relatives in the sea. The largest land snail, for example, is the 900-gram African giant snail. Its largest relative in the sea is the trumpet conch from Western Australia – a monster that can weigh as much as 18 kilograms!

Fish

By about 350 million years ago, the four main groups of fishes had appeared. These were the jawless fish; the 'placoderms' – ancient heavily armoured fish, now extinct; the first cartilaginous fish – ancestors of modern sharks and rays; and the bony fish, which quickly became the most widespread, varied and successful group of all.

The characteristic feature of the sharks is that their skeletons are made not of bone but of rods of gristle or cartilage. For this reason this ancient group is known as the 'cartilaginous' fish. Most of the sharks are predators, and their powerful jaws are lined with sharp teeth designed for stabbing and cutting. Most of the sharks live deep in the ocean waters. They come up to the surface to feed on shoaling fishes. They use their good sense of hearing to help detect their prey.

Skates and rays are related to sharks. They feed mainly on small fish, molluscs and crustaceans, and some species can stun their prey with electric shocks generated by specialized muscles along the sides of the body. Another group, the sting rays, have sharp poison spines at the base of the tail.

The only surviving descendants of the original jawless fish are the hagfish and the lamprey. These fishes have

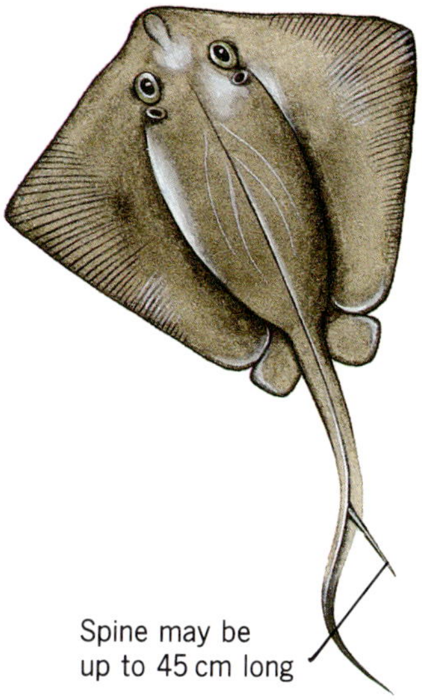

Above: Sting rays defend themselves by lashing their whip-like tails, armed with vicious poisoned spines.

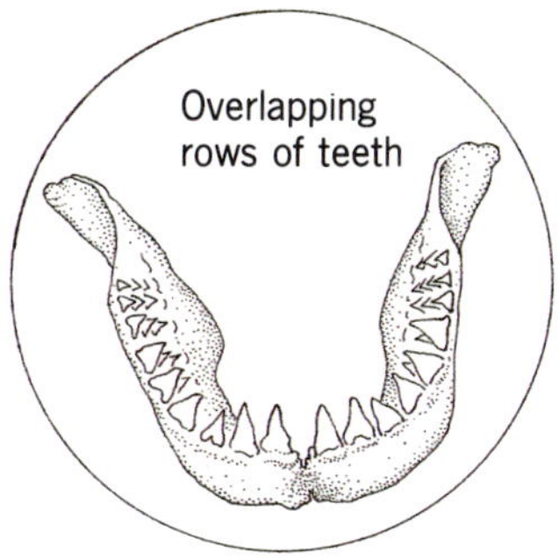

Above: A shark's teeth are arranged in overlapping rows. As the outer row wears out, it is replaced by a new row of teeth.

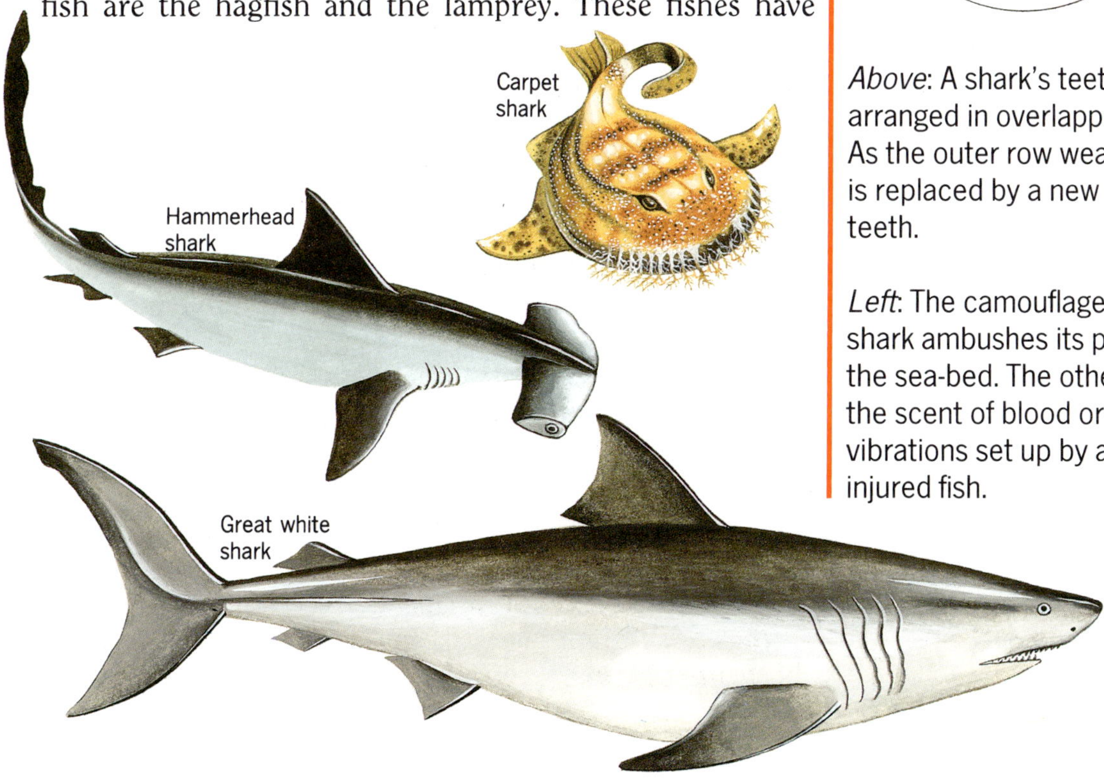

Left: The camouflaged carpet shark ambushes its prey on the sea-bed. The others follow the scent of blood or the vibrations set up by a sick or injured fish.

mouths adapted to rasping and sucking. They attach themselves to the body of another fish to feed on its blood. Feeding can continue without interruption because chemicals in their saliva prevent the host fish's blood from clotting. Hagfish are found in the sea-bed mud while lampreys are mainly freshwater fishes.

The ancient group of fishes called the 'lobe-fins' was believed to have died out 70 million years ago. But the scientists were proved wrong in 1938 when one of these strange, heavily-built fish, a coelacanth, was pulled up in a fisherman's net off the coast of South Africa!

Other 'living fossils' are the primitive lung-fish of Australia, South Africa and South America. Because they have lungs and can breathe air, they can survive long periods of drought, sealed in mud burrows beneath the beds of dried-out lakes. It may have been from creatures similar to these that the first land animals evolved.

Above: Box-fish, or trunk fish are well protected from predators. Their highly specialized scales form a hard shell-like covering over the head and body, giving the fish a square appearance.

Above right: Tropical fish are often brightly coloured.

The 'true' fishes – bony fishes – seem to have been successful right from the start. They very quickly found their way into every possible watery habitat.

Its bony skeleton gives the fish's body great strength and flexibility, while an internal gas-filled bladder like a small sausage-shaped balloon automatically adjusts the fish's buoyancy, enabling it to 'float' at any depth. (The sharks have no swim bladder. They sink if they stop swimming.) Because visibility is poor under water, fishes rely mainly on pressure waves to find their way around. The line of pits along a fish's side are tiny pressure sensors that serve as its main sense organs.

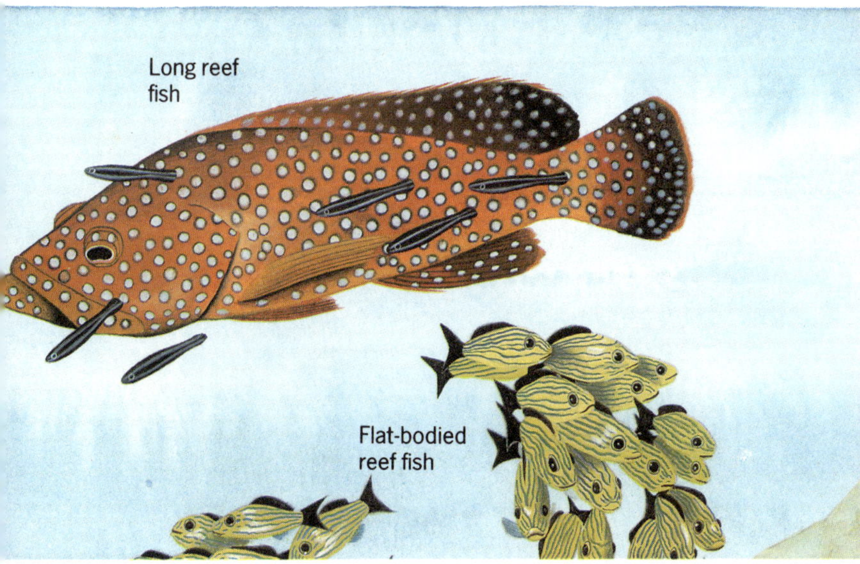

Above: Fishes are found all over the world. Some species survive in the salty oceans, others need fresh water environments.

The butterfly fish is found in still waters in West Africa. It feeds on crickets and beetles, living near the surface. Butterfly fishes may jump above the water using their wing-like fins.

The archer fish inhabits brackish coastal waters from the Persian Gulf to Australia. It captures perching insects for food by shooting jets of water from its mouth. When hit, the prey falls onto the surface of the water and is eaten.

Left: Shape and colour tell us about fishes. Some tropical fishes such as the long reef fish and the flat-bodied reef fish are well adapted to passing easily in and out of gaps in coral reefs. Fast-swimming predators like the marlin are streamlined. Silvery undersides make the herring hard to see from below, against the sea's sunlit surface, while its dark back hides it from seabirds overhead. This camouflage is called 'protective coloration'.

Amphibians and Reptiles

Amphibians spend part of their lives in water and part on dry land. They are descended from a group of animals that flourished about 350 million years ago and included the ancestors of true land animals.

There are three groups of modern amphibians – the tailless frogs and toads, the tailed salamanders and newts, and a curious group called caecilians.

Amphibians reproduce by laying eggs, but as their eggs do not have shells they must be laid in water, or at least in damp surroundings, so that they do not dry out. The eggs finally hatch into tadpoles, with fish-like gills and tails. They can live only in water, feeding on algae, but after a few weeks they go through a complete change of body shape and turn into four-legged, air-breathing adults.

The 5000 or so reptile species living on Earth today are all that remain of the vast numbers that dominated the

Above: There are some 2500 species of frogs and toads. Some arrow-poison frogs climb trees. The midwife toad carries its eggs on its back. Newts, like frogs, must return to water to breed.

Right: The crocodile, like its American relative the alligator, is a fierce predator. It hunts in the water, only its eyes and nostrils showing above the surface, but likes to sunbathe on river banks. Female crocodiles lay up to 60 leathery eggs in a hollow; alligators make nests of vegetation. Both take good care of their young.

Above: Lizards range in size from a few centimetres to the Komodo dragon, a giant of three metres. Some have frills of skin which are raised in displays. Others rely on warning colouring or speed.

Below: Snakes are the most recent reptiles to evolve. All snakes are hunters, killing by biting, by constriction (squeezing and suffocation) or by venom. In the most venomous snakes, the fangs are hinged to swing forwards as the animal strikes.

Viperine snake

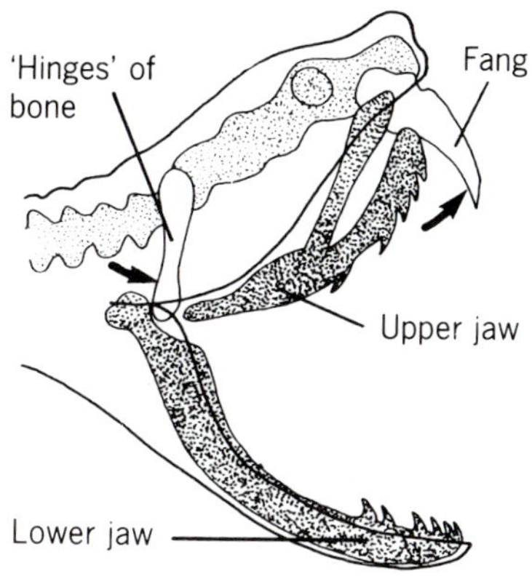

Earth for 140 million years, from the start of the Triassic period to the end of the Cretaceous. Snakes, crocodiles, tortoises and turtles, and lizards are reptiles. They are a kind of 'half-way' group between the fish and amphibians, and the advanced warm-blooded mammals and birds.

Reptiles are often referred to as cold-blooded. Unlike warm-blooded mammals and birds, their body temperature matches their surroundings. This is why most reptiles either live in warm regions or hibernate through the colder months.

Unlike the eggs of the more primitive amphibians, reptile eggs have leathery skins or shells, which means they can be laid on dry land.

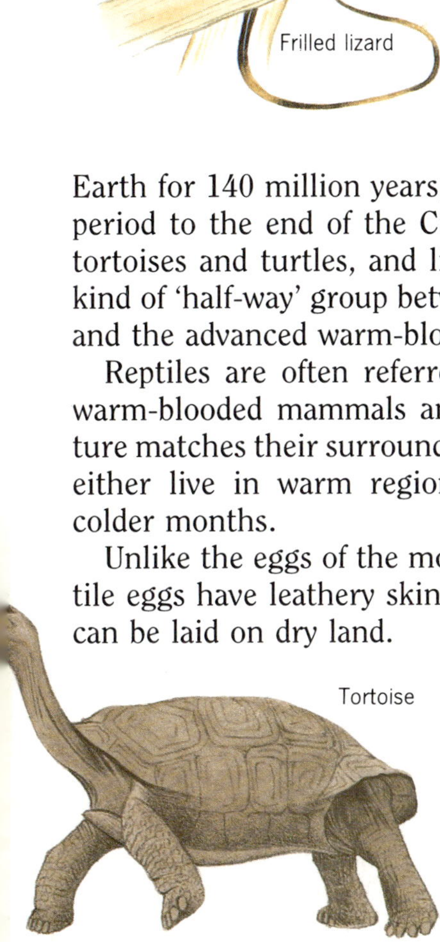

Left: Tortoises and turtles have changed little in 200 million years. Shells protect the animals from enemies. The Galápagos giant tortoise shown here can weigh over 200 kilograms.

The rook and crow (*above*) are large birds, feeding mostly on insects and carrion (dead animals).

Below: Some well known birds of America and Europe. There are about 9000 bird species.

Birds

The first birds appeared on Earth about 150 million years ago. They probably evolved from small dinosaurs that ran on their back legs like modern lizards do, and spent their time in the trees, scurrying about and jumping from branch to branch. Some may even have been able to glide on flaps of skin. At some point the reptile scales of these primitive creatures evolved into feathers – the one thing that makes birds different from all other animals.

The reptile ancestors of the birds were probably cold-blooded, which limited the range of habitats they could live in. But with a covering of feathers, birds were able to keep in more of their body heat, and so the evolution of

Bird of paradise

Condor

The condor has broad wings for soaring. The swallow has narrow wings for speed. The bird of paradise is gorgeously plumed but can fly only short distances.

Swallow

feathers was a major step on the birds' road to becoming warm-blooded. And once they made that change, they were able to spread into the high mountains, cold deserts and even the polar regions.

The other great advantage of feathers was that they made flight possible. One group of mammals, the bats, can also fly. They have wings made of thin elastic skin. But a bird's wing is a more complex piece of engineering, and can be tailor-made for many different kinds of flight.

The whole of the bird's body is designed for flight. Its skeleton is very strong to take the stresses of take-off and the impact of landing, but it is also very light. The bones are honeycombed with air spaces to save weight. The neck and skull and legs are long and bony, with no excess flesh. All the bird's weight is concentrated where it needs it most – in the massive breast muscles that power the beating of the wings.

Flying uses up a tremendous amount of energy, so birds must eat a great deal of food, and digest it very quickly, in order to keep their muscles fuelled.

HOW BIRDS FLY

Air rushing over the curved upper surface of the bird's wing travels farther and faster than air passing under the wing. This reduces air pressure above the wing, creating upward force or 'lift'. It is this force that keeps birds in the air.

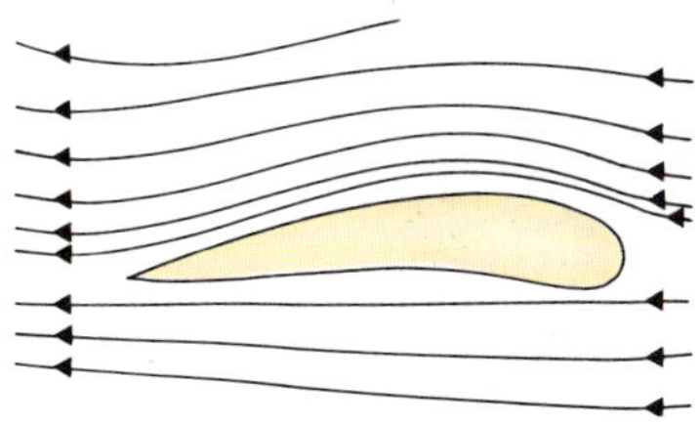

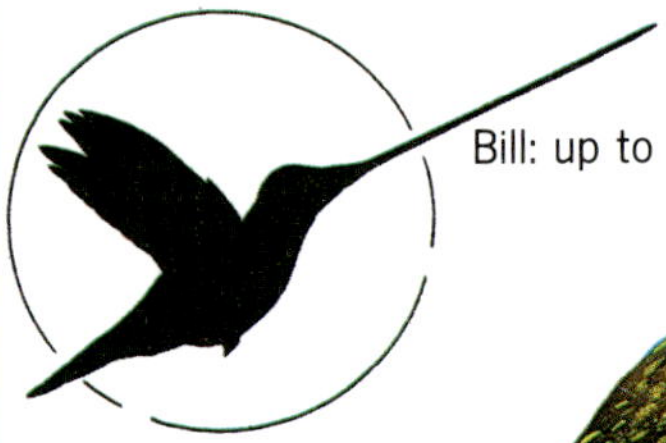

Above: The long bill of the South American sword-bill can reach inside the deep flower of the *passiflora* plant.

Right: Can you tell what foods these birds eat, from the shape of their bills? 1. Seeds (sparrow). 2. Flying insects (swallow). 3. Fish (kingfisher). 4. Pond animals (duck). 5. Carrion (crow). 6. Bark-dwelling insects (woodpecker). 7. Small mammals (hawk). 8. Seashore mud-dwelling creatures (curlew). 9. Insects (wren).

Below: The ostrich and cassowary are still common, but other flightless birds are now very rare.

A world of bird specialists

Birds more than any other animal group make it easy to see the effects of evolution at a glance. The short thick bill of a European hawfinch immediately reveals that its owner feeds on tough-shelled seeds and nuts. The sharp hooked bill of an owl or a hawk is that of a hunter, while the slender curved bill of a sunbird is perfect for reaching the nectar inside deep-belled flowers.

But other clues are not so obvious at first glance. The crossbill, for example, has a bill like a parrot, yet it lives in northern Europe. Only in winter is the secret revealed. While most other woodland birds fly off to warmer lands, with better food supplies, the crossbill continues feeding happily – using its powerful bill to slice into spruce and fir cones to get at the seeds inside. Its bill is perfectly designed to search out the only kind of seeds available in winter.

Although flight is one of the most characteristic features of birds there are quite a few flightless species. Some of the flightless birds are large, and rely on their size and speed, and in some cases kicking power, to protect them. The ostrich is an example. Others, like the kiwi of New Zealand, are nocturnal and secretive.

The most specialized flightless birds are the penguins of the southern oceans. Their bodies are smooth and streamlined and their wings are modified into stiff muscular paddles, with which they swim and dive with amazing speed and agility. They are protected from the cold by a layer of blubber (fat) beneath the skin, and by their dense waterproof plumage. Emperor penguins can dive for up to 20 minutes.

Above: Some unusual birds' nests. 1. Hole in tree sealed with mud. 2. Hardened saliva 'cup' nest. 3. Artificial island of stones. 4. Basket woven from grass stems. 5. Mud nest on fence post. 6. Woven grass nest hanging over water.

Left: Barn owls are solitary but useful birds as they hunt for mice and rats which can damage farmers' crops. Owls are nocturnal (they are active at night) and, unlike most birds, they have eyes set at the front of their heads. This allows them to judge distances well – an important skill for a bird of prey. Owls like to nest in dark places like tree hollows, belfries or barns.

Above: An African elephant. The elephant is the largest land animal. Elephants live in herds, led by females. The males live in a separate group some distance away.

Below: A female chimpanzee and baby. Primates must look after their young for many months after birth.

Mammals

The mammals are the most highly developed animals of all. Unlike other animals, female mammals feed their young on milk produced in their own bodies. Care of the young is very important in mammals. Most species produce only one or two young at a time – and in most cases they are quite unable to fend for themselves. Human babies, for example, are completely dependent on their mothers, while puppies do not even open their eyes until they are about ten days old. For this reason, many female mammals seek the safety of a den or burrow when it is time to give birth, and most will defend their helpless young fiercely if they are threatened.

However, there are exceptions, and the most remarkable is provided by the large grazing animals of the grasslands, such as wildebeests and giraffes. Within minutes of being born, young of these species can stand, walk and even run with the herd. It is a marvellous example of evolution fitting an animal to its environment. In open grassland there is nowhere to hide. If danger threatens from lions or hunting dogs, the only protection is to run.

Above: Dolphins are small whales. They are fast swimmers and feed on fish. Because dolphins are mammals, they have to surface at intervals to breathe air. They swim in groups or 'schools' and have their own form of communication.

There are many other differences between mammals and other animal groups. Mammals, for example, have a very efficient four-chambered heart. Their teeth are also very highly specialized, with cutting teeth at the front, holding or stabbing teeth at the sides, and grinding or shearing teeth at the back. Which combination of teeth a particular animal has depends on how it feeds. Cats have large canine teeth (fangs) for seizing and killing, and sharp cutting and shearing teeth for slicing through flesh and tough skin. Grazing animals have a simple chopping arrangement at the front of the mouth, and large flat or ridged teeth at the back for grinding their tough plant food. Mammals are also very adaptable. They have adapted to all kinds of environments, including the sea.

Below: The leopard is a powerful hunting mammal. Spots help to camouflage this big cat. Its smaller relative is the domestic cat, bred by humans into a variety of colours and patterns (*left*).

Criollo – a cattle pony from South America

Basuto – a tough pony from South Africa

Pony of the Americas

Australian pony

Above: The horse is an example of a species that has been dominated and changed by people. Horses have been tamed and bred for human purposes, from racing to carrying heavy burdens.

Endangered species

Animals and plants have been dying out quite naturally for millions of years. If this was not so, there would still be trilobites in the sea, tree-sized clubmosses covering parts of the land, and our modern birds would be sharing the skies with a variety of flying lizards.

The problem today is the way humans have completely taken over and dominated the natural world. A few animals will continue to die out naturally, but most of the animals and plants that are in danger today are threatened by us and not by natural events.

Right: The blue whale is the largest animal that has ever lived on Earth. Whales communicate over great distances by sound.

Some species are threatened by hunting. Crocodiles are hunted for their skins. Turtles are hunted for their meat. Whales are hunted for their oil and meat. Some birds are hunted for their beautiful feathers while others are trapped and sold to collectors who will pay huge amounts of money for a very rare tropical forest parrot.

The biggest problem of all, however, is that many animals and plants are simply being pushed off the face of the Earth by people and their domestic animals. In 1970 there were fewer than four thousand million people on Earth. By the year 2000 there will be about six thousand million.

Striped possum

ANIMAL SIZES

Above: If animals like the blue whale, the little striped possum (*top*), and the large land mammals shown below are to survive, we must protect them. All the world's animals need room to share the planet with us.

1. Animal dies and sinks to the sea- or lake-bed

2. Hard parts become buried under sand, silt or mud

3. Bones are slowly replaced by hard mineral crystals

We know about long-dead animals from their fossil remains. Fossils are found in rocks such as sandstones, mudstones and limestones. These rocks were once soft sands or muds. A dead animal may become fossilized (*above*) and millions of years later be uncovered by scientists.

Top right: The fossil *Archaeopteryx*, a reptile with feathers. This ancient creature may possibly have been the link between reptiles and birds.

Prehistoric Life

Life on Earth has not always been the same as it is today. The familiar plants and animals that we see around us have changed greatly since life first began, millions of years ago.

Scientists have learnt about prehistoric life by studying fossils. Fossils are the remains of plants and animals that have been turned into rock and so preserved. Many common fossils can be very beautiful objects that show a great deal of fine detail, like fossil shells with surface patterns, whole insects trapped in amber, or skeletons of tiny fish preserved in fine mud. Fossils can be very ancient.

The early stages in the history of life all took place in the sea. There was no life on land at all for many thousands of millions of years. Eventually, about 400 million years ago some plants and small animals moved out of the water and onto the shores. These animals were amphibians.

These first amphibians lived in warm, wet swamps, where there were tall plants and large insects. Just like their living relatives, the frogs and salamanders, they had to live very close to water in order to stop their skins from drying out. Their eggs were also laid in water.

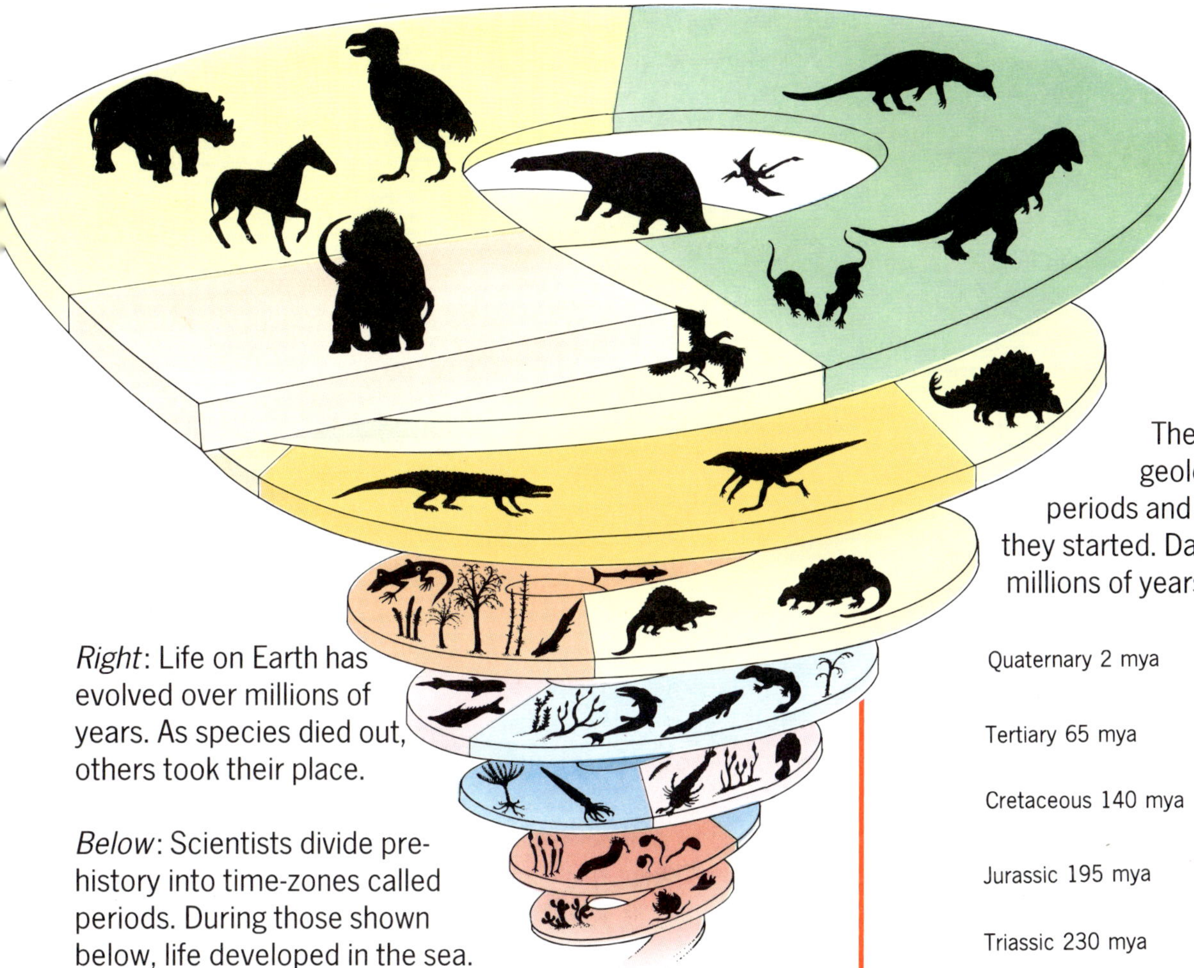

The main geological periods and when they started. Dates in millions of years ago.

- Quaternary 2 mya
- Tertiary 65 mya
- Cretaceous 140 mya
- Jurassic 195 mya
- Triassic 230 mya
- Permian 280 mya
- Carboniferous 345 mya
- Devonian 395 mya
- Silurian 435 mya
- Ordovician 500 mya
- Cambrian 570 mya

Right: Life on Earth has evolved over millions of years. As species died out, others took their place.

Below: Scientists divide pre-history into time-zones called periods. During those shown below, life developed in the sea.

Two hundred million years ago, huge, reptile-like monsters ruled the Earth. Today, we call these creatures dinosaurs, from Greek words that mean 'terrible lizard'. Some dinosaurs were as large as several houses. Other dinosaurs were no bigger than a chicken.

Some of the biggest animals ever to live on Earth were the plant-eating dinosaurs. One of these giants was *Apatosaurus*, once known as *Brontosaurus*, or 'thunder lizard'. Its legs were as thick as tree trunks, and it was 25 metres long from its tiny head to the tip of its long tail. Other

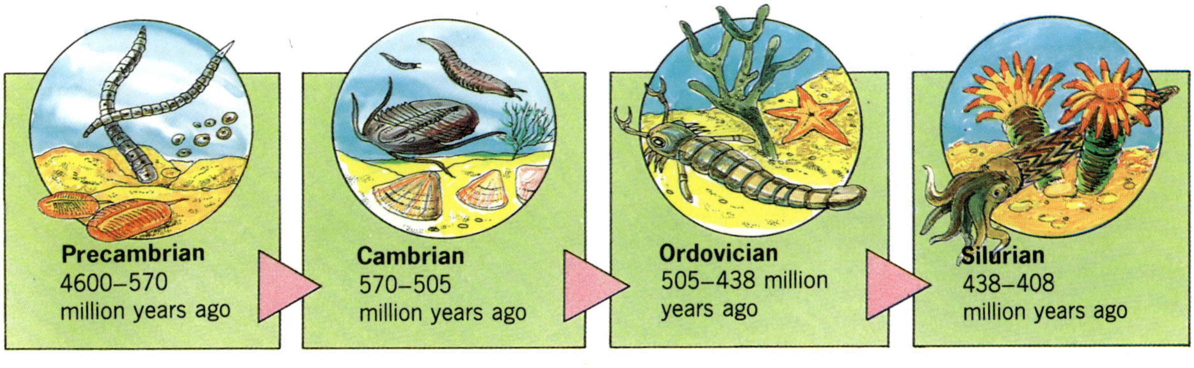

plant-eaters included *Iguanodon*, which walked upright and had 'hands' with spiky thumbs, and the duck-billed dinosaurs called hadrosaurs. The armoured dinosaurs, such as *Triceratops* and *Stegosaurus*, were also plant-eaters. Some had huge, bony plates to protect them; others sprouted horns.

One of the biggest unsolved mysteries is why, 65 million years ago, the dinosaurs suddenly died out. Some scientists think that the climate on Earth may have grown too cold for them. Others believe their food-plants died. After the dinosaurs died out, there were hardly any large animals on land at all. There were birds (descended perhaps from the reptile-bird *Archaeopteryx*), and also lizards, crocodiles and turtles. There were a few rat-sized and cat-sized hairy animals. These creatures were the mammals, which had lived in the undergrowth during the whole of the age of the dinosaurs. They had first come on

Above: *Eogyrinus* was a Carboniferous amphibian four metres long.

Below: Several coelurosaurs, small predatory dinosaurs of the Jurassic period.

the scene 200 million years ago, but had been overshadowed for millions of years by the dinosaurs. Now that the dinosaurs had all died out, their chance had come.

Above: Early woodland mammals of Palaeocene times. *Planetotherium* was a gliding squirrel-like creature. Centre is the plant-eater *Barylambda* and on the branch *Plesiadapis*. Bottom right is the fruit-eater *Taeniolabis*; bottom left, an early shrew.

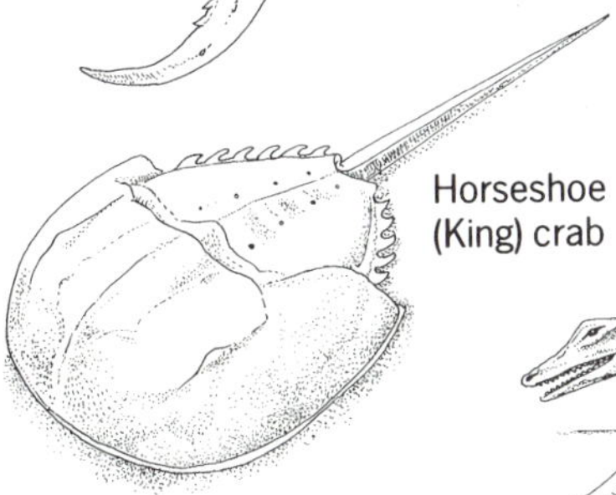

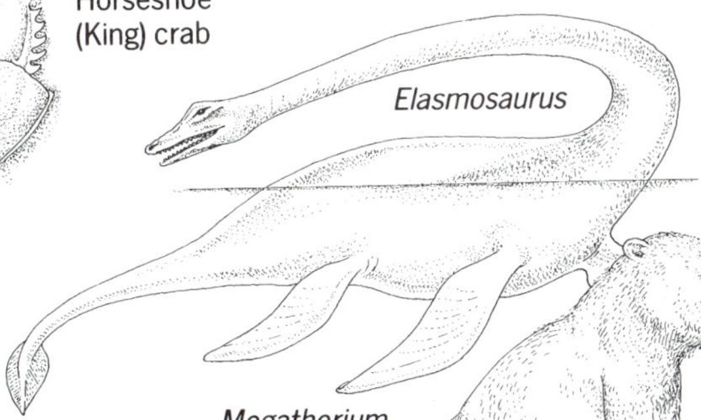

The tuatara and king crab (*above*) have not changed for millions of years. The sea reptile *Elasmosaurus* and the giant sloth *Megatherium* (*right*) could not adapt to the changing world and died out.

SOME CURIOUS PREHISTORIC MAMMALS

Hyracotherium – dog-sized ancestor of the horse.
Diatryma – huge meat-eating flightless bird.
Baluchitherium – largest land mammal ever, eight times the weight of a rhinoceros.
Amphicyon – a dog the size of a bear.
Glyptodon – a giant armadillo.
Sabre-tooth – big cats with long stabbing teeth.
Woolly mammoth – relatives of modern elephants. Frozen mammoths are found in the icy ground of Siberia.
Megatherium – giant ground sloth of South America.

First Humans

Our earliest ancestors were ape-like creatures. They lived in the forests, climbing and running on all fours. Over many millions of years these animals changed. Some apes moved down from the trees and hunted for food on the open plains. They began to walk upright on their back legs. This meant their front legs, or arms, were free to make and carry things.

The human story really begins just under four million years ago, in Africa. A one-metre tall creature known to scientists as *Australopithecus afarensis* is the oldest-known species of human. Other species of *Australopithecus* are also known from Africa, and they lived up to about one million years ago.

Australopithecus died out a million years ago. Already, however, 'true' humans had arrived on the scene. The first of the new species was *Homo habilis*, or 'handy man', who first lived in Africa two million years ago.

Fossils of stone tools have been found near the bones of *Homo habilis*, suggesting that 'handy man' was the first

Right: *Homo habilis* or 'handy man' appeared about 2 million years ago. *Homo habilis* and *Australopithecus* seem to have lived side by side in Africa until *Australopithecus*, died out.

Below: *Australopithecus* fossils have been found in Africa. These early humans lived almost 4 million years ago. They could walk upright and may have discovered how to use sticks and bones as tools or weapons.

Above: Making tools. The first tools were pebbles picked up from the ground. Later, people chipped away flakes of flint to make cutting tools with sharp edges. These tools were used for cutting and scraping, and also as arrowheads.

Below: Our earliest known ancestors were ape-like. The shape of the human skull has changed during the course of time. We have larger craniums and smaller jaw-bones than our ancestors.

tool maker. Greater intelligence and skill might also have allowed these humans to hunt better and to find more food than *Australopithecus*, and this may explain why the earlier type of human died out.

The next human species – *Homo erectus*, or 'upright man' – first lived in Africa about one million years ago. *Homo erectus* was larger than *Homo habilis*, being about 1.5 metres tall and stockily built. These people still had rather primitive faces with no chin and heavy bony ridges over the eyebrows. However, their brains were only slightly smaller than the brain of a modern human.

Home erectus spread out all over the world from Africa.

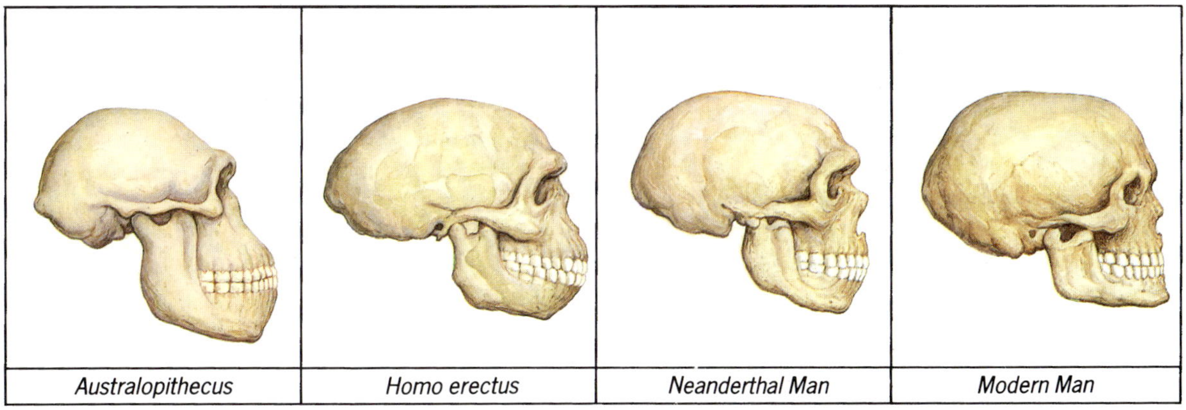

Above: Only humans discovered how to make fire. Fire gave the first people light, warmth and a feeling of safety.

In China, these humans lived in caves and made a variety of tools for hunting. They also made fires for cooking the meat. This is shown by layers of ash in the caves.

By the time *Homo erectus* had died out, the last human species had arrived and taken over the world. This was *Homo sapiens*, or 'wise man' – the group to which we belong today. One of our early relatives was Neanderthal man, who lived in Europe until about 35,000 years ago.

Neanderthal man had a heavier skull than living humans, but his brain was just as big, if not bigger! He walked fully upright, and made excellent tools. Far from being a brute, he was able to make carvings of the animals he saw about him in stone and bone. Tribes of these early people lived in Europe during the later ice ages, when their short stocky bodies helped to keep out the cold. They sheltered in caves, and made themselves warm clothing out of animal skins.

Modern *Homo sapiens* lived at the same time as Neanderthal man, but in warmer parts of the world such as North Africa and the Middle East. As the ice sheets melted, modern humans spread out into Europe and Asia. The modern humans made better tools than the Neanderthals, as well as beautiful paintings and carvings. The Neanderthals died out. After the end of the last ice age, about 11,000 years ago, the people living in the Middle East began to farm their land. Civilization had begun.

The story of human life has taken in all just 15 million years, beginning with the appearance of an ape-like crea-

FIRST FOOTPRINTS

Is this the oldest human fossil? This trail of footprints was found in Tanzania, Africa, in 1976. They were made in mud some 3.75 million years ago and are preserved in volcanic ash. The footprints prove that there were humans around then. Only humans walk upright on the soles of their feet. These prints might have been made by an *Australopithecus* family. They probably lived near lakes and rivers, feeding mainly on plants. The discovery of these footprints suggests that Africa was the birthplace of humankind.

ture called *Ramapithecus*. Little is known about this early primate, for only a few bones have been discovered. *Ramapithecus* was followed by *Australopithecus* four million years ago, *Homo habilis* appeared two million years ago, and *Homo erectus* one million years ago. Neanderthals and modern humans only came onto the scene about 100,000 years ago.

Above: Neanderthals wore animal skins for warmth. They made good stone tools.

Below: Cave paintings at Lascaux in France, produced by early modern humans.

HISTORY

Bust of Pericles

ANCIENT CIVILIZATIONS

Civilization began with the first farmers around 11,000 years ago. Later great empires arose in Egypt, Greece, Rome and China. (See page 64.) Remains and ancient writings tell us of these times.

THE MIDDLE AGES

The Middle Ages in Europe lasted from the fall of the Roman Empire until the 1400s. (See page 67.) An unsettled and changing period, witnessing the spread of the Christian and Muslim faiths.

THE RENAISSANCE

The 'rebirth of learning' in Europe was a time when ancient knowledge and new ideas came together. (See page 70.) It affected art, science and literature.

EXPLORATION AND EMPIRE

European exploration by sea revealed a New World, America. Europeans went in search of trade and to found colonies. (See page 72.)

GROWTH OF INDUSTRY

The agricultural and industrial changes that began in the 1700s altered people's lives. The modern world had started. (See page 76.)

THE AGE OF REVOLUTION

In the 1700s and 1800s people demanded freedom and independence. This was the age of revolutions (See page 78.)

WORLD WARS
Two world wars in the 20th century caused terrible destruction and resulted in millions of deaths. (See page 80.)

THE MODERN WORLD
In modern times, the world has seen great changes in power, dependence and influence. Every continent has been affected. (See page 84.)

OUTLINE OF WORLD HISTORY
On pages 88–101 you will find a **Time Chart** of important historical events and a **Who's Who in History**.

Above: A wall painting of a pharaoh. An Egyptian king was an absolute ruler and was regarded as a god. Everyone in Egypt obeyed his commands.

Below: The funeral procession of a pharaoh on its way to a tomb in Egypt's Valley of the Kings. Four oxen pull the funeral boat bearing the dead ruler's mummy. The Egyptians believed in an after-life.

Ancient Civilizations

Civilization began when people no longer had to spend all their time searching for food. Thousands of years ago groups of people began joining together to form communities. Farming and trade developed as they settled in one area, instead of wandering from place to place. As people grew more prosperous, they built cities, temples and roads. More than 5000 years ago, people settled along the banks of the river Nile in Egypt. Every year the river flooded the surrounding lands, leaving a rich silt in which farmers could grow their crops. In time, a great civilization arose.

The rulers of Egypt were called pharaohs. When a pharaoh died, he was buried in a tomb deep inside a huge pyramid. With him were buried all the things the Egyptians thought he would need in the next world, such as clothes, furniture and jewels. The body itself was preserved in bandages as a 'mummy'. We know about life in Ancient Egypt from the remains and wall paintings in such tombs. The Egyptians studied mathematics and astronomy, they worshipped many gods, and they invented the picture writing called hieroglyphics.

The Ancient Greeks built one of the greatest of all civilizations. They developed art, music and poetry and about 2500 years ago they set up a new form of government in

the city of Athens. It was called democracy, meaning 'rule by the people'. The Greeks were great athletes. Their Olympic Games were named after Mount Olympus, home of Zeus and the other Greek gods.

The most lasting of all ancient civilizations arose in China over 2000 years ago. The emperor set up a strong central government. Cut off from the rest of the world, the Chinese developed their own philosophy and art. They made many advances in science and technology centuries before such inventions were known in the West.

Most civilizations in ancient times had strong armies to protect them against invaders. Mighty empires also spread their way of life by conquest. According to legend, the city of Rome was founded in 753 BC. It grew larger and strong-

Above: Imperial officials on a tour of China.

A Roman apartment block. Wealthy families lived on the ground floor, poorer people above.

Roman engineers building an aqueduct, a bridge for carrying water. The Pont du Gard in southern France was built like this around 19 BC.

er until by about 140 BC the Romans ruled all the countries around the Mediterranean Sea. Their empire eventually stretched from Britain in the west to Asia Minor in the east and across to North Africa. Everywhere they went, the Romans built fine towns and cities linked by a network of well constructed roads. They borrowed many ideas from the Greeks, but their way of life was the most advanced the world had ever seen.

The great empires of the past grew so powerful that their rulers felt they would last for ever. But none did. Some civilizations grew weak and fell apart. Others were destroyed by enemies. Only the ruins of these great civilizations now remain.

TIME CHART

8000 BC	First farmers and towns in Middle East
3000 BC	Sumerian civilization, Middle East Indus Valley civilization, Asia
2600 BC	Minoan civilization, Crete First pyramids in Egypt
c.1766 BC	Rise of Shang dynasty, China
1600 BC	Mycenaean civilization, Greece
900–750 BC	Rise of Greek city states
776 BC	First Olympic Games
c. 720 BC	Height of Assyrian empire
509 BC	Roman republic
323 BC	Death of Alexander the Great
214 BC	Great Wall of China built
27 BC	Augustus, first Roman emperor
AD 30	Crucifixion of Christ
AD 300	Mayan civilization, South America
AD 476	Fall of Roman Empire

Right: The ruins of the Colosseum in Rome. In this great open-air arena the ancient Romans cheered gladiator combats.

Middle Ages

Above: From about 800 onwards the Vikings not only ravaged Europe, they also made hazardous voyages in order to trade, establishing colonies in North America and Russia.

Below: A lord's castle was a community in the Middle Ages. It defended his lands and his household.

When Roman rule ended in the 5th century AD, the many different tribes in Europe who had lived under Rome's protection were left to look after themselves. It took about 1000 years for settled, civilized life to return, and this period of turmoil is called the Middle Ages.

Without Roman armies to protect it, Europe was overrun by barbarians. Fierce tribes such as the Goths and Vandals sacked and burned towns. Later, in the 800s and 900s, Viking raiders sailed in their ships from Scandinavia to plunder many coastal areas and to seize land in Britain. Soon the ancient art and learning of the Greeks and Romans was forgotten, except by Christian monks in their monasteries and by Arab scholars.

Above: In the Middle Ages books were produced by hand. The pages were made not of paper, but of animal skins or parchments. The skins were dried and cleaned so all hair was removed from them. The parchments were sold to scribes or writers who would laboriously copy texts. Many mistakes might be made in the process. The finished sheets were passed to the binder who would stitch them together and bind them in boards covered with leather.

Few people could read and write at this time. Among the better educated people were the monks. They spent many hours copying religious texts. Often the written page would be decorated with paint or gilding. These are called illuminated manuscripts.

Books were large and so precious that they were often kept chained up.

TIME CHART

814 Death of Charlemagne
1000 Vikings discover America
1066 Normans conquer England
1096 First Crusade to the Holy Land
1100s First universities founded in Europe
1241 Mongols invade eastern Europe
1248–70 Seventh and last Crusade
1271 Marco Polo sets out for China
1337 Start of Hundred Years' War
1347 Black Death in Europe
1363 Tamerlane begins conquest of Asia
1453 Turks capture Constantinople

For safety, people banded together under the protection of strong leaders, or kings. Poor peasants worked on the great estate, or manor, of a rich noble or knight. They were his vassals, and had to work for him, or provide him with some of their crops, in return for his protection. The nobles in turn were vassals of the king. In return for the monarch's protection, they supplied him with their peasant vassals as soldiers in time of war. This arrangement is known as the feudal system. In France and Germany the feudal system dominated life in the Middle Ages, and it spread eastwards to central and eastern Europe. There it lasted well into the 19th century.

Life in the Middle Ages was often harsh and cruel. The peasants had to obey their lord; the Church, too, was rich and powerful. During the Middle Ages as the strength of Islam grew, the Christian Church called on people to fight a holy war or 'crusade' against the Muslims in the Holy

Land. There were seven crusades in all. Several expeditions were prevented from reaching the Holy Land by illness and disaster. However, the crusades did bring new knowledge about the East and opened up trade links.

Most people lived in dark, smoky huts and had barely enough to eat, especially in winter. Little was known about hygiene or medicine; terrible plagues swept the land, killing many thousands of people.

The worst and most famous outbreak of plague during the Middle Ages was the Black Death. The disease was bubonic plague and it was spread by fleas from the black rats which often lived on ships. The Black Death reached Europe from Asia in 1347. All countries were affected by it and perhaps as many as a third of Europe's entire population died. Whole communities were destroyed.

Despite such disasters, slowly learning spread. Great cathedrals were built. Art and poetry developed. Universities and schools were founded. Government became more settled, trade flourished. With the voyages of discovery in the 1400s and the Renaissance, or 'rebirth of learning', the Middle Ages came to an end.

Above: A stained-glass window showing France's national heroine, St Joan of Arc. Inspired by heavenly voices, she took the role of a soldier and led the French to victory against the English in the Hundred Years' War. She won five battles but was captured and burnt as a witch in 1431.

Below: Seamen during the Middle Ages had few good maps. From the late 1200s charts became more accurate and reliable, following the introduction into Europe of the Chinese floating, magnetic compass.

With the increase in trade, the need for maps grew. This map was made for the French king in about 1375. Information on this chart about central Asia and China was based largely on the writings of Marco Polo.

Above: Before the 1450s books were handwritten and available only to the rich and priests. After the invention of movable type by Johannes Gutenberg, printed books became much cheaper and many more people could afford them.

Art and sculpture flourished during the Renaissance with the help of rich, noble families. Federigo da Montefeltro, Duke of Urbino, (*below*) commissioned paintings from the artist Piero della Francesca for his grand court.

Renaissance

During the 13th century, the seafaring Italian cities of Venice and Genoa opened up new trade routes to the East through Constantinople. Merchants began to make huge profits from the increase in trade. Contacts with the East gave them a wider outlook and a new interest in collecting rare and exotic things. Wealth and fashion led to astonishing advances in learning and the arts.

This period in Western civilization is called the Renaissance, a word meaning ‘rebirth’. A new, adventurous spirit began to make way for an age of exploration, discovery, and scientific thought.

The Italian merchants and nobles competed to make their cities brilliant centres of learning and the arts. They sent agents all over Europe to bring back rare manuscripts by famous ancient Greek and Roman authors. Many old books were found in monastery libraries where they had long been forgotten. Few people could understand the ancient languages in which they were written and so scholars translated them into Italian. More and more people rediscovered the ideas and discoveries of Greek and Roman civilization.

Scientists such as Copernicus and Galileo questioned the old ideas about the Universe. They studied the stars and planets through the newly invented telescopes. They observed that the Earth revolved around the Sun and not the Sun around the Earth as had been thought. Erasmus and other ‘humanist’ thinkers taught that human beings were important, and not just weak, miserable creatures ruled by God. Explorers such as Columbus brought back new knowledge from their voyages.

Above: Rich Renaissance families often entertained guests at country villas where hunting was a popular pursuit. In the evenings they might discuss philosophical matters.

The Renaissance also saw great changes in the arts. In medieval painting, figures were flat and stylized against plain gold backgrounds. But around 1300 an artist called Giotto began to paint more realistic figures, making them more solid and setting them against backgrounds that looked like the real world.

By the end of the Renaissance, painters, sculptors and architects were known far and wide by name. Artists such as Michelangelo, and Leonardo da Vinci recaptured the beauty of 'classical' Greek sculpture and architecture.

In 1495 the friar Savonarola became ruler of Florence, a very rich Italian city. Objecting to the literature and art, he built bonfires (*below*) on which books and precious items were burned, and called many to repent of their sinful lives.

Above: Early European navigators braved the oceans in tiny sailing ships, like these of Vasco da Gama's expedition to India in 1497–9. Disease was rife and many men died.

Exploration and Empire

To the ancient peoples of Europe, 'the world' meant the lands around the Mediterranean Sea. Only the Phoenicians dared sail out into the cold, grey Atlantic Ocean beyond. Perhaps the first European to reach the Americas was the Irish monk St Brendan in the 6th century AD, who sailed west from Ireland in a boat made of leather.

In 1002 the Vikings sailed in their small, fragile ships as far as North America. But until the use of the magnetic compass in the late 1200s, long sea voyages were very dangerous.

To reach the East, with its gold, spices and silks, European merchants had to travel overland. In 1275 Marco Polo reached China and brought back astonishing tales of what he had seen. It was the Portuguese who discovered that they could reach India by sailing round the coast of Africa. In 1492 Christopher Columbus tried to find a shorter route to Asia by sailing west, across the Atlantic. Instead he reached America. By 1522 Ferdinand Magellan's sailors had sailed right round the world.

In 1519, the same year in which Magellan left Spain on his voyage, Hernando Cortés sailed from Cuba in the West Indies to land on the Central American coast. In the 30 years that followed, a few thousand Spanish adventurers

Above: The *Santa Maria*, flagship of Christopher Columbus's voyage to the New World in 1492. Though only 24 metres long, carrying 40 men, it was the largest of his three ships. No pictures of *Santa Maria* survive, but it was probably a three-masted carrack like this.

Left: An early European map of South America, showing the southern part of the continent, to Cape Horn. The first European to sail around the tip of South America into the vast Pacific Ocean was Ferdinand Magellan, during the first round-the-world voyage of 1519–1522. Spain and Portugal led the European exploration of South and Central America. They set up trading posts and conquered large empires. Some Europeans searched for mines and fabulous treasures of gold and silver. Others came to plant crops, such as sugar. The local people, the Amerindians, were often treated harshly.

Right: When the Spanish *conquistadors*, led by Francisco Pizarro, explored Peru in 1533, they discovered the empire of the Incas. These people of South America had the most advanced civilization in the New World. The Incas were great builders. An Inca mountain town, like this one, had stone houses, paved roads and rope bridges. With no wheeled vehicles, the Incas used llamas as pack animals.

Below: An Indian chief, in ceremonial costume, drawn in about 1585 by a European visitor to America. The Europeans who settled in North America in increasing numbers from the 1600s took more and more land from the native Indians. Because the Indians resisted, there was fighting between Indians and Europeans which worsened as the settlers moved west.

Right: A Dutch merchant ship of the 17th century battles through a storm. Europeans on voyages of discovery set up trading posts and then founded colonies. From these colonies grew large overseas empires. There was great rivalry between the seagoing nations of Europe – chiefly, Spain, Portugal, Holland, France and Britain.

(conquistadors) conquered the first great European overseas empire. In the Americas the Spaniards found great civilizations which had grown up quite independently of the rest of the world. The most important were the empires of the Aztecs in Mexico and the Incas of Peru. Within a few years, the Spaniards had almost totally destroyed them as they conquered and converted the local people to Christianity. Spain was enriched by important silver mines in both Mexico and Peru.

After this, explorers went out from Europe eager to find lands to settle as colonies. The Portuguese also built an empire in South America. The French and British explored North America. The Dutch sailed to the East Indies and found Australia and New Zealand. In the 1700s James Cook mapped the South Seas and neared the frozen continent of Antarctica.

The last continent to be explored was Africa. During the 1800s several explorers, of whom the greatest was David Livingstone, crossed the unknown 'Dark Continent'. The European powers competed to set up colonies in Africa, but by the late 20th century, these European empires had come to an end.

Above: Drawings like this one of red honeysuckle recorded the finds made on the voyages of Captain Cook (left).

MAP OF VOYAGES OF DISCOVERY

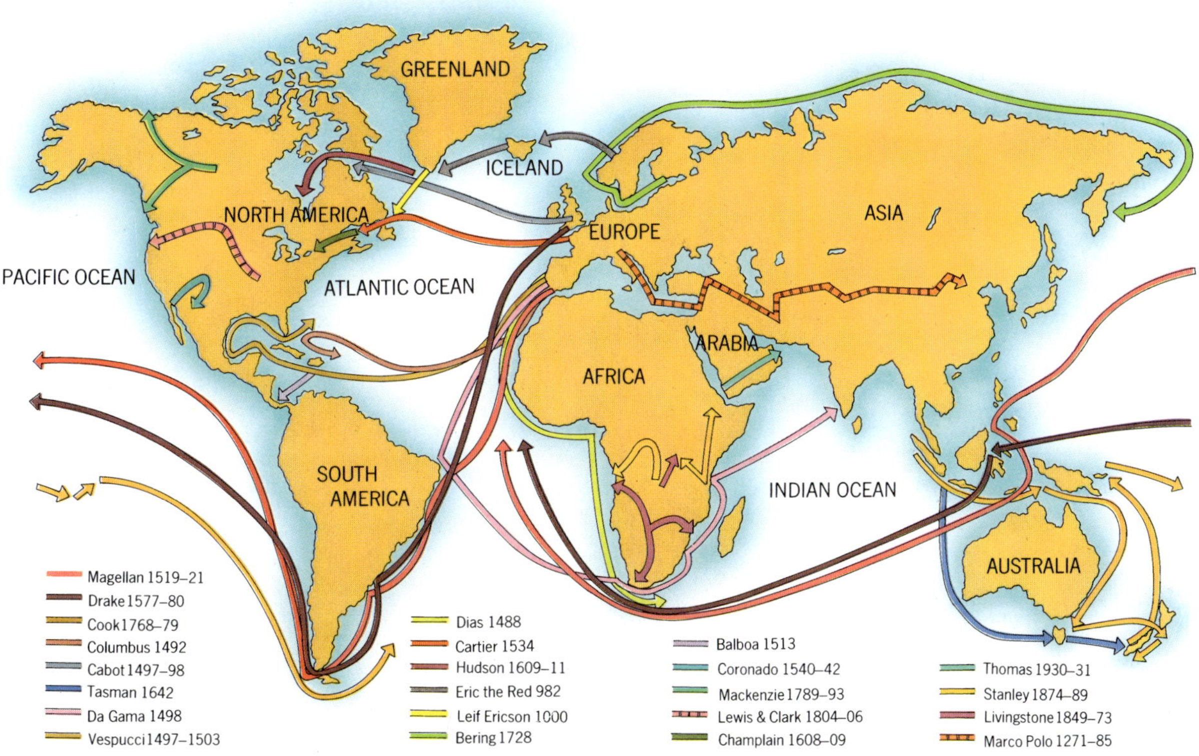

CHRONOLOGY

1708 Thomas Newcomen's steam engine used for pumping water from mines
1709 Abraham Darby smelts iron ore with coke
1733 John Kay's flying shuttle speeds hand-loom weaving
1757 James Brindley builds first completely artificial canal
1759 Bridgewater Canal built
1767 James Hargreaves' spinning jenny makes finer yarn
1768 James Watt's steam engine
1769 Richard Arkwright's water frame for spinning through rollers
1771 First cotton-spinning factory at Cromford
1779 Samuel Crompton's mule combines the water frame and the jenny
1783 Henry Cort's puddling and rolling process makes possible the large-scale production of wrought iron
1785 Edmund Cartwright's mechanical power loom
1802 Richard Trevithick's high-pressure engine, the origin of all steam locomotives
1825 George Stephenson's Stockton and Darlington Railway
1829 Stephenson's *Rocket*
1830 The Liverpool and Manchester Railway (first passenger service) opened

Growth of Industry

Until the 1700s most people worked on the land. They grew their own food and made cloth and other goods by hand in their own homes. There were no factories and few large towns. The Industrial Revolution changed all this. It began in Britain, a country rich in minerals like coal, iron, tin and copper. Britain also had many rivers to transport heavy, bulky goods and raw materials. Many canals were built too. Later, with the start of the railways, Britain improved its transport system dramatically.

The first industry to be mechanized was cotton manufacture. Inventions such as the spinning jenny produced more thread than could be handled by weavers, so a power loom was invented to speed up weaving. The new cotton machines needed a better source of power than windmills and waterwheels. James Watt provided this with his development of the steam engine. By 1800, 500 of his engines were in use – some pumping water, the rest providing power to run textile mills and iron furnaces.

Then new machines made it possible to produce goods very cheaply in factories but life in these factories and cot-

Right: Ironworks at Coalbrookdale, England, the site of the world's first iron bridge (1782). The use of iron and steel for engineering and construction was one of the great changes brought about by the Industrial Revolution. Factories, foundries, mills and mines spread across the countryside.

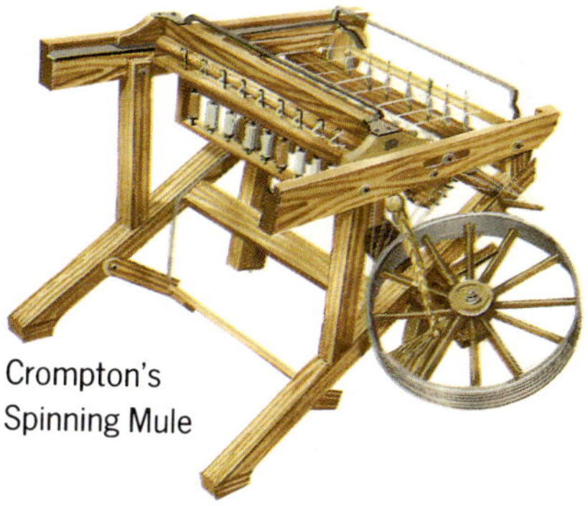

Crompton's Spinning Mule

Hargreaves' Spinning Jenny

ton mills was hard and dangerous. People worked 13 hours a day for low wages. Sometimes they were killed or crippled by unsafe machines. Children had to work as well, joining the women who dragged heavy coal tubs along coal mine tunnels. Towns grew quickly as people flocked from the countryside looking for work. Most lived in badly built slum houses.

After 1840 laws were made to improve conditions for workers, especially women and children. Factory owners were forced to fence in dangerous machinery. Trade unions were started to look after the workers' interests and to campaign for higher pay and better conditions.

During the Industrial Revolution Britain led the world in manufacturing and trade. Britain became the 'workshop of the world'. Other countries, particularly the United States and Germany, soon developed their own industries and challenged Britain.

Above: Machinery like Hargreaves' Spinning Jenny and Crompton's Spinning Mule speeded up the manufacturing process of textiles. Work formerly done by hand at home was, by the later 1700s, done in mills by steam-driven machines.

Below: An industrial town of the 19th century. Heavy goods were transported by canal in horse-drawn barges. Smoke from factory chimneys polluted the air above the workers' grimy houses.

Above: Simón Bolívar's troops defeat the Spanish at Ayacucho in 1824, freeing Peru from Spain.

Above: A French revolutionary. After the King's execution in 1793, France suffered a 'reign of terror'.

George Washington (*right*, mounted) led the American armies to victory over the British during the American War of Independence (1775-83). He became the first American president.

The Age of Revolution

If a country has a revolution, its government and laws are overthrown, often by war and bloodshed. Two of the most famous revolutions in history happened in America and France in the late 18th-century.

From the 1600s, the British had set up 13 colonies on the east coast of America. Eventually the colonists wanted to govern themselves, and fought a war of independence against British rule. In 1776 they founded their own republic, the United States of America. The British agreed to independence at the Treaty of Paris in 1783.

Meanwhile, discontent was growing in France, where the people felt that they were ruled unfairly. The king, Louis XVI, did not seem to care that many were poor and hungry, and heavily taxed. In 1789, fighting broke out in

Paris, and soon the rebellion against the king spread throughout France. In 1793 King Louis and his queen, Marie Antoinette, were put to death.

Over the next 50 years the new spirit of independence was to spread to many countries in Europe and to the Spanish colonies in South America.

In 1805, a young Venezuelan called Simón Bolívar took a vow to free his country from Spanish rule. Between 1811 and 1825, he and his followers fought a bitter war against the Spanish rulers in South America. In time, his armies freed not only Venezuela but the whole of northern South America. Six new republics were born: Venezuela, Colombia, Ecuador, Peru, Bolivia and Panama.

In Europe, hardship or the desire for freedom from foreign rule sparked other revolutions: by Poles, Belgians and Italians in 1830, and by Austrians, Hungarians, Italians and Slavs in 1848. The next major revolutions came later, in Portugal in 1910, and in 1917 when the Russians overthrew their tsar.

Above: The battle of Navarino, 1827, helped win Greece's independence from Turkey. An allied fleet of British, French and Russian ships defeated a Turkish-Egyptian fleet off the coast of southwest Greece at Navarino Bay destroying 60 ships.

Right: The Italian patriot Giuseppe Garibaldi (1807–82) led 1000 'Redshirts' to conquer the Kingdom of the Two Sicilies in 1860. Garibaldi helped to bring about Italy's unification in 1861 under Victor Emmanuel.

World Wars

Wars in the 19th century were mainly local affairs involving only two or three states. They scarcely affected other countries. World War I was a new kind of war, fought by many countries. Its effects were felt all round the world.

In August 1914, when World War I began, thousands of men – Germans, Austrians, Turks on one side, British French and Russians on the other – rushed eagerly to join the armed forces. People on both sides sang and cheered as the soldiers marched off to fight. But by the end of 1914 this mood had changed. Instead of rejoicing people were shocked and horrified at the destruction. The war had become a dreadful disaster.

Right: World War I quickly became a stalemate. Bogged down in trenches where conditions were extremely unhealthy, soldiers fought and lived in seas of mud among the corpses of their comrades and enemies. Rats and lice were common in the trenches and they speeded the spread of disease.

The two sides spent four years in the trenches in northern France, fighting over the same patch of ground. Soldiers were killed in thousands, mown down by enemy machine guns, as they tried to advance a few metres over the muddy wasteland. Here, Canadian troops fight off an attack at the second battle of Ypres in 1915. The misery and futility of trench warfare shocked both troops and civilians.

In the east the war was less static than in the west because the front was much longer. The Germans managed to occupy much of western Russia. Heavy Russian losses and defeat in the fighting helped to bring about a revolution in Russia in 1917.

ARMOURED WARFARE

Tanks made their first appearance on the battlefield in 1916. However, these new armoured vehicles were never used in large numbers. Though slow and clumsy, the first tanks might have made a breakthrough, smashing through the maze of trenches and barbed wire that crossed western Europe.

British SE 5

Left: World War I was the first war in which aircraft played an important part. Airships dropped bombs on towns and factories.

German Zeppelin

British Fairey Swordfish

Both sides had guns so powerful that they could fire shells for hours on end, until everything within range had been destroyed. A single machine gun could slaughter dozens of men in minutes. Armies could not move forwards against such guns. So they dug themselves lines of trenches. The trenches partly protected soldiers from gunfire, but did not save them from poison gas attacks. Troops were issued with gas masks to protect them against poisonous fumes. Not even aircraft or tanks (both new weapons) could break the stalemate.

At sea, steam 'iron clads' had thick, metal armour but mines and torpedoes were a real danger. Merchant ships were frequent targets and by 1917 Britain was close to starvation. In April 1917 German submarines attacked American ships carrying supplies and food to Britain and France. This brought the United States into the war on behalf of the Allies (the British and the French). Fortified by the American soldiers and weapons, the strength of the Allies outweighed that of the Germans and in 1918 the Germans and their allies surrendered. About 10 million soldiers were killed in World War I. The financial cost was so great that war debts continued long after 1918. People called it 'the war to end all wars'. But it was not. An even more terrible war lay in the future.

EVENTS OF WORLD WAR I

1914 June 15 Assassination of Archduke Franz Ferdinand at Sarajevo
Aug. 1 Germany declares war on Russia
Aug. 4 Britain declares war on Germany
Aug. 30 Germans defeat Russians at Tannenberg
Sept. 12 French and British halt German advance at Battle of the Marne

1915 Dec. British withdraw from Gallipoli

1916 Feb.–July German attack on Verdun
May 31–June 1 Naval battle of Jutland: indecisive
June–Sept. Brusilov offensive
July 1–Nov. 18 Battle of the Somme

1917 Mar. 3 Russia makes peace with Germany at Brest-Litovsk
Mar. 11 British occupy Baghdad
Apr. 6 US enters war against Germany.

1918 Mar. Great German offensive begins
Oct. 28 Mutiny in German navy at Kiel
Nov. 9 German Emperor (Kaiser) Wilhelm II abdicates
Nov. 11 Ceasefire

Above: The scene at Pearl Harbor on 7 December, 1941. Japan attacked the US Pacific fleet and destroyed 18 warships. Although the Japanese had crippled the US navy, they also forced the Americans into the war.

Below: Adolf Hitler, leader of Nazi Germany, attends a Nazi rally.

The Second World War (1939–45) was in fact two wars; one fought in Europe and along the coast of North Africa (against Germany), the other in the Pacific (against Japan). Out of 50 million casualties, 35 million were civilians, including 20 million Russians, 6 million Jews and $4\frac{1}{2}$ million Poles. At the end of the war European countries were bankrupt and the western USSR was in ruins. Only the United States seemed to remain strong.

Many Europeans became conquered peoples when, between 1939 and 1941, Adolf Hitler ordered the German armies to invade Poland, Norway, Denmark, the Netherlands, Belgium, France, Yugoslavia and Greece. Millions of Jews, gypsies, Communists, and others whom the Nazis hated, died in terrible concentration camps.

Britain and its Empire fought back. In 1941 Russia joined the fight against Hitler, after German armies invaded the USSR. From 1941 Britain had a powerful new ally when the USA entered the war after the Japanese attacked the naval base of Pearl Harbor. The Allies (Britain, USA and Russia) gradually got the upper hand, as they fought the Axis powers (Germany, Italy and Japan).

Armies fought across Europe and in Asia, while naval war was fought in the Atlantic and Pacific oceans. Submarines, tanks and aircraft dominated the fighting. The close of World War II saw the first long-range rocket weapons – the German VI flying bomb and V2 rocket – and, finally, the atom bombs which were dropped on Japan in 1945, ending the war.

German Messerschmitt Me 262

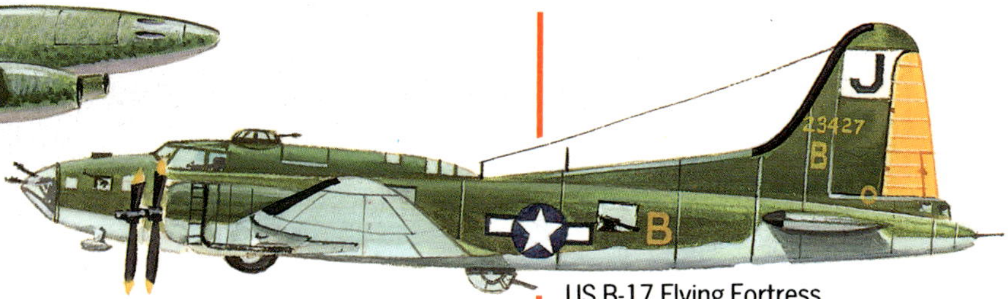

US B-17 Flying Fortress

Above: The German Messerschmitt Me 262 was the first jet fighter. Its speed startled Allied pilots. Bombing raids on enemy cities were carried out by heavy bombers such as this US B-17 Flying Fortress.

EVENTS OF WORLD WAR II

1939 Sept. 1 Germany invades Poland

1940 May 10 Germany invades Belgium, the Netherlands and Luxembourg
May 26–June 4 British evacuated from Dunkirk
June 10 Italy declares war against France and Britain
Aug.–Sept. Battle of Britain

1941 June Germans invade Russia
Dec. 7 Japanese attack on Pearl Harbor, Hong Kong, Malaya and the Philippines

1942 June Battle of Midway
Oct. Battle of El Alamein

1943 Jan. Leningrad relieved after a 17-month siege
Feb. German army surrenders at Stalingrad
Sept. Allies land in Italy

1944 June Allies invade France
Oct. US invades the Philippines

1945 May 8 VE Day: Victory in Europe
Aug. 6 Atom bomb dropped on Hiroshima
Aug. 10 Japan surrenders

French AMC

British A-9

Armoured warfare played a very important part in World War II. Both sides used large formations of tanks, particularly in the land battles in North Africa, the USSR and in Europe.

Below: The Allied invasion of western Europe took place on D-Day, 6 June 1944. Thousands of troops landed on beaches in Normandy, France, supported by huge naval and air forces. By August, Paris was liberated from the Germans, and an end to the war in Europe was in sight.

Right: During the early 1950s discontentment with the repressive communist government in Hungary mounted. Demands were made for an end to policies which had done much to destroy the economy since World War II and to limit personal freedom. In October 1956 fighting in the streets of Budapest quickly spread to a nation-wide revolution. The Russians acted swiftly to suppress with force the people's demands for freedom. Many were killed.

The Modern World

TIME CHART

1945 End of World War II
1947 India and Pakistan become independent
1949 Communist rule in China
1950–53 Korean War
1956 Hungarian uprising
1957 European Common Market founded
1967 Six-Day War (Israel and Egypt)
1968 Soviet army crushes democracy movement in Czechoslovakia
1973 Arab-Israeli War
1975 End of Vietnam War
1979 Iranian revolution establishes Islamic Republic
1979 USSR invades Afghanistan
1980–88 Iran-Iraq War
1988–89 Democratic revolutions in Eastern Europe

The United Nations, set up in 1945 to keep world peace, actually has little real power. The world is dominated by two 'super powers', Russia and the United States. Since 1945 they have competed for influence and have built up a stock of nuclear arms. Europe was separated into the communist East, for many years under Russian control, and the democratic West where the European Community helped to bring prosperity to its members. Former colonies in Africa, Southeast Asia and the West Indies became independent.

In the Far East Japan is an economic 'super power' whose manufactured goods are sold all over the world. China is a communist state which, under Mao Tse-tung's leadership (1949–1976), underwent enormous changes. The present government has opened trade links with the West but is still opposed to democracy. The countries of Indo-China – Cambodia, Laos and Vietnam – have been torn by terrible wars as the communists took over.

In the Near East, Saudi Arabia, a poor country 50 years ago, has larger oil deposits than any other country and is

Left: A street scene in Lagos, the capital of Nigeria. Modern buildings, cars and street lighting provide a stark contrast with the simple, rural lifestyle that the majority of Nigerians lead, herding cattle or growing cash crops such as cocoa and peanuts. However, in recent years since the exploitation of oil reserves and economic growth, the hope of employment in mining and manufacturing industries has drawn many to the large cities, leading to overcrowding in some areas.

now very rich. The Jewish state of Israel, founded in 1948, survives, though surrounded by hostile Arab countries. Iran is in a troubled state after the overthrow of the Shah (1979) and the setting up of an Islamic republic; it was at war with Iraq from 1980 to 1988. Russian troops occupied Afghanistan in an attempt to support a communist government there. Lebanon has been torn by civil war.

In the Americas the United States leads the fight against communism, and resists further moves towards communism in the countries of Latin America (only Cuba is communist). Much of Latin America is still poor though some countries, such as Brazil, have great natural wealth which is often misused (as when the Amazon forests are destroyed for farm land and timber).

Africa is now made up almost entirely of independent black-ruled states. The exception is South Africa, which has a policy of *apartheid* (racial discrimination).

Since 1945 the world has experienced two major 'secondary' wars: in Korea and Vietnam.

In 1945 Korea had been divided into a communist North under Russian influence, and a non-communist South which had American support. In 1950 the communists attacked the South. South Korea appealed to the United nations for help, and an army, mainly American but provided by 15 countries, was soon fighting the North. China sent 780,000 soldiers to help the North Koreans. After three years of fighting, there was a ceasefire, and peace was restored.

About three-quarters of the world's population live in developing countries where disease and poverty are widespread. During the second half of the 20th century there has been a growing awareness of the needs of these countries. Some Western governments have set up aid programmes, and charities are at work in many places. Through these, local people are supplied with food, medicine and expertise. A Red Cross health programme in Angola (*below*) helps mothers nurse and feed young children.

Above: Refugees flee fighting in Vietnam. The Vietnam War began as a war against France in 1946. In 1954 Vietnam was divided. Civil war between the communist North, and the non-communist South helped by the USA, lasted until 1975 when the communists captured the South.

Below: East-West relations improved during the late 1980s. In 1987 Gorbachev and Reagan both agreed to reduce numbers of nuclear missiles.

In 1954 the French left their former colony of Vietnam which, like Korea, was then divided into a communist North and a non-communist South. The Vietcong (Vietnamese communists) waged guerrilla war against the government in the South. The Americans aided the South Vietnamese government and eventually became involved in the war. They began to bomb northern cities and used chemical weapons against the Vietcong. In the end the Americans pulled out of a war they could not win, and in 1975 Saigon, the southern capital, fell to the Vietcong. Vietnam was united as a communist country.

A direct telephone link was set up in 1963 between Moscow and Washington to allow the Russian and US leaders to discuss immediately any issues which might lead to war. In the same year Russia, America and Britain signed the Test Ban Treaty, which stopped nuclear tests above ground. This was the start of 'peaceful coexistence', the recognition by both sides that differences must be sorted out by talking and not by war. Since the coming to power in 1985 of the Russian leader Mikhail Gorbachev, there have been signs of new freedoms and economic changes in the USSR. In addition, in 1989 dramatic political changes swept through the countries of Eastern Europe, which had been ruled by the communists since the 1940s. After widespread demonstrations, hardline governments were replaced by reformists, restrictive laws were abolished and the demolition of the Berlin Wall was begun. In turn, there has been some progress towards disarmament and a more peaceful future for the world.

Below left: This map shows the member countries of the European Community.

Below: The United Nations sends peace-keeping forces to the world's troublespots, but has no army of its own. These Royal Marines are serving in Cyprus.

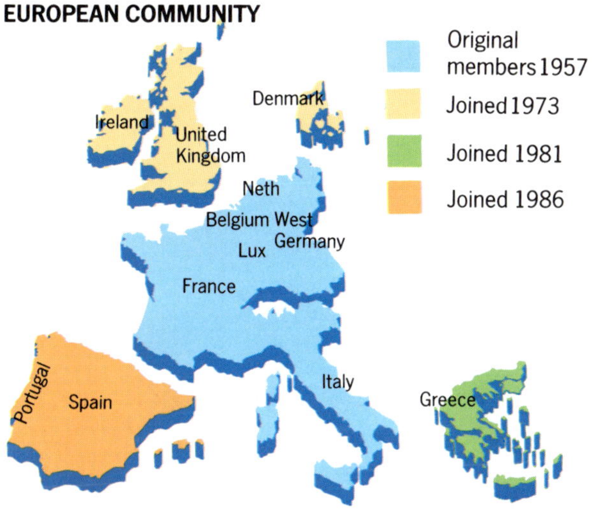

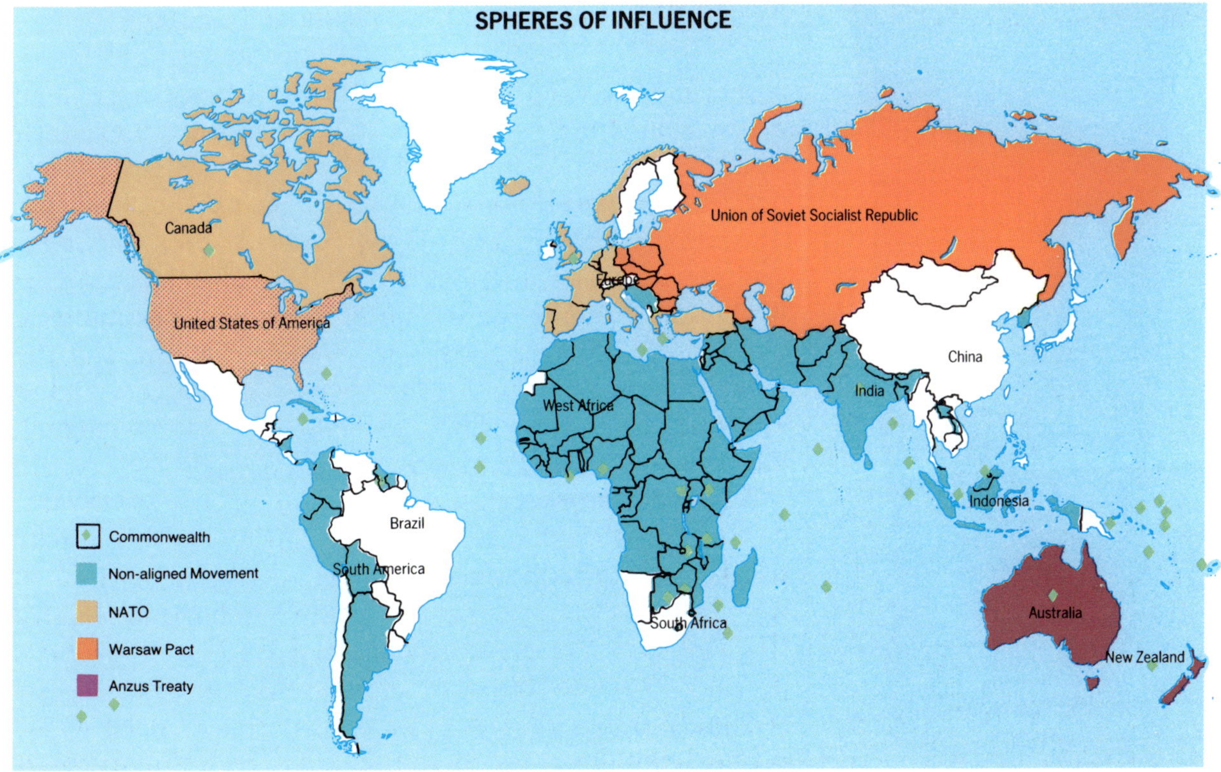

Time Chart

EUROPE

BC

*c.*6500	Farming begins in Greece and the Aegean
*c.*4000	Farming develops in Britain
*c.*3000	Windmill Hill culture in Britain
*c.*2000	Bronze Age in northern Europe
*c.*2000–1200	Minoan and Mycenean civilization in Crete and Greece
*c.*750–550	Greeks and Phoenicians colonize Mediterranean and Black Sea lands
660	Byzantium founded
509	Roman republic founded
477	Athens starts rise to power
*c.*380–300	Work of Plato, Euclid and Aristotle
*c.*327–300	Main period of Roman expansion
27	Augustus becomes Emperor of Rome

AD

77	Roman conquest of Britain
101–107	Roman Empire increased to maximum over Europe
284–305	Reign of Diocletian. Empire reorganized and divided into East and West
370	Huns from Asia invade Europe
*c.*400–*c.*600	Angles, Saxons and Jutes migrate and settle in Britain
410	Goths sack Rome
597	St Augustine lands in England
*c.*600	Slavs move into Balkans
711	Muslims invade Spain
795	Vikings raid Ireland
800	Charlemagne crowned
817	Partition of Charlemagne's empire begins
899–939	Wessex kings reconquer Danelaw
1054	Break between Greek and Latin churches
1066	Battle of Hastings
1073–85	Quarrel between Holy Roman Empire and Papacy begins
1170	Thomas à Becket murdered
1215	Magna Carta
1296–1336	Anglo-Scottish wars
1337–1453	Hundred Years' War in France
1347–50	Black Death

AMERICA AND AUSTRALASIA

BC

3372	First date in Mayan calendar
*c.*3000	Agriculture in Tehuacan Valley in Mexico. First pottery in Mexico.
c.1500	Beginning of Eskimo culture
*c.*900–100	Olmec culture in Middle America
*c.*800–400	Burial mound period begins with Adena culture
*c.*500–100	Mogollon and Hohokam cultures and Desert culture in North-West America
*c.*400	Navigation among Pacific islands
*c.*300	Maya civilization in Yucatán and Central America

AD

*c.*200–400	Hopewell culture replaces Adena in North America
*c.*400	Incas established on parts of South American Pacific coast Teotihuacán at its height
*c.*500–700	Regional cultures thrive after Hopewell decline
*c.*700–800	Temple mound period begins
*c.*800	Zenith of Classic Maya civilization
*c.*900	Anasaki and Hohokam cultures flourish in North America
1002	Leif Ericsson explores North American coast
1100	Polynesian islands colonized
1151	End of Toltec culture in Mexico
1189	Last known Norse visit to North America
*c.*1200	Thule Eskimo migration to eastern Canada and Greenland
1200	Hunac Ceel revolts against Maya
*c.*1325–1520	Aztecs found Tenochtitlan and begin civilization in Mexico

AFRICA AND THE NEAR EAST

BC

*c.*9000	Farming begins
*c.*4000–3500	Invention of wheel, plough and sail in Mesopotamia and Egypt
*c.*3500	Early writing in Mesopotamia and Egypt
*c.*2780	First pyramid built in Egypt
*c.*2300	Semites found Assyrian and Babylonian Empires
*c.*2000	Hittite civilization in Turkey
1361	Accession of Tutankhamun
1300	Medes and Persians move into Iran
500	Bantu people spread to East Africa
*c.*500–330	Achaemenid Empire in Persia
470	Hanno sails down African coast
334–323	Campaigns of Alexander the Great
*c.*6	Birth of Christ

AD

*c.*30	Crucifixion of Christ
226–636	Sassanid Empire in Persia
429–535	Vandal Kingdom in northern Africa
527–565	Justinian emperor of Byzantium
540	Persian-Byzantine War begins
570	Birth of Muhammad at Mecca
636–43	Arab conquest of Syria, Egypt and Persia
700	Arabs capture Tunis – virtual end of Christianity in North Africa
969	Fatimids conquer Egypt
980	Arabs settle on East African coast
1055	Seljuk Turks capture Baghdad
1061	Almoravid dynasty established in North Africa
1096–99	First Crusade; Kingdom of Jerusalem established
1196–1494	Marimid dynasty in Morocco
1258	Mongols sack Baghdad
1271–95	Travels of Marco Polo
*c.*1300	Ottoman Turkish expansion begins
1308–1405	Career and conquests of Timur (Tamerlane)
1345	Ottomans first cross the Bosphorus into Europe

ASIA

BC

*c.*6000	Rice cultivation in Far East
*c.*2500	Start of Indus Valley civilization
*c.*2350	Yao dynasty in China
*c.*2150	Aryans invade Indus Valley
*c.*1766–1000	Shang dynasty in China
*c.*1000	First Chinese dictionary
*c.*1000–500	Zhou dynasty in China
*c.*600	Early cities in Ganges Valley
563	Birth of Buddha
551	Birth of Confucius
327	Alexander begins invasion of India
321–184	Mauryan dynasty in India
214	Building of Great Wall
*c.*200BC–*c.*220AD	Han dynasty in China
184–72	Sunga dynasty in India

AD

*c.*74	China opens silk trade
220–264	Period of Three Kingdoms in China
230	Sujin: first known ruler in Japan
304–8	Huns invade China
265–317	Western Chin dynasty
*c.*320	Gupta Empire in Ganges Valley: 'Golden Age' of Hindu culture
*c.*300	Buddhism spreads in China
407–553	First Mongol Empire
*c.*520	Decimal system invented in India
618–906	T'ang dynasty in China
663	Japanese leave Korea
711–13	Muslims conquer Samarkand and Indus Valley
932	Wood block printing in China
960–1280	'Golden Age' of arts in Japan
1206	Genghis Khan becomes ruler of Mongolia
1206–80	Mongol conquests
1363	Tamerlane moves into Asia
1320–1413	Tughluk dynasty in Delhi
1368–1644	Mung dynasty in China
1369–1910	Korea: I dynasty
1398–1399	Tamerlane invades Delhi and massacre follows
1405	Death of Tamerlane

Above: King Alfred the Great, king of Wessex in 871, defeated Danish invaders.

Above: Genghis Khan, a fierce tribal leader from Mongolia who conquered most of central Asia.

Above: Those who disagreed with the new leaders, Danton, Marat and Robespierre, during the French Revolution were in danger of meeting their end at the guillotine. After the king was executed in 1793, the Revolution became more extreme. During the Reign of Terror which followed, civil and political rights were withdrawn and 18,000 people were sentenced to death.

EUROPE

1431	Joan of Arc burned as a witch
1453	Constantinople falls to Ottoman Turks
1455–85	Wars of the Roses in England
1521	Condemnation of Martin Luther. Beginning of Protestantism
1529–39	Henry VIII's Reformation Parliament and dissolution of the monasteries
1588	Spanish Armada dispersed
1598	Edict of Nantes
*c.*1600–1650	Scientific work of Kepler, Galileo and Descartes
1605	Gunpowder Plot discovered
1618–48	Thirty Years' War
1642–48	Civil wars in England
1643–1715	Reign of Louis XIV
1660	Monarchy restored in Britain under Charles II
1665	Great Plague in London
1666	Great Fire of London
1682–1725	Reign of Peter the Great, Tsar of Russia
1707	Union of England and Scotland
*c.*1730	Wesley brothers found Methodism
1755	Lisbon earthquake
1756–63	Seven Years' War
1789	French Revolution begins
1799	Napoleon seizes power in France
1800	Union of England and Ireland
1808–1814	Peninsula War
1812–29	Greek War of Liberation
1813	Battle of Leipzig
1814	Napoleon exiled to Elba
1815	Battle of Waterloo; Congress of Vienna
1825	Stockton-Darlington railway completed
1830	July Revolution in Paris
1834	'Tolpuddle Martyrs' in England
	Carlist wars in Spain
1845	Irish potato famine
1848	Year of Revolutions throughout Europe
1851	Great Exhibition, London
1854–56	Crimean War
1859	Darwin's *Origin of Species*
1870–71	Franco-Prussian War
1912–13	Balkan Wars
1914	World War I begins
1916	Easter Rising in Ireland
1916	Battle of the Somme

AMERICA AND AUSTRALASIA

*c.*1400–1525	Inca civilization in Andes
1492	Christopher Columbus crosses Atlantic and reaches America
1493	Newly discovered lands divided between Spain and Portugal
1497	John Cabot discovers Newfoundland
1513	Vasco Nuñez de Balboa discovers Pacific Ocean
1521	Hernándo Cortés conquers Tenochtitlan
1522	First circumnavigation of the world by Magellan's expedition
1533	Pizarro conquers Peru
1586	Francis Drake sails to West Indies
1607	English found colony of Virginia
	Henry Hudson explores Canada
1608	French colonists found Quebec
1619	First black African slaves arrive in Virginia
1620	*Mayflower* puritans (Pilgrim Fathers) settle in New England
1645	Tasman discovers New Zealand
1722	Dutch navigator Jacob Roggereen discovers Samoa and Easter Island
1755–1763	French and Indian Wars
1768	English navigator James Cook discovers and explores east coast of Australia
1770	Botany Bay
	Boston Massacre
1772–1775	James Cook circumnavigates Antarctica
1773	Boston Tea Party
1775–1783	American War of Independence
1776	American Declaration of Independence
1787	United States Constitution signed
1788	First convicts transported from Britain to Australia
1789–1797	George Washington, first President of United States
1791	American Bill of Rights
	Division of Canada into French and English speaking parts

AFRICA AND THE NEAR EAST

1405–1413	Civil war in Ottoman Empire
1453	Fall of Constantinople to the Turks. End of Byzantine Empire
1455–57	Ca Da Mosto explores West Africa
1468	Sonni Ali captures Timbuktu Shonghay Empire founded in West Africa
1471	Portuguese seize Tangier from Muslims
1482	Portuguese settle Gold Coast
1485	Batholomew Diaz rounds Cape of Good Hope
*c.*1500–1870	African slave trade
1505	Portuguese colonize Mozambique
1517	Turks capture Cairo – end of Mameluke Empire
1534	Turks capture Tunis, Baghdad and Mesopotamia from Persia
1554–56	Turks conquer coast of North Africa
1571–1603	Bornu Empire in Sudan reaches height
1574	Portuguese begin to settle coast of Angola
1578	Battle of Al Kasr Al-Kabil in Morocco
1595	First Dutch settlements on Guinea coast
1626	First French settlements on Madagascar
1652	Capetown founded by Dutch
1660	Rise of Bambara Kingdom on upper Niger river
1697	French complete conquest of Dutch in Senegal
1705	Husseinite dynasty founded in Tunis
1713	Start of most active period of British slave trade
1714	Karamanli dynasty in Tripoli
1715	French take Mauritius
1723	British take Gambia
1795	British take Cape of Good Hope from Dutch
1798–1799	Bonaparte's expedition to Egypt Battle of Pyramids Battle of Nile
1801	Islamic Kingdom of Sokoto founded in West Africa
1802–11	Portuguese explorers cross Africa from west to east
1818	Zulu Empire founded in South Africa

ASIA

	Mongol Empire disintegrates
1411–1442	Ahmadabad built in western India
1467	Start of 100 years of civil wars in Japan
1498	Vasco da Gama reaches India
1513	Dutch reach Canton
1522–1680	Mughal expansion in India
1556	Battle of Panipat
1557	Portuguese settle at Macao in China Akbar the Great, Mughal emperor, unifies northern India
1570	Nagasaki port opened
1577	So-nam Gya-tso becomes Tibetan Dalai Lama
1590	Hideyoshi unifies Japan
1595	Dutch settle on Guinea coast of Japan
1600	East India Company founded
1603	Tokugawa appointed shogun in Japan
1615–1620	Military tribe the Manchus attack northern China
1621	Nurhachi in China expels Ming
1632–53	Shah Jehan of India builds Taj Mahal
1644–1912	Manchu dynasty rules China
1661	British acquire Bombay
1676–78	Sikh uprising in India
1707	Death of Aurangzeb Disintegration of Mughal Empire in India
1751	Clive takes Arcot; start of British power in India
1756	'Black Hole' of Calcutta
1757	British rule in India
1775–82	British and Marathas at war
1787	Rice riots in Edo, Japan
1792	China invades Nepal
1814	First modern Shinto sect in Japan. India and Nepal fight over borders
1839–42	Opium War; Britain takes Hong Kong
1845–48	Anglo-Sikh wars in India
1850–64	Revolt in China
1856	Anglo/Chinese War begins
1857–59	Sepoy Rebellion in India against the British
1858	Government of India transferred to British Crown
1862	Cambodia becomes French
1868–1912	Meiji period in Japan

Above: The American Civil War

Below: The opening of Japan's first railway station.

Above: Two historical posters show different aspects of war – the banner of Lenin and Stalin of the 1905 Russian Revolution, and a recruitment campaign for the British army. For hundreds of years war has been going on somewhere in the world nearly all the time. Wars have been fought for different reasons.

EUROPE

1917	Bolshevik Revolution in Russia begins
1918	Ceasefire on western front World War I ends
1922	Mussolini takes power in Italy Irish Free State established
1926	General Strike in Britain
1927	Charles Lindbergh makes first trans-Atlantic solo flight
1933	Hitler becomes German Chancellor
1936–39	Spanish Civil War
1938	Germany annexes Austria Munich pact
1939	World War II begins
1940	Battle of Britain
1941	Germany invades USSR
1944	Normandy Landings (D-Day)
1945	Defeat of Germany Cold War begins United Nations formed
1948	North Atlantic Treaty Organization (NATO) formed
1955	Warsaw Pact formed in opposition to NATO
1957	USSR launches first space satellite. Treaty of Rome: formation of the European Community
1961	Berlin Wall built First man in space: Yuri Gagarin of Russia
1965	Vietnam War begins
1968	Soviet troops invade Czechoslovakia Northern Ireland crisis begins
1972	Britain assumes direct rule in Ulster. Greek–Turkish conflict in Cyprus
1975	Death of General Franco; Prince Juan Carlos crowned king of Spain 'Cod War' develops over fishing rights
1982	Britain at war with Argentina over Falkland Islands
1985	Mikhail Gorbachev becomes leader of USSR
1989	Berlin Wall dismantled Free elections in Poland and Hungary. Fall of communist Romanian dictator Ceausescu Political change throughout Eastern Europe
1990	Lithuania, Latvia and Estonia demand independence from USSR

AMERICA AND AUSTRALASIA

1793	First free settlers arrive in Australia
1803	Louisiana Purchase
1817–30	Careers of Simón Bolívar and José de San Martin
1848	Californian Gold rush begins
1846–48	USA–Mexico War
1861–65	American Civil War
1867	United States purchases Alaska from Russia Dominion of Canada formed
1868	Ten year war between Cuba and Spain
1869	First trans-continental railway completed in USA
1876	Battle of Little Big Horn
1881	Peace declared between New Zealand settlers and Maoris
1895–98	Spanish–American War
1901	Commonwealth of Australia established
1903	Wright brothers: first powered flight Alaska's boundaries determined
1907	Dominion of New Zealand established
1909	American Robert Peary reaches the North Pole
1911	Mexican Revolution
1914	Panama Canal opened
1917	United States enters World War I
1926	Canberra becomes capital of Australia
1929	Wall Street Crash begins Great Depression
1941	Pearl Harbor, Hawaii attacked by Japanese United States enters World War II
1943	Argentinian Revolution led by Juan Peron
1955	Rebellion in Argentina
1957	Race riots in southern United States
1959	Communist Revolution in Cuba
1962	Cuban missile crisis
1964	Civil Rights Bill in United States
1965	Australia–New Zealand free trade agreement
1969	Neil Armstrong lands on the Moon
1973	Military coup in Chile
1976	Papua–New Guinea gains independence from Australia
1981	First Space Shuttle

AFRICA AND THE NEAR EAST

1822	Liberia in West Africa founded as colony for freed US slaves
1824–27	War in Gold Coast, Ghana
1830	French invade Algeria
1835	Great Trek of Boers inland from Cape of Good Hope
	Transvaal founded
1838	Boers defeat Zulus in Natal
1853–56	David Livingstone crosses Africa
1869	Suez canal opened
1880–81	Boer uprising; Transvaal becomes independent
1882	Britain occupies Egypt
1885	German East Africa established
1890	Rhodesia founded by Cecil Rhodes
1893	Ivory Coast becomes French
1899–1902	Anglo-Boer War
1910	South Africa becomes a dominion
1920	Palestine comes under British rule
1922	Egypt becomes independent
1949	*Apartheid* policy adopted by South Africa
1952	Mau Mau rebellion
1956	Suez Canal dispute
1960	Seventeen African states become independent
1961	South Africa becomes a republic
1962	Algeria becomes independent
1963	Organization of African Unity formed
1967–1970	Nigerian Civil War
1973	Arab states impose oil embargo
1974	Angola and Mozambique become independent
1979	Shah of Iran deposed
	Ayatollah Khomeni rules
1980	Rhodesia gains independence as Zimbabwe
	Iran-Iraq War begins
1984	International aid to Ethiopia
1985	Severe famine in East Africa
1988	Nelson Mandela's 70th birthday spent in prison
	Iraq-Iran War ends
1989	Ayatollah Khomeni dies
1990	Nelson Mandela released from prison
	Namibia gains independence

ASIA

1895	Treaty of Shimonoseki – Japan gains Formosa
	Korea gains independence
1896	Anglo-French agreements in Siam (now Thailand)
1900	Nationalist Boxer rebellion in China
1904–5	Japan at war with Russia
	Tibet open for trade
1905	Battle of Tsushima
1910	Japan annexes Korea
1912	China becomes a republic
1919	Nationalist movement in India
1924	New Chinese government led by Sun Yat-sen
1927	Civil war in China
1931	Japanese occupy Manchuria
1934–35	Mao Tse-tung's Long March
1937	Japanese capture Shanghai and Peking
1945	Atomic bombs dropped on Hiroshima and Nagasaki
1946	Civil war in Indochina
1947	India, Pakistan, Burma and Indonesia independent
1949	Communist regime in China
1950–53	Korean War
1954	French lose battle of Dien Bien Phu
1959	Uprising in Tibet
1965	India and Pakistan at war
1965–73	American troops fight in Vietnam
1966–68	China's 'Cultural Revolution'
1970	USA invades Cambodia
1971	Bangladesh becomes independent
1973	End of Vietnam War
1979	Russian forces move into Afghanistan
1987	Indian troops war with Tamils in Sri Lanka
1988	Soviet troops withdraw from Afghanistan
	Benazir Bhutto becomes Pakistan's first woman president
1989	Burma changes name to Union of Myanmar
	Emperor Hirohito of Japan dies
	Chinese government suppresses student pro-democracy demonstrations: many killed
1990	Pro-democracy demonstrations in Nepal

Above: In May 1953 the New Zealander, Edmund Hillary and Tenzing Norgay, a Nepalese Sherpa, became the first people to reach the summit of Mount Everest in the Himalaya range, the highest mountain in the world.

Above: John F. Kennedy was the youngest president of the United States of America when he was elected in 1961. His term in office was brutally curtailed when Lee Harvey Oswald shot and killed him in Dallas on November 22, 1963.

Who's Who in History

Agricola, Gnaeus Julius (37–93) Roman soldier, governor of Britain 78–84. Carried Roman conquest to the farthest northern point of the empire, when he defeated Caledonians at Mt Graupius somewhere near Aberdeen, Scotland, in 83.

Akbar the Great (1542–1605) Grandson of Babar, he was the greatest Mughal emperor of India and a fine military commander who expanded the empire. Akbar was respected for his justice and religious tolerance.

Above: The sacking of Rome.

Alaric (370–410) Leader of the Visigoths, ravaged Thrace to the gates of Constantinople (Istanbul) at the end of the 4th century. In 410 Alaric sacked Rome – he died soon after in southern Italy.

Alexander the Great (356–323 BC) Became king of Macedon at 20 and then set out to conquer the world. By 323 BC, his empire stretched from Greece to the River Indus in Pakistan and south to include Egypt – he was one of the world's greatest military commanders.

Alfred the Great (849–899) Became king of Wessex in the south of England. He led the Saxons to victory over the Danish invaders.

Alva, Duke of (1508?–1582?) Spanish governor of the Netherlands during the reign of Philip II. He attempted to crush Calvinism in the Netherlands and allowed thousands to be sentenced to death for their faith by the courts. Opposition was fierce and finally the Spaniards had to admit defeat by accepting the independence of seven northern Protestant provinces.

Archimedes (287–212 BC) Greek mathematician and engineer, discovered principles of buoyancy and the lever. Calculated accurate value of pi (ratio of circle's circumference to its diameter). His military defensive devices prolonged the siege of Syracuse by the Romans. He was reputedly killed by a Roman soldier because he would not stop the experiment upon which he was working when the Romans broke into the city.

Ashoka (273 BC–232 BC) The greatest of the Mauryan emperors. He brought peace and order to his huge empire which covered most of India.

Assurbanipal (died *c.* 626 BC) The last great king of Assyria, he completed the conquest of Egypt and Babylon. After his reign the empire collapsed.

Atahualpa (1500?–1533) The last leader of the Incas, he came to the throne in 1532. He was captured and executed by the conquistador Francisco Pizarro.

Atatürk, Kemal (1881–1938) Turkish general and statesman – founder of modern Turkey. Atatürk was a general in World War I; he overthrew the Sultan and turned Turkey into a republic, becoming its president in 1923. Forbade the wearing of the fez (hat) and discouraged women from using the veil.

Augustine, St (died 604) Italian missionary who brought Christianity to Britain. He became the first archbishop of Canterbury in 601.

Augustus (273 BC–AD 14) Heir of Julius Caesar and the first Roman emperor. He strengthened Rome through good government after a century of civil war.

Babar (1483–1530) Mongol descendant of Genghis Khan, he became ruler at Kabul when aged 21. From there set out upon the conquest of northern India to establish the Mughal empire which lasted until the coming of the British to India in the 18th century.

Becket, Thomas à (1118–1170) Friend and Chancellor of Henry II. The king made him archbishop of Canterbury, but he then quarrelled with the king over the balance of Church and state power. He was murdered in Canterbury Cathedral by followers of the king. Subsequently made a saint.

Bede, the Venerable (673–735) English monk and scholar. His *History of the English Church and People* written in medieval Latin is one of the first source books of English history. It was translated into English by King Alfred the Great.

Bismarck, Prince Otto von (1815–1898) Prussian statesman, prime minister of Prussia and then Germany from 1862 to 1890. He is the creator of modern united Germany. He was known as the 'Iron Chancellor'.

Boudicca (Boadicea) (died AD 62) Queen of Iceni tribe of Britain, she revolted against the Roman occupation. Only defeated after a major campaign that endangered Roman control of Britain.

Buddha (Siddhartha Gautama) (563–483 BC) Founder of Buddhism, well-born Indian who renounced worldly pleasures and sat under a *bodhi* tree until mysteries of life were unfolded to him.

Above: Statue of Buddha.

Burton, Sir Richard (1821–1890) Eccentric British traveller and explorer. One of first Europeans to enter Mecca (holy city of Islam) in disguise. Discovered Lake Tanganyika with Speke. Wrote more than 50 books including a translation of the *Arabian Nights*.

Caesar, Julius (100–44BC) Roman statesman and general. Conquered Gaul and wrote his account – *De Bello Gallico*. Defied orders of the Senate and crossed the River Rubicon with his army to invade Italy and become dictator. Assassinated by his political rivals and in the power struggle that followed Augustus emerged victorious to become first Roman emperor.

Calvin, John (1509–1564) One of the greatest religious reformers of the 16th century. His ideas were more extreme than Luther's and often controversial, but his influence spread quickly all over Europe.

Canute (994–1035) Son of Sweyn Forkbeard of Denmark. King of England from 1016 to his death. Strong king who restored order to the country after a period of weakness. The famous story of Canute telling the sea to stop has often been misunderstood. He wished to demonstrate the limit of kingly power to foolish courtiers, who said he could do anything.

Castro, Fidel (1927–) Cuban Marxist, overthrew President Batista (1959) and became Cuba's leader.

Catherine II, the Great (1729–1796) Deposed her mad husband Tsar Peter III of Russia and became empress (1762). Strengthened power of nobility; captured Crimea, Black Sea coast and much of Poland.

Charles V (1500–1558) Holy Roman emperor from 1519. King of Spain as Charles I from 1516. Ruled over more of Europe than any other Habsburg. Abdicated 1556.

Cheops (c. 2600 BC) He had the Great Pyramid built – the largest stone monument the world has seen. It contains 2,300,000 blocks of stone with an average weight of two-and-a-half tonnes each.

Churchill, Winston S. (1874–1965) British soldier, statesman and author. First lord of admiralty 1911–1915 and 1939–1940, chancellor of exchequer 1924–1925. Britain's wartime prime minister 1940–1945 and PM again 1951–1955. Also a writer – he won the Nobel prize for literature in 1953.

Above: Churchill (left) with Roosevelt and Stalin at the Yalta Conference in 1945.

Claudius I (10 BC–54 AD) Became Roman emperor from 41 AD after the assassination of Caligula. During his reign he established a good system of government and extended the empire.

Cleopatra VII (69–30 BC) Queen of Egypt from 51 to 30 BC. Caesar supported her against a rival claimant to the throne. She became his lover and bore him a son. After his death she became the lover and later wife of Marcus Antonius. Attempted but failed to captivate Augustus and in 30 BC committed suicide. Her great beauty is almost certainly a later exaggeration but she did use her attractions to keep her throne.

Clive, Robert (1725–1774) British soldier who did much to bring India under British control in the 18th century. Governor of Bengal (1764–1767). On his return to England he was censured for misgovernment and corruption, and said that in retrospect he was astonished at his own moderation. Committed suicide.

Columbus, Christopher (1451–1506) Genoese navigator who discovered Cuba (the New World) in 1492. Made four trips to New World but never realized he had found a new continent. Died in poverty.

Confucius (Kongfuzi; Great Master Kong) (c. 551–479 BC) Chinese philosopher who preached absolute justice and moderation. The *Analects* are his collected sayings. Confucianism has been the greatest influence upon Chinese philosophy.

Cook, James (1728–1779) British navigator. First person to sail south of Antarctic Circle. Explored Pacific, charting coasts of New Zealand and Australia. Died in a scuffle in Hawaii.

Above: Aztecs seized by Cortes' soldiers.

Copernicus, Nicolaus (1473–1543) Polish astronomer who developed the idea of a Sun-centred solar system. Considered to be the founder of modern astronomy.

Coronado, Francisco Vásquez de (1510–1554) Spanish explorer in the American Southwest. He led an expedition in 1540 to claim the legendary riches of the Seven Cities of Cibola for Spain.

Cortés, Hernando (1485–1547) Greatest Spanish conquistador – who conquered Mexico (the Aztecs) in 1519–1521 with a mere 550 men. He ruled as governor until 1530.

Cranmer, Thomas (1489–1556) English reformer and archbishop of Canterbury. He promoted Protestantism in England and was responsible for the first prayer book which was published in 1549. He was imprisoned under Queen Mary I and finally burned at the stake.

Crockett, Davy (1786–1836) American frontiersman, politician and folk hero. He was killed at Alamo.

Croesus (died 546 BC) The last king of Lydia in Asia Minor. He is known for his powerful military leadership and his vast wealth.

Cromwell, Oliver (1599–1658) Leader of the Roundhead (Parliamentary) faction in the civil war in England. Brilliant soldier and great statesman. Had Charles I executed and ruled as lord protector of England (1653–1658).

Curie, Marie (1867–1934) With her French husband **Pierre** she discovered two radioactive elements in uranium ore. Their discovery of these elements, which they called radium and polonium, won them the Nobel Prize for Physics in 1903 which they shared with Becquerel, a French scientist who discovered natural radioactivity.

Danton, Georges Jacques (1759–1794) Lawyer and revolutionary who became a leader in the French Revolution of 1789. He helped organize the Reign of Terror and was himself guillotined on Robespierre's orders.

Darwin, Charles Robert (1809–1882) English naturalist whose major work, *The Origin of Species*, proposed the theory of evolution by natural selection. This was utterly opposed to the ideas of the Church and caused furious arguments.

Above: Portrait of the young Charles Darwin.

Davy, Sir Humphry (1778–1829) English chemist who was also an important inventor, best remembered for his miners' (Davy) lamp. Using electrolysis he isolated potassium, sodium, barium, strontium and magnesium. Proved chlorine to be an element.

De Gaulle, Charles (1890–1970) French general and statesman. Only French soldier who successfully withstood the German panzer tank tactics of 1940. After the fall of France in 1940 he organized the Free French movement from London. President of France from 1945 to 1946 and during the important period from 1956 to 1969, with a new constitution (the Fifth Republic). Granted full independence to France's African colonies in 1960 and ended the war in Algeria in 1962.

Drake, Sir Francis (1543–1596) English adventurer, plundered Spanish settlements in America. Sailed round the world in 1577–1580. Burned a Spanish fleet at Cadiz in 1587 and helped to defeat Spanish Armada in 1588. He died in the West Indies.

Edison, Thomas Alva (1847–1931) American inventor who patented nearly 1300 inventions including phonograph, electric light bulb and electricity generating station. He also invented a moving picture.

Edward, the Black Prince (1330–1376) Son of Edward III, he 'won his spurs' at the Battle of Crècy. Regarded as the greatest knight of his age. He died a year before his father and his son became king of England as Richard II.

Above: Portrait of Albert Einstein.

Einstein, Albert (1879–1955) German-born theoretical physicist, made greatest scientific advances since Newton over 200 years earlier. In 1905 used quantum theory to explain photoelectric effect, produced famous $E=mc^2$ equation relating mass to energy, explained Brownian motion thus confirming atomic theory of matter, and expounded special theory of relativity. Published general theory of relativity in 1916 (replaced Newton's gravitational theory) and unified field theory in 1929. Became Swiss citizen 1901, American 1940 (as a Jew could not work in Germany in 1930s). Reluctantly persuaded President Roosevelt to begin atomic research 1939. Fought for world peace. Nobel physics prize 1921.

Elizabeth I (1533–1603) Queen of England from 1558. Skilled politician who supported Protestantism.

Ericsson, Leif (c. 970–?) Viking explorer who crossed the northern Atlantic in about 1000 to found the colonies of 'Woodland' and 'Vinland' – possibly Newfoundland and Maryland in North America.

Eugène of Savoy, Prince (1663–1736) Austrian general, born in France, who with Marlborough won many victories against the French in the War of Spanish Succession. Napoleon considered him to be one of the greatest generals of all time.

Faisal I (1885–1933) Arab statesman who led the Arab revolt against Turkish rule in 1916. In 1921 he became king of Iraq.

Fawkes, Guy (1570–1606) English conspirator who was caught trying to blow up the Houses of Parliament on 5 November, 1605. He was executed for treason.

Ferdinand of Aragon (1452–1516) As king of Aragon he united most of Spain under his rule. He established the Inquisition in Spain and expelled the Jews.

Ford, Henry (1863–1947) American car manufacturer who pioneered methods of mass production to make cheap cars.

Fox, Charles James (1749–1806) British politician, arch opponent of George III. One of few British parliamentarians to support the French Revolution.

Franco, Francisco (1892–1975) Leader of the Nationalist Army during the Spanish Civil War. After the Loyalist forces had been defeated in 1939, he became supreme ruler and dictator. During his leadership there was some improvement in the living standards of the Spanish people. He declared that after his death Spain would be ruled by King Juan Carlos.

Franklin, Benjamin (1706–1790) American statesman and scientist and one of the founding fathers of the USA. He invented bifocal glasses and the lightning conductor.

Frederick II, the Great (1712–1786) King of Prussia from 1740, brilliant general. Fought Empress Maria Theresa in War of Austrian Succession.

Freud, Sigmund (1856–1939) Austrian psychiatrist whose theories of the conscious and subconscious mind have had a major influence upon modern psychiatry.

Fry, Elizabeth (1780–1845) Quaker who became an active reformer of English prisons. She was also concerned with raising standards in nursing and education.

Galileo Galilei (1564–1642) Italian scientist and the first to combine theory and experiment in a modern scientific way. He discovered the principle of the pendulum and of falling bodies. He developed the telescope and noticed sun-spots. He discovered four Moons orbiting Jupiter. Through his observations he confirmed Copernicus' view that the Earth moves round the Sun.

Gandhi, Mohandas Karamchand (1869–1948) Indian lawyer and Hindu spiritual leader; worked for independence from Britain, largely by non-violent civil disobedience; jailed several times; assassinated by Hindu fanatic because he preached peace with Muslims. Known as *Mahatma*, great soul.

Garibaldi, Giuseppe (1807–1882) Italian patriot who played a major part in the struggle to bring about the unification of Italy (1861). His most famous feat was the conquest of the kingdom of the Two Sicilies in 1860 with 1000 men (Redshirts). Twice tried to conquer Rome (1862, 1867). Fought for France (1870–1871).

Genghis Khan (*c.* 1162–1227) Great Mongol leader and conqueror who fought for and ruled over the largest land empire in history which, by the time of his death, stretched from present day Iran in the west to China in the east. His title, Genghis Khan, meant Ruler of All Men.

Gladstone, William Ewart (1809–1898) British Liberal statesman who was four times prime minister of Britain. Failed in several attempts to persuade Parliament to agree to Home Rule for Ireland. When, as an old man in 1894, he went to resign, Queen Victoria, who disliked him, kept him standing throughout the interview.

Hammurabi the Great (died 1750 BC) Sixth king of the first Babylonian dynasty, he conquered all Mesopotamia. He was a great builder and his code of laws was not surpassed until Roman times.

Hannibal (247–183 BC) Greatest of Carthaginian soldiers and statesmen. Crossed the Alps (with elephants) to invade Italy, where he defeated the Romans in many battles. He was himself defeated at Zama in 202 by the Romans and was later exiled. He committed suicide so as not to fall into Roman hands.

Harun-al-Raschid (?–AD 809) Caliph of Baghdad from 786–809, he was one of the greatest and most splendid of the Abbasid rulers made famous through the pages of the *Arabian Nights*.

Herodotus (c. 484–424) Greek traveller and writer, called the 'Father of History'. Recorded customs, manners and traditions of peoples in places he visited.

Hitler, Adolf (1889–1945) Nazi German dictator 1933–1945. His ambition to rebuild Germany into a powerful empire, and his hatred of the Jews led to World War II and millions of deaths.

Above: Joan of Arc kneels before the French king.

Joan of Arc (Jeanne d'Arc) (1412–1431) The peasant girl who 'heard voices' and led the French armies against the English in the Hundred Years' War. She was burnt as a witch by the English.

Johnson, Samuel (1709–1784) English writer and debator who was renowned as a wit. He produced his Dictionary in 1755. One of the most famous biographies is James Boswell's *Life of Johnson*.

Justinian I (483–565) Great Byzantine emperor, he became emperor of the eastern empire in 526 at Constantinople, and reconquered much of the old western empire (Italy) which was then in the hands of the barbarians. Published a new legal system.

Kenyatta, Jomo (c. 1889–1978) Kenyan nationalist leader who spent much of his life campaigning for Kenyan independence from British rule. His book *Facing Mount Kenya* was a landmark in African nationalism. He became the first prime minister and then president of an independent Kenya (1963).

King, Martin Luther (1929–1968) Campaigner for civil rights in America. He advocated passive resistance to the segregation of blacks.

Kitchener, Horatio Herbert (1850–1916) British soldier who won the battle of Omdurman in 1898. Governor-general of Sudan, recapturing Khartoum from Muslim fanatics. British commander in South Africa during the Boer War (1900) and was secretary of state for war in 1914. His features became famous on the World War I poster 'Your Country Needs You'. Drowned when ship hit mine.

Kublai Khan (1216–1294) Grandson of Genghis Khan, he completed the Mongol conquest of China and founded the Yuan dynasty.

Lenin, Vladimir (1870–1924) Russian revolutionary who was exiled from Russia from 1895–1917. He founded the Bolshevik (later the Communist) party. Allowed across Germany in a sealed train after the February Revolution, he then led the October Revolution. Fell ill and lost control of government in 1922. Succeeded by Stalin in 1924.

Above: Lenin addresses a political meeting.

Leo the Great (?–AD 461) First great pope who obtained from the Emperor Valentinian III an edict to the effect that papal decisions had the force of law. He was traditionally credited with stopping Attila the Hun's westward advance.

Livingstone, David (1813–1873) Scottish missionary and explorer of Africa who became a hero of Victorian England. After crossing the Kalahari Desert and travelling down the River Zambesi, he sought sources of Congo and Nile rivers. Feared lost, he was found by Stanley. In a speech to Cambridge undergraduates he called upon them to go out as missionaries to Africa and a generation was to follow his advice. Died still exploring.

Louis XIV (1638–1715) King of France from 1643, he established a magnificient court at Versailles. He ruled as an autocrat and aimed to be supreme in Europe. His persecution of the Huguenots led hundreds of thousands to flee the country. Many were craftsmen or businessmen and France suffered when they fled.

Louis XVI (1754–1793) King of France from 1774. The decadence and isolation of the court, the bankruptcy of the country and the unwillingness to reform government systems during his reign were some of the causes of the French Revolution which broke out in 1789. The king and his wife Marie Antoinette were extremely unpopular and were executed by the revolutionaries.

Loyola, St Ignatius (1491–1556) Basque nobleman, soldier and theologian. After being wounded in battle, experienced religious conversion that led to his founding of the Society of Jesus (Jesuits).

Luther, Martin (1438–1546) German reformer who spoke out against the greed of the Church which was leading the people astray. Taking the Bible as his authority, he put emphasis on being saved by faith rather than by good works. His stand was the beginning of Protestantism. He translated the Bible into contemporary German and wrote many hymns and prose works.

Mao Tse-tung (1893–1976) Chinese communist leader who defeated the Nationalists, under Chiang Kai-shek, in 1949 to rule all China. His revolutionary method was constantly to upset the Chinese establishment and after his death the Maoist notion of continuous 'cultural revolution' was rejected.

Maria Theresa (1717–1780) Austrian empress of Holy Roman empire from 1740. Defended her right to the throne in the War of Austrian Succession, 1740–1748. Her husband, Francis of Lorraine, was recognized as emperor in 1748.

Marx, Karl (1818–1883) German Jewish philosopher who in his writings laid the foundations of communism. In 1848 (with Engels) he published the *Communist Manifesto*. His doctrine in *Das Kapital* (1867) revolutionized political thinking.

More, Sir Thomas (1478–1535) English lawyer and statesman who was made chancellor by Henry VIII. His book *Utopia* published in 1516 describes an ideal society. He refused to recognize the king as head of the Church and was executed for treason.

Nasser, Gamal Abdel (1918–1970) Egyptian revolutionary and army officer. Helped depose King Farouk (1952). While president from 1956 tried to modernize country. Nationalized Suez Canal.

Nehru, Jawaharlal (1889–1964) Indian statesman who played a leading part in the nationalist struggle to gain independence from Britain. Prime minister of India from 1947–1964. He was one of the founders of the political movement known as Non-Alignment.

Above: Nehru, India's first prime minister.

Nelson, Horatio (1758–1805) British naval hero, lost eye and arm in battle. Destroyed French fleet at Battle of Nile (1798), won Battle of Copenhagen (1801), destroyed another French fleet at Trafalgar (1805), dying in moment of victory. Created viscount, 1801. Love affair with Emma, Lady Hamilton created a scandal.

Nero (37–68) Roman emperor from 54 to 68. Rebuilt city after the great fire and was wrongly depicted by later Christian writers as playing the lyre while Rome burnt. His reign was characterized by many acts of great cruelty. He led a dissolute private life and committed suicide in 68 when the army revolted.

Nightingale, Florence (1820–1910) English reformer, became nurse. Against great opposition from the military commanders she organized nursing reforms during the Crimean War when she became known as the 'Lady with the Lamp'. Her system of sanitary barrack hospitals was to be adopted worldwide.

Nkrumah, Kwame (1909–1972) African nationalist, he founded the Convention People's Party. Became Ghana's first prime minister at independence and its first president when it became a republic in 1960. He was ousted in a coup in 1966 and died in exile in Guinea.

Park, Mungo (1771–1806) Scottish explorer who twice went to west Africa in search of the source of the Niger. In 1806, while travelling down the Niger, he was drowned at Bussa.

Pasteur, Louis (1822–1895) French chemist, established bacteriology as science – devised method of gentle heating (pasteurization) to kill micro-organisms in wine and beer. Showed air to contain spores of living organisms. Proposed germ theory of disease. Developed inoculation of animals against anthrax and rabies.

Above: The scientist Louis Pasteur.

Pericles (c.490–429 BC) Greatest Athenian of its 'golden age', he led Athens from 460 to 430 BC and was responsible for making Athens the 'most beautiful city in the world'. He died in 429 BC of the plague.

Pizarro, Francisco (c.1478–1541) One of the greatest of the Spanish conquistadors, he conquered the Inca empire of Peru in 1528 with only 180 men, capturing and murdering their leader, Atahualpa. Assassinated.

Plato (427–347 BC) Greek philosopher who was a pupil of Socrates and teacher of Aristotle. Enshrined his philosophy in his *Dialogues*. Platonism, stressing idea of the good rather than material appearances, has had a profound influence upon philosophy.

Polo, Marco (1254–1324) Venetian merchant who travelled to the court of the great Mongol emperor Kublai Khan in Cathay (China). Returned to Venice in 1295, after 24-year absence, a wealthy man. Described journeys in *Travels* which astonished the Europe of his day.

Above: The explorer Marco Polo.

Ptolemy I Sotor (?–283 BC) Half-brother to Alexander the Great and one of his most trusted generals. Ptolemy took Egypt as his 'share' of Alexander's empire when Alexander died. He founded the Ptolemaic line of pharaohs which lasted until the time of Julius Caesar.

Above: Sir Walter Raleigh.

Raleigh, Sir Walter (1552–1618) English soldier and courtier who established the first colony of Virginia and introduced the habit of smoking to England. Explored Guiana region of South America and was executed by James I after failing to find gold.

Rhodes, Cecil John (1853–1902) British statesman. As a young man went out to South Africa for his health. He made a fortune in diamonds, became prime minister of Cape colony and created Rhodesia between 1890 and 1895. Disgraced over Jameson Raid in Transvaal (1896).

Richelieu, Cardinal Armand Jean du Plessis (1585–1642) French statesman who became the first minister of Louis XIII from 1624–1642 and virtually ruled France. He curbed the old nobility, broke the independent power of the Huguenots and extended France's boundaries and power in Europe.

Robespierre, Maximilien (1758–1794) Leader of the Jacobins in the French Revolution, became the most important figure in the 'Reign of Terror'. Almost a dictator for a time, he himself was denounced and guillotined.
Roosevelt, Franklin Delano (1882–1945) Four times president of the USA, he was responsible for the 'New Deal' in the 1930s to help end the Great Depression. He led his country through the Second World War until his death in 1945. He was a polio victim and spent his last years in a wheelchair.
Savonarola, Girolamo (1452–1498) Italian priest who denounced the corruption of Florentine society, led a rebellion against Pope Alexander VI. Captured and executed for sedition and heresy.
Shaka (1787–1828) He became king of the Zulus in 1818 and devised new military strategy and new weapons, creating a standing Zulu army of *impis* (regiments). His military conquests caused a dispersal of his people that had widespread effects throughout southern Africa.

Above: Portrait of William Shakespeare.

Shakespeare, William (1564–1616) England's greatest dramatist, whose plays and poetry have had a profound effect upon the English language and have been translated into most languages in the world.
Stalin, Joseph (1879–1953) Dictator of the Soviet Union 1924–1953. Exiled or executed anyone who opposed him. Established 'five-year plan' to improve the economy in 1928. Led his country during World War II.
Stuart, Charles Edward (1720–1788) Known as the 'Young Pretender' to the British crown. Son of James Edward Stuart and grandson of King James II. Led the unsuccessful 1745 invasion of Scotland in an attempt to bring about a Jacobite rebellion against the Hanoverian dynasty. Defeated at Culloden (1746), lived rest of his life in exile.

Sun Yat-sen (1866–1925) Chinese revolutionary who overthrew the Manchu dynasty and turned China into a republic. He was president of China from 1921 to his death. His ideas inspired a later government.
Tamerlane (1336–1405) Name means 'Timur the Lame'. He created a huge Mongol empire from Turkey to India and north to Moscow. A brilliant soldier, he was feared for his ruthlessness.
Toussaint L'Ouverture, Pierre Dominique (1743–1803) Haitian liberator, born of African slave parents, became leader of French republican rebels. Gained control of island and ruled well until overthrown by French military intervention (1802).
Trotsky, Leon (Lev Davidovich Bronstein; 1879–1940) Russian revolutionary. Minister under Lenin (1917). Organized Red Army in civil war of 1918–1921. Opposed Stalin – exiled 1929. Assassinated in Mexico – on Stalin's orders.
Victor Emmanuel II (1820–1878) King of Sardinia. Leader in war against Austria and struggle for unification of Italy. First king of Italy (from 1861) guided by Cavour, his chief minister.
Walpole, Sir Robert (1676–1745) Britain's first prime minister and one of the longest-serving (1721–1742). His general motto was 'let sleeping dogs lie'.
Wesley, John (1703–1791) English Christian evangelist who rode through England on preaching tours. He was the founder of the Methodist Church.

Above: John Wesley preaching a sermon.

Wilberforce, William (1759–1833) English reformer and evangelist who spent his life campaigning to end the slave trade and slavery. Achieved this goal in 1833.
Zoroaster (Zarathustra; c.660 BC) Persian who founded the religion of Zoroastrianism – said to have written its sacred book, *Avesta*.

THE ARTS

PAINTING AND DRAWING
Painting and drawing are two of the most ancient arts, going back to Stone Age times. (See page 104.)

SCULPTURE
An artist who makes sculptures is called a sculptor. There are many forms of sculpture. (See page 110.)

ARCHITECTURE
Architecture is the art of designing and making buildings. Architects are engineers as well as artists. (See page 112.)

LITERATURE
Every continent has its writers and storytellers, poets and playwrights. (See page 116.)

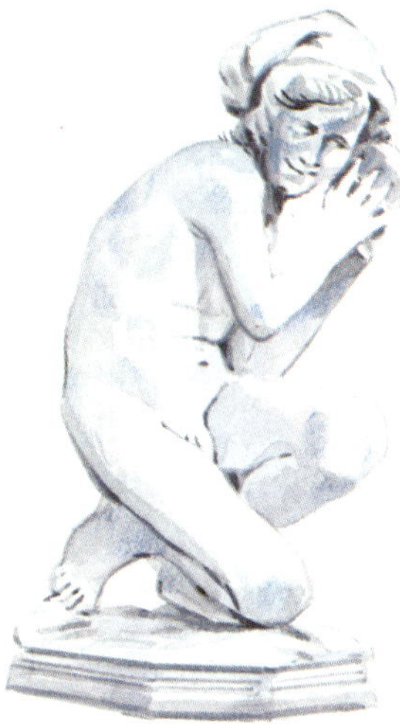

MUSIC
Music is an international means of artistic expression. Almost everyone enjoys listening to and making music. (See page 122.)

DANCE
Dance can be a simple, primitive art form or highly stylized as in ballet. (See page 126.)

CINEMA AND TV
During the 20th century the modern arts of film and television have developed. (See page 130.)

CRAFTS
Making things with one's hands is very satisfying. Some crafts are as old as civilization. (See page 134.)

THEATRE
Theatre arts include acting on stage, film and television. Opera, dance and ballet are also forms of theatre. (See page 120.)

Painting and Drawing

Above: The Gleaner, 1885 by the Dutch artist Vincent Van Gogh. This powerful drawing shows a peasant woman, with knotty joints and stiff limbs after years of hard backbreaking work. The artist is showing us real life through sympathetic eyes.

Right: An artist's tools include brushes, pencils, palette knives and various kinds of paint such as water-colours, acrylics and oils.

Below: A few examples of the many ways of shading with a pencil, a stick of charcoal and a brush and wash.

No one knows when people first began painting. The oldest known paintings were made by Stone Age artists in caves thousands of years ago. They mostly show hunters chasing animals. The artists may have thought that the pictures would magically bring them good hunting.

Much later, people started to decorate their homes and temples with paintings. The Egyptians and Greeks loved painted vases and pottery. They also painted scenes of everyday life on the walls. Wall paintings made on wet plaster are known as *frescoes*. The Chinese invented a system of picture-writing and made beautiful pictures on silk and plaster.

During the Middle Ages in Europe most paintings were done for churches. Painters mostly painted stories from the Bible. Their pictures were rather stiff-looking. But

AN ARTIST'S EQUIPMENT

Above: It was the intention of Van Gogh to use art to convey feelings both through the images used in the painting and through the use of colour. In this work, entitled *The Yellow House*, the medium is traditional oil paint.

Left: David Hockney, an English artist, has used coloured crayons for this work, *Dr Eugen Lamb, Lucca 1973* (detail). By a system of interlacing lines Hockney has managed to blend the colours in the eye of the spectator. Hockney is a versatile modern artist whose works range from large acrylic paintings to prints, drawings and operatic sets.

Right: Part of a water-colour sketch, by British artist Philip Wilson Steer, of Haresfoot Park in England. Water-colours can run into one another to give a 'watery' effect.

Above: Pastel is a major painting technique. Pastels are made from natural pigment, powdered and bound together with gum or resin. Pastels retain their purity and delicacy of colour as seen in Odilon Redon's *Vase des Fleurs* (A Vase of Flowers). Using pastels, an artist can achieve a wide range of colours directly, whereas oil paints have to be mixed and may lose the clean effect. Many famous artists such as Edgar Degas and Jean Chardin used pastels for subtle and realistic portrait painting.

then Italian painters, such as Giotto, Fra Angelico and Botticelli, began to paint in a more natural way. Their Bible characters looked like real people. In the 1400s Florence and Venice became great centres of the Renaissance – the 'rebirth' of learning. Florence was the home of three of the greatest artists of all time: Michelangelo, Leonardo da Vinci and Raphael.

The Renaissance period saw a change in style and emphasis in painting. Rich noblemen and dukes in the Italian city states vied for acclaim and prestige through the decoration of their courts and the commissioning of paintings and sculptures. They patronized many artists. The skilled artist was treated no longer as a master craftsman but became a well respected gentleman.

The Renaissance fostered the idea of the universal man who was knowledgeable in many subjects. The breadth of knowledge of artists such as Leonardo da Vinci and Michelangelo is apparent in their paintings. Both studied anatomy for themselves, dissecting animals and human corpses. Their discoveries are seen in their natural depiction of people, whereas medieval artists painted figures in a flat and unnatural way.

Brunelleschi, a famous Renaissance architect, made the important discovery of perspective. This is the way in which objects in the distance appear smaller. The use of this knowledge gives depth to pictures.

During the Renaissance painters often took scenes from history, and Greek and Roman legends as their subjects. They also painted portraits of people from life, and realistic

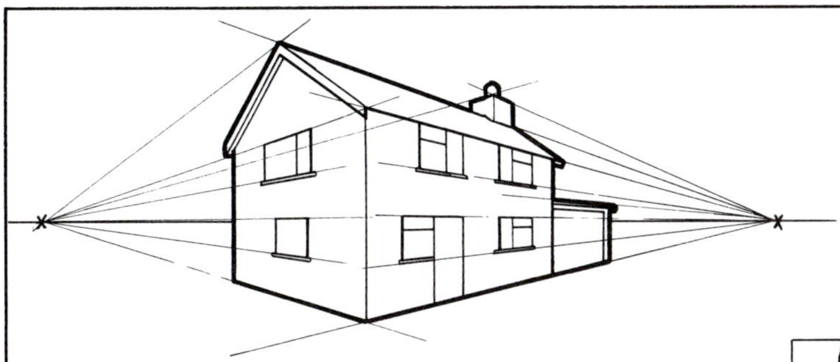

SOME LAWS OF DRAWING
Left: The 'vanishing point' where parallel sides of the walls meet. *Below left:* Using a pencil to work out proportion and (*below*) a grid to copy accurately.

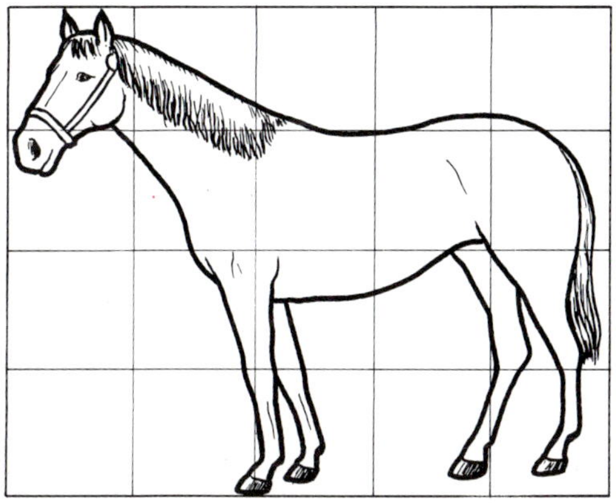

Above: The School of Athens by Raphael is an example of a fresco. Frescos are paintings made on fresh plaster using pigments mixed with water. The colours used for such paintings are mainly earth colours, which have duller tones than those used in oil painting. Fresco painting became very popular during the Italian Renaissance of the 1400 and 1500s. It was used to decorate the walls and ceilings of many palaces and public places.

Above: A medieval painting showing Middle Eastern astronomers at work.

Right: The Cook by the Dutch artist Jan Vermeer (1632–75). He often painted people at their everyday work, like this domestic servant preparing a meal. Vermeer's paintings are almost all of the inside of people's homes. Like many painters, Vermeer made little money from his work in his lifetime, when his paintings were not highly thought of. He died a poor man but today his paintings are highly valued and are sold for enormous sums of money.

Above: Detail from a self-portrait by Rembrandt van Rijn (1606–69). The greatest of all Dutch painters, Rembrandt was a miller's son. A large number of his pictures are of himself or of old people – he was fascinated by the timeworn faces of the elderly. Rembrandt's paintings movingly explore the way a person's appearance changes with age and experience.

scenes from nature. Rubens, a Flemish painter, was the first great master of landscape painting. Dutch and Flemish painters were also fond of showing amusing scenes of country life.

Patrons liked to have their portraits painted. Rembrandt, a Dutch painter of the 1600s, painted hundreds of portraits, including several famous self-portraits (pictures of himself).

During the 1700s many artists painted people in family groups, often against a background of a garden or a fine house. Caricaturists drew humorous sketches, making fun of the famous. Constable and other painters painted naturalistic landscapes.

But styles of painting began to change once again as artists experimented with new ideas. One important change was called Impressionism. Impressionist painters (most of whom were French) loved to paint light and shadow. Painters tried to show things in a painting which a photograph could not show. They tried to express feelings and ideas. By the early 1900s some artists were making pictures as designs and shapes, rather than copies of objects. This is called abstract painting. Probably the greatest 20th-century painter was Picasso who painted in a number of different styles.

Below: This painting of *Gare St Lazare* by Claude Monet was painted in the Impressionist style. This style of painting originated in France. It aims to give the viewer an immediate impression of an object or event rather than sharply defining shapes. It shows how objects are changed by the effects of light and colour.

Above: The Spanish artist Picasso (1881–1973) was, unlike so many artists, rich and famous during his life.

Below left: Sunday Afternoon on the Island of La Grande Jatte, 1886, by the French Post Impressionist artist Georges Seurat (1859–91).

Above: This is part of one of a series of Picasso's paintings of weeping women, inspired by the artist's horror at the tragic events leading up to World War II.

Above: Abraham, Moses and Samuel, three Old Testament figures carved in stone in the 1200s, stand over the door of Chartres Cathedral, France.

Above: Michelangelo's marble *Pietà*, a famous and sympathetic sculpture of Mary and the dead Christ.

Right: These huge Hindu statues of Buddha in Sri Lanka date from the 11th century.

Sculpture

Sculpture is the art of making shapes and models. Early sculptors modelled animal shapes in wood and bone, and also made statues (models of gods or humans).

The Ancient Egyptians cut huge figures of solid rock, and there is wonderful ancient sculpture too in the Far East, India and in Central America. But the masters of sculpture were the Ancient Greeks. They decorated their temples with marble statues of athletes, heroes and gods. Never before had the human body been represented so naturally in art. Roman sculptors copied the Greeks. Their work is not so beautiful, but the faces on the statues are more like those of ordinary people. Sculptors often made stone portraits, showing a person's head and shoulders. These are known as 'busts'.

In the Middle Ages wood carvers and stone masons decorated churches with figures of saints. Often their carvings were brightly painted, though today almost all traces of the colours have disappeared. They also showed people going about their everyday work. During the Renaissance, or 'rebirth of learning' in the 1400s, sculp-

tors such as Michelangelo, in his figures of the dying slaves, imitated the 'classical' lifelike styles of the Greeks.

Lifelike sculpture continued to be popular until the present century. Most modern sculptors do not copy the human body or natural shapes so closely. Instead some make patterns or shapes which express feelings and ideas. This kind of sculpture is called 'abstract'. They also experiment with different materials: wire, plastic, even junk.

Sculpture is done in two ways: by *carving* and *moulding*. In carving, the sculptor cuts into a block of wood or stone with sharp tools. In moulding, he or she makes a model in soft clay, then bakes the clay to harden it. From the hard model the sculptor makes a mould, and pours into it wet concrete or hot, liquid metal (such as bronze). When this hardens, a perfect 'casting' of the model is left.

Some modern sculptures have moving parts, and are known as 'mobiles'. A 'relief' is a kind of raised picture made by cutting into a flat piece of wood or stone.

Above: These impressive *moai* statues were carved with stone hand picks from *tuff* (volcanic rock), hundreds of years ago, by the people of Easter Island, in the South Pacific Ocean. Today there are over six hundred still standing. They range in height from three metres to twelve metres.

Left: Picasso's small-scale model for a huge steel figure which he sculpted in 1965. The full-size construction now stands outside the Civic Centre in Chicago, Illinois. Picasso used industrial and household materials to make some of his unusual sculptures. He produced more than 650 sculptures during his long career, including many highly original works.

GREEK CAPITALS

Doric

Ionic

Corinthian

Above: The three main styles of ancient Greek capital. Capitals are the decorated tops of columns.

Above right: The famous Greek Acropolis in Athens, with the ruins of the Parthenon Temple.

Below right: Sturdy Minoan architecture as it would have looked on Crete in 1700 BC.

Below: A post and lintel long-house 5000–3000 BC.

Architecture

The first great architects were the Ancient Egyptians. Their stone temples and tombs have lasted for thousands of years. Some people think the architecture of Ancient Greece was the most beautiful of all time. Greek temples were decorated with carvings and sculptures. The Greeks used different kinds of columns. The three main kinds were the Doric, Ionic and Corinthian styles, or 'orders'. These were later copied by the Romans. Many Roman buildings look like Greek buildings.

But the Romans were better engineers than the Greeks. Roman architects developed the arch and the vault, a roof supported by arches. The arch was a good way of spanning a wide distance quickly. By using the arch, the Romans were able to build taller buildings.

In Europe during the Middle Ages stone was the natural material for building strong castles and long-lasting cathedrals. At first architects followed Roman styles. This is called Romanesque architecture. But from around 1200 they began building tall, slender churches and cathedrals. The spires and pinnacles pointed to heaven. Pointed

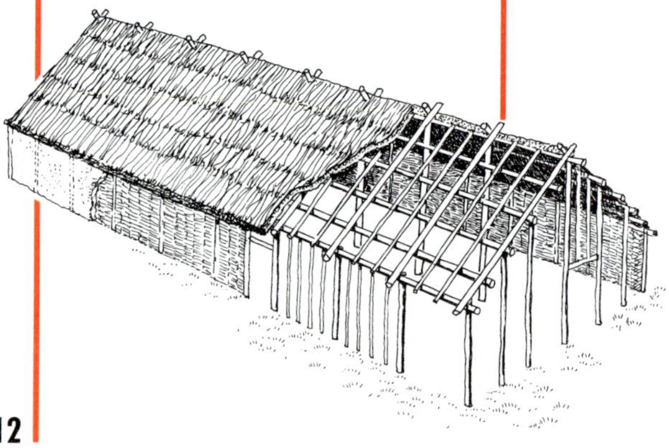

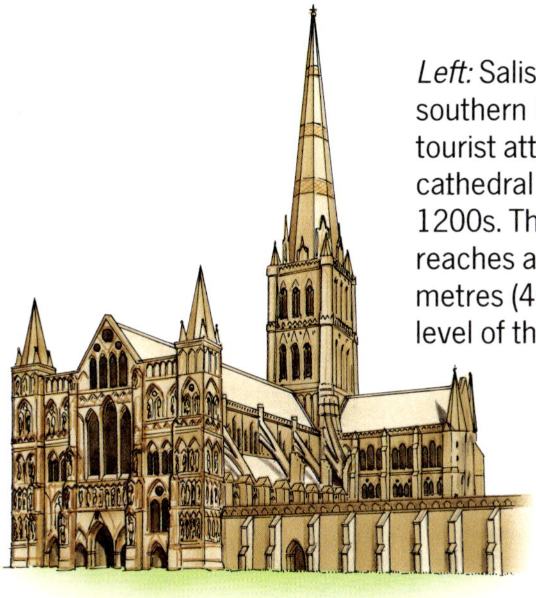

Left: Salisbury cathedral in southern England is a popular tourist attraction. The cathedral was built in the 1200s. The cathedral spire reaches a height of 123 metres (404 feet) above the level of the ground.

Above: The beautiful Duomo or cathedral in Florence, Italy, has a dome designed by the architect Filippo Brunelleschi. The buildings of Florence are among the finest architectural triumphs of Renaissance Europe.

Below: The Crystal Palace in London was designed by Sir Joseph Paxton for Britain's Great Exhibition of 1851. Made of steel and glass, it was startlingly modern for its day. It was built like a giant greenhouse in an amazingly short time.

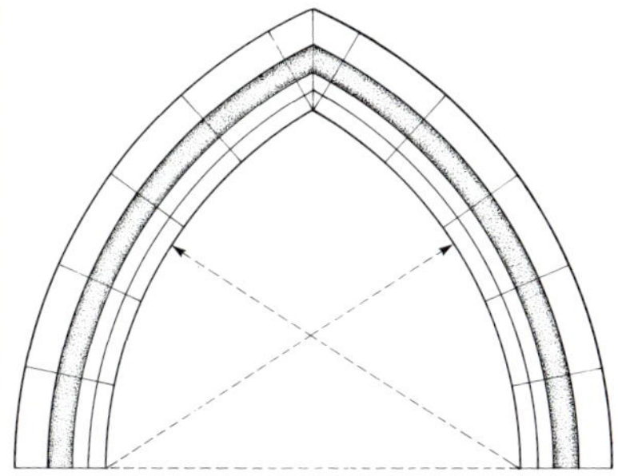

Above: From the mid 1100s to the 1400s, arches in many buildings were built like this. This Gothic style has a graceful, pointed arch.

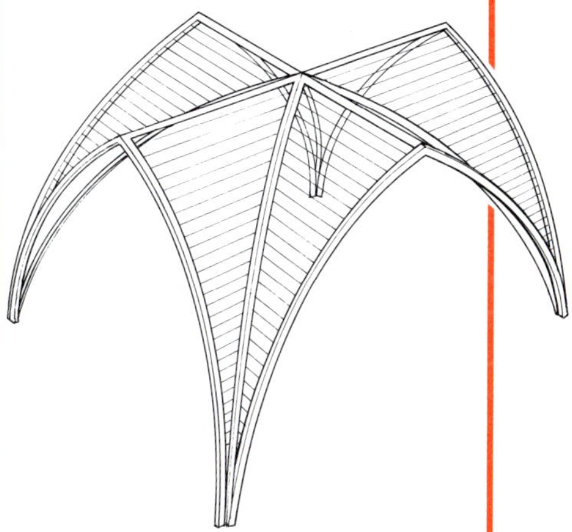

Above: A Gothic ribbed vault. The ribs carry the whole load of the vault.

Below: In a rounded arch, the *voussoir* stones and the middle keystone carry the weight.

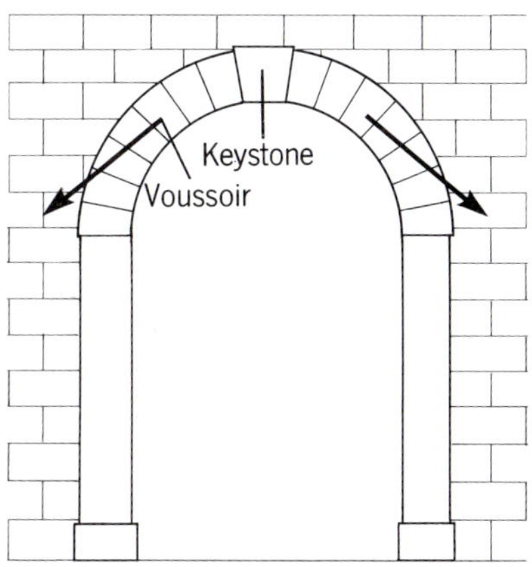

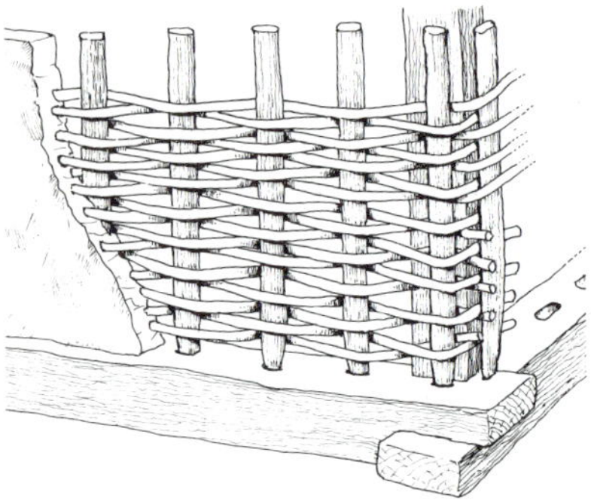

Above: From prehistoric times to the Middle Ages European homes had a wooden framework strengthened with light woven branches (wattle) which was covered with wet clay or mud (daub).

Above: Different regions have their own distinctive styles of architecture, which make use of natural building materials available in the locality. This is the Old Post Office at Tintagel, Cornwall, in southwest England. It is over 600 years old and is built of local stone with a thick and uneven slate roof.

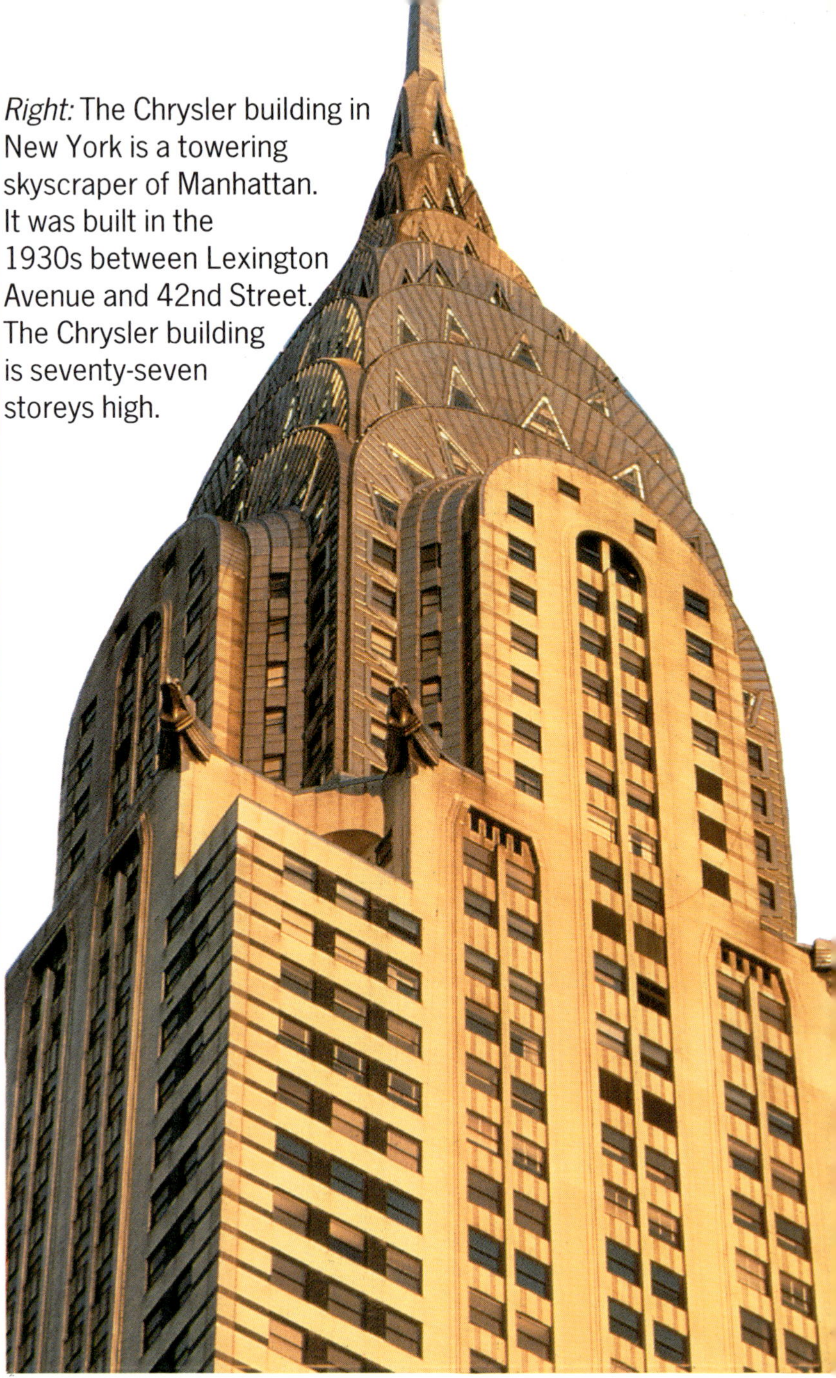

Right: The Chrysler building in New York is a towering skyscraper of Manhattan. It was built in the 1930s between Lexington Avenue and 42nd Street. The Chrysler building is seventy-seven storeys high.

arches were used instead of round ones. This is called the Gothic style. Around 1300 the Decorated style, with carvings and stained glass windows, became popular.

During the Renaissance architects returned to the Greek and Roman styles. They liked the simple and regular 'classical' designs. But in time more decoration was added. By the 1600s the Baroque style was fashionable. It was very ornate. Even straight stone columns were twisted into spiral shapes. During the 1700s architects designed many fine houses. Often they laid out parks and gardens as part of the design. The Victorians of the 1800s liked the medi-

Left: The Ross Office Tower in the modern city of Dallas in Texas. Dallas is one of the largest cities in the United States. Much of the city was rebuilt after World War II and today it has an impressive skyline of modern architecture. Buildings like this one are 20th century landmarks.

Below: The unfinished Church of the Sagrada Familia (or Sacred Family) which stands in the city of Barcelona in northern Spain. This unusual building is the work of the well-known Spanish architect, Antonio Gaudí. Gaudí designed the church and supervised its construction from 1884 until he died in 1926. Among Gaudí's other works, most of which were built in Barcelona, are the Casa Milá and the Casa Battló.

eval Gothic style of architecture, and so many of their buildings look like much older ones. The Houses of Parliament in London are a good example. A big change came about in the 1880s with the use of steel and reinforced concrete. The first very tall buildings, or 'skyscrapers', were built in the United States. Skyscrapers were soon being built in cities all over the world.

A modern architect may be asked to design a single house, a shopping centre, an office building or a new housing estate. Steel, concrete, glass, plastics and brick are the chief materials used.

Literature

Above: Homer (700 BC) was a great Greek poet, who wrote the epics (long poems) the *Iliad* and the *Odyssey* about Greek and Trojan adventures.

Above: An illustration to the *Canterbury Tales* by Geoffrey Chaucer. These two pilgrims are a ploughman and a shipman.

Literature is the way we communicate our thoughts and ideas in words. Literature does not have to be written down. Oral (spoken) literatures began in prehistoric times, when people first told stories. The storyteller memorized each story and poem, and taught it to his or her children, who in turn passed the stories on to their children. Later, after the invention of writing and of alphabets, stories could be written down and so literature as we know it today began.

The invention of the printing press in the Middle Ages was a great advance. Before then any book had to be written by hand, and making copies was a slow process. As more people learned to read, literature developed and became more important. In the 1800s the spread of libraries and improved schooling for all brought literature within the reach of everyone.

Literature can do many things besides tell a story. It can describe a person's feelings. It can explain how something came about. It can persuade the reader to a different point of view. Literature can both teach and entertain. Literature that deals with made-up stories is called *fiction*. Literature that deals with real events (a history or travel book, for example) is *non-fiction*.

Right: The Italian poet Dante (1265–1321), who wrote a long poem in three parts called the *Divine Comedy*.

Above: The famous pair from the early 17th century novel *Don Quixote*, a major work by the Spanish writer, Miguel de Cervantes. The hero, Don Quixote, and his companion Sancho Panza, set out in search of romantic adventure.

Above right: William Shakespeare (1564–1616) is recognized as the greatest English poet and playwright. He was born, lived and died in Stratford-upon-Avon in Warwickshire. His plays have been translated into many languages.

Much of the literature of ancient times has been lost. The greatest storytellers of ancient times were the Greek Homer and the Roman Virgil. They created epics (long adventure-poems) about gods, wars and heroes. The first writer to use everyday English (rather than the French or Latin used by the Church and the king's court) was Geoffrey Chaucer in the 1300s. In the 1500s English literature enjoyed a period of great creativity. Many writers wrote plays for actors to perform, and the greatest of these playwrights was William Shakespeare.

The essay is a short composition giving the writer's personal view of a subject. Biography is someone's life-story written by another person. (Autobiography is a person's life written by that person.) A short story is, as the name suggests, a short piece of fiction. Longer pieces of fiction are called novels. The novel became popular in Europe from the late 1600s; one of the first novels was Robinson Crusoe, written by Daniel Defoe in 1719. The great age of the novel came in the 1800s, with writers such as Jane Austen, Emily Brontë and Charles Dickens.

Below: The German Romantic writer, Johann Wolfgang von Goethe (1749–1832). Goethe was a brilliant scholar, a playwright, critic, journalist, theatre manager, poet and scientist. He wrote a famous version of the German legend of the magician Faust, who sold his soul to the devil in return for knowledge and earthly power. In Goethe's version, Faust is saved from damnation.

Left: The humorous writer Samuel Langhorne Clemens (1835–1910) used the pen-name Mark Twain. He wrote books about American life, including *The Adventures of Huckleberry Finn.*

Right: Charles Dickens (1812–70) is Britain's greatest novelist. He wrote about industrial England. His books include *Great Expectations* and *David Copperfield.*

Novels are written in prose (as are the articles in this encyclopedia). Poetry, or verse, differs from prose in several ways. It has a more musical sound, and is arranged in lines which may follow a special rhythmical arrangement called *metre*. Some poetry rhymes (the words at the

Below: The Charge of the Light Brigade at the battle of Balaclava in 1854 inspired a famous poem by Alfred, Lord Tennyson (1809–92).

Left: An illustration from Alice's adventures *Through the Looking Glass*, the sequel to *Alice in Wonderland* by Lewis Carroll (Charles Lutwidge Dodgson 1832–98). Lewis Carroll created a unique fantasy world. In everyday life, he was a shy man who taught mathematics at Oxford University.

ends of lines sound the same, giving the poem additional rhythm). But not all poetry rhymes. Poetry is generally more personal than prose. It often reflects the innermost feelings of the poet. Famous poets in English include John Milton, Alexander Pope, William Wordsworth, John Keats, Alfred Lord Tennyson and T. S. Eliot.

Different forms of poetry include narrative poetry (which tells a story) and dramatic poetry (which may be in a play or may tell a story in verse through a conversation between the characters). Lyric poetry expresses the writer's thoughts or emotions; they may be joyful, as in an ode, or sad at the loss of a dead friend, as in an elegy.

Literature that makes us laugh by showing us how ridiculous some 'serious' things really are is called satire. A good example of satire is Jonathan Swift's book *Gulliver's Travels*. Another, more recent, satire is George Orwell's *Animal Farm*.

Many writers have written especially for children. They include Lewis Carroll (who wrote *Alice in Wonderland* for a friend's young daughter), Kenneth Grahame (*Wind in the Willows*) and A. A. Milne (*Winnie-the-Pooh*).

One of the joys of literature is that each writer has something different to say, and every generation finds something new and valuable in the literature of the past. Every continent has its great literature. Europe has produced great writers in English, French, German, Russian, Italian, Spanish and other languages. Chinese, Indian and Japanese writers have been important in the history of Asian literature. Since the 1800s American literature has developed steadily, and today it is the foremost literature in English. New writers have emerged in Canada, Australia, South America and Africa. Today, in addition to writing books, authors also write scripts for the theatre, films and television.

Above: Rudyard Kipling (1865–1936) was a British poet, short-story writer and novelist. Many of his stories are set in India. His books include *Kim*, the *Just So Stories* and *The Jungle Book*.

Above: The French writer George Sand (1804–76). Her real (married) name was Amandine Aurore Lucile Dudevant, but from 1832 she wrote novels under a pen-name. She was a campaigner for greater freedom for women. Other woman writers of the period used pen-names to disguise their identity.

Theatre

Above: The 2300-year-old open-air Greek theatre at Epidaurus.

The first theatres were in Ancient Greece. People sat in the open air on a hillside, while actors and dancers performed on a space called the orchestra. A changing room behind the actors, called the skene, later became a stage and from this comes the modern word 'scenery'.

In the Middle Ages religious plays were performed in town squares or on carts wheeled through the streets. In the early 1600s, the Globe Theatre in London, where Shakespeare's plays were performed, had a stage jutting out into the audience. Later, stages were given a 'picture frame' surround. The oldest indoor theatre still in use is the Teatro Olimpico in Vicenza, Italy, completed in 1585.

PUPPET THEATRE

Puppets have been used in theatre in the East and West for hundreds of years. In Asia, shadow-puppets play out stirring dramas. String-puppets or marionettes, shown here, were popular in medieval Europe and were often used by travelling showmen who performed traditional dramas. Glove puppets were also used, as in the English Punch and Judy show. Other forms of drama have taken over puppet plays and have developed the techniques of puppet theatre.

Below: This is the kind of theatre, with tiered seats all around the stage and made mostly of wood, in which Shakespeare's plays were first performed in the late 1500s and early 1600s.

Left: Kabuki is a traditional form of Japanese theatre and one that is very popular. This kind of drama developed in Japan at the same time as Shakespeare was writing his plays in England. There is usually not much scenery on the stage, but the acting is very exaggerated. Kabuki includes the wearing of colourful masks, costumes and make-up. The acting style is very dramatic and the stories are often about historical or national events.

France's Comédie Française, founded in 1680 in Paris, is the oldest national theatre in the world.

The two main forms of drama are tragedies (plays with sad endings) and comedies (ones with happy endings). Scenery and costume became very important in the 1800s, but today a playwright (someone who writes plays) may create a drama which needs little scenery but relies on lighting, sound effects and the skills of the actors.

Below: A large modern theatre is an elaborate building equipped with the latest technology. Many people work behind the scenes preparing costumes, making scenery and fixing the lighting. A theatre company works as a team.

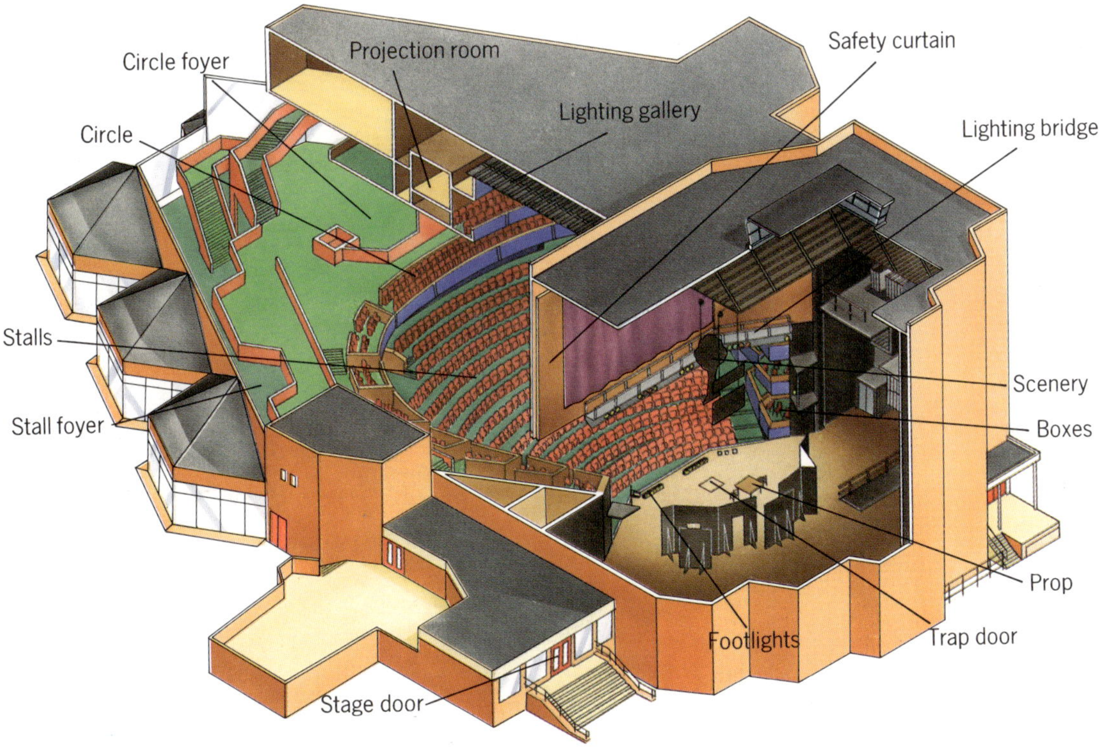

Above: A Roman wall-painting or fresco showing a music lesson.

Above right: An Italian lute player from the Renaissance period.

Music

Music is a set of sounds arranged in a way that is pleasant to hear. It has *rhythm* (a beat) and usually *melody* (a tune). People make music to show their feelings. When they are happy, they whistle or sing. Sadness, too, can often be best expressed in music.

Music can be heard in natural sounds, such as bird songs. Many sounds have their own rhythm. Think of your own heart beating. These rhythms can be copied by people beating with a stick on a stone, or on a drum. Music is made up of *notes* that may be long or short, loud or soft, high or low.

Above: A brass instrument (trumpet) and a woodwind instrument (recorder).

Right: Russian folk musicians with violins and cellos.

The earliest musical instrument was the human voice. Musical instruments have been made for thousands of years. There are three main groups of instruments. Wind instruments are played by blowing down a hollow wooden or metal tube with holes cut in it. By covering some holes with the fingers, different notes are produced. Wind instruments include flutes, clarinets, oboes, bassoons, trumpets and horns. Stringed instruments have strings stretched across a hollow box. The strings are bowed, as in a violin, or plucked, as in a guitar, to make different notes. Short strings make high notes and long strings make low notes. Stringed instruments include violins, violas, cellos, basses, guitars, banjos, lutes and mandolins. Instruments such as drums, cymbals and bells, which are hit with hammers or sticks, are called percussion instruments. A large group of people playing instruments together form an orchestra. There are now electronic instruments which can reproduce the sounds of the other instruments, so a musician can now be his or her own 'orchestra'.

At first music had a simple melody and rhythm. But by the Middle Ages it had grown more complicated. Two or three tunes were played together. This made a richer sound and was called counterpoint. But it was difficult to remember without writing it down. Notes can be written down in order on a *scale*. Eastern and Western music use different scales – so Chinese music, for example, may sound strange to European ears at first.

Above: A 17th century engraving showing an organ-maker carrying the parts needed to make an organ.

Below: An organ and a harpsichord from the late 1700s to the early 1800s era, the time of Beethoven.

Organ

Harpsichord

THE ORCHESTRA
A full-sized modern concert orchestra is usually arranged in this semi-circular formation. The stringed instruments are closest to the conductor, with violins to the left, basses and cellos to the right. Percussion and brass are in the centre, furthest from the conductor. It is very important that all the players can see the conductor who directs the performance.

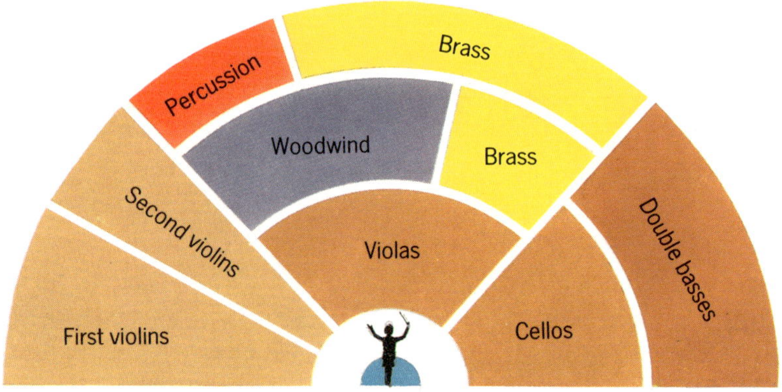

Above: Ludwig van Beethoven.

Below: Mozart listens as Beethoven plays the piano.

People who make up music and write it down are called composers. Two great composers of counterpoint were Bach and Handel who both lived in the 1700s. Much great music has been written for orchestras by composers such as Haydn, Mozart, Beethoven and Brahms. They wrote symphonies (long pieces of music for orchestras) and chamber music (for smaller groups of instruments). They also wrote choral music, for choirs to sing. Some composers have written operas, which are musical plays in which all the words are sung.

People often call this kind of music 'classical' music. But there are many other kinds of music, including folk songs, jazz and pop music. Folk music has developed from

Left: A jazz band of the early 1900s. Jazz music was first played in America. It was influenced by West African rhythm, gospel songs and spirituals and European classical harmony. Originally played at funerals, early jazz has a mournful sound. Famous jazz musicians include Duke Ellington, Louis Armstrong and Ella Fitzgerald.

ELVIS PRESLEY
Elvis Presley (1935–77) was a leading rock and roll star from 1956 when his first hit record *Heartbreak Hotel* was launched. He was especially popular in America. His songs were influenced by blues music. He was well known for controversial live performances which often offended adults although they were popular with young fans. He died at the age of 42.

Above: In the 1960s the Beatles (from left to right Paul McCartney, Ringo Starr, George Harrison and John Lennon) became pop music super-stars. The group members were all born in Liverpool. The last to join the band in 1962 was Ringo Starr, the drummer. The others played the electric guitar and all of them sang. The main song-writers were McCartney and Lennon. By the late 1960s the Beatles had become the most popular band in rock music history.

the songs people made up for themselves and sang when working or entertaining themselves. Jazz musicians often make up or 'improvise' the music as they play together. Beginning in the 1800s, jazz had its origins in the music of American black people. Black music also had a considerable influence on pop music, particularly through rock and blues, which reached wide audiences through radio, TV and records from the 1950s.

Today, thanks to the wonders of electronic sound recording, more people can listen to music, of all kinds, than has ever been the case before. Even so, a 'live' performance by an orchestra, a soloist or a band still has a special excitement of its own. Modern music is very different from the music of the 1800s. It has difficult rhythms and sounds, and often requires electronic instruments such as synthesizers as well as wind, stringed and percussion instruments.

Above: Dancers perform in a production of the classical ballet *Swan Lake*.

Above: Egyptian dancers are shown in tomb-paintings.

Below: An Arabian classical dancer.

Dance

Dancing is as old as humankind. Thousands of years ago people often told stories by dancing. They danced to bring rain and to make crops grow. War dances made them feel brave before a battle.

In time, dancing became an art. Today, dancers take part in religious ceremonies in many parts of the world. In parts of Asia, almost all traditional dance has a religious significance. In India there are temple dancers who devote their lives to the sacred dances, some of the most ancient

Right: Ballet flourished at Louis XIV's court at Versailles in the second half of the 17th century. The 'Sun King' himself was an enthusiast and is shown here dancing in costume as the Sun.

in the world. Many folk dances are still danced today. From country folk dances developed other forms of dance, including ballet.

Ballet is dance performed on the stage. It may tell a story or act out an idea or feeling. Classical ballet is based on a number of set positions and movements which a choreographer (a dance arranger) arranges in various ways for each dance. Modern ballet allows the dancers more freedom of movement. Some of the best ballet music, such as that for *Swan Lake*, was written by the Russian composer Tchaikovsky.

Ballet began over 450 years ago in Italy and France as part of court entertainments. Dances at court became

Above: In classical ballet, the young dancer has to learn five basic positions from which all movements begin. Ballet shoes (right) are blocked at the toe so the dancer can balance on the point.

Below: A scene from the 1970s film of the ballet *Tales of Beatrix Potter*, with dancers dressed as animal characters from the children's stories.

Above: Highland dancing is part of Scotland's culture. Tartan kilts are worn and music is played on the bagpipes.

more elaborate than those of the country village. Professional ballet was born with the founding of the Royal Academy of Dancing by King Louis XIV in France in 1661. In the 20th century the Russian ballet led the way, and famous dancers such as Pavlova, Nijinsky and Rudolf Nureyev became international ballet stars.

Modern dance, based on natural free body movements, was developed in the early 1900s. The American dancer Isadora Duncan helped to make this new dance technique popular. The modern dance movement has influenced other styles of dancing.

Many people enjoy dancing for the fun of it. Country and folk dancing continues centuries-old, traditional

Left: Temple dancing is part of religious ritual in South East Asia.

Right: European folk dancers usually wear traditional costume. Folk dances are still performed at annual festivals in many countries.

Left: Flamenco is a Spanish folk dance. In some of the dances the movements of the man and woman are meant to represent those of a bull-fighter and his cape.

Below: The movements and costumes in modern dance aim to create a mood rather than telling a story as traditional ballet often does.

Above: The more natural movement and style of modern dance, which were developed in the 1920s and 1930s in America and Germany, have influenced traditional ballet in recent decades. Choreographers have explored and adopted modern dance techniques, and have experimented with ideas from jazz and rock and roll to provide an extensive, challenging range of dance.

Left: A Kenyan Masai woman wearing tribal dress dances with small steps.

dances. Ballroom or social dances include dances as different as the waltz (invented in the 1800s) and Latin American dances such as the tango and samba. Popular dances change frequently with musical styles, from the jive of the 1950s to the latest disco dance craze of today.

The musical theatre, films and television have helped to make dance more popular. Theatre dance includes modern and chorus line routines. No screen dancers have equalled the success of the Hollywood stars Fred Astaire and Ginger Rogers, who tapped and twirled through a string of hit dance movies in the 1930s.

Cinema and TV

Above: Movie and television films are made of lots of separate scenes. Each scene may involve several 'takes', which are marked on a clapper-board to keep them in order.

Right: An Illinois cowboy tries to shoot a villain on the screen, believing that the cinema picture is real.

Below: The *Cinematographe* machine, built by Louis and Auguste Lumiere, was being used for public film showings by the 1890s.

'Moving pictures' were first shown in the 1890s. Soon films were so popular that people were crowding into cinemas to watch them. At first films were silent and rather jerky. 'Talking pictures' appeared in 1927 with the release of *The Jazz Singer*.

Hollywood in California, USA, became the centre of the movie industry in the 1930s. Later, when television began to rival the cinema in the 1950s, the big film studios switched to making TV programmes as well as films. Today, the cinema has regained some of its popularity, though weekly audiences are still not as huge as they once were. Hollywood produced the film stars – actors such as Clark Gable, Clint Eastwood, Marilyn Monroe and Meryl Streep – whose names and faces are known all over the world through their screen roles.

Working in the world of film and television is not all glamour, however. There is much hard work to be done,

both before and behind the cameras. Acting is a difficult profession, yet there are always lots of students training in drama schools and hoping one day to become stars.

The person who decides how a story is made into a film is the director. The producer looks after the business side. And apart from the actors and cameramen, there are people to look after scenery, lighting, costumes, make-up and 'stunts'. Sometimes a studio set, with artificial scenery, is used. But films are often 'shot' (filmed) out of doors or 'on location'. When filming is over, the best parts

Above: Cartoons are made up of separate pictures or 'frames' run off a reel, so the picture appears to move.

Above left: A 'still' picture from the black and white film *King Kong*. Although King Kong appears to be much larger than the buildings, he was in fact a small-scale model of a gorilla. Different-sized models of King Kong were used in the film and he was made to move using electric wires.

Left: A television camera crew shooting film on location in Tenerife.

Right: The American Civil War story of *Gone with the Wind*, made in 1939, was a blockbuster. The film starred Vivien Leigh and Clark Gable and was made using a new colour process called Technicolor, which made the elaborate costumes and sets seem more realistic.

Above: Charlie Chaplin in *The Gold Rush*, made in 1925. Chaplin wrote, directed and starred in nearly all his films. He is most remembered dressed in a shabby suit, hat and shoes and for his shuffling walk. The films of this comic genius are classics.

of the film are edited (cut up and stuck together) to make the finished version. When the shooting is finished, the sound-track is put together by the dubbing editor. This may include music and sound effects as well as dialogue.

Like movies, television programmes are also made either in a studio or outdoors, on location. TV programmes were first broadcast regularly in 1936 and from the 1950s television quickly replaced radio as the most popular form of home entertainment. Programmes include news and current affairs, documentaries, nature series, drama, comedy, sport, children's programmes, films, and serials or 'soaps' which often attract the largest viewing audiences of all.

Sophia Loren

Robert Redford

Marlene Dietrich

Dustin Hoffman

Julie Andrews

Eddie Murphy

Right: The cinema created an industry, and a 'star' system'. These six famous film stars span the history of 'talking pictures' from the 1930s to the present.

Left: John Logie Baird was the first person to show true television pictures in 1926. However, his televisor (shown here) was overtaken by its rival the electronic Marconi-EMI television, which was then mass-produced.

In the early days of television, almost all programmes were 'live'. Most TV programmes nowadays are recorded. Video recording on tape was invented in the 1950s. Today, even in live recordings such as sports programmes, videos are used to produce slow-motion action replays. Videos allow us to record a programme from the television at any time and watch it later. We can also make our own videos or buy or hire them to watch at home.

Since communication satellites were first launched in the 1960s, it has been possible to broadcast 'live' TV pictures around the world. Events such as the Olympic Games can be seen as they take place, by many millions of people. In the 1990s cable and satellite TV stations are greatly increasing the number of TV channels a viewer can receive at the push of a button.

RECORD-HOLDERS

FIRST TALKING PICTURE
The *Jazz Singer* (1927) was the first movie with sound.

MOST SUCCESSFUL FILMS
Gone with the Wind (1939) and *ET* (1982) rank as the most successful films of all time.

MOST PLAYED CHARACTER
Dracula has appeared on screen in over 150 characterizations; 69 actors have played Sherlock Holmes on film.

MOST OSCARS
Walt Disney (1901–66) won 20 Oscar awards for his films.

LARGEST CINEMA
The world's biggest cinema theatre is in Detroit, Michigan, U.S.A.

MOST POPULAR TV SHOW
BBC's *Andy Pandy* ran from 1950 to 1970 even though only 26 shows were made. *Coronation Street* has run on ITV since 1962.

BIGGEST AUDIENCE
2500 million people watched the TV coverage of the Los Angeles Olympic Games in 1984. 126 million Americans watched the final transmission of *M*A*S*H* in 1983.

Left: A television cameraman filming live sporting events at the 1984 Olympic Games held in Los Angeles.

Crafts

In ancient times people began to develop skills in various crafts such as weaving, pottery, wood carving and metalwork. These skills blended scientific discovery and artistic imagination. They made civilization possible.

The craft-workers of the past mastered the techniques of forging, casting and shaping metal. They learned how to decorate the surface of metal objects with fine engraved designs and how to make jewellery using gemstones and gold. Such works of art became highly valued and were regarded as treasures. Often they were buried alongside a dead king, in the belief that he would be able to wear his finery in the next world.

All the civilizations of the world have produced craftwork of great beauty. Sometimes the objects tell a story or have a religious or magical significance. The ancient Greeks decorated vases and pots with pictures of heroes and warriors from legend.

Glass was first used to glaze beads around 4000 BC. Around 250 BC Syrian glass-makers learned how to blow bubbles of glass on the end of blowpipes in order to make jugs, goblets and dishes. The Romans brought the art of glass-blowing to Europe, where Venice later became a centre of glass-making.

The people who mastered these craft skills guarded their knowledge. In the Middle Ages they formed guilds, or associations, to protect the secrets of their craft. Today, many people enjoy trying some of these crafts themselves as a hobby for relaxation and satisfaction.

Above: A finely decorated Celtic bronze shield (top), inset with stones and about 2000 years old. Also a Viking amulet made of silver and depicting a face with large, staring eyes. Its shape is that of the hammer of the Norse god, Thor.

Right: A mosaic in a Turkish church showing Christ. Mosaics are pictures made from coloured pieces of glass or stone, often cemented to walls, ceilings or floors.

Above: A colourful embroidered figure made centuries ago by Peruvian Indians living in the Pre-Inca period in South America.

Above right: Violin-makers carve violins out of solid pieces of wood. No nails or screws are used, only glue holds the violin together.

Below: Clay pots are 'thrown' on a potter's wheel. The lump of soft, wet clay spins on the wheel while the potter shapes it with the hands.

Right: The ancient Greeks were famous for their beautiful pottery work. This vase dates from thousands of years BC.

MAKING A POT ON A WHEEL

SCIENCE AND TECHNOLOGY

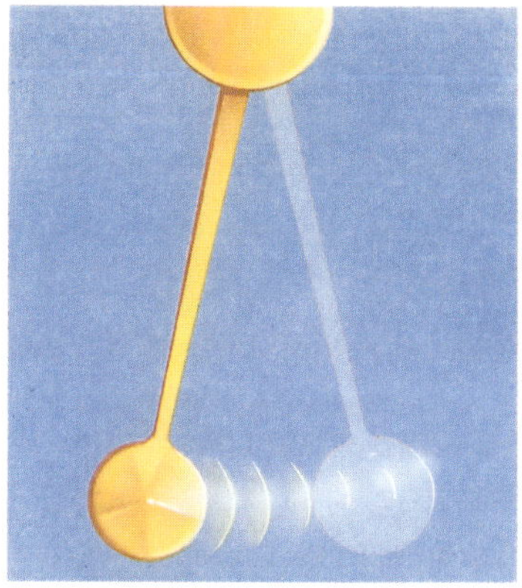

ATOMS AND MATTER
Everything in the Universe is made of matter and all matter is made of atoms. What goes on inside the atom? (See page 138.)

ELECTRICITY AND MAGNETISM
How are electricity and magnetism linked? Electricity changed people's lives. Today we would find it hard to live without electric power. (See page 142.)

SOUND
Sound travels like ripples on a pond. It can travel through air, and through solids and liquids. All sounds are made in the same way – by vibrations. (See page 145.)

ELECTROMAGNETIC WAVES
These forms of radiation include cosmic rays, gamma rays, X-rays, infra-red waves, microwaves and radio waves. (See page 147.)

ELECTRONICS
The electronics revolution has given us radio and TV, computers and robots. Many daily activities involve electronics. (See page 149.)

ENERGY
Heat, light, electrical energy, mechanical energy, chemical energy: energy can be changed but not destroyed. (See page 153.)

MEASURING
When early people started to measure, count and calculate, science in its first stages had begun to develop. (See page 156.)

CONSTRUCTION
Since ancient times people have been builders. Roads, dams, bridges and buildings have shaped our world. (See page 158.)

CHEMISTRY
The Greeks thought there were four elements. Modern chemists studying matter have found over 100 elements. (See page 160.)

MINERALS AND MINING
Rocks are made of minerals. From rocks come the ores from which metals are made and used for many everyday objects. (See page 164.)

TEXTILES
Some fibres come from plants and animals. Others are artificial and are formed from chemical processes (See page 168.)

MACHINES
Machines work for us. The simplest machines such as levers and pulleys are thousands of years old. (See page 170.)

INVENTIONS
Throughout history, people have invented things – from the wheel to the microchip and other modern marvels. (See page 172.)

FORESTRY AND FARMING
Forests and farmland are vital to human life, especially in an overcrowded world. Crops vary according to soil and climate. (See page 176.)

SCIENCE GLOSSARY
An A to Z of common scientific terms, with explanations of what they mean. (See page 178.)

Atoms and Matter

Below: If you pour hot water (liquid) onto ice cubes (solid), you will see water vapour forming as the steam (gas) condenses. Water is actually a mineral, but the only mineral that is found naturally in a liquid form.

Next time you see a kettle of water boiling, watch the steam rising from it. Heating water turns it from a liquid into a gas called steam. However, the 'steam' that we say we see is not really the gas – it is a cloud of tiny water droplets called water vapour. The true steam forms immediately above the kettle spout. About 2.5 centimetres above the spout, this gas meets colder air and condenses into water vapour. If the water vapour meets a cold surface, such as a window pane, it turns into even larger drops of water. Frozen water, in the form of ice cubes from your refrigerator, will melt slowly in your favourite drink

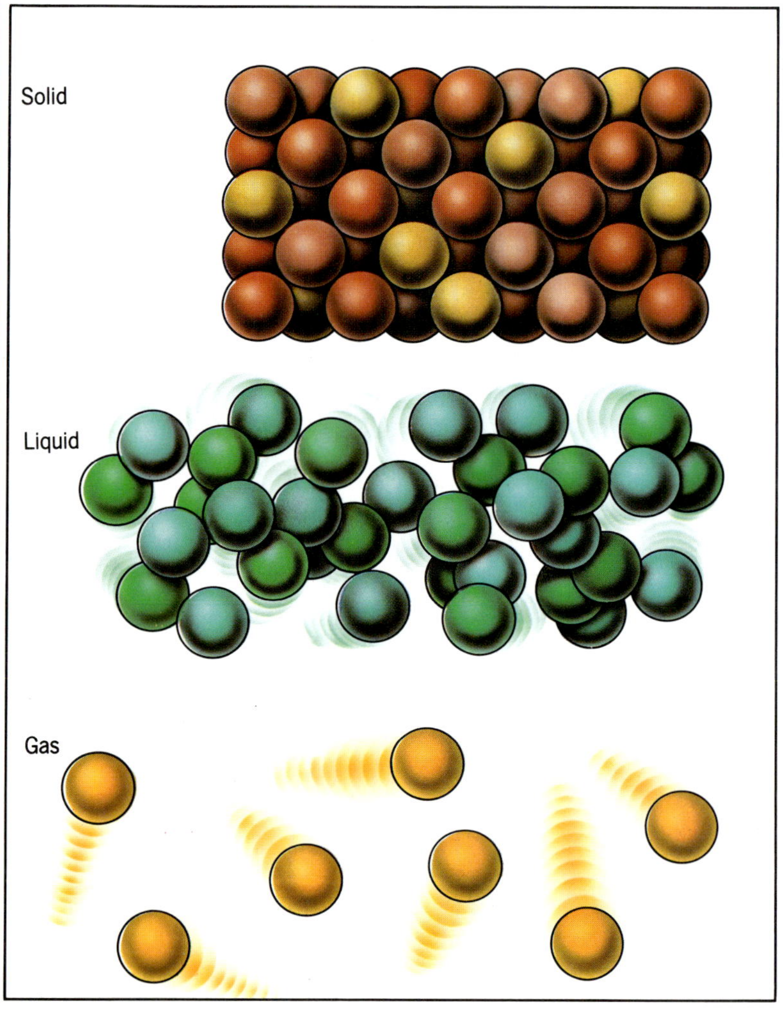

Right: Whether something is a solid (for example a brick, which cannot move of its own accord), a liquid (which flows of its own accord), or a gas (which is lighter than liquids or solids), depends on the energy of the atoms and molecules that make it up. In a solid the particles have a low energy and only move very slightly, so the object stays fixed. In a liquid the particles have more energy and move about, this means the liquid changes shape and can flow. In a gas, the particles have a high energy and move about freely, this means that a gas will fill the whole of a space containing it.

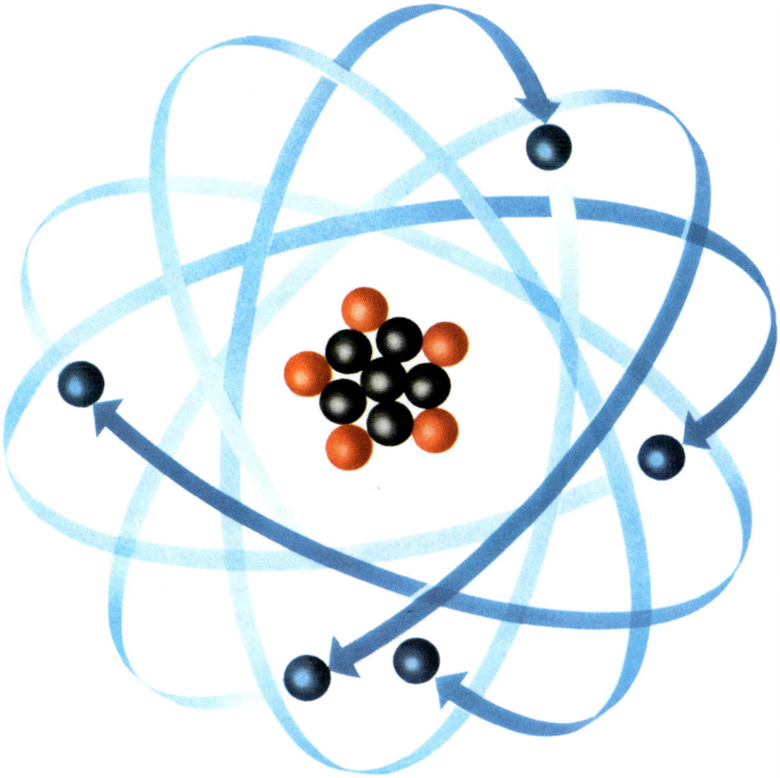

Left: The atom itself consists of a nucleus, or centre, around which move particles called electrons – like planets around a sun. The nucleus contains protons (which carry a positive electric charge) and neutrons (which carry no charge).

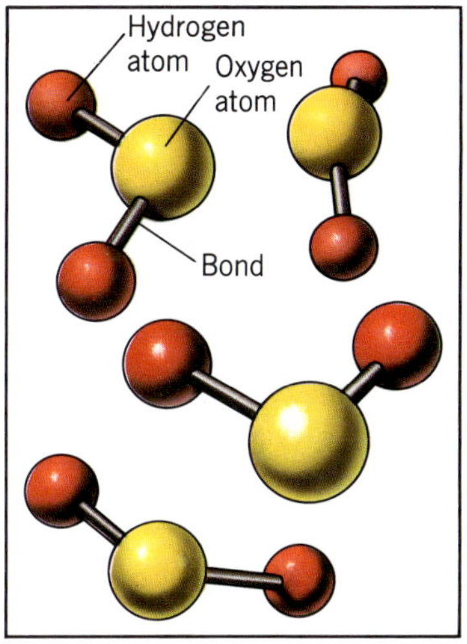

Above: Like all elements, water is made up of molecules. Shown here are four water molecules. Each one has one oxygen (O) atom linked, or bonded, to two hydrogen (H) atoms. From this comes the chemical name for water, H_2O.

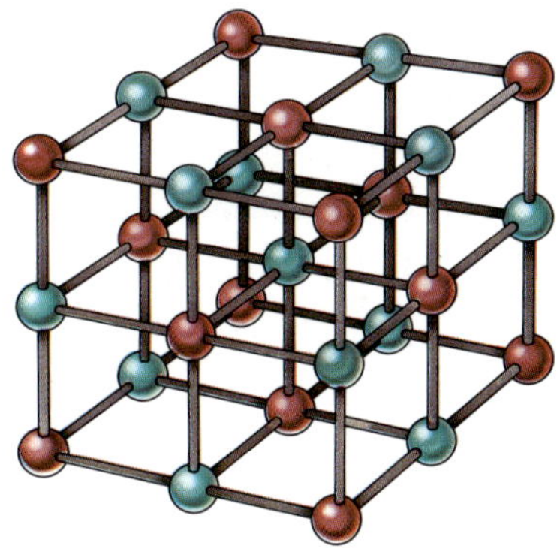

Above: A model of a sodium chloride (common salt) molecule. Sodium and chlorine atoms are linked to form a square lattice pattern.

and turn back into water because the temperature outside the refrigerator is much warmer. Although they seem so different, steam, water and ice are simply three forms of the same substance – one a gas, one a liquid and one a solid. These are called 'the three states of matter'.

Just one tiny drop of water contains about 10,000 million, million, million even smaller parts called molecules. Steam, water and ice all have the same kind of molecules. Each molecule of water is made up of still tinier parts called atoms. An atom is about one hundred-millionth of a centimetre across. A water molecule has two atoms of hydrogen and one atom of oxygen. This is why scientists give water the shorthand name H_2O. Substances differ from one another because their molecules contain different kinds and numbers of atoms. Sugar is made of atoms of carbon, hydrogen and oxygen. Substances which contain more than one kind of atom are called compounds. Sugar and water are both compounds.

Elements are substances that are made of just one kind of atom. For example, the element gold contains only gold atoms in each of its molecules. Gold, silver and lead are examples of solid elements. Elements such as oxygen, hydrogen and chlorine are gases, and mercury is a liquid. Just as heating ice turns it into water without altering its mol-

Above: When heated, glass softens, proving that it is not a true solid but a congealed liquid. It can be moulded and blown to make many objects.

Above: Seen from space, most of the Earth's surface is covered with water.

ecules, solid, liquid or gas elements can be changed in form. If liquid mercury is heated enough, it turns into a gas. If it is cooled a great deal, it turns into a solid. Heating the solid turns it back into a liquid again. All these forms of mercury contain exactly the same molecules. There are fewer than 100 natural elements and everything in the known Universe is made of one or more elements.

All elements are made up of atoms. Every atom has a nucleus – a small inner core made up of protons and neutrons. The number of protons in the nucleus of an atom determines what element it is. Around the nucleus circle tiny negative electrons. Most atoms are very stable. Strong forces bind the protons and neutrons together in their nuclei (plural of nucleus). But some elements have nuclei that tend to decay, or break apart. We call these radio-

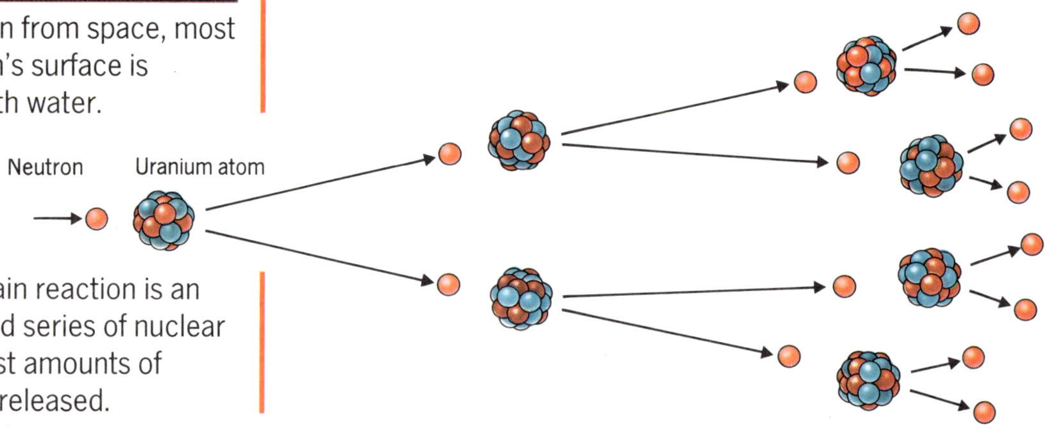

Right: A chain reaction is an uncontrolled series of nuclear fissions. Vast amounts of energy are released.

active elements. One radioactive element is radium, discovered by Marie and Pierre Curie. When a radium atom decays, it gives off an alpha particle – a bundle of two protons and two neutrons. Because it has lost two protons the atom is no longer an atom of radium. It is now an atom of another element called radon. But radon is radioactive too. After a while the radon atom gives off an alpha particle and becomes a polonium atom.

These three steps – from radium to radon to polonium – are just part of a long chain of radioactive decay that starts with the element uranium and ends up with lead. Ordinary lead is not radioactive, so the decay stops there. Not all of the radioactive elements give off alpha particles. Some of them give off beta particles – electrons made in the nucleus of the atom.

The sum of protons and neutrons in an atom is called the element's 'mass number'. The heavier the element, the greater its mass number. Uranium is the heaviest natural element – it is about two and a half times as heavy as steel.

Marie Curie, the Polish scientist, worked on radioactive elements with her French husband Pierre. They discovered two new elements: polonium and radium. Marie Curie died in 1934 of leukemia, as a result of handling radioactive materials.

Left: Nuclear power is the energy released when radioactive atoms are split. Inside a nuclear reactor, this splitting takes place under controlled conditions, producing heat to generate electricity. But in nuclear weapons the energy is released in a violent explosion.

Below: The international symbol for radioactive substances is displayed wherever they are being used or stored.

Right: Once people thought that thunder and lightning were signs of the gods' anger. But lightning is actually a giant spark of natural electricity. A flash of forked lightning is produced by the electrical charges in the raindrops of a cloud. It streaks to Earth in a fraction of a second.

Electricity and Magnetism

Electricity is an invisible form of energy that is stored in electrons and protons. Electrons have a negative electric charge, protons have an equal positive charge. In normal atoms there is an equal number of electrons and protons, so there is an equal amount of negative and positive electricity. To make electricity we must create a situation in which there are more negative or more positive electrons in something and so create an imbalance.

There are two forms of electricity – static and current. 'Static' means 'stationary'. In static electricity the electrons are not moving. In current electricity the electrons are in motion. Current electricity can be produced by a battery or by a machine called a generator. The batteries that we use in toys, torches and radios are 'dry' batteries that have an outer case made of zinc. Inside the case, a layer of manganese dioxide surrounds a carbon rod. The

STATIC ELECTRICITY

Static electricity can be made by rubbing a balloon with a cloth. Electrons move from the cloth to the balloon, making the balloon negatively charged (–) and leaving the cloth positively charged (+). The negatively charged balloon will pick up little bits of positively charged paper because unlike charges attract each other.

Right: A 'dry' battery and bulb make up a 'circuit'. Current flows from the positive (+) terminal to the negative (–) one. A car battery contains plates of lead and lead oxide, suspended in weak sulphuric acid. Electricity is produced when the plates and acid react.

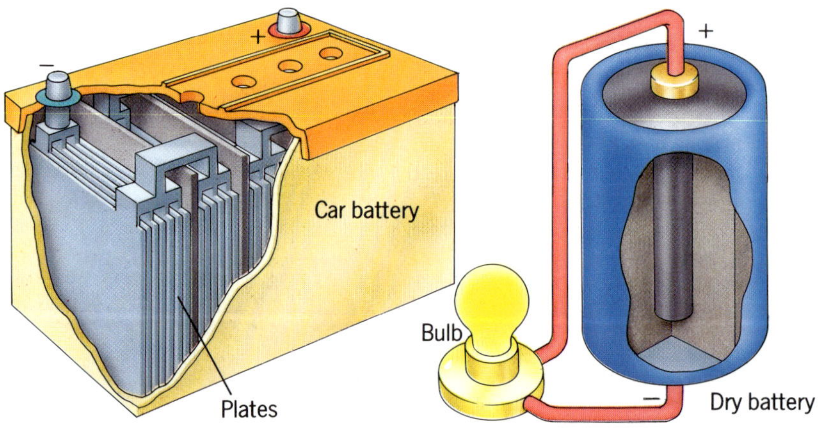

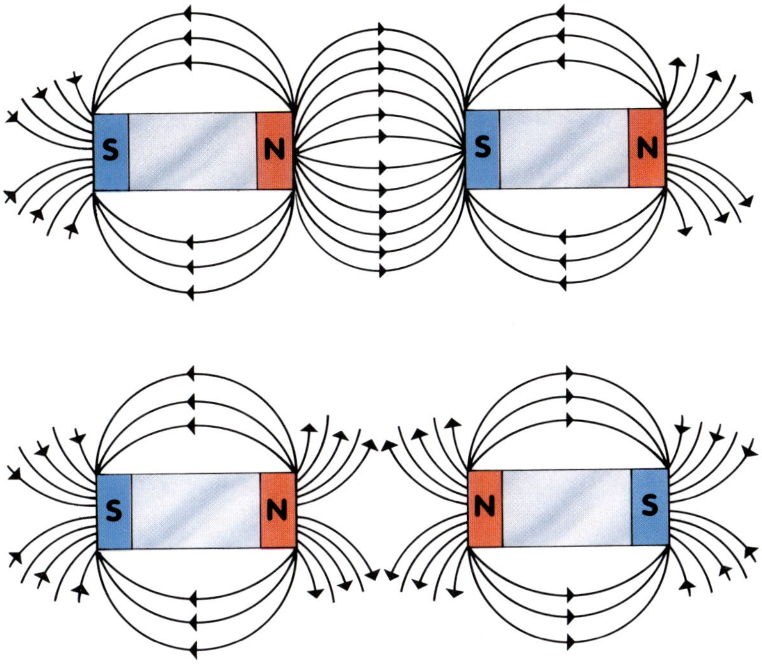

rest of the space is filled with ammonium chloride. The zinc, carbon and ammonium chloride react together to produce electricity. The manganese dioxide absorbs hydrogen formed as a by-product. Dry batteries must be thrown away when their chemicals are exhausted and they produce no more electricity.

Magnets are made of iron or steel (steel is an alloy that contains a lot of iron). They can only attract things made of iron, cobalt, nickel or steel, so we say that these metals are magnetic. A magnet's influence is limited to an invisible force field, or magnetic field spreading out in lines of magnetic force from the ends of the magnet.

We call the ends of a magnet the poles. One is the 'north' pole and the other the 'south' pole. Two magnets held with like poles facing will be pushed apart by their magnetic fields, while a north pole of one magnet will be attracted to the south pole of another. If any magnet is suspended in the air so that it can turn freely, it will always line up with its north pole pointing in a northerly direction. Magnets behave in this way because the Earth has a magnetic field all around it. A magnet suspended in this field will line up along the lines of magnetic force.

In 1820 a Danish scientist called Hans Oersted noticed that when electric current was flowing along a wire, it produced a magnetic field around the wire. This magnetism produced by an electric current is called electromagnetism. Coils of wire used to produce magnetism became known as electromagnets.

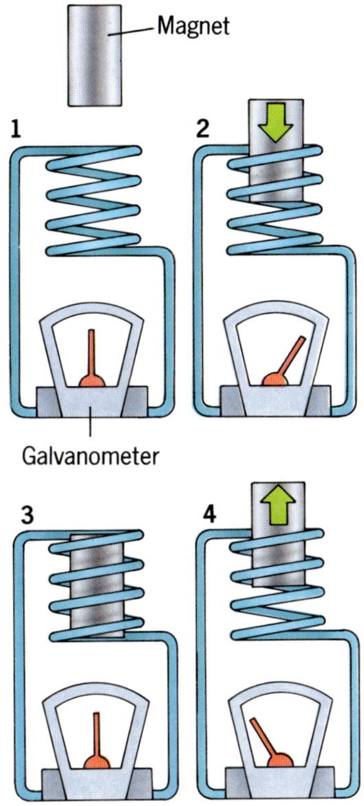

Above: Faraday used a wire coil, magnet and galvanometer to show how current flows when the magnet is moving.

Above left: 'Like' poles of magnets repel; 'unlike' poles attract.

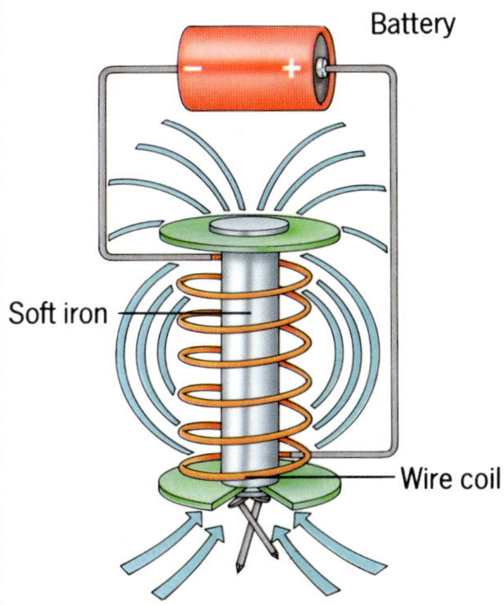

Above: An electromagnet is made by wrapping a wire coil around an iron bar connected to a battery.

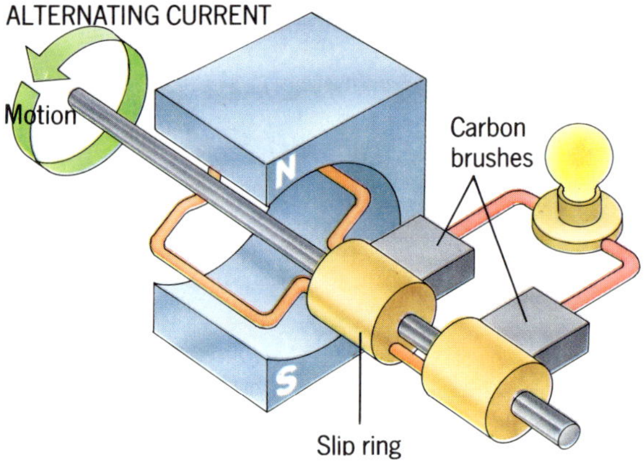

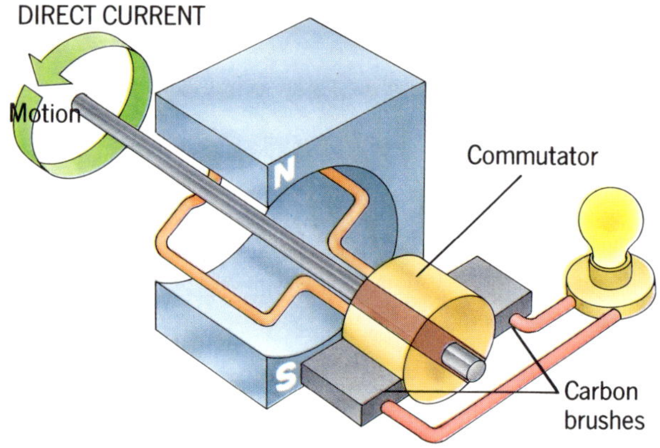

Above: Generators have a coil held between two magnetic poles. When the coil turns, electricity is produced. AC generators connect to the circuit by a slip ring and carbon brushes. DC generators connect by a commutator.

Below: The frequency of alternating currents is measured in cycles a second.

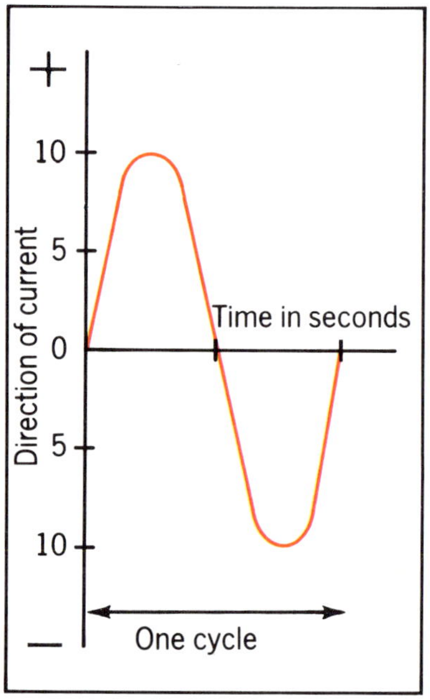

Right: An electric motor. A current turns the coil into an electromagnet, which the magnet poles force to spin.

After the discovery that electricity could produce magnetism, scientists began to wonder whether the reverse might be possible – could magnetism be used to make electricity? In 1830 a British scientist called Michael Faraday found that current was produced in a coil of wire when a magnet was moved in and out of it. He had found a way to turn mechanical energy, the movement of the magnet, into electrical energy. The faster the magnet was moved in and out of the coil, the greater the current it produced. Current flowed first one way and then the other to give an alternating current – AC. Later, a mechanical engine was used to move the magnet and the first simple electricity generator had been made. Direct current – DC, similar to that from a battery, can be obtained from a generator by using a device called a 'commutator'. This makes the current flow continuously in the same direction.

As Faraday continued with his experiments, he found that a wire suspended in a magnetic field would move if a current was passed through it. This was exactly the opposite to what happened in a generator. Faraday had established the principles on which electric motors work.

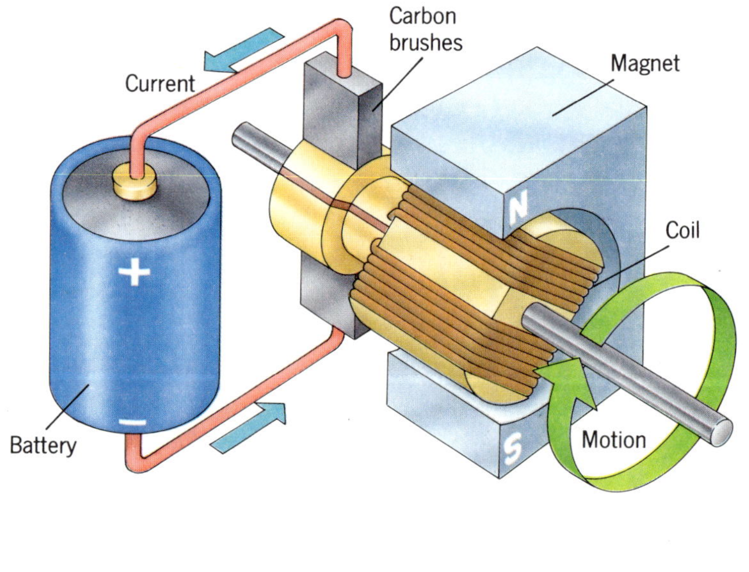

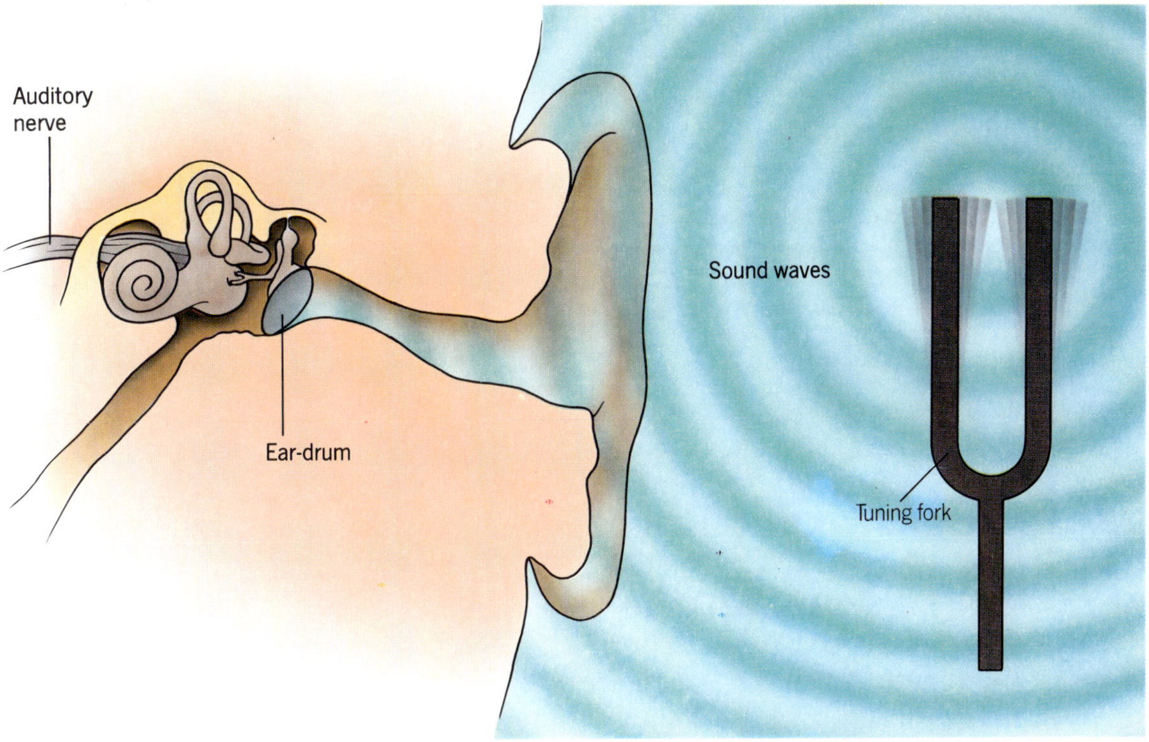

Sound

Above: Sound waves from a vibrating object (a tuning fork, say) are collected by the ear. The ear drum vibrates and sends messages along the auditory nerve to the brain.

Sounds travel in waves that push through things and spread out from the source of a noise, rather like ripples on a pond when a stone is dropped in. We hear sounds when the waves reach our ears. An echo is reflected sound waves that bounce off a rock face or high wall.

Frequency is the number of waves passing a fixed point every second. It is measured in units called hertz. One hertz is equal to one complete wave, or cycle, per second. The volume of sound – how loud it is – depends on how much energy the vibrations pass on through the air. Sound waves can be shown as wavy lines on a special instrument called an oscilloscope. Loud sounds make higher waves than softer ones. The height of the waves shown on the oscilloscope is called the amplitude of the sound.

In order to make a recording, sound vibrations must be converted into a form that can be stored. A microphone turns sound into bursts of electric current called 'signals'. The signals, which vary according to the loudness and frequency of the sound, are passed to an amplifier, which makes them powerful enough to 'cut' a record. A special cutting needle called a stylus vibrates in tune with the sig-

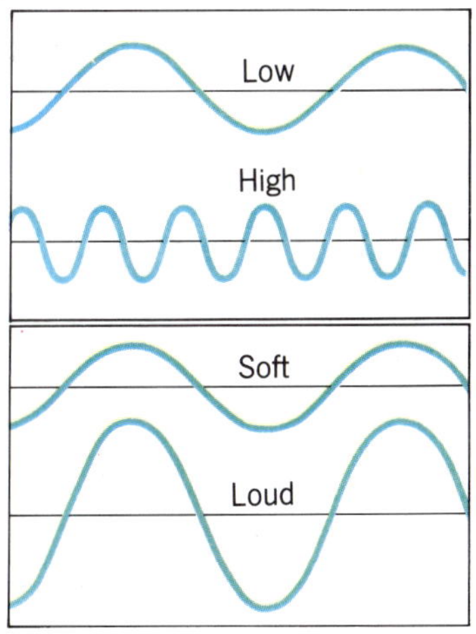

Above: On an oscilloscope the waves close together show high-pitched sounds. Lower pitched sounds have longer and wider waves.

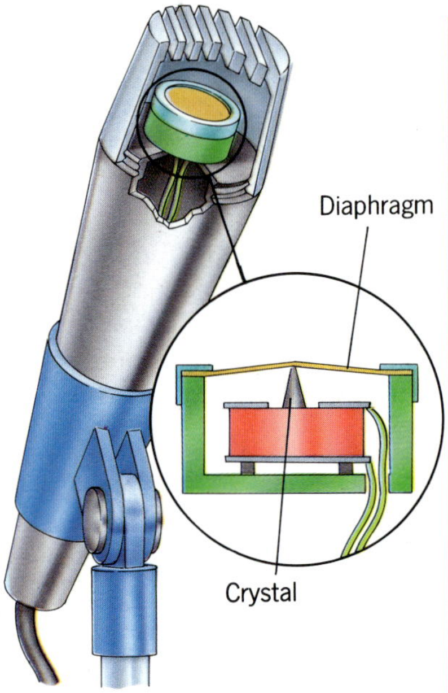

Above: In a microphone, sound waves hit a diaphragm (a thin plate) which vibrates. A crystal (in this example) turns sound into electrical signals.

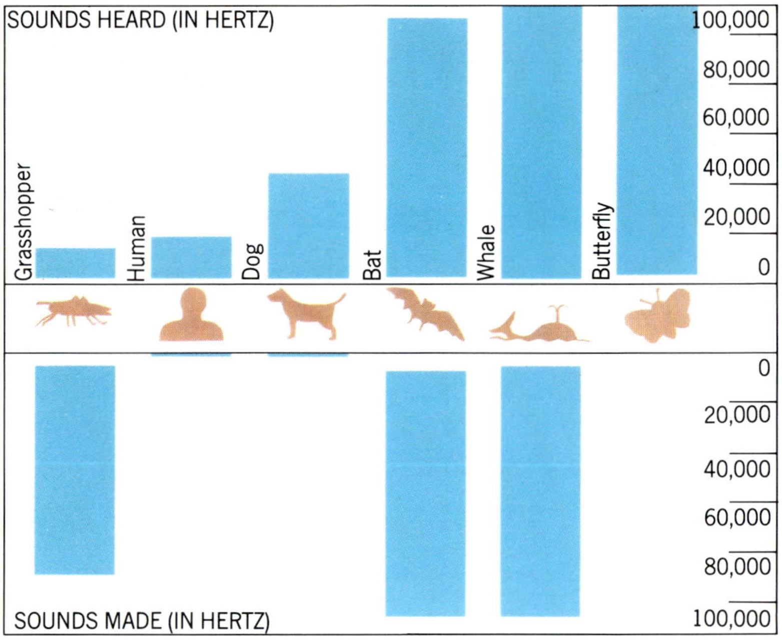

Above right: The range of sounds made and heard by different animals.

nals it receives and marks the pattern of signals into the sides of a soft, plastic master disc. From this one disc many more records can be copied. To make a cassette tape, the electrical signals are converted into bands of magnetic pattern on tape. A compact disc stores information in millions of tiny pits on the surface of the disc.

Record, disc or cassette players convert the stored messages back, firstly to electrical signals and then to vibrations of air that we can hear. A record player picks up the stored messages with a stylus and cartridge, a cassette player has sensitive magnetic heads which the tape is wound around, and compact discs are 'read' by laser beams. The electric signals that these devices produce are fed to the amplifier inside the player which makes them strong enough to vibrate the loudspeaker. The loudspeaker's vibrations are passed on to the air and the vibrating air hits our ears as sound.

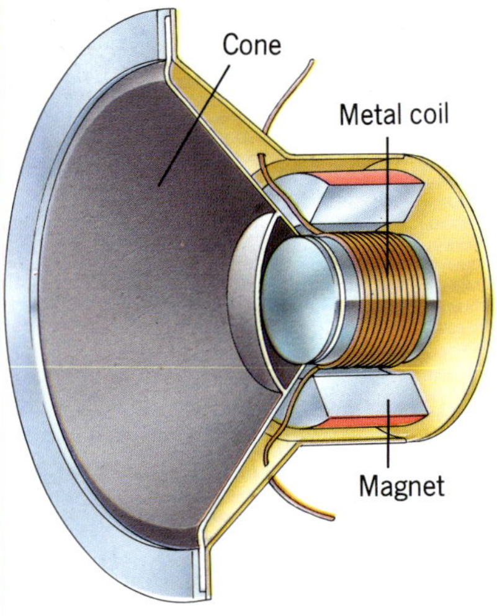

Below: A loudspeaker turns signals back into sounds.

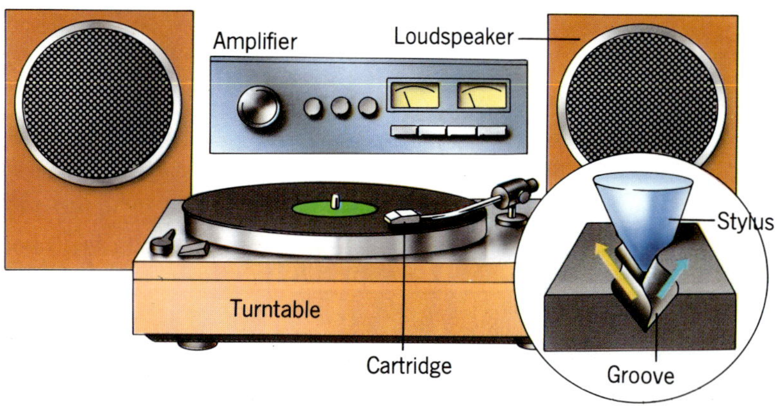

Right: In a record player, the stylus vibrates as it follows the grooves.

Electromagnetic Waves

Our Universe is full of the waves of energy that make up the electromagnetic spectrum. These various types of wave are very important to us and yet our senses can detect only a small proportion of them. We can see ordinary visible light and feel the heat of infrared waves, but radio waves, ultraviolet (UV) and X-rays pass right through our bodies without us knowing it. All the waves travel at the same speed – the speed of light – but their wavelengths vary. Cosmic rays are less than one hundred million-millionth of a metre in length, while radio waves can be several kilometres long.

The radio waves that we know best are those that bring us music and speech through our radios. But there are other radio waves flashing continuously through space. Some come from distant stars, others are created by lightning. The shortest type of radio waves are microwaves. Microwaves pass messages between satellites and are used by radar systems to detect distant objects. Their most familiar use is for cooking food in microwave ovens. The shorter waves of the electromagnetic spectrum are more penetrating and some are harmful to our bodies. X-rays are valuable in medical examinations, but too much exposure to them is harmful.

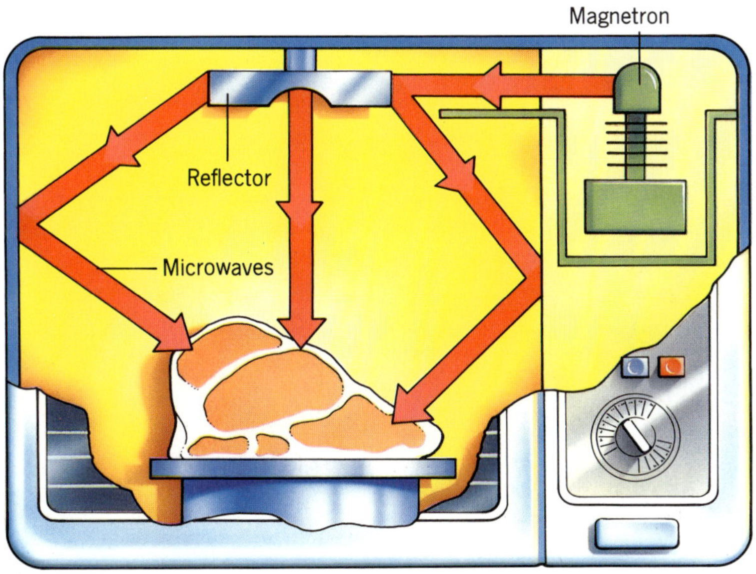

Above: Ultraviolet light from the Sun gives pale skins a 'tan'. Much of this UV light (which can be harmful) is absorbed by the atmosphere.

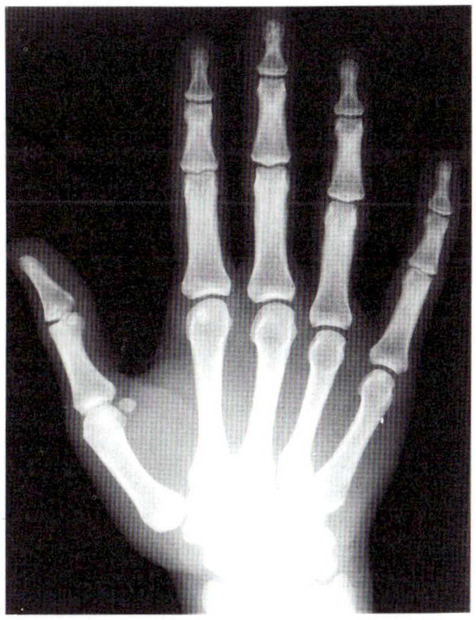

Above: X-rays are used in medical photographs. When the X-rays pass through our bodies, bones, teeth and some other parts show as shadows on the photographic plate.

Left: Inside a microwave oven the magnetron reflects microwaves off the oven's metal walls. These waves agitate the water molecules in the food. The friction causes heat, which then cooks the food.

Sun
Galaxies
Supernova
Visible light
Radio waves
Satellites
Microwaves
Radio telescope
Gamma rays
Satellite tracking station

Electronics

Left: The Earth's atmosphere shields us against harmful rays. Without light from the Sun, there would be no life. Without radio waves, we would not enjoy modern telecommunications.

Below: Sections through two transistors. The arrows represent the flow of electricity. If a transistor is made of two pieces of silicon, electricity can flow in one direction but not back again (**1**). Such transistors act like diode valves ('di' means 'two') and change AC into DC. The other transistor (**2**) is made of a sandwich of three differently treated pieces of silicon. Minute amounts of impurities are added to the silicon making it unstable and allowing electrons to flow from one layer to another in one direction only. The centre of the sandwich will convert a tiny change in electric charge into a big change in current. In this way the transistor amplifies the signal. The diagram on the right shows a transistor connected to a circuit.

Before we can enjoy the sounds and pictures from signals gathered by our radio and television aerials, the signals need to be amplified. The signals must make changes in the flow of electricity strong enough to make the radio or television speaker vibrate. Early radios and televisions had large glass valves to control the flow of electricity and amplify signals.

Smaller radios and televisions were made possible by the invention of the transistor in 1947. Transistors do just what valves do, but they are smaller, cheaper and more reliable. Transistors consist of a sandwich of three specially treated pieces of silicon. Silicon is a 'semiconducting' material, which means that it allows electricity to flow through it, but not as easily as a conductor such as copper.

The sounds of a radio programme begin their journey to your radio at the microphone. Microphones convert the sound waves that pass into them into electrical signals. The signals are amplified (strengthened) and sent to a transmitter. Transmitters produce special radio waves called 'carrier' waves. Transmitter aerials radiate the carrier waves with their signals to a receiving aerial in a radio. Tuning your radio picks out the signal coming from the station you want to listen to from the others. Inside a radio, signals are separated from their carrier waves and then turned back into sounds by the loudspeaker.

Broadcasting stations use 'long', 'medium' and 'short' waves. Long and medium waves are between 10,000 and 100 metres long. These waves tend to follow the curve of the Earth's surface. But short waves between 10 and 100 metres long bounce off a layer called the 'ionosphere' high up in the atmosphere. The waves are reflected back down

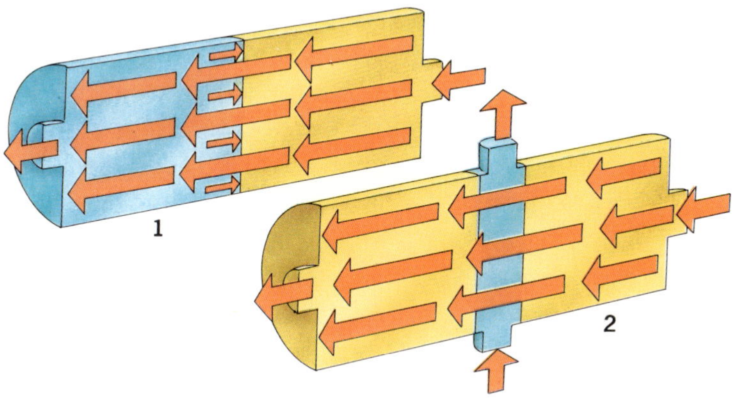

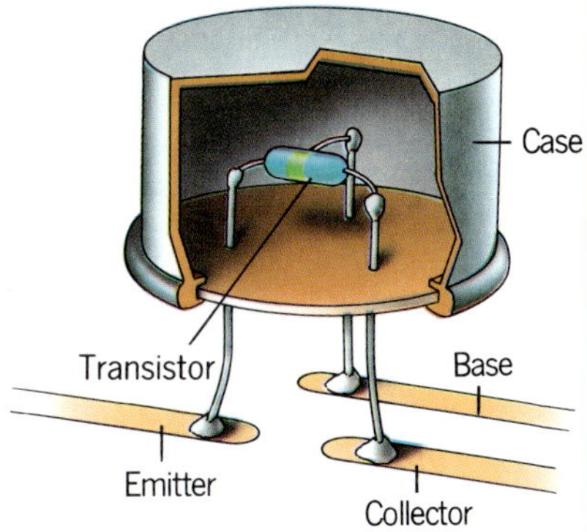

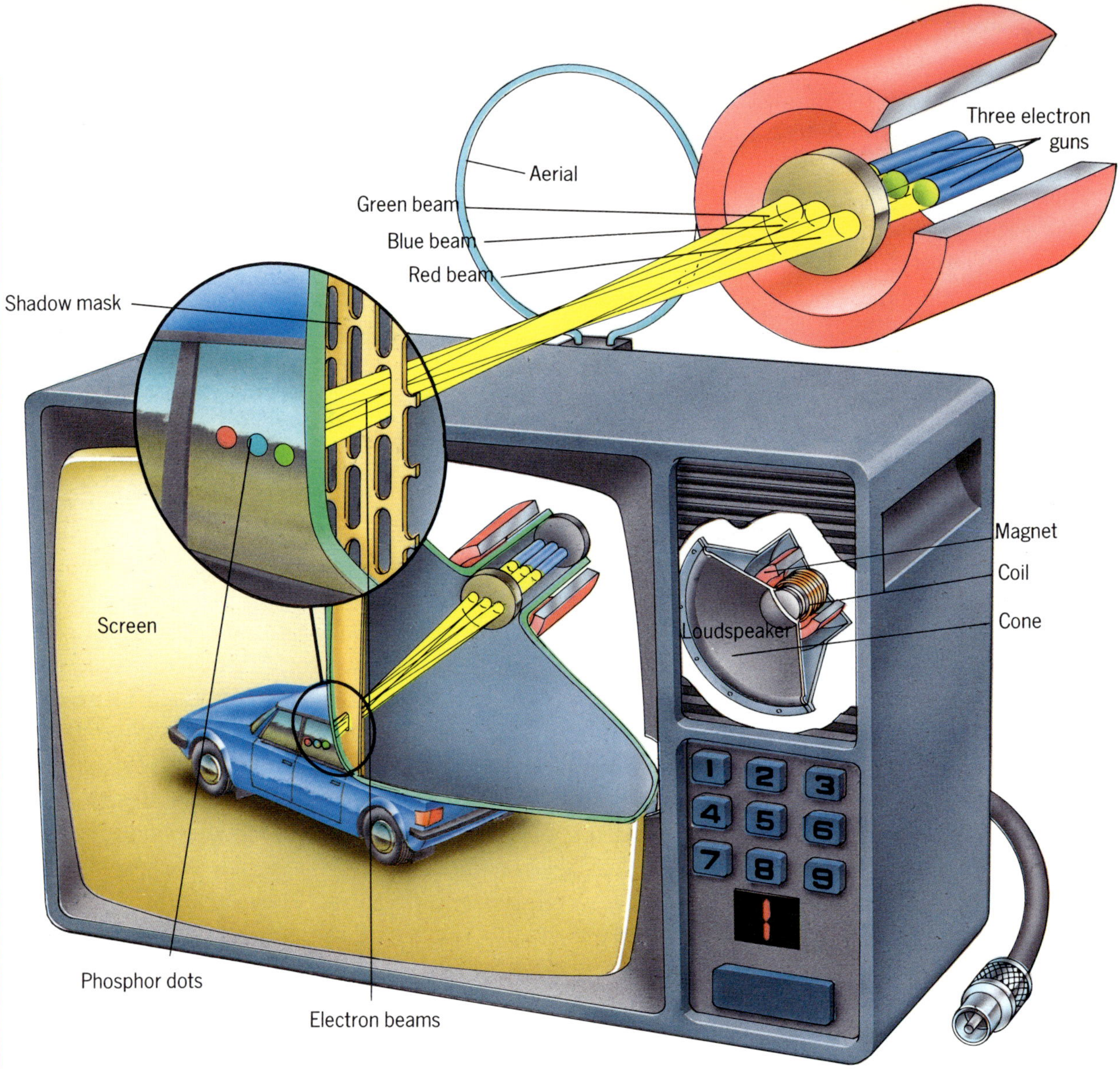

Above: How television works. The inside of your television screen is coated with chemical phosphor dots. The screen is actually the wide end of a cathode ray tube. Electrons pass easily through the vacuum in the tube. An electron 'gun' fires electrons onto the back of the screen when it receives a signal. This makes the dots glow and combinations of these dots form a picture. A colour television has three guns – one for each of the colours.

to Earth, far from the transmitter. Because of this, short waves are used for long-distance broadcasting. VHF ('very high frequency' waves) and UHF ('ultra high frequency' waves) travel straight through the ionosphere into outer space.

Television, computers, telecommunications: all these marvels make use of new technology. A television programme begins wherever a camera films an event. Colour television cameras use special mirrors to divide the light they receive into three simple colours – red, blue and green. Combinations of these colours can produce any other colours in our televisions. Beams of the three colours are turned into electronic signals. These are transmitted on very high frequency carrier waves and can be 'bounced' off satellites high above the Earth.

The first 'transistor' radios in the 1950s contained tran-

THE BINARY CODE

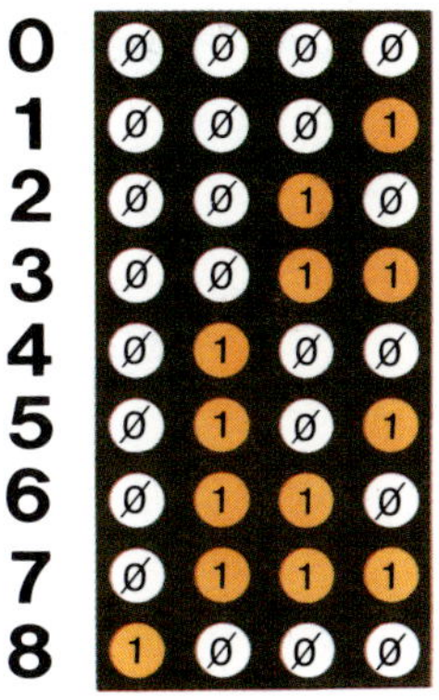

Everyday counting and calculation uses the decimal system which is based on the numerals 0–9. However, computers can only work on information in the form of binary code. This number system uses only 1s and 0s indicated by electrical pulses: 0 = no pulse and 1 = a pulse. On the diagram from right to left, the first column stands for units of 1, the second for 2s and so on. When we type on the keys of a computer keyboard we make small electrical currents flow through tiny circuits in microchips and so the computer works.

sistors as separate parts joined together by wires to form an electrical circuit. But by 1960, it had been discovered that different components, including microscopic transistors, could be put together into just one little piece, or chip, of silicon to form a whole electrical circuit. These complete 'integrated' circuits opened the way for very small radios, smaller televisions, pocket calculators and 'micro' computers.

The silicon that is used to make chips is produced from a special type of sand. It is melted at 1420°C and long cylindrical crystals, ten centimetres in diameter and one metre long, are grown from it. These cylinders are sliced into thin wafers, each of which is divided into 500 chips, five millimetres square. Each of these chips has even

Above: A watch can give a lot more information than just the time!

Below: A silicon chip, compared to the size of cherries.

Right: A laser beam cuts through a steel sheet.

Below: An operation to seal a detached retina is carried out using a laser.

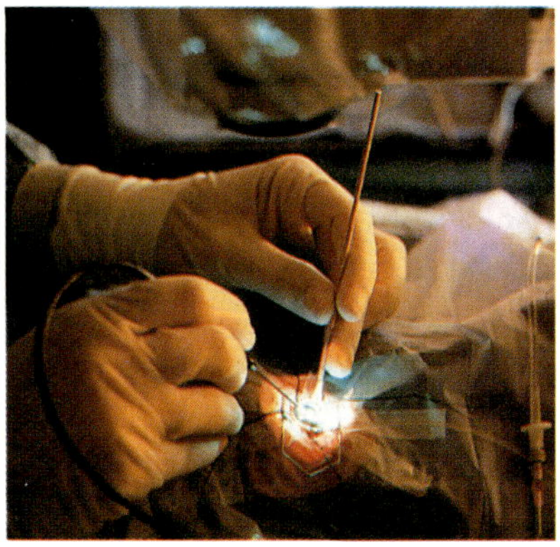

LASER COMMUNICATION
Pulses of laser light can be sent along ultra-thin glass fibres. The light is reflected back each time it hits the fibre's surface, so the signal it carries remains strong. A cable made of 100 fibres is only 10 mm thick, yet it can carry nearly a million phone conversations at once. The sending of light through glass fibres is known as 'fibre optics'.

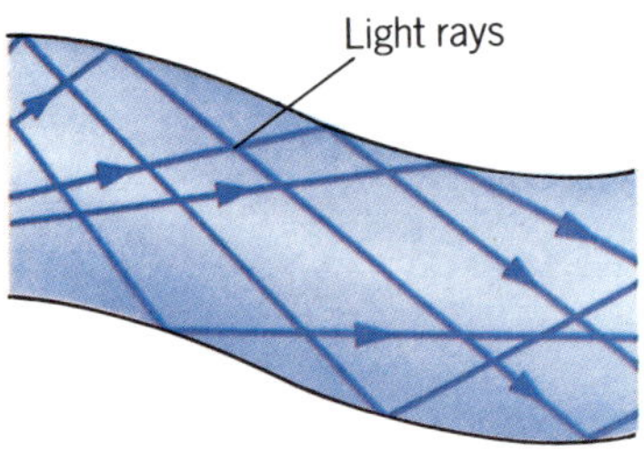

smaller transistors and connecting channels 'etched' onto it, using metals and other materials which stick to the surface of the chip. The process is repeated many times to give several layers and produce a complete circuit.

Lasers

Ordinary light spreads out in all directions and its beams fade as they travel. A laser beam looks like a straight rod because it is made of very intense beams which stay almost parallel and keep their intensity over very long distances.

Since the discovery of the laser in 1960, a whole new way of sending messages and storing information has been opened up. Laser beams can be used to transmit telephone calls, television broadcasts and computer data. They also 'read' visual or audio information stored on special discs and are used in laser printers to make books and newspapers. Lasers can cut metal and repair human tissue.

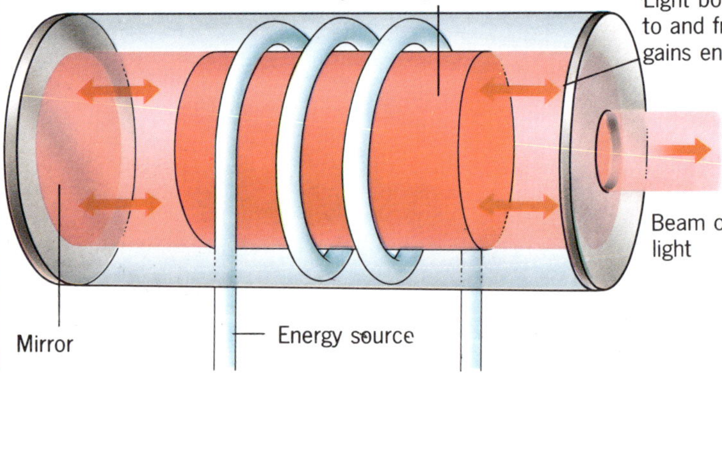

Right: Atoms of the laser crystal or tube of gas are excited by energy from the electrical discharge. They bounce off the mirrors, gaining energy, and are emitted as a coherent beam of laser light.

Energy

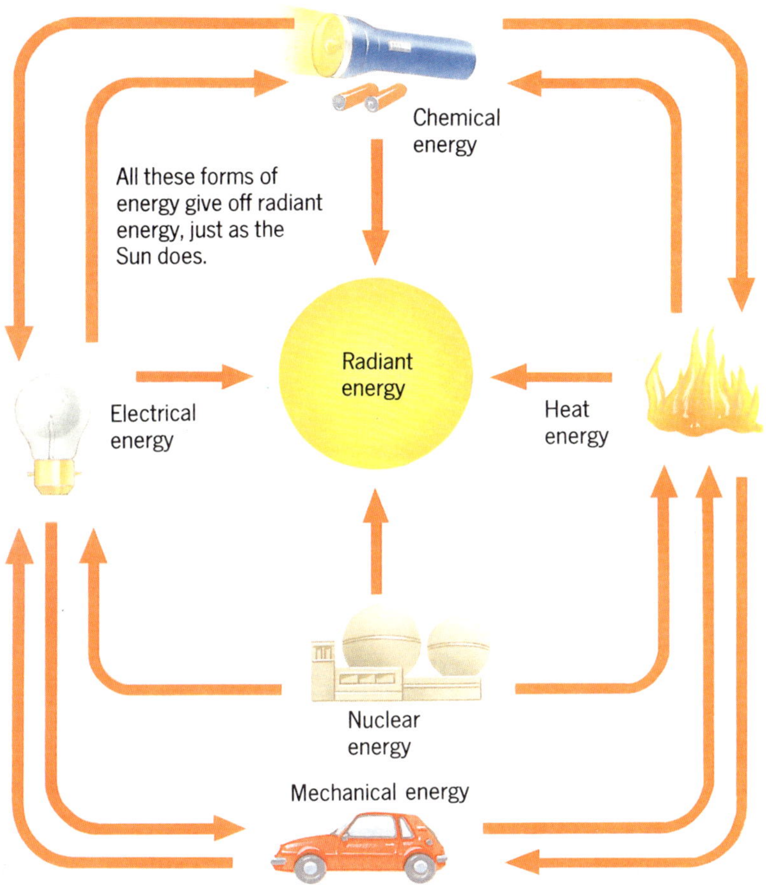

It is not easy to explain what energy is. Energy does not have a shape like a log of wood or a taste like a bar of chocolate, and yet both these things have energy in them. It is easier to say what energy does – if we burn the wood its heat energy can keep us warm, and if we eat the chocolate we can use its chemical energy to enable us to run. Energy means being able to do *work*. The many different forms it takes enable us to do different types of work. Heat and chemical energy are just two forms. Other forms include light, electrical and mechanical energy.

The total amount of energy in the Universe remains the same because energy cannot be created or destroyed – it can only be changed from one form to another. Heat can be transformed into mechanical energy in a steam engine, chemical energy is released as heat energy when fuel burns, and electrical energy can be converted into sound and light energy, for example in radios and lamps.

Above: A moving snooker ball has kinetic energy. As it hits another ball, it gives some of its energy to that ball.

Left: Nearly all the energy on Earth has come from the Sun. And all forms of energy can be changed into other forms. Every form of energy can be turned into heat, but most of this heat energy cannot be recaptured and changed back into a form that can be used. Instead it spreads out in the molecules of the air.

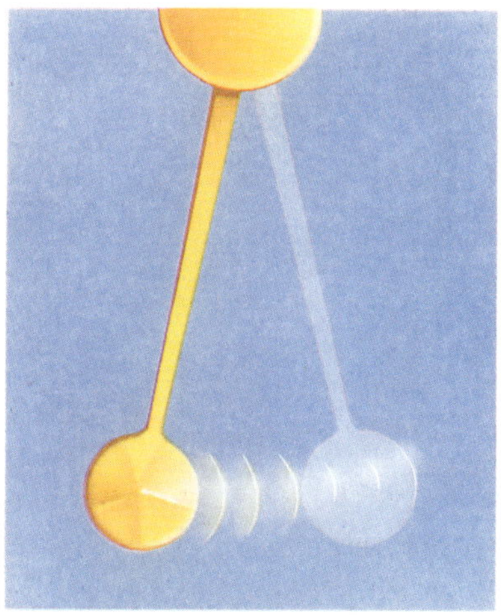

Above: A pendulum at the top of its swing has potential energy. As it moves, the energy becomes kinetic.

Above: An electric hot plate produces heat energy which moves through the pan by *conduction*, to heat the water.

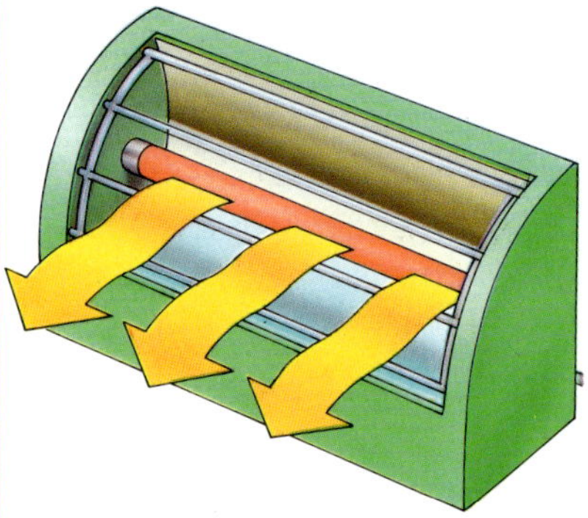

Above: An electric bar heater produces heat energy in the form of *radiation*.

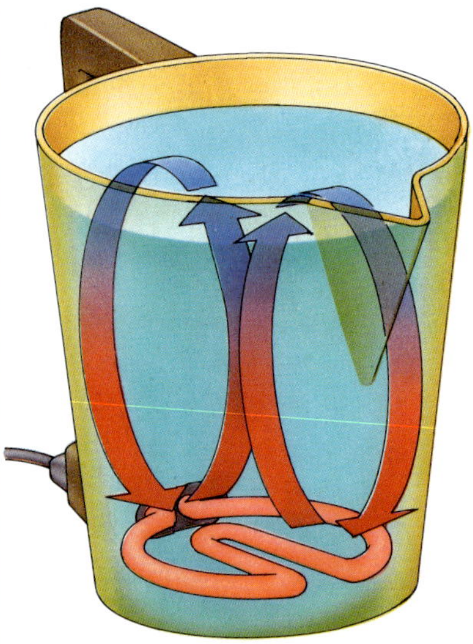

Above: Water in a kettle is heated by *convection*. Currents circulate, heating the water.

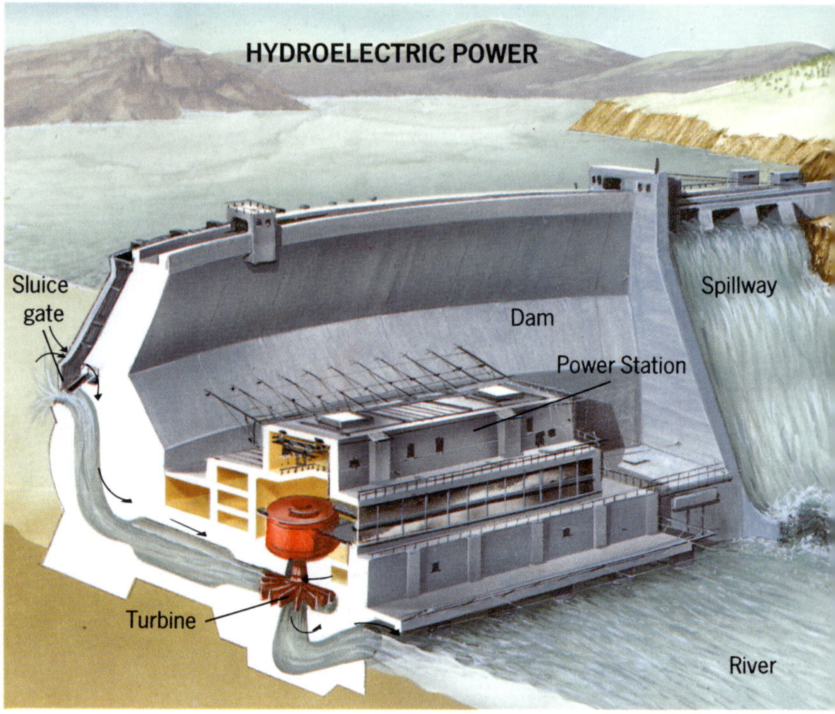

The most obvious source of energy on Earth is the light and heat we receive from the Sun. Energy from the Sun is captured and stored by plants, using photosynthesis. This energy forms the first link in a food chain that supplies all animals. Energy is transferred at each link.

Whatever form energy takes, we can think of it as being in one of two states. Kinetic energy is energy that is used for activity or moving. Potential energy is stored energy. Usually, a store of potential energy can be released as useful kinetic energy. For example the wound-up spring in a clockwork toy has potential energy that can become moving kinetic energy and drive the toy.

A hydroelectric power station converts stored potential energy into kinetic, electrical energy that we can use. Water held back behind a dam contains a great deal of energy – it has the potential to turn the turbines in the hydroelectric power station. As water is released from the top of the dam, it falls down and loses its stored energy. As it falls faster and faster, it gains kinetic energy and this energy turns the turbines and generators. The electrical energy they produce can be used to give us heat, light and sound – all different forms of flowing, kinetic energy.

Nuclear power is the energy released when radioactive atoms are split. Inside a nuclear reactor, this splitting is controlled to produce heat to generate electricity. What happens in a nuclear reaction is quite different from the

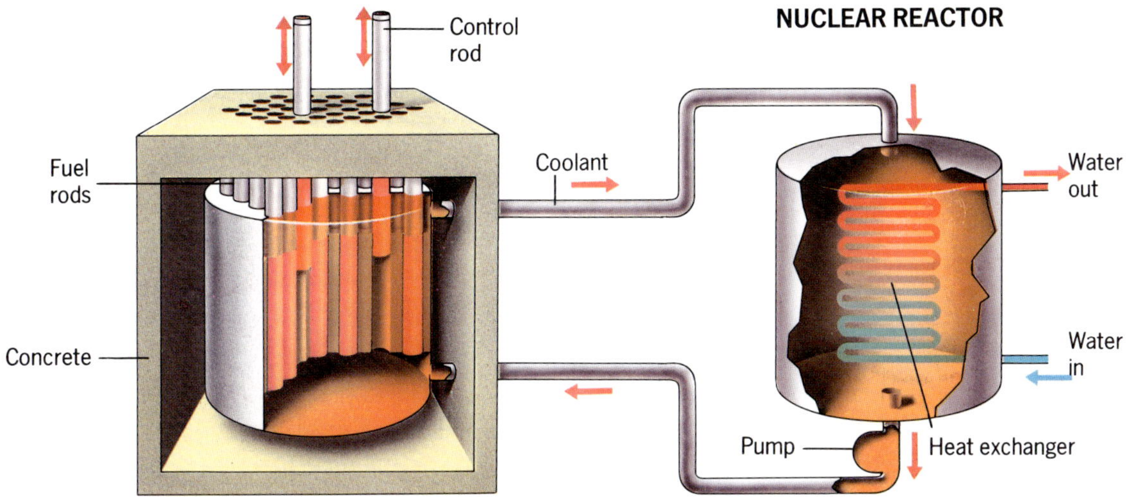

way in which energy is released from other sources of chemical energy. Burning ten kilograms of coal releases chemical energy as heat and leaves ten kilograms of ash plus smoke. But in a nuclear reaction, some of the actual fuel substance is turned into energy, so that there is less total matter left at the end of the reaction.

Nuclear power (*above*), hydro-electric power (*far left*) and coal (*below*) are all used to provide electrical energy. Without this power supply, life today would be very different.

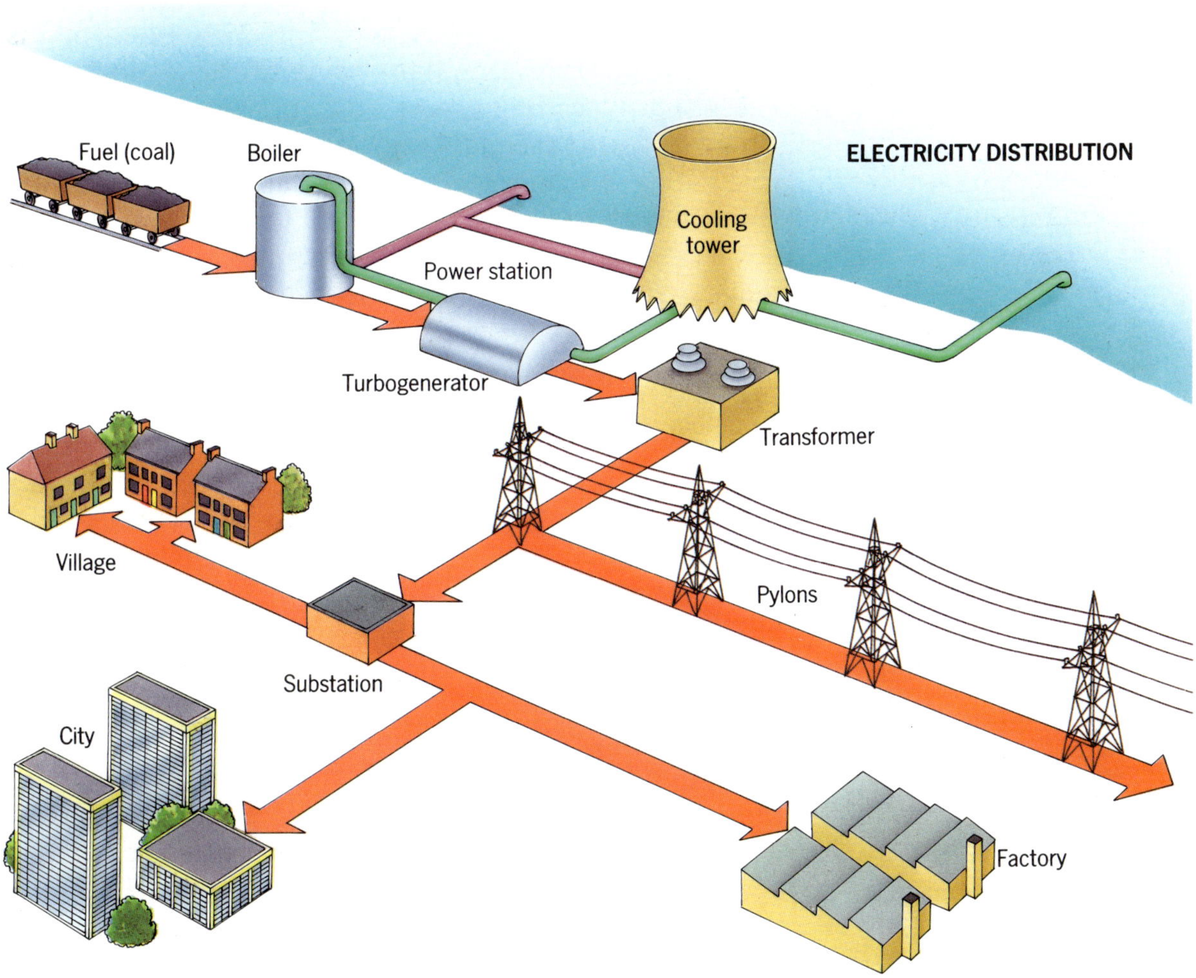

Measuring

At first, people measured distance with rods and knotted cords. Weights and volumes were based on the different containers used for holding wine and grain. Units of measurement were often based on the human body, and there were many different ones. The metric system (1791) was an attempt to standardise weights and measures. A metre was originally one ten-millionth of the distance from the North Pole to the Equator.

Priests in ancient Babylon and Egypt studied the Moon and stars in order to draw up calendars. These astronomer-priests could predict eclipses.

The Egyptians used geometry when building the Pyramids. The great mathematicians of Greece, who included Euclid and Pythagoras, made many important discoveries. The Greeks knew that a circle is made up of 360 degrees, a figure probably chosen by the Babylonians. Using geometry, they calculated the size of the Earth. No matter what its shape, a triangle has angles that always add up to 180 degrees. This was first proved by Euclid about 300 BC.

Two useful early aids to mathematics were logarithms (invented in 1614) and the slide rule (1621). Blaise Pascal's calculating machine of 1642 was ahead of its time. Electronic computers did not appear until 1946.

Computers count using only two symbols, 0 and 1. This 'binary code' was first described in 1679 by Leibnitz. The numerals we use today come originally from India. They reached Europe, by way of the Arabs, around AD 1000.

Above: Two sides of an algebra equation should always balance, like a pair of scales. If we call the large blocks x and each of the small blocks 1, we see that $2x + 3 = 11$. Remove 3 from either side and $2x = 8$. By halving both sides of the equation, we find that x balances 4, so $x = 4$.

Below: The Greek scientist Archimedes lived about 250 BC. He discovered how to find volume (the space taken up by an object) by putting the object in water. Archimedes had to find out if the king's crown was pure gold. While taking a bath he realized that the water spilling over the bath's edge must have the same volume as his body. So he put the crown and the same weight of pure gold in water, to check if each displaced the same amount of water. (They didn't. The king had been cheated.)

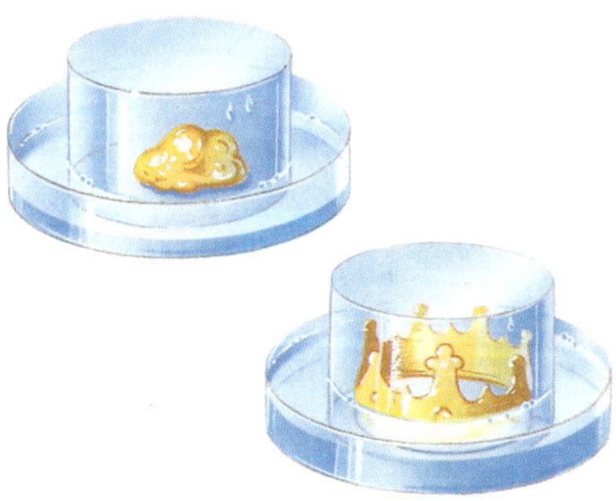

Below: In 1642 the French scientist Blaise Pascal built a mechanical calculating machine. It used sets of dials.

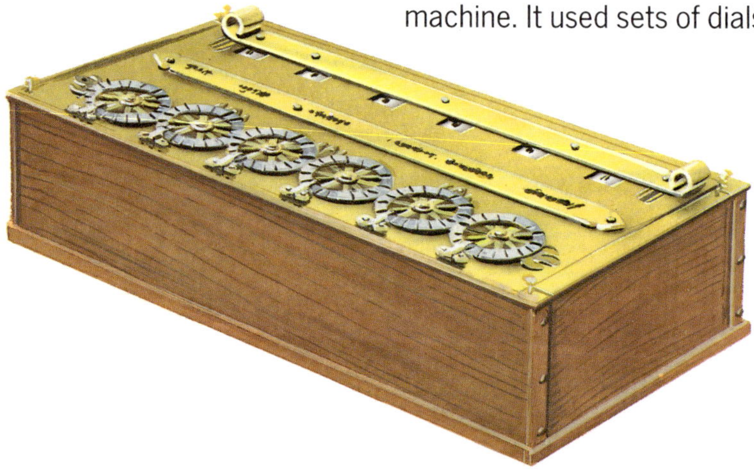

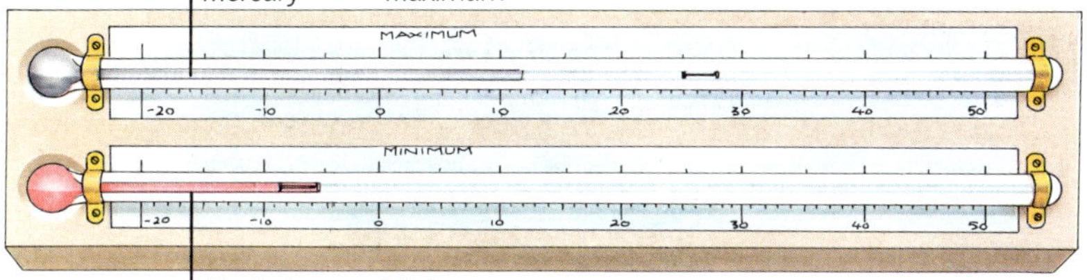

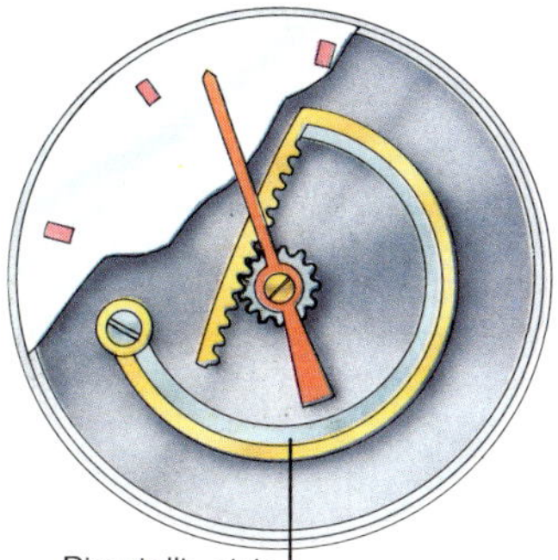

Above: Maximum and minimum thermometers indicate the highest and lowest daily temperatures recorded. They have to be reset each day.

Above right: The two metals that form the bimetallic strip in oven thermometers expand at different rates. When heated, the strip bends moving a pointer on a dial.

Left: People first measured time by means of sundials, sand glasses, candles and water clocks. By the 1300s mechanical clocks, worked by heavy weights, were in use and from the 1600s pendulum clocks were found in the homes of the wealthy. They were crude compared to modern quartz and atomic Caesium clocks. (The latter should be accurate to 1 second in 300 years.)

Below: Light travels at 300,000 km/sec. The diagram illustrates how long it takes light to travel across the Atlantic, from the Moon, the Sun and the nearest star.

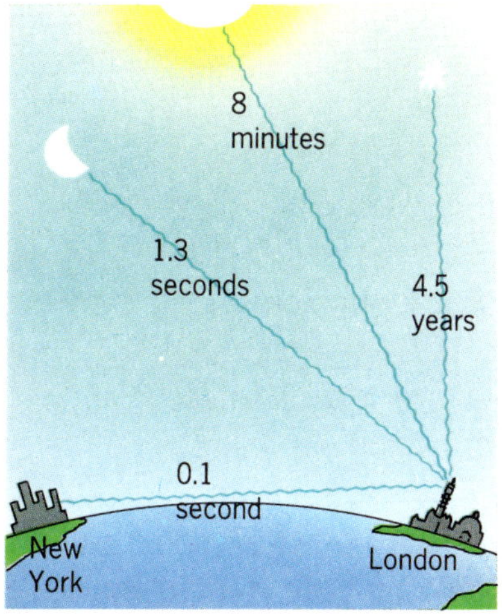

MAKING A SUNDIAL

On a sunny morning fix a straight stick in the ground. Every hour, place a marker on the ground at the tip of the stick's shadow. Notice how the shadow shortens as noon approaches, and then lengthens again. Try to decide just when the shadow was shortest. Did your 'sundial' agree with 'clock' noon? Remember that Summer Time is one hour ahead of 'sundial' time.

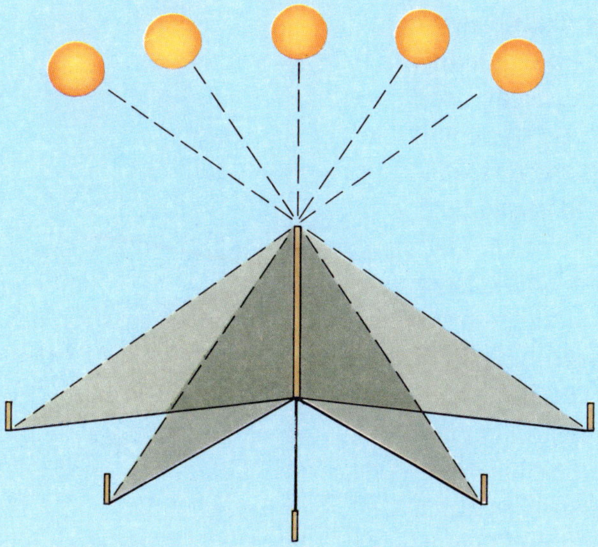

Right: Egyptian pyramids were built from millions of tonnes of stone. Cranes had not been invented, so the stones had to be dragged to the site and hauled up ramps on sledges to be laid in position. No cement was used and a set square and plumb line were essential tools. The pyramids were finely measured.

Above: Medieval builders at work. To build a vault, stones were laid along wooden centrings. A specially shaped keystone was hoisted by a pulley to complete the arch. When the mortar, used as a cement, had hardened, the centrings were removed leaving the vault in place.

Right: The Greeks built temples supported by rows of tall columns. The buildings were decorated with sculptures and carving. European architects of the 'neo-classical' period in the 1700s imitated Greek styles.

Construction

Construction means 'building'. The art and science of building is called architecture. The first great builders of the ancient world were the Egyptians. They used mathematics to design their pyramids and temples, but slave labour to build them. Muscle power also built the cathedrals and castles of the Middle Ages.

Many people think that Greek building was the most beautiful of all. Greek styles of architecture were copied by later architects. The Romans were good engineers: they built excellent bridges, aqueducts and roads. They also

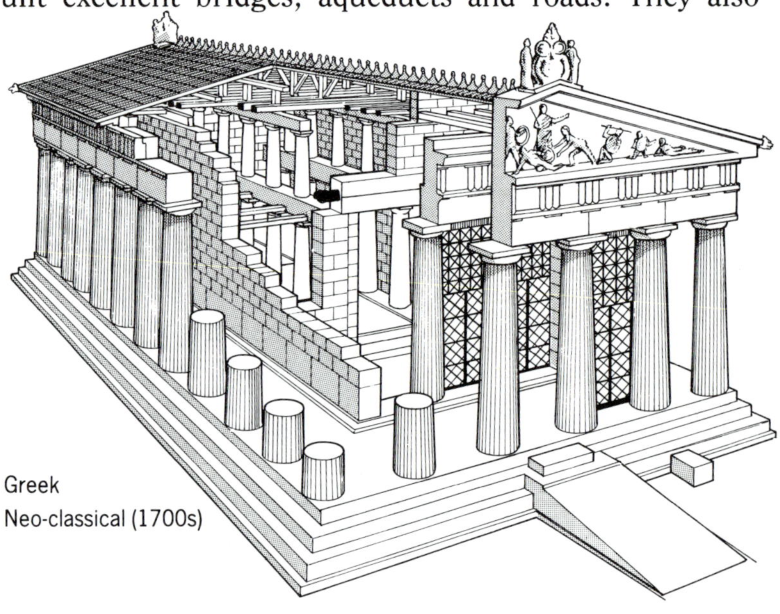

Left: Much modern construction is made possible by using tower cranes to raise and lower heavy loads.

developed the vault and the arch in their buildings.

A great change in construction methods came in the 1800s. Steel and reinforced concrete were important new materials. The first towering skyscrapers were erected in the United States and soon these very tall buildings could be seen in cities everywhere. In the 20th century, powered cranes, mechanical excavators, tunnelling machines and road-surfacing equipment speeded up construction. One of the largest construction projects of today is the boring of the Channel Tunnel, linking Britain and France.

The people who design (plan) buildings are called architects. In the construction industry architects and engineers work closely together. Modern architects use a variety of materials, including concrete, bricks, glass, steel and plastics. They design buildings in many styles, from family houses to huge office blocks in which hundreds of people work. For more about architecture, see page 112.

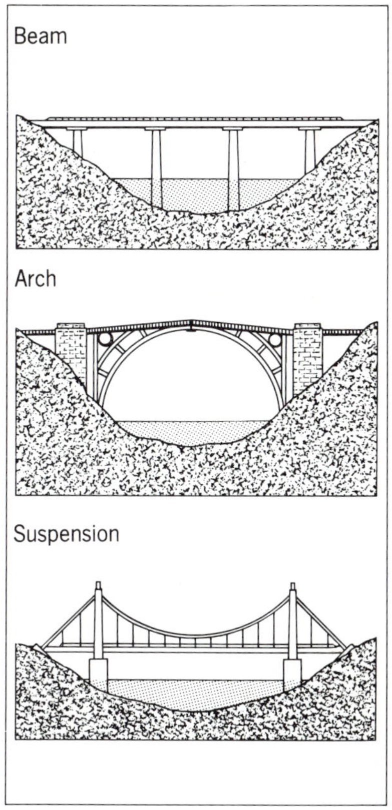

Above: The beam bridge is the simplest and oldest design. The arch can span a wider gap, but very long bridges are usually suspension types, hung from thick steel cables.

Left: A cement mixer is a common sight on building sites. It churns cement, sand, gravel and water to make concrete which hardens and holds structures firmly.

Right: Suspension bridges are built with towers and cables which support the weight of the bridge and its traffic.

Above: This painting by Joseph Wright shows an alchemist at work with his assistants. Alchemy was a medieval mixture of astrology, primitive chemistry and religion. Modern chemistry is based upon it.

Below: In a molecule the bonds that join atoms are formed from atoms 'sharing' electrons. Here a sodium atom and a chlorine atom share an electron, to form a molecule of sodium chloride (salt).

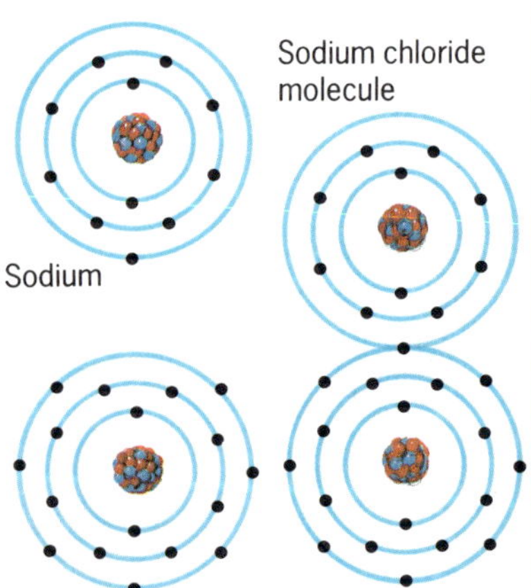

Chemistry

Chemists investigate the properties and structure of all the matter that makes up the Earth and the Universe. They also study the way in which different substances react together, and how new substances are made.

There are fewer than one hundred different elements making up all known substances. We call something an element if it cannot be split up into a simpler substance. Groups of atoms, joined together by chemical bonds, are called molecules. If all the atoms in a molecule are alike they form an element, if different elements are combined they form a compound.

Chemists use a simple shorthand system to refer to the atoms of various elements. The system used now was invented by the Swedish chemist J. J. Berzelius in 1813. It uses the first letter of the English or Latin name of each element to represent an atom of that element. So the symbol for carbon is C, phosphorus is P, oxygen is O and so on. If two elements have the same initial letter, then a second letter is added – manganese is written as Mn and magnesium is Mg. Compounds are represented by combinations of letters: CO_2 is the gas carbon dioxide – one atom of carbon combined with two of oxygen, H_2O is water – two atoms of hydrogen and one of oxygen.

An acid can be a strong corrosive, burning liquid, or an everyday substance, such as lemon juice or vinegar. Sub-

Left: These branches reveal the devastating effects of acid rain on conifer forests. The 'acid' is a weak sulphuric or nitric acid that forms when compounds from industrial waste from factories and power stations, and exhaust fumes from vehicles, are dissolved in the moisture in the air. The droplets of moisture often fall as rain hundreds of miles away from the factories that gave off the harmful smoke. Damage is done both when acid rain falls directly onto the leaves or needles of plants and trees, and when it seeps into the ground where it will damage the roots. Acid rain pollutes lakes and rivers, which may affect fish and other wildlife. Action is being taken to reduce the amount of waste gas poured into the atmosphere by the industrial nations of the world.

stances that are the opposite of acids are called bases. If acids and bases are mixed together, they form new substances called salts. Bases which will dissolve in water form alkalis. These react with acids to neutralize them, producing a salt and water.

Both acids and alkalis are very important industrial chemicals. Large amounts of sulphuric acid are used for making fertilizers, for removing rust from metals before they are processed, and for manufacturing dyes and detergents. Sodium hydroxide (caustic soda) is used in making paper and soap and in the production of aluminium.

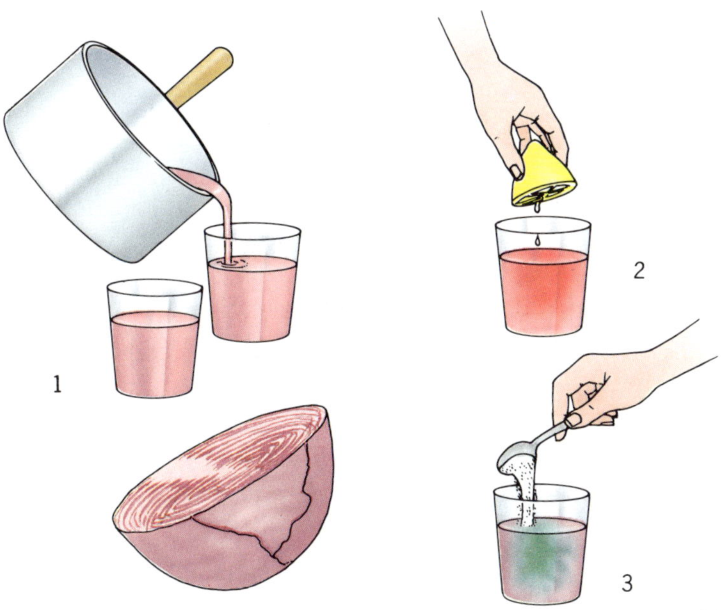

MAKE AN ACID/ALKALI INDICATOR

Cut half a red cabbage into strips. Put the strips into a bowl, pour hot water on *very* carefully, and let the mixture cool. Strain the liquid into two clean glasses (**1**). Add a few drops of water to the cabbage solution. This shows the neutral colour of the indicator. Now add a few drops of lemon juice to one glass to show its acid colour (**2**) and some washing soda to the other glass to show its alkaline colour (**3**). Other acid/alkali indicators include litmus paper and methyl orange.

Oil is a fossil fuel, formed within the Earth's crust. We need oil for generating the various kinds of power we use. Oil drives our cars, planes and ships. It is also used to make detergents and plastics.

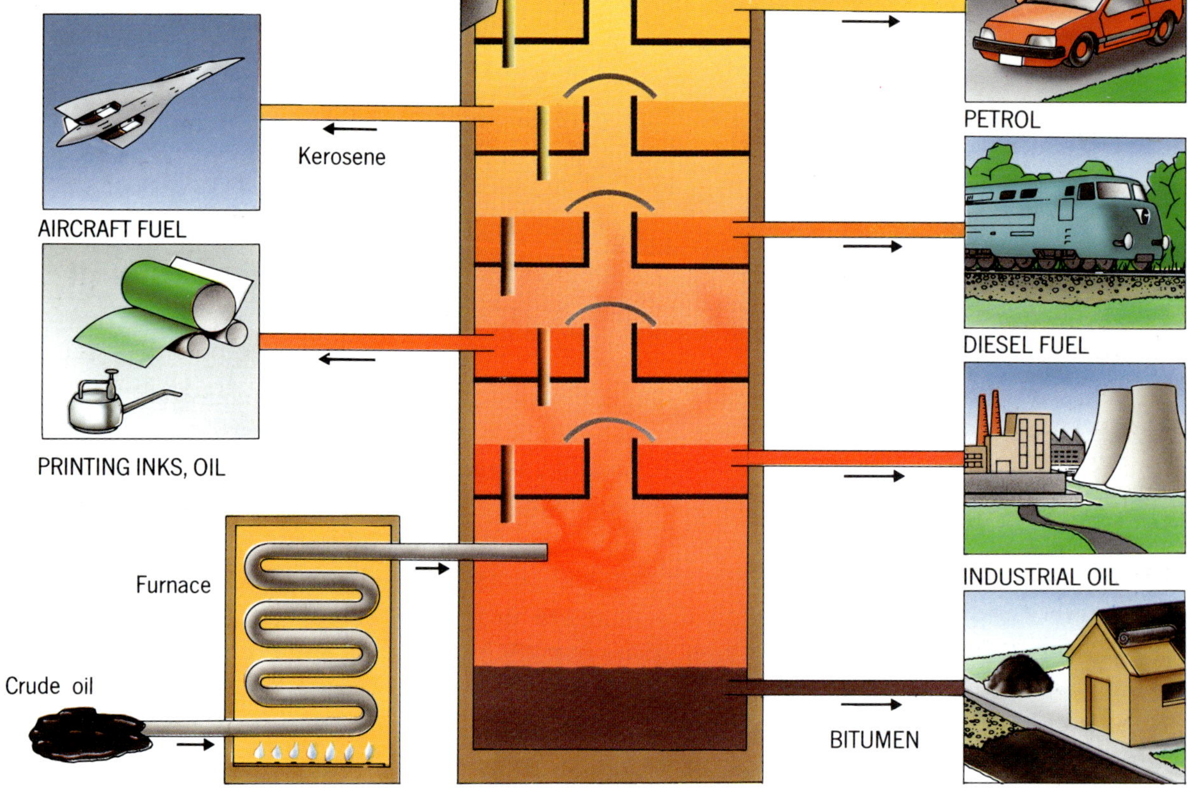

Above: Crude oil is broken down into its various 'fractions' (parts) by 'fractional distillation'. The crude oil is heated to a vapour which passes up a tower. Different products can then be drawn off. Towards the top of the column come kerosene for aircraft fuel, diesel oil and petrol. Right at the top, fuel gas comes off. Heavy products, such as asphalt for road-making and heavy fuel oils, sink to the bottom. Each fraction is used for a different industrial task.

Solids from Liquids

If a spoonful of sugar is added to a glass of water, the crystals soon disappear completely. The sugar has dissolved forming a solution with the water.

Not all substances will dissolve in water. Some mix in, but their physical form remains unchanged. Powdered chalk behaves like this – when mixed with water its particles stay floating in the liquid for a short time to produce a milky mixture called a 'suspension'.

Colloids are a special type of solution. Molecules disperse but do not form a true solution. A colloid made in water is given the name 'emulsion'. Paints are emulsions and so is milk, which is an emulsion of fat in water.

To collect a solid from a solution, salt from sea water for example, we must use a process called evaporation. By warming sea water in a dish we drive off molecules of water as a vapour. As the water in the dish dries up – evap-

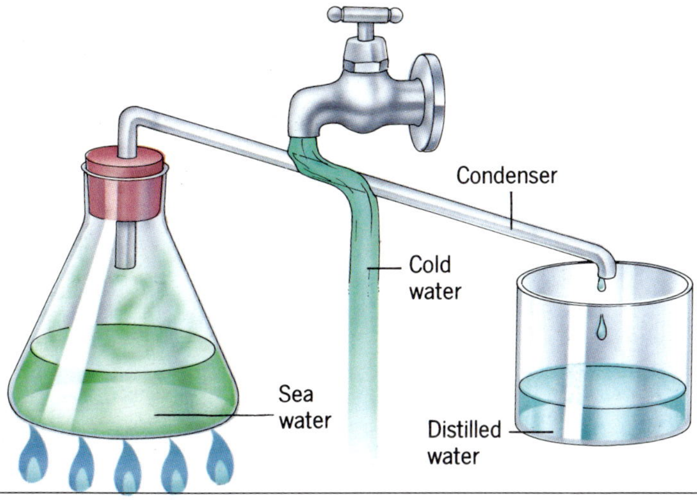

DISTILLATION
Distilling fresh water from salt water is the process çarried out on a large scale at 'desalination plants'. In these plants sea water is changed into drinkable, unsalted water. This diagram shows the process working on a small scale. Sea water is heated in the flask and turns to vapour. This rises to the top of the flask and into the condenser channel, which is cooled by the tap. As the condenser cools the vapour, it turns back into liquid and collects as distilled water in the beaker.

orates – crystals of salt begin to form and are left behind in the dish. To collect the water, we must use a method called distillation. Distillation is a useful industrial process.

Plastics

All plastics belong to a family of chemicals called 'polymers' – materials that have long chain-like molecules made up of hundreds of similar units linked together. There are two main kinds of plastics – 'thermosetting plastics' and 'thermoplastics'. Thermosetting plastics do not melt when heated. They get even harder. Thermoplastics, such as polystyrene and PVC, can be melted and hardened again.

Below: Thousands of everyday household products are made from the chemical by-products that come from oil. Plastics and artificial textiles such as nylon and polyester are oil-based. Detergents, soap, paint and cosmetics contain oil chemicals. Oil is used to make synthetic rubber, animal feed and the vinyl in records and floor coverings.

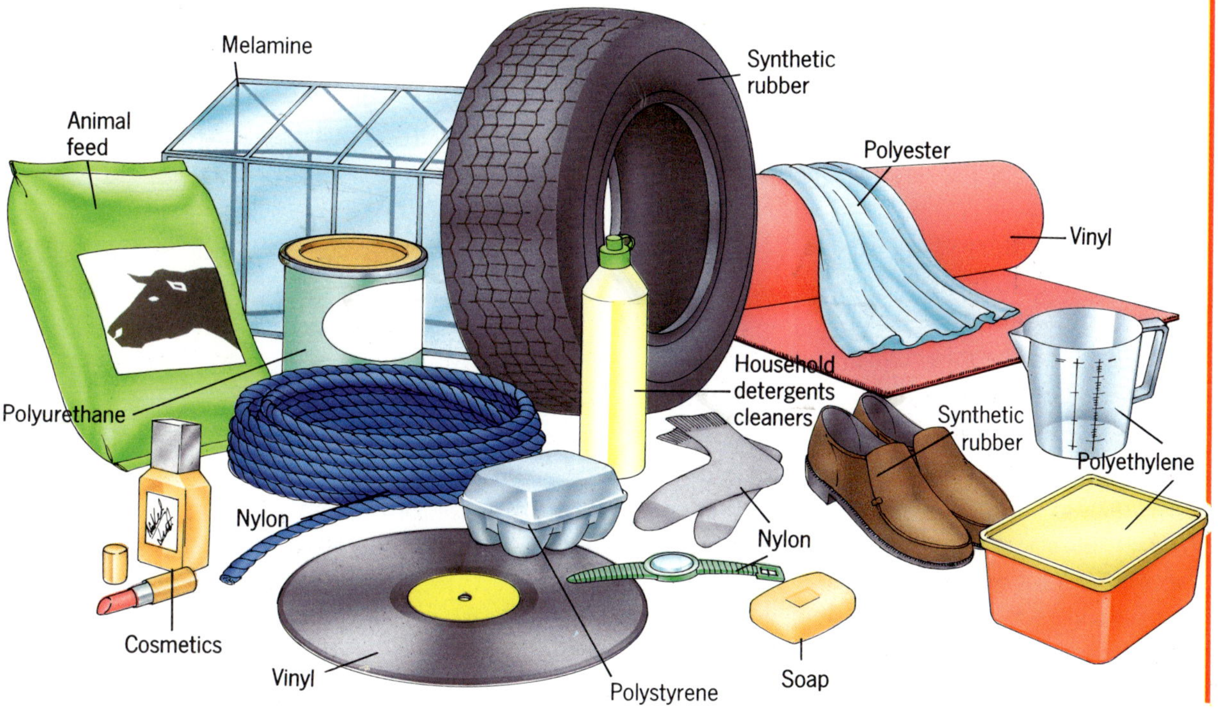

Above: Magma or molten rock from deep below the Earth's crust is forced out through a volcano's vent during an eruption. When it cools it forms various kinds of crystalline rock. Flat sheets of lava are the result of highly fluid magma, whereas sticky magma may form jagged rocks. Pumice comes from frothy acid lava which contains many bubbles of gas. Following very rapid cooling the lava solidifies into a glassy rock. Pumice is sometimes used as an abrasive, and for grinding and polishing metals and stones.

Right: Sedimentary rocks are formed from mud, sand or animal shells and bones. Over millions of years, hard rocks result. This diagram shows how sedimentary rocks can be changed by heat and pressure. They are then known as metamorphic rocks. Shale becomes slate when subjected to pressure, while limestone can change to marble if heated enough.

Minerals and Mining

All rocks are made of crystals of various minerals. Usually the crystals are too small to see and thin slices of rock must be examined under the microscope to reveal them. Quartz is the mineral most often found – it makes up 90 per cent of all rocks. Agates found inside many pebbles on the beach are one form of quartz and sand is another. The small grains of sand are actually tiny pieces of quartz that have been worn away from rocks by the action of the sea and the wind over the years.

There are nearly three thousand minerals found on Earth. All but a few of these form special shapes called crystals when conditions are suitable. Most naturally-occurring crystals contain combinations of the elements which make up the Earth's crust, although a few, such as crystals of gold and silver, are made of just one element. The largest single crystal ever found was a crystal of the precious gemstone beryl. It was found on the island of Madagascar in 1976. It measured 18 metres in length by more than 11 metres across and weighed in at a staggering 380,000 kilograms!

The crystals of about eighty special minerals are known as 'gemstones' because of their beautiful appearance and their value. Many gemstones are used just for making jewellery while others have less glamorous, but still very

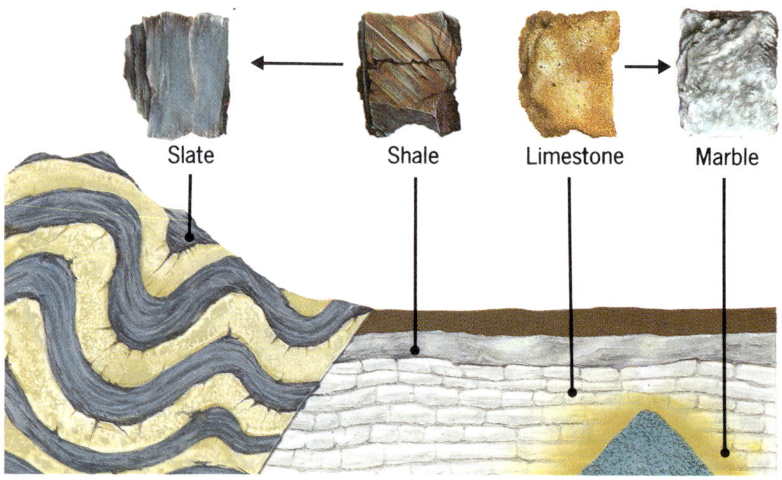

Calcite (hexagonal) Zircon (tetragonal) Sulphur (orthorhombic) Rhondonite (triclinic)

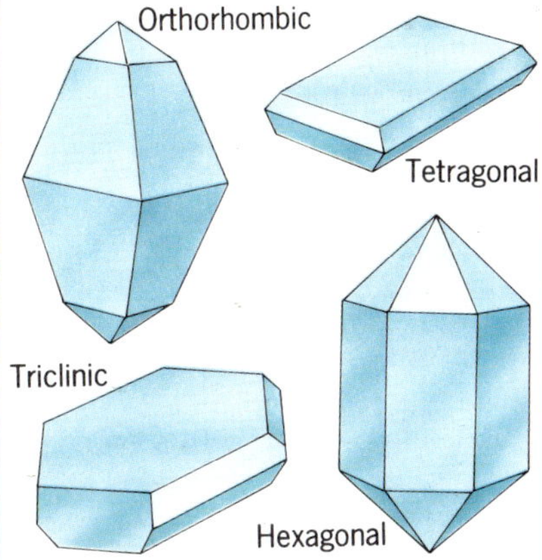

important, uses as well. The most valuable gemstone is the diamond. A diamond is a crystal of carbon; it is an extremely hard substance that can cut through many materials, including glass. Industrial diamonds are used in the manufacture of drilling and cutting tools, while other stones are used to make styli (plural of stylus) for record players. The finest diamonds are cut and polished for jewellery. Ruby crystals were the first substances used to make laser beams.

Marble, which has very regular crystal patterns, is formed when limestone is heated to very high temperatures deep in the Earth. Some minerals, like marble, are obtained from shallow holes called quarries. Others must be dug from mines deep below ground.

Above and above left: Most of the Earth's minerals have regular structures of crystals. There are six main 'systems' (types) of mineral crystal shape, based on the size, shape, number and angle of the faces of each crystal. Examples of some of the systems are shown here. The different crystal shapes make the general appearance of one type of mineral very different from another.

HARDNESS OF MINERALS

Some minerals are harder than others. A harder mineral can scratch a softer one. In 1822, a German scientist named Friedrich Mohs devised a hardness scale. He listed minerals from softest (number 1) to hardest (number 10). The scale, named after Mohs, is used to determine the hardness of minerals and any other substances.

Minerals from Softest to Hardest	Scratch Test for Hardness
1. Talc	Crushed by a fingernail
2. Gypsum	Scratched by a fingernail
3. Calcite	Scratched by a copper coin
4. Fluorite	Scratched by glass
5. Apatite	Scratched by a knife
6. Orthoclase (Feldspar)	Scratched by quartz
7. Quartz	Scratched by a steel file
8. Topaz	Scratched by corundum
9. Corundum	Scratched by diamond
10. Diamond	Scratches all common material

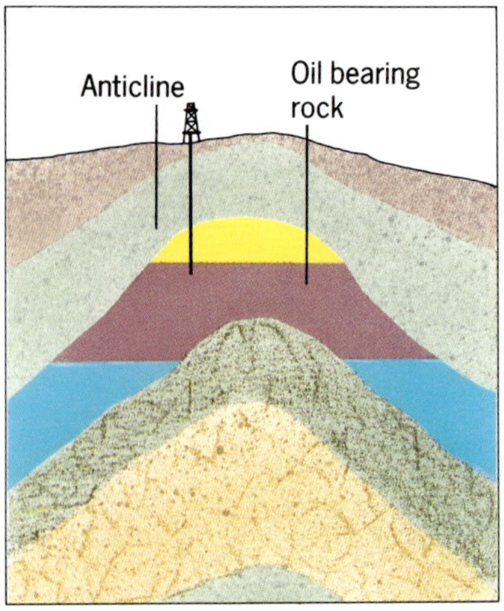

Above: Oil reserves form when oil seeps up through porous rock and is trapped by an impervious non-porous layer. If an arch or 'anticline' of impervious rock prevents oil seeping upwards, a pool of oil is trapped below.

Right: An oil production platform. Offshore wells provide about 20 per cent of the world's oil, despite being more expensive to build.

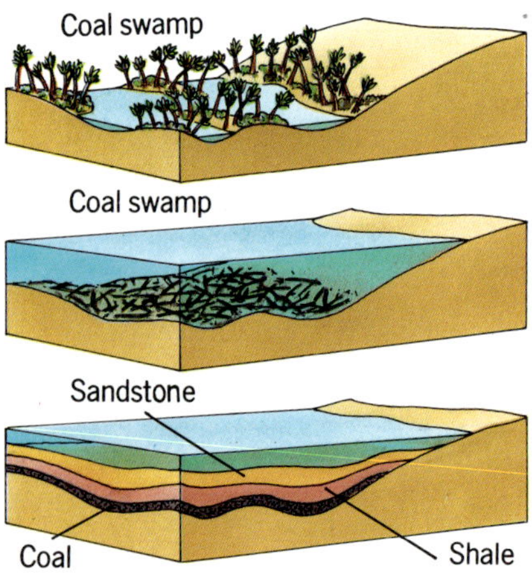

Above: Seams (layers) of coal formed as swamps containing plant and animal remains sank and were squeezed by layers of rock above them.

Oil and Gas

Areas with oil and natural gas beneath them are not easy to find. Oil has been discovered under the deserts of the Middle East, the swamps of South America, under icefields and under the sea. Geologists survey likely areas using magnetometers and gravitometers which measure the magnetism and hardness of the rock formations below. A seismograph survey, to show how various layers are arranged, is carried out by setting off a small explosion on the surface and recording the shock waves that are bounced back from the Earth's crust beneath. Deposits of natural gas are often found lying just above a layer of oil-bearing rock.

Oil is reached by drilling a well. A drilling rig on land has a huge tower called a 'derrick' to house the equipment. On an offshore rig the derrick is often carried on an enormous floating platform. Once oil has been found at sea, a production platform is set up to store oil or gas in its tanks and pump it ashore. Pipelines carry oil and gas to terminals on land. Oil goes on to the refinery while gas can be pumped to homes and factories.

Coal

The Sun has shone down on the Earth for millions of years, providing energy for plants and animals. Over many centuries, living things have died and their remains have been buried by movements of the Earth's crust, which have caused the land to sink. Deep down, under great pressure, the remains and their stored energy have formed our 'fossil fuels' – peat, coal, oil and gas.

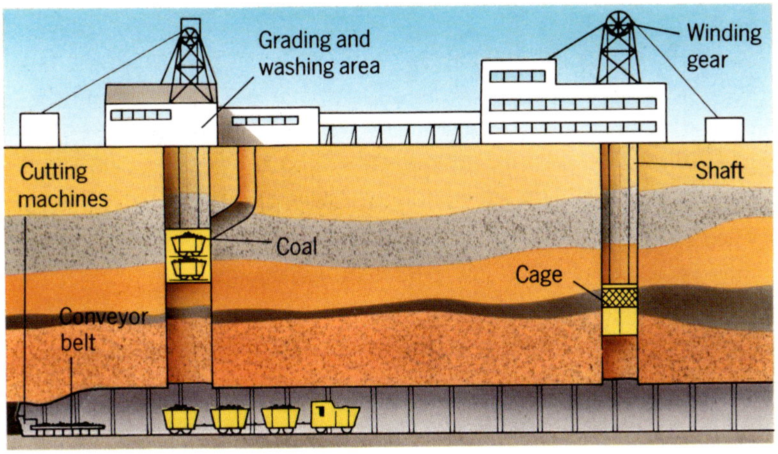

Left: In a deep coal mine, shafts are sunk to reach the coal seams. At the coal face, miners use cutting machines to remove the coal, which is taken by conveyor belts along tunnels to be loaded in carts and taken to the surface.

Coal started to form about 350 million years ago. The remains of swampy forests were compressed and hardened by sand and rocks which were piled on top of them. Gradually the layers of vegetation turned into layers or 'seams' of coal, separated by rock. In some places there are 30 or 40 different seams, one above the other.

Coal took over from wood as the main source of fuel for the industrial furnaces of the 18th century. With the invention of the steam engine, coal became the fuel of the Industrial Revolution in the 19th century and later it was used in coal-fired power stations that generated electricity.

Iron and Steel

Iron and steel are two substances that we use in very large quantities. Steel is an alloy of iron with carbon and another metal such as manganese, chromium or nickel.

Iron, like most metals, is found in the ground combined with other elements, in the form of an 'ore'. Oxides of iron are the ores used in steelmaking. The first step is to extract iron from the ore by 'smelting'. The smelting process heats the ore to a very high temperature and turns the iron in the ore into liquid metal.

Steel-making takes out some of the carbon, which the liquid iron contains, and adds other metals to make an alloy. Most steel is made by a process called 'oxygen steel-making'. Molten iron is poured from enormous ladles, which can hold up to 100 tonnes, into a simple furnace – a large steel vessel lined with heat-resistant bricks. Scrap metal and other ingredients may be added. Then oxygen, or an air and oxygen mixture, is blown straight down on to the metal. Any carbon in the metal burns out in this oxygen. Steel is used to make many objects from engines to bulldozer parts and from cans to girders.

LINZ-DONAWITZ STEEL-MAKING

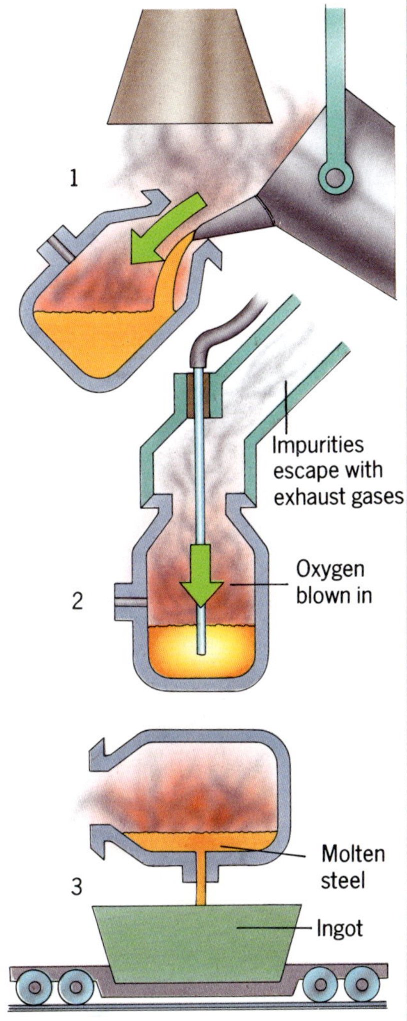

Making steel by the 'Linz-Donawitz' method. The furnace is 'charged' (filled) with scrap and molten iron. It is heated to melt the iron. Oxygen is blown into it to make extra heat to burn out impurities and, after about 20 minutes, molten steel is poured from the furnace into ingots.

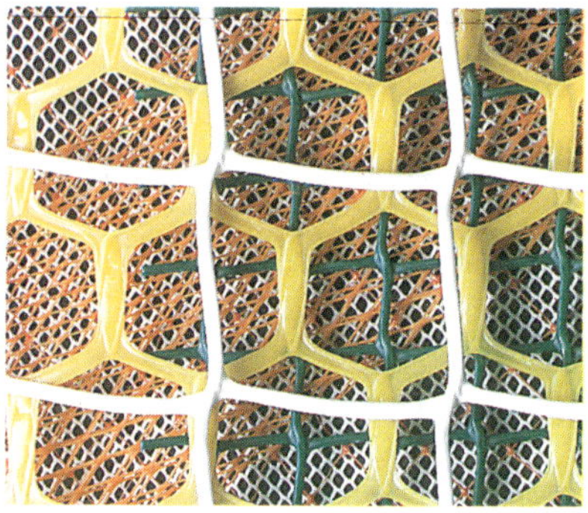

Above: Three kinds of net, all made from moulded or woven plastics.

Below: To make nylon fibre a chemical called caprolactam is heated under pressure to make long polymer filaments, which are turned into chips, melted and pumped through tiny holes. The threads harden in cool air, then they are twisted together to make nylon yarn.

Textiles

The materials that we use to make our clothes are made from threads or fibres which are woven into cloth. Some are 'natural' fibres from animals, plants or even minerals, while artificial fibres are manufactured.

The two most common types of plant fibres are cotton and flax. Cotton fibres come from inside the seed pod or 'boll' of cotton plants. Flax plants produce the fibres that are used to make linen cloth. The lower parts of the stem and the roots of the plants provide the best fibres.

Wool and silk are the best-known animal fibres. Wool comes from the soft hair – the fleece – of a sheep. But other animals also provide wool for clothing. For example, some goats provide mohair and some kinds of rabbits provide angora. Silk comes from the cocoons of the silkworm. The caterpillars of the silk moth spin more than 1000 metres of silk around themselves in about three days. This silk thread can then be unwound and used to make soft fabric that is both shiny and strong.

Artificial fibres are sold under many brand names such as Terylene (polyester) and Courtelle (acrylic). All artificial

MAKING NYLON

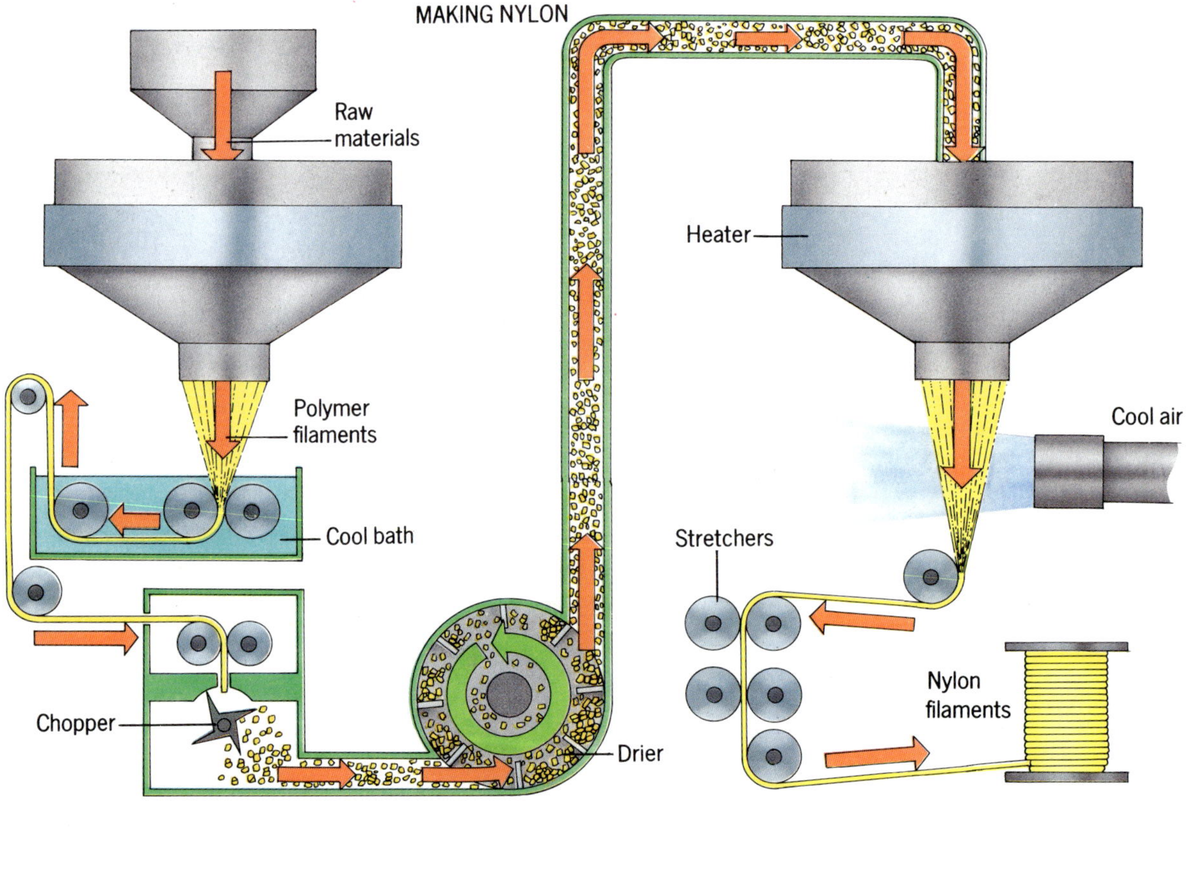

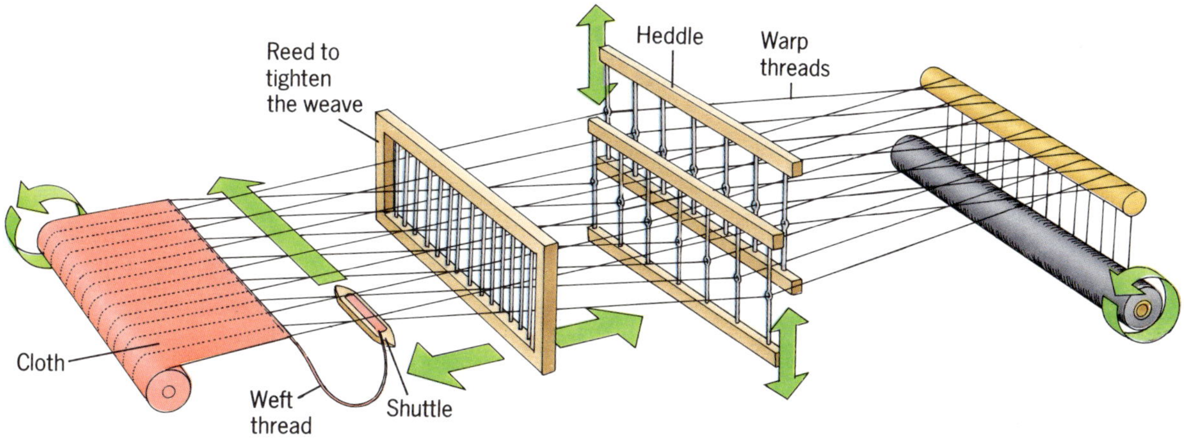

fibres are slightly different but they can be divided into two main types: cellulose fibres; which are made from cellulose extracted from natural fibres of trees and plants, and synthetic fibres, which are made from coal and oil products. The cellulose fibres used to make rayon, acetate and triacetate fabric come from the wood of spruce trees and from cotton linters (short cotton fibres). Synthetic fibres, such as polyester and acrylic, are made from chemicals called polymers (see page 163).

Natural fibres must be cleaned and washed before being spun (twisted) into long threads of yarn. Man-made fibres are also spun: cotton polyester is a mix of natural and synthetic fibres, for example. The yarn is then woven into cloth. Not all fabrics are made by weaving. Knitting is a different process that entwines loops of yarn in rows.

Above: Weaving intertwines threads to form patterns under and over one another on a machine called a loom. The threads of the cloth that run lengthwise are fixed to the loom and are called warp threads. Weft threads are woven under and over the warp threads. The weft threads are carried to and fro across the warp threads by a shuttle, although modern shuttleless looms use a jet of air or water to carry them.

Below: Silk is a natural fibre. It is spun by the larva of the silk moth from a liquid produced in its body. When it reaches the air, the liquid hardens to form a fine thread of silk.

Below: Cotton thread is made from the fluffy fibres of the cotton plant.

Machines

Objects cannot start or stop moving by themselves, they need a force to push or pull them. One such force is gravity, a natural force that pulls everything towards the Earth. In order to produce the forces needed to move things, people have invented various machines to help them. Some machines, such as cars, lifts and cranes, have complicated parts and need electricity or petrol to drive them. Others are very simple and rely only on muscle power. Levers, pulleys, slopes and wheels are all examples of simple labour-saving 'machines'. They let us get more movement for less effort.

As long ago as 4000 BC, the people who built Stonehenge probably used tree trunks as rollers under the huge rocks they moved. Because friction (rubbing) was reduced between a heavy load and rough ground, the load was easier to push or pull along.

No one knows exactly who took the next step and invented the wheel, but in about 3000 BC in Asia, people were using carts which had two solid wheels joined together by a pole called an 'axle'. These early wheels were much more useful than rollers, because the axle could be

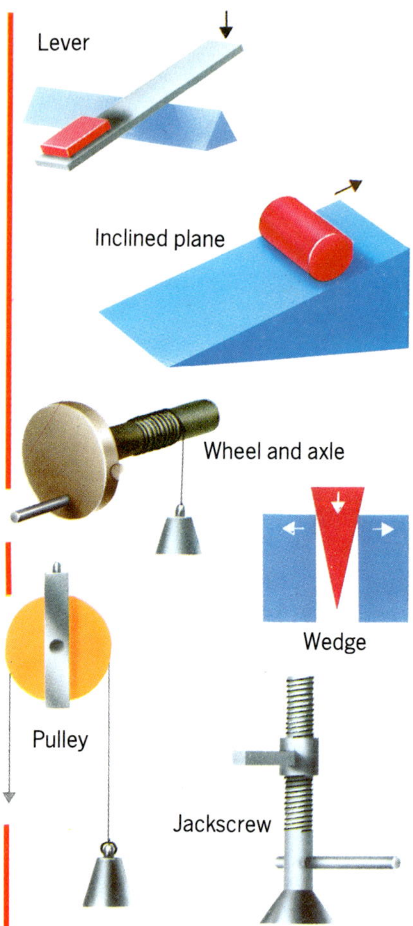

Above left: Levers are among the oldest machines. So are the inclined plane – a form of ramp – and the wedge. The invention of the wheel made possible other devices such as the pulley, and the wheel and axle.

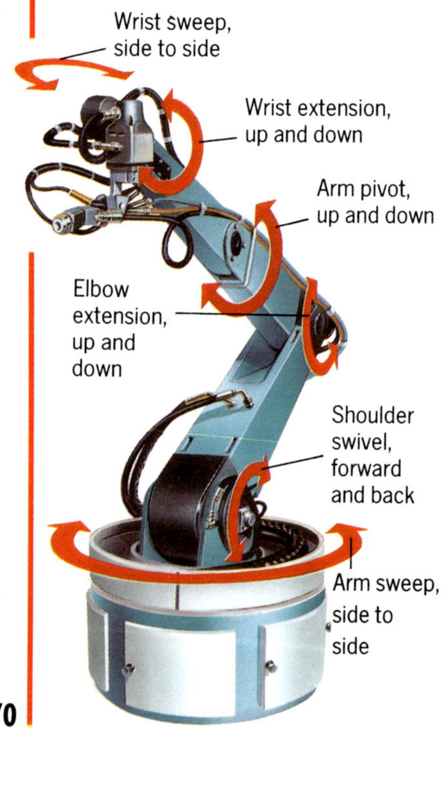

Left: Robots are used in manufacturing industry. This computer-controlled mechanical arm is worked by hydraulic motors making it swivel, move and perform routine tasks.

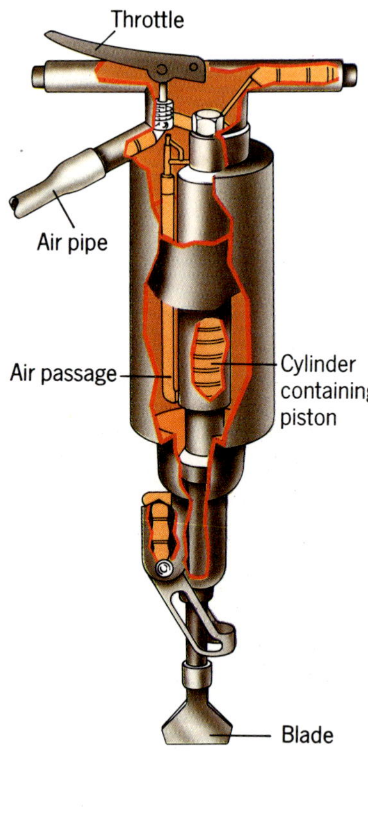

Right: The pneumatic drill uses the force of air compressed in a cylinder to drive the blade.

fitted to the cart and move along with it. Later, in about 1750 BC, lighter wheels with spokes radiating from a centre 'hub' were made in Egypt.

Although people greased the wheels, it was not until the 19th century, when 'ball bearings' were invented, that the problem of reducing friction between wheel and axle was solved. Ball bearings are small steel balls which fit between the centre hub of a wheel and the axle, reducing friction so the wheel turns easily.

The first motorcycle, built by Gottlieb Daimler in 1885, comprised a petrol engine fitted to a wooden bicycle frame. A modern motorcycle (*above*) is a more complicated machine. Its engine is similar to a car's, and may be cooled by either air or water.

Left: A mechanical excavator. The boom moves the rear bucket up and down while twin hydraulic arms raise and lower the front scoop. The rear bucket has a large capacity and can rotate as required. By using its independently controlled vertical stabiliser legs, the excavator is able to stand steadily on uneven ground. It can dig down more than 4 m and lift 900-kg loads. Machines like this can tackle all kinds of large-scale construction jobs, but they are expensive to maintain.

Inventions

Above: This 5000-year-old cart from Sumeria (Iraq) has wheels made from tree trunks.

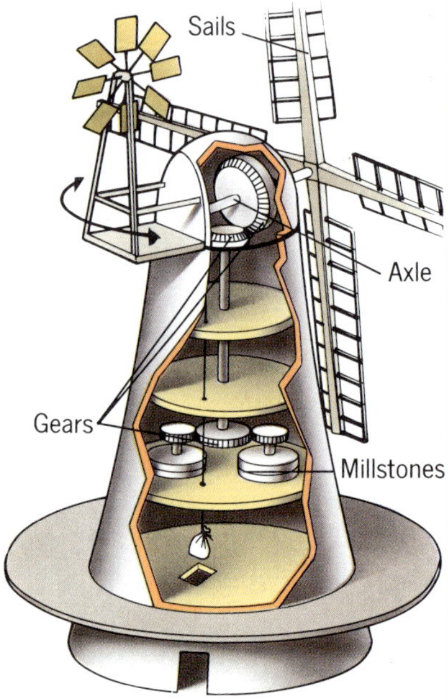

Above: Wind power has been used for over 1000 years.

Even in the Stone Age some people must have been better than others at making tools. Probably they were more curious and inventive than others too.

It was almost certainly one of these early 'experts' who first discovered how to make metal tools. Perhaps he found a lump of natural copper and tried hammering it. Copper is soft and easily shaped, especially when it has been heated in a fire.

Metal-working was an almost magical secret. Metal weapons (made first of bronze, later of iron) were so much better than stone weapons that people everywhere wanted them. This led to increased trade.

The smith, the 'master of metals', became an important person. Other crafts also appeared: those of the weaver, the stone mason, the potter, the glass-blower and the carpenter. Many of the tools they used looked much like those you would find in a modern tool box.

With better tools, people could make better household goods and better houses to live in. Early inventors devised the first simple machines. Some of these devices (such as the screw press, the lever and the winch, for example) have remained almost unchanged ever since. With new skills, human beings were able to become machine-builders.

Above: Gutenberg's first printing press was adapted from a wine press.

Domestic Inventions

Domestic life began when people became farmers and gave up a nomadic (wandering) life for a settled home. Farming provided a reliable food supply, as well as materials (such as cotton and wool) with which to clothe people and make their homes more comfortable.

The ancient civilizations of India and Rome set high standards of comfort and hygiene. For example, the Romans had drains, piped water, baths and central heating in the houses of the rich and in public buildings. Such luxuries were unknown in medieval Europe, when home life was draughty, dirty, smoky and almost certainly smelly. Domestic conveniences, such as those known by the Romans, had to be re-invented in the 1800s.

Science played little part in home life until the 1700s when the Industrial Revolution began to change the way people lived – the clothes they wore, the food they ate, the entertainments they enjoyed, and the homes they lived in.

Many of the domestic inventions of the past 100 years are now so much part of our daily lives that we seldom stop to think about them – electric light, for instance. Since the 1800s advertising has done much to speed domestic invention, by encouraging people to buy new gadgets and to eat new 'convenience' foods.

The Industrial Revolution

For a long time most goods were made by hand, usually in the worker's home and often by a family working together. But as new machines came into use, people began to work in factories. In the textile industry, Kay's Flying Shuttle (1733) made weaving much quicker and led to Hargreaves' invention of the Spinning Jenny (1764). Now spinners could keep up with the weavers. Next a spinning machine was made by Arkwright which was worked by waterpower. The first factories were successful because they made good use of waterwheels. But it was steam power that really caused a change in the means of production and so in the lives of people in Europe and North America.

Transport

Until the 1700s no one had ever travelled faster than a horse could run or a ship be blown by the wind. Then came the Industrial Revolution and the Age of Machines.

Now speed became important for trade. A transport race began. Among the most important inventions were the

Right: Richard Arkwright's 'water frame' of 1769 was the first spinning machine to use water power and not human power.

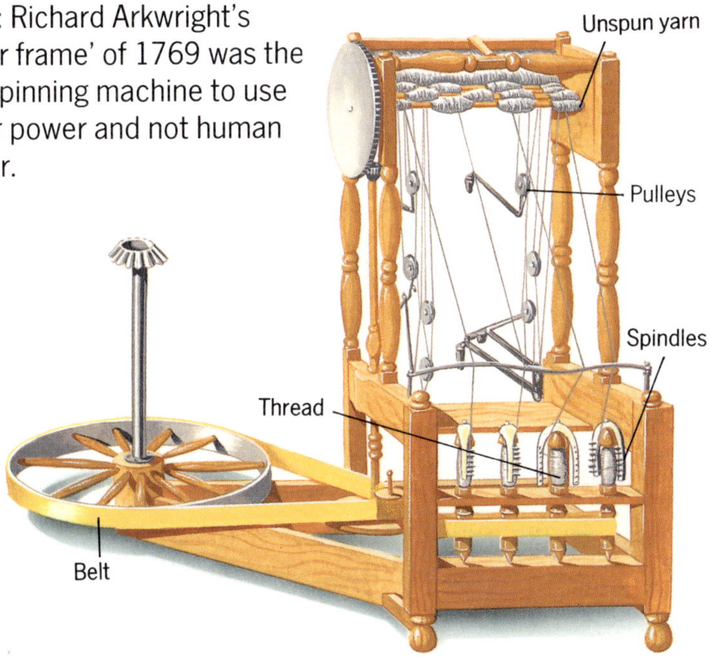

Below: Savery's steam engine, invented in 1698, was used to pump water out of mine shafts. Water was boiled producing steam. The steam passed into a chamber where it was cooled by cold water so that it condensed. This made a vacuum which acted as a suction and pumped the water upwards into a tank above the mine.

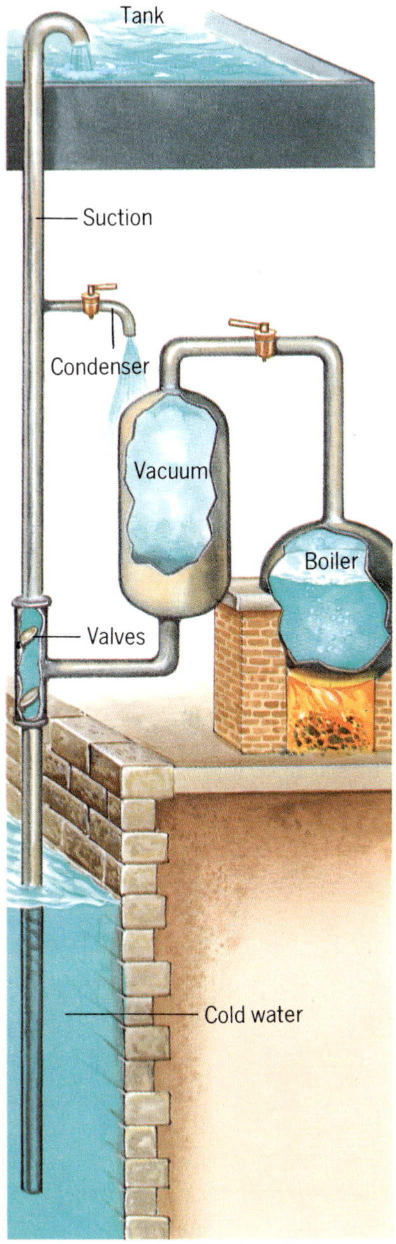

Above: The mountain bicycle has a strong but light metal frame, with thick pneumatic tyres for good grip.

Above: Alexander Graham Bell invented the telephone in 1875.

Above: John Logie Baird's first television projected an image through holes in a disc.

balloon (1783), the steamship (1807), the steam railway (1825), the motor vehicle (1885), and the aeroplane (1903). Travel became faster and simpler, and changed people's way of life.

In the 20th century many people in the richer countries enjoy the luxury (and the fumes and traffic congestion) of personal transport by car. They also use advanced public transport systems such as underground railways and monorails. In poorer countries horses, oxen and camels still carry people and goods. Yet supersonic jets circle the world in a few hours. The space age that began with the first artificial satellite in 1957 has taken astronauts to the Moon (1969) and sent spacecraft to explore the planets in our solar system.

Fighting Disease

In ancient times no one knew what caused disease, because there were no scientific tools to help doctors understand the body's secrets. One of the first, and most important, medical instruments was the microscope. With its help, doctors could learn more about anatomy (how the body is made) and physiology (how the body works). The dissection of animals and then human bodies was another way scientists could study parts of the body.

The Ancient Egyptians and Jews knew that good food and cleanliness were vital for 'public health'. But dirt and poor hygiene remained the doctor's enemies until the

1800s. Only slowly was it realized that better housing, good sanitation, improved childcare and a proper attention to diet could prevent people from becoming ill.

Today most countries have a health service with hospitals, dental surgeries and clinics. Doctors, nurses and dentists are trained to use advanced machinery and sophisticated drugs. Thanks to the work of the World Health Organization, once deadly diseases such as smallpox have been conquered. Other diseases such as cancer and AIDS still await a cure, and much remains to be done, especially in poorer countries.

Communications

Communication is the transport of ideas. It is the way we learn. Civilization grew as ideas spread. From the time of the first Stone Age cave painters to today's mass media, such as radio, cinema and television, communications have changed the ways in which people think and behave.

No one knows when language began. Perhaps people first began to speak by imitating natural sounds such as bird cries or the sound of water. Certainly spoken language came thousands of years before writing. Information had to be passed on by word of mouth until the invention of the first writing – picture signs – over 5000 years ago. The development of writing meant that knowledge could be recorded in books and information passed on from generation to generation.

The development of numbers was almost as important as words. At first, people worked out a number system and simple weights and measures to help them weigh grain or measure land. Later mathematicians and astronomers devised calendars and learned how to calculate distance and time with more and more accuracy. Through their work people discovered more about the world and the Universe beyond.

The last 500 years have produced two communications explosions. The printing revolution made books available to all. And in the last 100 years science has given us amazing new ways of message-sending and message-storing. Inventions such as photography, the telephone, sound recording, radio, television and computers are the 'keys' to the modern world. They give us instant communication. Word processors, photocopiers and fax machines have become part of our everyday lives. Information can be stored and 'called for' at the touch of a switch. People's faces and voices can be recorded and preserved for ever.

Above: Radar can track distant objects using radio waves.

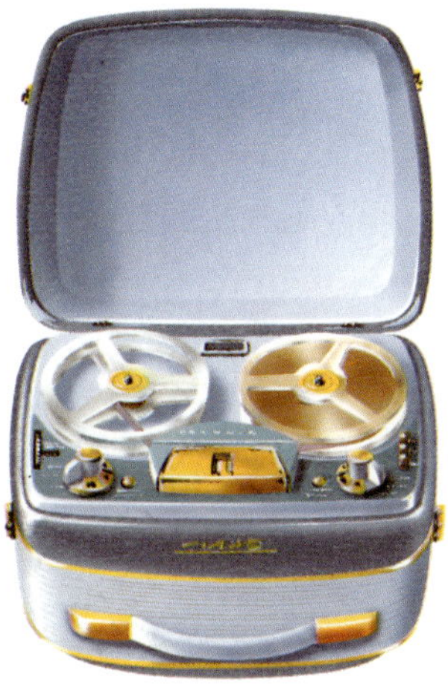

Above: A 1960s reel recorder. Today these are much smaller.

Below: The SR-71A Blackbird is the world's fastest plane.

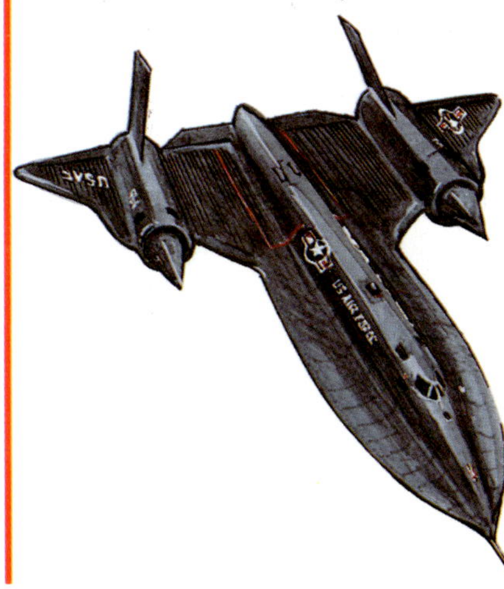

Right: Once trees have been felled for timber, the logs or trunks are often floated down river to the saw mill. There they are cut up for various uses: furniture, construction, paper-making and musical instruments are just some of them. Planned forestry replaces the trees that are cut down, planting new, young trees in their place. Hardwood forests, such as the Amazon Forest in Brazil, are suffering as trees are not being replanted.

Below: Felled timber is lifted by a hydraulic scoop onto this fork-lift timber loader.

Forestry and Farming

There are about 20,000 different kinds of tree and about 1000 of them produce good timber. In cold lands the forests are mainly of conifers, such as pines and firs. These trees produce softwood. In the hot, wet lands close to the Equator there are tropical forests of trees such as ebony and mahogany, whose wood is very hard.

Farming

Primitive farmers grew just enough food for themselves. They had no tractors and used wooden ploughs pulled by

Right: From early times farmers have rotated crops so that the soil is rested and the risk of a build-up of plant disease is lessened. Shown here are two kinds of rotation. One uses a strip-field system. In the other case a new crop is planted in each field in successive seasons.

oxen or horses. They harvested by hand, using sickles. In winter in northern Europe they had to kill most of their animals because there was no food for them. In hot, dry lands crops could be grown only near rivers, where irrigation helped water the fields.

In the 1800s and 1900s machines were invented to do the work of people and animals. There were better ploughs, seed drills, threshers and reapers. Turnips and clover were grown as food for the animals in winter, and bigger, heavier animals were bred. Improved 'crop rotation' – growing different crops on the same land from year to year – was good for the soil. Fertilizers, which helped to enrich the soil, and chemicals, to kill insect pests, allowed farmers to grow larger, healthier crops.

The most important crops are cereals (such as rice, wheat and maize), sugar, fruits, vegetables, coffee, cocoa and tea. Cotton is grown for its fibre and oil. Fish, bees and fur-bearing animals, such as mink, are also farmed.

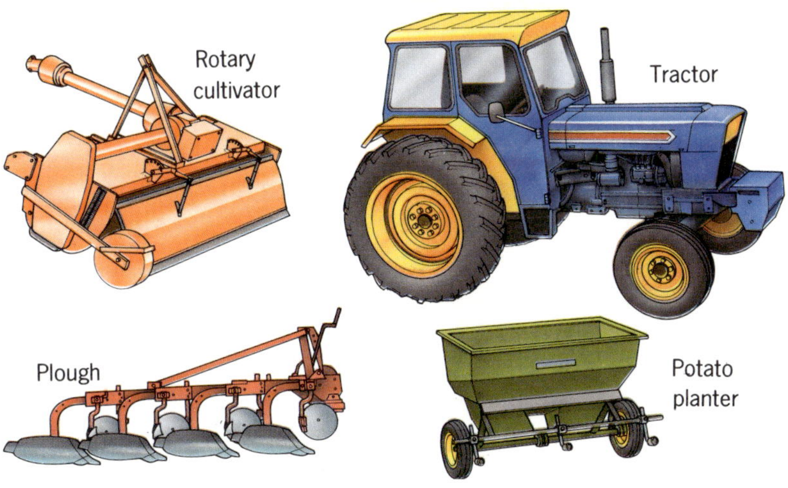

Today, about half of the world's people are farmers. Many of these, especially those living in poorer countries, practise 'subsistence' farming, growing only enough to feed themselves. Other farmers specialize in one crop grown for sale (cash crop). In Africa one of the most important cash crops is cocoa (*left*). Cocoa trees grow in the coastal region of West Africa where the equatorial climate is hot and wet. When ripe, the pods are harvested. The beans are extracted and left to ferment, and then dry in the Sun. Finally they are packed in bags for shipment. Cash crop farmers are vulnerable as they are dependent on world demand and prices for their income.

In developed countries agriculture has become more mechanized and scientific as farms have increased in size. Farm machinery has largely replaced human and animal power. By the 1800s threshing and reaping machines had been introduced and by the 1840s combine harvesters were in use. Cultivators (*left*) can be fitted to tractors to do different jobs such as seed-drilling. Fertilizer sprays and manure spreaders help farmers increase their yield while combine harvesters gather in the grain crop, saving time, and cutting on the cost of human labour.

Science Glossary

Acid A chemical substance that will dissolve in water, producing hydrogen IONS: acids are neutralized by ALKALIS to form SALTS.

Acid rain Rain water with too much acid in it caused by industrial pollution in the air. Plants are killed and buildings eroded by acid rain.

Adaptation The slow process of change that adjusts an animal to fit into a particular set of living conditions.

Alkali Any of a number of substances which are strong BASES, including soluble metal hydroxides. Alkali metals, sodium and potassium, form caustic alkalis. Alkalis react with acids to form SALTS and water.

Alloy Metal consisting of a mixture of one metal with another metal or non-metal, for example brass is an alloy of copper and zinc.

Alpha particle One of the three types of RADIATION emitted by some radioactive substances, consisting of two PROTONS and two NEUTRONS.

Alternating current (AC) Electric current that rapidly changes direction from a maximum in one direction through zero to a maximum in the other direction.

AMP Short form of 'ampere', the unit used to measure electric current.

Amphibian ('two-lives') A backboned animal that lives both on land and in the water, for example a frog or a salamander.

Amplitude The maximum value (or maximum height of the waves) of anything that goes back and forth in a cycle, for example alternating current or sound waves.

Anode The positive terminal through which electric current goes into a liquid (called the electrolyte) during ELECTROLYSIS.

Asteroid Another name for a minor planet – one of the thousands of small bodies circling around the Sun, measuring from a few metres to a thousand kilometres.

Atmosphere The envelope of gases that surrounds the Earth (or any other planet, star or moon).

Atom The smallest part of an ELEMENT that can take part in a chemical reaction. It consists of a positively charged central NUCLEUS surrounded by orbiting ELECTRONS.

Aurora A display of coloured light high in the Earth's ATMOSPHERE. It is caused when particles from the Sun make the gas in the atmosphere glow. This usually happens near the Earth's poles.

Axis The imaginary line through the centre of a spinning star or planet. Think of a pointed stick pushed through an orange and then spun like a top. The Earth spins on a tilted axis.

Bacteria ('small-stick') Simple, microscopic creatures that are made up from single CELLS. These cells are often stick-shaped. Some bacteria cause disease, others are helpful.

Base A substance that reacts with an ACID to form a SALT and water. All ALKALIS are bases.

Battery An electrical cell formed from different metals in certain liquids that react together to give out an electric current.

Beta particles Fast-moving ELECTRONS emitted by some radioactive substances, more penetrating than ALPHA PARTICLES, but less penetrating than gamma rays.

Big bang The theory most astronomers use to explain how the UNIVERSE began. Everything that exists now was crushed into a superhot ball that exploded about 17,000 million years ago.

Big crunch What may happen in thousands of millions of years' time if the UNIVERSE collapses. But it is more likely to go on expanding for ever.

Binary Code A system of numbers that uses only 0s and 1s. Computer programmes work by the on-off currents of an electrical binary code system.

Binary star A pair of stars turning around each other. They may take a few hours if they are very close, or thousands of years if they are far apart.

Black hole An object with such strong GRAVITY that LIGHT WAVES cannot escape from it. Anything pulled inside a black hole is lost for ever.

Boiling point The temperature (different for each substance) at which a liquid turns into a gas.

Camouflage Disguise, produced by colour or pattern or shape, which makes an animal hard to see and may protect it from predators.

Carnivore ('flesh-eater') An animal that lives by eating other animals rather than by eating plants.

Cartilage The tough, elastic gristle in animal bodies. A layer of cartilage makes joints work smoothly. In sharks, the SKELETON is made entirely of this material, and not of bone.

Cathode The negative terminal through which electric current goes into a liquid (called the electrolyte) during ELECTROLYSIS. See ANODE.

Cell The smallest living unit. Animals and plants are built of cells. Some may have just one. Others, such as humans, are made of many. A human adult has about 60 million million cells.

Chemical symbol A shorthand method of naming an ELEMENT, using a formula. The symbol is usually formed from the first letter or letters of the element name so the symbol for hydrogen is H and the symbol for manganese is Mn.

Chip A thin slice of semi-conducting material, usually silicon, that contains all the parts that make an electronic circuit.

Chlorophyll The green chemical that gives plants their colour. It enables a plant cell to capture energy from the Sun and turn it into food.

Chloroplast The microscopic packages inside green plant cells that contain CHLOROPHYLL. Inside the tiny sacs the chlorophyll is converted into carbohydrates by the process of photosynthesis.

Cold-blooded The term used to describe an animal that cannot automatically keep its body at operating temperature by burning fuel (sugar) stored in the body. A cold-blooded animal remains at about the same temperature as its surroundings.

Colloid A chemical substance with large MOLECULES which disperse in liquid to form a solution that has different properties from a true SOLUTION. Gelatine, starch, glue and plastics are examples of colloids.

Combustion (burning) A chemical reaction that occurs when a substance combines with oxygen and produces light, heat and flames.

Comet A mixture of crumbly rock and ice a few kilometres across, which travels around the Sun. If it comes near the Sun the heat makes DUST and gas pour off in a long glowing 'tail'.

Compound A chemical substance that contains two or more ELEMENTS combined together, for example salt consists of sodium and chlorine.

Concave Curved inwards. A concave lens is thicker at the edges than in the middle.

Condensation The liquid formed when a vapour or gas is cooled.

Conduction The process of passing heat from MOLECULE to molecule that allows heat to be transferred from one part of a substance to another.

Conductor A substance, such as copper, that will allow electricity to flow along it.

Constellation A group of stars making a pattern in the sky. Some constellations were named thousands of years ago. There are 88 covering the whole sky.

Convection The movement of heat from place to place in a flowing liquid or gas.

Convex Curved outwards. A convex lens is thinner at the edges than in the middle.

Corona The faint halo of DUST and gas above the Sun's bright surface. It can be seen during a total ECLIPSE of the Sun.

Crystal A solid substance that has a definite, symmetrical shape that is formed by the arrangement of its ATOMS and MOLECULES.

Current electricity The movement of ELECTRONS along a CONDUCTOR that produces a flow of electricity.

Deciduous tree One that sheds all or most of its leaves at roughly the same time every year. Deciduous is the opposite to evergreen.

Density How heavy a substance is for its size. It is calculated by dividing the MASS of a thing by its volume. Each substance has a particular density.

Dicotyledon A plant that starts off with two tiny leaves when it first sprouts from the SEED.

Direct current (DC) Electric current that always flows in the same direction.

Display Any kind of animal behaviour that has a particular meaning. Courtship display is used to attract a mate; threat display to frighten off an enemy, and so on.

Distillation A way of separating or purifying liquids by heating them until they boil and condensing the vapour produced back into a liquid which is collected.

Dust The name given to tiny particles, usually made of carbon, about one thousandth of a millimetre across. These form huge dark NEBULAE in space.

Dwarf star Either an ordinary small dim star (red dwarf), or the dying remains of a bright star (white, brown or black dwarf).

Eclipse When the Moon passes in front of the Sun and blocks its light from Earth (eclipse of the Sun), or the Moon passes into the Earth's shadow (eclipse of the Moon).

Ecosphere The region around the Sun where it is neither too hot, nor too cold, for life to exist.

Edentate ('toothless') A South American MAMMAL with small teeth, or no teeth at all. Examples include anteaters and sloths.

Electrolysis Passing electricity between two terminals (electrodes), through a liquid that contains IONS, in order to produce a chemical change at the terminals.

Electromagnetic waves Waves of energy that include a range of different wave-lengths from short cosmic rays to long radio waves.

Electron The part of an ATOM which spins around the solid centre or 'nucleus'. Very hot atoms can lose electrons, and invisible clouds of electrons are sent into space by the Sun. A flow of electrons is an electric current.

Elements Substances made of only one kind of ATOM. There are two main groups of elements: metals and non-metals.

Ellipse The shape of a planet's ORBIT as it goes around the Sun. An ellipse is oval or egg-shaped. The distance from the planet to the Sun varies as it moves once around its orbit.

Evaporation The way in which liquid turns into vapour as fast-moving molecules escape at the surface of the liquid.

Evolution ('unfolding') The development of plants and animals over a long period of time. Animals and plants *evolve* as a result of changes in their living conditions and in themselves.

Fission The splitting of atoms and the releasing of large amounts of energy that takes place in nuclear reactors or atomic bombs.

Food chain The natural links between animals and what they eat. A simple example is cat-bird-spider-fly – each one eats and obtains energy from the next one down the chain.

Fossil The remains of an animal or plant, or its imprint, left in the rocks of the Earth's surface. The best fossils are found in limestone and mudstone.

Frequency The number of waves or cycles that occur in one second. A frequency of one HERTZ is one cycle per second. Frequency of sound waves determines their pitch, frequency of light waves determines their colour.

Friction The force that holds back two surfaces that are sliding across one another. Bicycle brakes for example use friction to stop motion.

Fruit The fleshy part of a plant, which forms a container for the SEEDS.

Fungus A large family of 'plants' that includes mushrooms, toadstools, moulds and the plate-like crusts that grow on woodland trees. They are not true plants as they contain no CHLOROPHYLL.

Galaxy A 'star city'. It is where stars are born and die. Even a small galaxy contains several million stars – the largest may contain a million million.

Gas A physical state of matter, in which a substance has a definite mass, but no definite volume or shape. It will fill the space it occupies.

Giant stars May be either much hotter and brighter than the Sun (white or blue giants), or cool red stars that have puffed up to an enormous size (red giants).

Gill The breathing organ of an animal that lives in water. It takes oxygen from the water just as an animal's lung takes oxygen from the air.

Gravity The force which pulls all objects down to the surface of the Earth (or any other planet or moon, or a star).

Greenhouse effect The result of Solar energy being trapped in the Earth's atmosphere causing too much carbon dioxide and raising average world temperatures.

Habitat The natural living place of an animal or plant. Examples are ponds, woodland, grassland, deserts and forests.

Half-life The time it takes for the RADIOACTIVITY of a substance to decrease to half its original value.

Hertz The unit used to measure frequency, equal to one cycle per second.

Hibernate To spend the winter in a kind of deep sleep. The animal slows down its heartbeat and other body systems and lives off stored body fat until the spring.

Host An animal or plant that is used by another animal or plant as a source of food. The PARASITE lives on, or in some cases inside, the host.

Inertia The property of an object that makes it stay still, or resist stopping if it is already moving.

Instinct A built-in ability to do certain things without having to learn them or be shown. Baby turtles instinctively head for the sea as soon as they hatch out.

Insulator Either a substance that will not allow heat to pass through it, or one that will not allow electricity to pass through it.

Intelligence Quickness of mind, or ability to think and work things out.

Invertebrate An animal that does not have a backbone.

Ion An ATOM that has an electrical charge because it has lost or gained ELECTRONS.

Isotope A form of an ELEMENT that has a different number of NEUTRONS in the nuclei of its atoms from the 'usual' form. This gives it different properties, for example whether or not it is radioactive.

Kinetic energy The energy an object has because it is moving.

Larva The grub of an insect. The insect is a larva from the moment it hatches from the egg until the time it turns into a pupa. (The final stage is when the adult insect emerges from the pupa.)

Lightning The result of water and air molecules in clouds rubbing together, making an electrical charge.

Light waves A ray of light is made up of light waves. There are about 2500 waves in every millimetre of blue light, and about 1500 in every millimetre of red light. This means that each different light colour has a different 'wavelength'.

Light-year The distance a ray of light travels through space in a year – about nine and a half million million kilometres. Light is the fastest thing in the Universe.

Liquid One of the physical states of matter. It takes the shape of the container it is in.

Litmus paper Paper coloured with a purple dye obtained from lichens, used in laboratories to test whether a solution is an ACID or an ALKALI.

Local group The collection of about 30 GALAXIES which includes our own Milky Way Galaxy.

Magnetism A force found in planets, stars and even whole galaxies. The huge amounts of iron at the centre of the Earth cause the magnetic force which makes compass needles point towards north and south.

Magnitude The word an astronomer uses to describe the brightness of a star or planet. The smaller the magnitude number, the brighter it is.

Mammal An animal that gives birth to live young and feeds the baby on milk produced in the mother's body.

Marsupial A group of primitive mammals whose babies are born at a very early stage but then finish off their development in a pouch on the mother's abdomen.

Mass The amount of matter in an object. On Earth the mass of an object is the same as its weight. On the Moon, the object will have the same mass as on Earth but a lower weight because of the weaker pull of the Moon's gravity.

Metamorphosis The word means 'change of shape' and it describes the changes in an insect's life from egg to LARVA to pupa and finally to adult. At each change, the insect grows a totally new kind of body.

Meteor The streak of light seen when a meteoroid – a particle between the size of a grain of sand and a pebble – burns up as it rushes into the ATMOSPHERE from space. Many meteoroids come from COMETS.

Meteorite The rocky or metallic remains of a meteoroid that hits the ground before it burns up. Not many are found, because most look like ordinary stones.

Migration Animals' regular journey to a particular place in order to breed and raise young, or in some cases to search out better food supplies. Whales are an example of animals that migrate.

Milky Way The patchy band of pale light which circles the sky. It is hard to see from towns, but shines out in country skies. It is our view of the stars in our GALAXY.

Molecule The smallest particle of a substance that can exist on its own. For example, a molecule of water is made of one atom of oxygen joined to two atoms of hydrogen.

Monocotyledon A plant that starts off with just one tiny leaf when it first sprouts from the SEED.

Monotreme A MAMMAL that lays eggs. The only living monotremes are the platypus and echidna of Australia and New Guinea.

Moon or **satellite** A large natural object which orbits around a planet. The planet Saturn has 24 moons. Earth has only one natural Moon, but thousands of artificial satellites also orbit our planet.

Natural selection A natural process in which the animals best equipped for a particular set of living conditions will be the most successful breeders. Their good features are therefore passed on to the new generation.

Nebula A huge cloud of DUST or gas, or a mixture of both. Some nebulae are many LIGHT-YEARS across. Nebulae are the birthplaces of the stars. To begin with they are just cold dark patches, but when stars form inside them they can shine brightly.

Neutral A substance that is neither an acid nor an alkali. A neutral solution has pH value of 7 and does not change the colour of LITMUS PAPER.

Neutron An uncharged atomic particle found in the nuclei of all ATOMS, except those of hydrogen.

Neutron star All that is left after a GIANT STAR explodes. It is completely made up of NEUTRONS, and these are crushed together into a hot ball the size of a small ASTEROID.

Nova A 'new' star – really a very faint star that suddenly shines out thousands of times more brightly. This happens when gas passes from one star to another and explodes.

Nucleus The positively charged centre of an ATOM. It is made of one or more PROTONS and, except in the case of hydrogen, one or more NEUTRONS.

Orbit The invisible path which a planet follows around the Sun, or a satellite follows around a planet. Orbits are never perfect circles, but ELLIPSES.

Ovary The tough case in the middle of a flower that contains and protects the eggs (ovules). It is the ovary that usually swells.

Oxidation The process in which a substance combines with oxygen.

Palaeontologist ('expert-on-ancient-life') A scientist who studies FOSSILS and the history of life.

Parasite A plant or animal that depends completely on another plant or animal in order to stay alive. Liver flukes and worms living inside the bodies of larger animals are examples of parasites.

Photosynthesis The word means 'building with light'. It is the chemical process that takes place in green leaves. Water and carbon dioxide from the air are used to make sugars that are the main plant food. The process uses energy from the Sun which is absorbed by CHLOROPHYLL.

Penumbra The lighter edge of a shadow, where the bright object (such as the Sun) is not completely hidden. It is also the name for the lighter edge of a SUNSPOT.

Phase The shape of the sunlit part of the Moon, or some planets, that is seen in the sky. It can change from a thin curved 'crescent' to completely round or 'full'.

Photosphere The Sun's bright surface. Its temperature is 6000 degrees Celsius.

Pitch The quality of a musical sound that depends on the FREQUENCY of the vibrations which produce it. A note of high pitch has a high frequency, while a note of low pitch has a low frequency.

Placental A MAMMAL that gives birth to fully developed young. Most mammals are placentals, such as mice, dogs, horses, whales and humans.

Pole One of the two ends of a magnet at which the magnetic forces are strongest.

Pollen The male CELLS of a plant. When pollen is carried by the wind or by an insect to another plant, that plant may be fertilized. Then it can produce SEEDS that will grow into new plants.

Potential energy The store of energy an object has because of its position. It can be converted to KINETIC energy if the object begins to move.

Prehistoric Something that dates from before 'history' (that is, before the invention of writing).

Primary colours One of the three colours (red, green and blue) of light that, when mixed, can give light of any colour; OR one of the three colours of pigment or paint (red, blue and yellow) that can be mixed to give paint of any colour, except white.

Primate ('first') A MAMMAL of the group that includes monkeys, apes and humans. It is called the 'first' group because it is the most advanced.

Prominences Enormous bursts of red-hot hydrogen gas which shoot out from the Sun's surface. Some may last for weeks, others for days, before dying back to the surface.

Proton Positively charged atomic particle found in the NUCLEUS of all ATOMS. The number of protons in the atom gives a substance its atomic number.

Protozoan A member of the simplest of all animal groups – the primitive single-celled animals.

Pulsar A fast-spinning NEUTRON STAR sending out a beam of light waves and radio waves. This beam 'pulses', like the circling beam of a lighthouse.

Quasars Giant GALAXIES with centres hundreds of times brighter than ordinary galaxies. They are all thousands of millions of LIGHT-YEARS away.

Radiation (heat) The transfer of heat in the form of ELECTROMAGNETIC waves.

Radioactive Term used to describe unstable ELEMENTS whose NUCLEI split to emit ALPHA, BETA and gamma rays.

Radioactivity A radioactive element has unstable nuclei which split up and emit ALPHA, BETA and gamma rays. When the nucleus of an atom splits up it produces radiation in the form of rays or particles. Radiation in large doses is lethal.

Radiocarbon dating Also called carbon dating: a way of telling how old dead matter is. All living things give off small amounts of radiation, this amount decreases after the thing dies and so can be measured to find how long ago it lived.

Ram (**r**andom **a**ccess **m**emory) The part of a computer's memory in which programs and data are held temporarily. Programs and data in the RAM can be changed and stored by the person using the computer.

Red shift The colour-change shown by distant GALAXIES. They are moving away at thousands of kilometres a second, and their LIGHT WAVES are stretched out by the speed, making them look redder in colour than they really are.

Reflection The bouncing back of a sound or light wave as it hits a surface.

Refraction The bending of a ray of light as it passes from one substance to another, for example, from glass to air.

Reproduction The process of making new members of the same animal or plant SPECIES. Some species reproduce asexually, just by growing an additional replica of the parent, or by splitting into two identical copies. Others reproduce sexually, that is by joining together an egg from a female parent and SPERM from the male parent.

Reptile A group of cold-blooded animals that lay eggs on land. A few give birth to live young.

Repulsion The force that pushes objects away from one another. For example 'like' poles of a magnet repel each other.

Resistance The way in which an electrical circuit opposes the flow of electric current through it. Resistance is measured in ohms and is equal to the voltage divided by the current.

ROM (**r**ead **o**nly **m**emory) The part of a computer's memory that has its program permanently fixed, usually by the manufacturer. Users cannot program the computer to change this memory.

Rodent An animal of the mouse-squirrel-beaver-porcupine family. All rodents have big, chisel-like front teeth which they use for gnawing plant food.

Ruminant An animal such as a cow, goat or sheep that has a four-chambered stomach which enables it to process tough plant food. Ruminants feed, then later they cough up the food and chew it a second time. It is called chewing the cud.

Saliva The juice that is produced by glands in the mouth. It helps to soften food and make it slide down easily, but it also contains important chemicals that start the process of digesting the food.

Salt The chemical substance formed when a BASE reacts with an ACID.

Season Changes in the Earth's climate caused by the tilt of its AXIS. Each POLE leans towards the Sun for half the year, and away from the Sun for the other half. This brings summer and winter to each half of the Earth in turn.

Seed A small capsule containing a baby plant and a small store of food to give it a start in life.

Skeleton The framework of bone or cartilage that supports the body of a bird, mammal, fish, amphibian or reptile. Crabs, insects and some other animals wear their skeletons *outside* – in the form of a shell or horny outer layer.

Solid A physical state of matter, in which a substance has a definite mass, volume and shape.

Solar system The family of planets, moons and COMETS revolving around our Sun. There are probably countless other solar systems around stars in our GALAXY and elsewhere in the Universe.

Solar wind An invisible stream of atomic particles, especially ELECTRONS and PROTONS, which pour out into space from the Sun's surface.

Solution A liquid that contains a solid (or gaseous) substance completely dissolved in it.

Species A group of animals of the same kind, which can breed and produce more of their own kind. A robin, for example, is one species of bird, while a blackbird is a different species.

Spectrum The band of colours you see when light passes through a glass prism. A rainbow is a spectrum, produced by sunlight shining through raindrops.

Sperm The male sex CELLS, which combine with the female egg cell to fertilize it and so enable it to grow into a new plant or animal.

Spore The reproductive CELL of certain plants. Fungi, for example, reproduce by spores which drift on the wind and grow wherever they land.

Star cluster A group of stars containing from a few tens (an open cluster) up to hundreds of thousands (a globular cluster of stars.)

Static electricity Non-moving electric charge on an object, often produced by friction, for example shoes rubbing on a carpet.

Sunspot cycle A period of time, lasting about 11 years, during which sunspots (cool, darker patches on the Sun's surface) become very common (maximum activity) and then rare (minimum activity).

Supernova A colossal explosion which destroys a GIANT STAR. The outburst gives out as much light as thousands of millions of ordinary stars before fading gradually.

Tides These are caused by the force of GRAVITY of one body in space, pulling at the surface of a nearby body. The pull of our Moon causes tides in the oceans.

Transistor A semi-conducting electronic component that can amplify signals or turn AC into DC.

Transit When the inner planets, Mercury or Venus, pass in front of the Sun. They appear as a slow-moving black spot.

Tuber The swollen end of an underground stem, which can sprout to produce new plants. The most common example is the potato plant.

Tundra The region between the cold northern forests and the polar desert of bare rock, ice and snow. It is a region of thin soil which is always frozen, apart from the surface layer, which melts in summer and a carpet of grass and lichen grows.

Umbra The dark centre of a shadow, where all the light from the bright object is cut off. When the Moon passes into the umbra of Earth's shadow, it is ECLIPSED. It is also the name for the dark centre of a SUNSPOT.

Universe The whole of space and everything in it.

Vacuum A space in which there are no ATOMS or MOLECULES. (Perfect vacuums are impossible to make so it usually means a place where the pressure is much lower than that of normal air.)

Volt The unit used to measure electrical pressure.

Warm-blooded An animal that can maintain its body at full operating temperature by burning fuel (food) to create chemical energy.

Wavelength The distance between the peak of one wave and the peak of the next.

X-rays Very short electromagnetic waves which can cause a chemical change on photographic plates and are used in radiography by doctors.

TRANSPORT AND COMMUNICATIONS

SHIPS
From the first reed boats and log rafts, to sailing ships and iron steamships, supertankers and submarines. (See page 188.)

RAILWAYS
Why have electric and diesel trains replaced steam locomotives on the rails? (See page 192.)

CARS
Only a hundred years ago, the car was a new invention. It is now the most popular form of transport. (See page 196.)

FLIGHT
The aeroplane, in peace and war, has changed the 20th century. Jet travel has brought people closer together. (See page 200.)

PAPER AND PRINTING
Writing and the printed book made knowledge available to anyone who could read. (See page 204.)

PHOTOGRAPHY
Photography began in the 1800s. Ever since, people have enjoyed taking pictures. (See page 206.)

SIGNALS AND FLAGS

For centuries communication was possible only as far as human eyes could see a signal or a flag. (See page 208.)

TELECOMMUNICATIONS

When the first telephone call was made, a new era of instant communication dawned. (See page 210.)

COMPUTERS AND ROBOTS

Already computers control factory robots. Soon there will be machines that can think. How do computers work? (See page 214.)

MOBILE INDUSTRIAL ROBOT

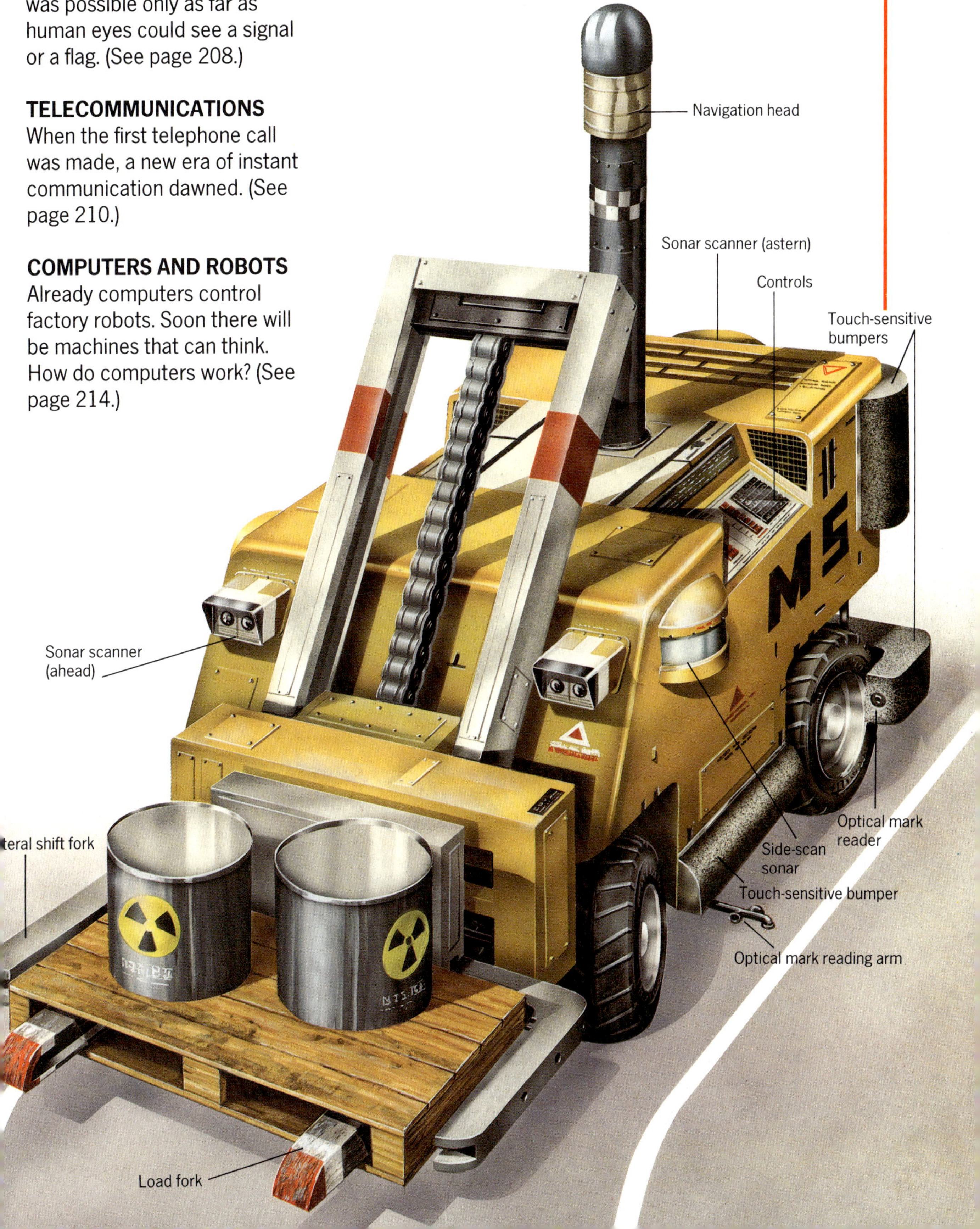

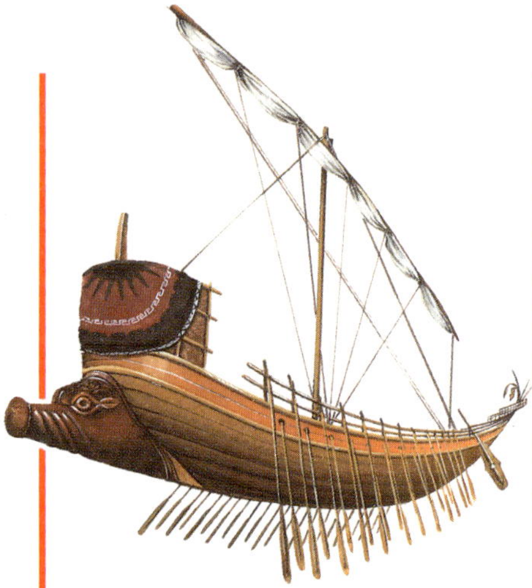

Above: The Ancient Greeks built biremes propelled by oars and with a sturdy ram attached to the bows.

Above right: Logs were hollowed out to make early boats or tied together to form rafts.

Ships

For thousands of years people have built ships to cross the oceans. Even in the Stone Age, sailors often sailed out of the sight of land. They learned to build craft from reeds and from logs. They learned to use sails as a means of power and, by following birds and studying the stars, began to master the skills of navigation (finding the way across the open ocean).

Until about two hundred years ago all ships were propelled by sails or by oars. For many years ships had only

Above: Viking longships were developed for the narrow fiords of Scandinavia. They had oars for use in calm waters and a single square sail which would be used in favourable winds on the open sea.

Below: A sixteenth-century galleon. The crew are setting the main sail.

Above: In 1838, *Sirius* was the first ship to steam all the way across the Atlantic.

Above left: Admiral Nelson's flagship *Victory* fought at the battle of Trafalgar in 1805.

Left: The *Charlotte Dundas*, built by William Symington in 1801, was the first successful power-driven ship.

one square sail on a single mast. They could only sail well with the wind and relied on oars to propel them when there was no wind. By the 1400s ships were built with several masts, one of which carried a triangular lateen sail which made sailing easier in all winds. From these developed the three-masted caravels and galleons.

Last of the sailing ships were the graceful and speedy clippers, which carried wool and tea from Australia or the Far East to Europe and America. The first true clipper was built in 1832. But by then steamships had already begun to appear. The first successful steamboat was Robert Fulton's *Clermont* (1807) which began the world's first regular steamship service on the Hudson River in the USA. Most early steamships were driven by paddle wheels. But the more efficient screw propeller replaced the paddlewheel from the 1830s. Steamships crossed the Atlantic, and a new age of fast, comfortable travel began.

Above: The only five-masted square-sail ship ever built was the windjammer *Preussen*. She presented a huge area of canvas to the wind.

Above: Gun-armed USS *New Jersey* is an old-style battleship. Most battleships now carry some form of guided missile.

Below: This US Navy aircraft carrier is nuclear-powered and carries up to 100 aircraft.

After the steam engine was invented, ships no longer had to rely on the wind. By the early 1900s steam turbines propelled huge ships built of steel. Most ships nowadays are propelled this way. They get up steam by heating water in oil-fired boilers. The steam spins the turbines, which turn the ship's propellers. Some ships are motor ships. They have a diesel engine to spin the propellers. A few speedy naval craft have gas-turbine engines, which work much like a jet engine.

Some of the most impressive ships ever constructed

Below: *Queen Elizabeth 2* was launched in 1967 as a replacement for the two famous Cunard liners, *Queen Mary* and *Queen Elizabeth*. *QE2* is used mostly as a cruise ship. She cruises at 28.5 knots (52.8 km/h) and normally carries up to 2000 passengers and 950 crew. More crew-members are employed in looking after the passengers than in working the ship.

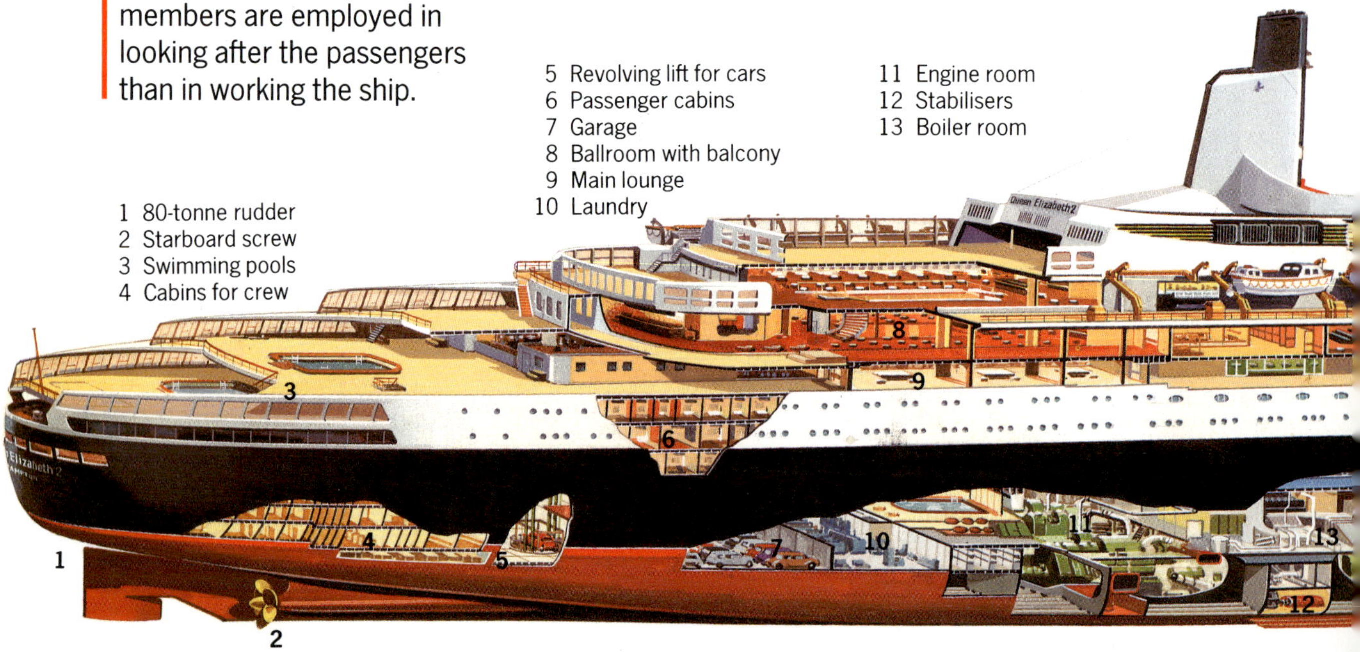

were the huge passenger liners of the 1930s such as the *Queen Mary* and *Queen Elizabeth*. Their rivals today are the nuclear-powered aircraft carriers and the even more enormous supertankers that carry oil around the world. These mammoth ships of 300,000 to 500,000 tonnes may be 380 metres long – yet need as few as 50 or so people to control them.

The first successful submarines were built in the 1890s, and these undersea craft played a big part in naval warfare in both World Wars. The first nuclear-powered submarine was the US Navy's *Nautilus* of 1955.

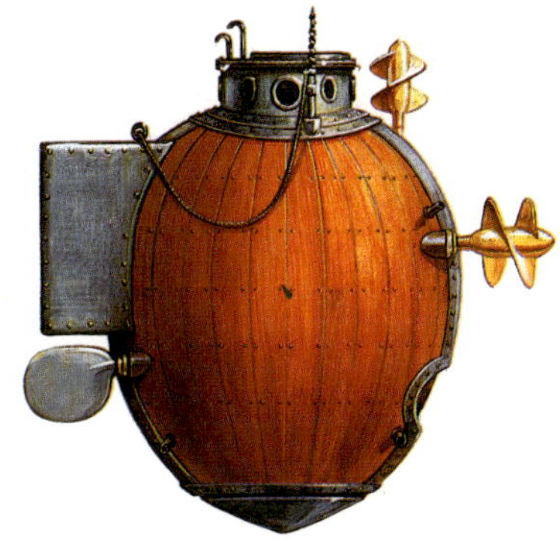

Above: David Bushnell built this small barrel-like submarine, called the *Turtle*, in 1775. It was used by the Americans to attack a British warship during the American War of Independence. It was manned by a single person working hand cranks to turn the propellers.

Below: Five navies (the United States, Soviet, Chinese, French and British) have nuclear submarines able to fire long-range ballistic missiles. Lurking on the seabed, they can launch rockets at land targets thousands of kilometres away. The other main class of nuclear submarine is the 'fleet hunter-killer', armed with advanced torpedoes to destroy enemy submarines.

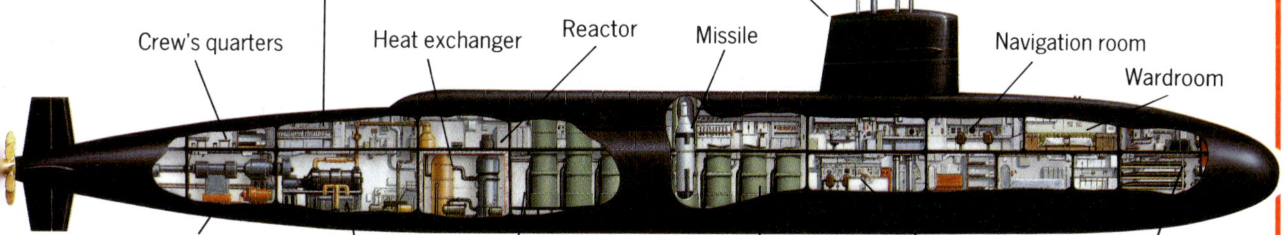

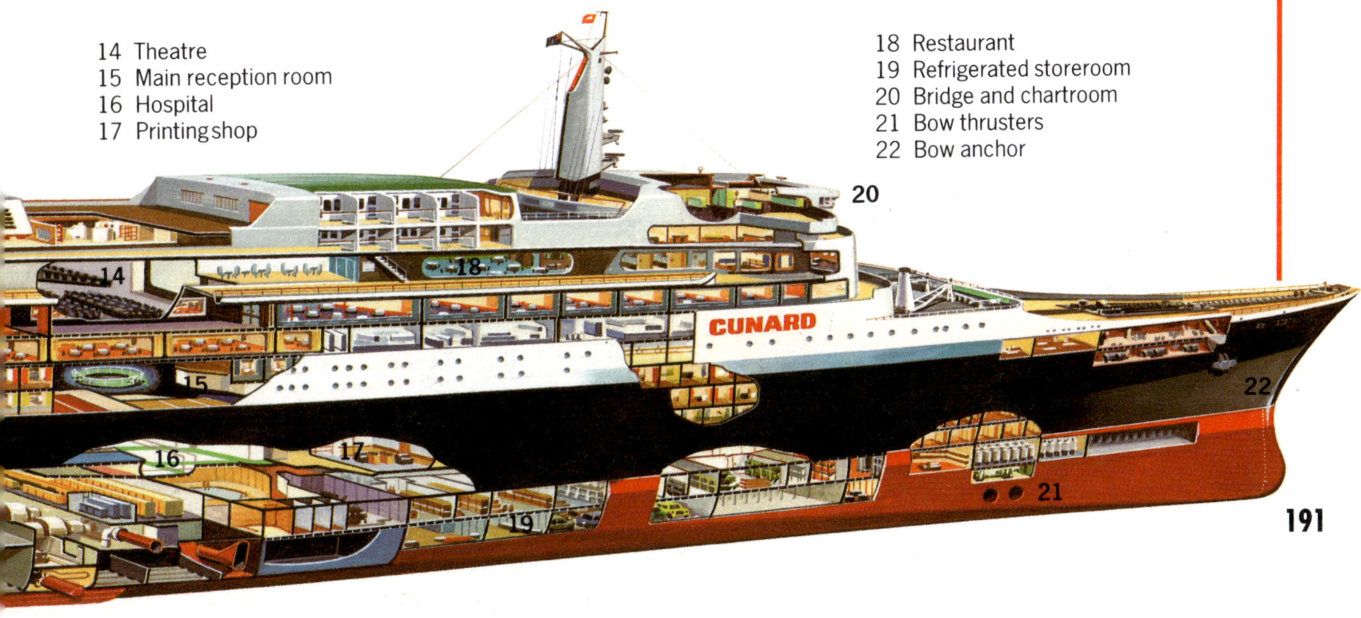

Shown below are three early rail locomotives. Despite a huge flywheel to smooth out the pounding of its single cylinder, Trevithick's locomotive of 1804 broke up the track. *Locomotion* was used on the Stockton and Darlington Railway in 1825. George Stephenson's *Rocket* won the British trials in 1829 for a locomotive to work the Liverpool and Manchester Railway. Until 1833, steam was used only for freight, with a horse-drawn coach service for passengers.

Railways

After the steam engine came into use in the 1700s, several inventors tried to build a steam-driven road carriage. A British engineer, Richard Trevithick, hit upon the idea of mounting a steam carriage on rails. Iron tracks had already been used in coal mines to make the heavy wagons move more easily.

The first public railway to use steam locomotives was the Stockton and Darlington Railway in northern

Trevithick's locomotive, 1804

Rocket, 1829

Locomotion, 1825

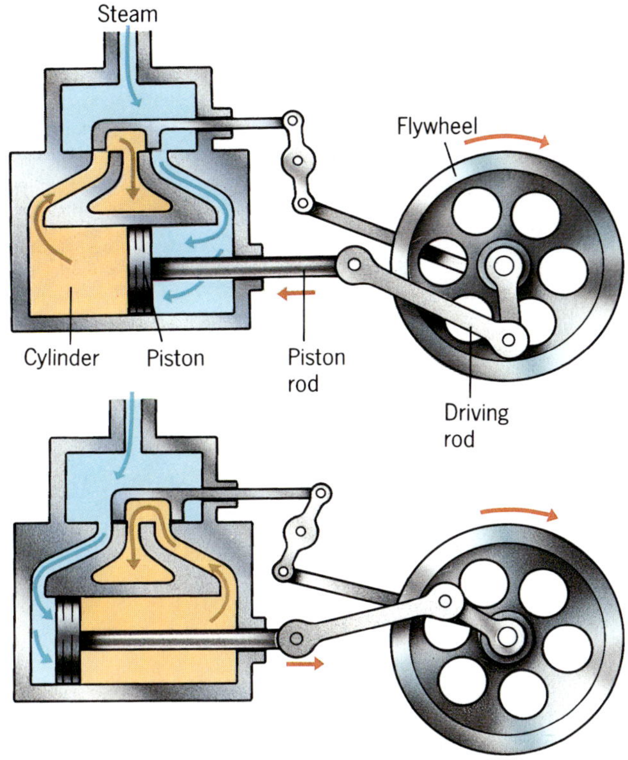

HOW THE STEAM ENGINE WORKS

In a steam engine, the pressure of expanding steam, given off by water heated by coal, is used to push a 'piston' to and fro in a hollow tube called a 'cylinder'. The piston is attached to a rod called the 'piston rod'. As the piston rod goes out and in it drives another rod called the 'driving rod'. It is the driving rod that turns a wheel called the 'flywheel'. The flywheel evens out the movements of the driving rod. It goes on turning steadily even when the piston is at the end of a stroke and is not pushing. In a steam locomotive, the driving rod of each piston is attached to a driving wheel. The largest steam locomotives, such as the US 'Big Boys', used 20 tonnes of coal and 44 tonnes of water an hour.

England. It was opened in 1825. George Stephenson built the track and its first locomotive, called *Locomotion*. The railway age had begun.

Bigger and more powerful steam locomotives were built. But they all worked in much the same way. Coal burning in a firebox heated water and turned it to steam.

Mallard, 1938

Mallet, 1914

Big Boy, 1940s.

Above: This diagram shows how a railway wheel runs along the metal rail. The rail rests on a sleeper or tie.

Left: Three famous steam locomotives. Britain's *Mallard* set a steam speed record of 202.73 km/h (126 mph) in 1938. The French *Mallet* 2-8-8-8-4 of 1914 had three sets of driving wheels. The US 'Big Boys' were the biggest locomotives ever built.

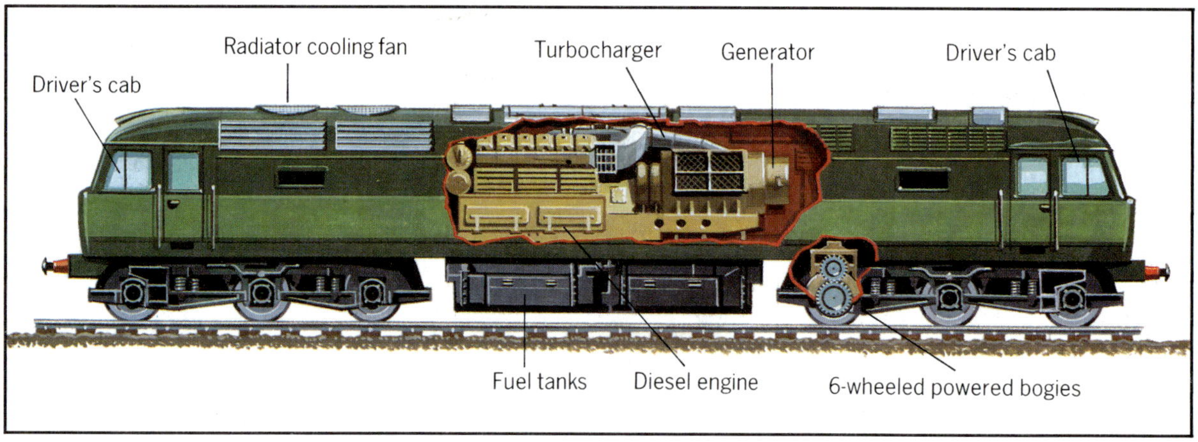

Above: A modern diesel locomotive. A diesel engine drives an electricity generator which in turn powers the motors that drive the sets of bogie wheels. The first diesel locomotive was built in Germany in 1912.

High-speed trains have revolutionized rail travel. The world speed record for a train is 480 km/h (298.27 mph) set by a French TGV in 1989. Britain's Electra, West Germany's ICE and Japan's Bullet train (*right*) can all operate at speeds above 200 km/h (124.28 mph).

Below: The Channel Tunnel will link Britain and France. High-speed trains will run through the undersea tunnel, carrying passengers in their cars inside double-decked wagons. Buses and trucks will also be carried.

The pressure of the steam forced large pistons to and fro in cylinders. The pistons were connected to the driving wheels and turned them round.

From the early 1900s steam locomotives were steadily replaced by diesel and electric locomotives which are cleaner, quieter and cheaper to run. Today, few steam trains remain.

Diesel locomotives are powered by oil-burning diesel engines similar to those used in large trucks. Electric locomotives are driven by powerful electric motors. They are connected to an electricity supply by overhead wires or by a 'live' third rail.

Right: A monorail. The Listowel and Ballybunion Railway in Ireland was the first monorail and ran for 35 years. The Schwehebahn at Wüppertal in West Germany opened in 1901. Each of these represents one of the two different kinds (the straddled rail and the suspended system) still being experimented with throughout the world. Monorails are cheap to erect and run. They can carry people swiftly into and out of city centres.

The monorail shown here runs in Tokyo, Japan. Bogie trucks run along a single rail. Coaches are suspended from arms curving down from one side of each bogie.

The first electric underground railway, or subway, was opened in London in 1890 (*left*). Steam trains had been used on underground lines in London since 1863. The tunnel, circular in section, carried the first of what Londoners came to call tube trains.

Left: A modern underground station. Modern tunnelling techniques can drive railways almost anywhere deep underground, below buildings, sewers and rivers. The first subway in the USA opened in 1904 in New York. The New York subway is the busiest in the world, though London has the longest route covering 408 km (254 miles).

In 1770 a Frenchman named Nicolas Joseph Cugnot built a steam tractor (*right*). It could run for 15 minutes at the slow speed for just over 3 km/h (1.86 mph). It was not very useful, but it was the first self-propelled road vehicle.

Below: Benz' three-wheeler of 1888 was the first petrol car to be produced as a standard model for sale.

Cars

Until the 1880s there were no automobiles. Two German engineers, Karl Benz and Gottlieb Daimler, built the first cars in 1885 and 1886. These had petrol engines, like most modern cars. Later, some cars were built with steam engines; others were driven by electricity from batteries. But in the end the petrol engine won.

At first, cars were hand-made and expensive. It was not until 1908 that they began to be made cheaply. In that year Henry Ford started to mass-produce his famous and successful *Model T*, called the 'Tin Lizzie'. It marked the beginning of the modern car industry.

A modern car is a collection of 10,000 or more separate parts. These parts make up several basic units: the body,

Above: The Rolls-Royce Silver Ghost of 1906 was a luxury car. It cruised at well over 80 km/h (50 mph).

Left: During the 1930s car makers concentrated on making cars larger and more comfortable. Some of the finest high-performance cars of all time were made during this period. This is a Duesenberg SJ of 1934.

the engine and the transmission are the main units. The transmission carries power from the engine to the driving wheels. The other units are the steering, the braking and the suspension.

Most cars have a (closed) *saloon* body. Sports cars may have an open body. They often have a soft top – a folding roof which can be clipped over the passenger compartment to give protection from the weather. Cars today are designed for economy, comfort and safety. In a low-speed crash the body crumples but the passenger compartment remains intact.

Above: The Model T Ford was built in many versions from 1908 to 1927. This is a 1923 'Fordor' sedan.

Left: The 1920s and 1930s saw the great age of record-breaking attempts in cars like Sir Henry Segrave's Sunbeam. Most attempts were made on flat beaches or dry lake beds.

FASTEST CARS

	km/h	mph
1898 Jeantaud electric car	63.15	39.24
1899 Jenatzy's *La Jamais Contente*	105.88	65.79
1922 Sunbeam	215.25	133.75
1927 Sunbeam (Henry Segrave)	327.97	203.79
1932 Napier-Campbell (M. Campbell)	408.73	253.97
1935 Campbell Special (M. Campbell)	489.74	304.31
1937 *Thunderbolt* (G. Eyston)	502.12	312.00
1947 Railton (J.R. Cobb)	634.40	394.20
The following were jet- or rocket-powered cars		
1964 *Bluebird* (D. Campbell)	648.00	403.1
1963 *Spirit of America* (C. Breedlove)	655.73	407.45
1964 *Green Monster* (A. Arfons)	863.75	536.71
1965 *Spirit of America* – Sonic 1	988.12	613.99
1970 *Blue Flame* (G. Gabelich)	1016.09	631.37
1983 *Thrust 2* (R. Noble)	1019.43	633.46

In 1898 a Frenchman reached the amazing speed of 63.15 km/h (39.4 mph) in an electric car. Many of the early record holders were electric and steam cars. Land-speed records have to be timed by officials from the International Automobile Federation. In 1963 Craig Breadlove set the record driving a three-wheeled jet. This vehicle did not conform to the official requirements which specified that the vehicle must have four wheels. The salt flats at Bonneville, in Utah, USA, are often used for land-speed records as they offer an ideal surface for hundreds of square miles.

Right: The main parts of a typical car engine.

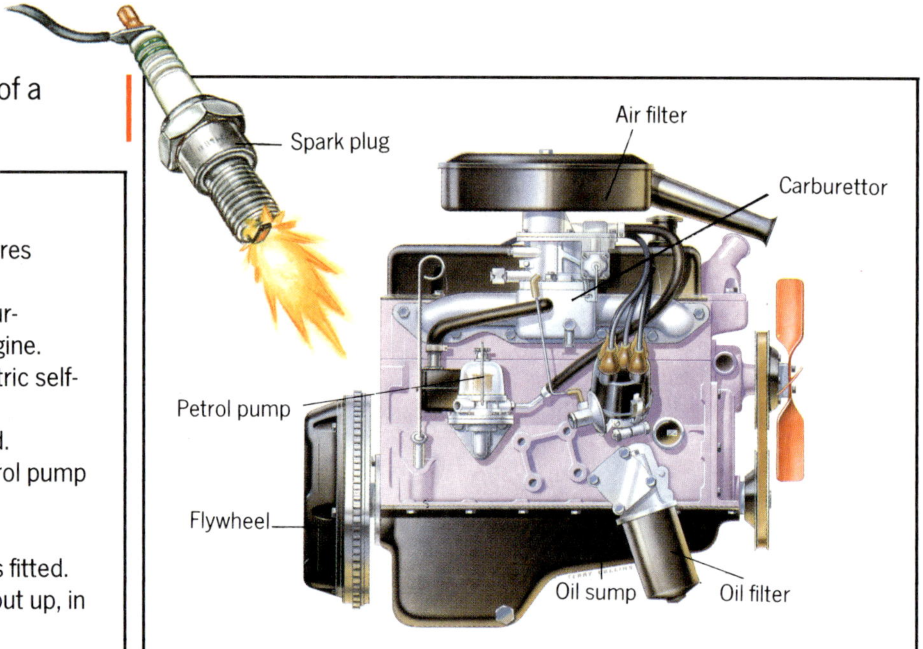

MODERN INTERNAL COMBUSTION ENGINE

MOTORING FIRSTS

1895 First pneumatic tyres introduced.
1896 First car with a four-cylinder petrol engine.
1896 First car with electric self-starter.
1904 First silencer fitted.
1906 First roadside petrol pump set up in America.
1915 First mechanical windscreen wipers fitted.
1919 First traffic lights put up, in Detroit, USA.
1924 First motorway opened, running from Milan to Varese in Italy.
1927 First white lines running down the centre of the road, introduced in Britain.
1935 First parking meter set up, in Oklahoma, USA.
1967 First racing car fitted with 'high-wing' aerofoils.

An ordinary car engine consists of thousands of separate pieces and may have as many as 150 moving parts. There are four or more closed tubes, or cylinders, in which pistons can travel up and down. A mixture of petrol and air is burned in the top of the cylinders. The gases produced push the pistons down. The movement of the pistons turns a rod called a crankshaft.

THE FOUR-STROKE CYCLE

Most cars have four-stroke engines – the piston goes through four up-and-down strokes. First the inlet valve opens and as the piston moves down it draws in the petrol-air mixture from the carburettor. This is the 'induction' stroke. Next the piston moves up compressing the mixture (squeezing it into a smaller space). In the next stroke a spark from the sparking plug sets fire to the mixture. The explosion forces the piston down and turns the crankshaft which powers the car's driving wheels. The up-and-down movements of the pistons turn the crankshaft. Lastly the exhaust stroke starts when the exhaust valve opens, the piston rises, and the burnt gases are pushed out.

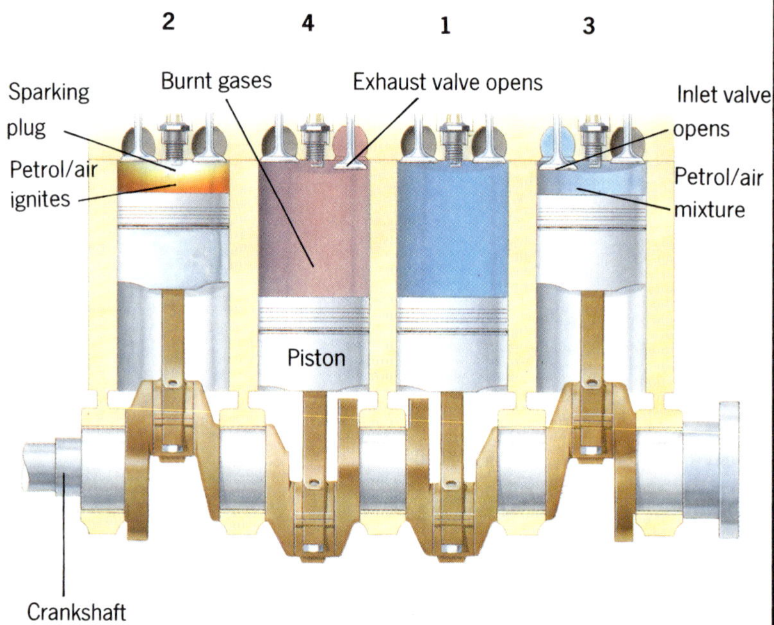

Above: In the 1950s American cars were enormous chromium-plated 'gas-guzzlers'. This is the Ford Edsel, which was unsuccessful because no one liked its design. Cars like this used a lot of fuel and became uneconomical in the 1970s when the price of oil rose sharply. Smaller 'compact' cars replaced them.

A car's transmission system carries the turning motion of the engine from the crankshaft to the driving wheels, which may be at the front or at the rear of the car. The most common system consists of a clutch, a gearbox, and shafts connecting the gearbox to the driving wheels. The clutch connects the gearbox to the engine. By changing the gears in the gearbox, the driver can make the car go faster or slower for the same engine speed.

Trucks and buses are often powered by diesel engines, invented by Rudolf Diesel in 1893. (A diesel engine is ignited by the heat of compressed air rather than by an electrical spark.) Another development is the rotary engine invented by Felix Wankel in 1956. The motor car has become the most important means of personal transport used in the 20th century. It has changed the look, sound and smell of our cities.

Above: The German Volkswagen Beetle, first built in the 1930s, is the biggest selling car of all time.

Left: The modern saloon car has a streamlined body. It is designed to withstand a collision and to give passengers a comfortable ride.

Right: Otto Lilienthal controlled his gliders by swinging his body.

Below: The Montgolfier balloon in which Jean Pilâtre de Rozier and the Marquis d'Arlandes became the first aviators in 1783. This was the first balloon to carry passengers.

Below: Leonardo da Vinci drew this sketch of a helicopter-like machine in the 1500s.
A practical flying machine could not be built in his day.

Above right: Orville and Wilbur Wright built their own aircraft. The first flight for their *Flyer* aeroplane in 1903 lasted only 12 seconds. But by 1905 the Wrights could stay aloft for 30 minutes.

Flight

For thousands of years, people have envied the ability of birds to soar through the air. Taking a lesson from nature, they even tried to copy birds by strapping crude wings to their arms and leaping off hills and high buildings. No matter how hard human beings flapped, they could never stay airborne. Human muscles are simply too weak and their bodies too heavy to stay aloft.

The conquest of the air began in 1783 when the Montgolfier brothers sent up a hot-air balloon. Later balloons were filled with hydrogen gas or helium, a gas discovered in 1895. Helium was much safer because, unlike hydrogen, it does not catch fire.

The de Marcay-Moonen, 1911 – the world's first practicable aeroplane with folding wings. The wings folded back against the fuselage. Folding-wing aircraft would later prove invaluable in service on aircraft carriers.

Left: A World War I 'dogfight' between German and British fighter planes.

Below: Two fighter planes. Conflict in the air added a new dimension to war.

German Albatross

British Sopwith fighter

Henri Giffard's cigar-shaped steerable airship (1852) had a steam engine driving a propeller. But steam engines were too heavy for use in aircraft. Petrol engines, being smaller and lighter, were used in the successful Zeppelin airships of the early 1900s, which could carry passengers across the Atlantic. However, in the 1930s a series of crashes brought the airship story to a close.

Otto Lilienthal experimented with a large kite-like glider in the 1890s, and his flights inspired the Wright brothers in America. On December 17, 1903, the Wrights' *Flyer* made the first controlled and powered man-carrying flight by an aeroplane.

Aeroplane development was rapid. Newspapers offered prizes for record-breaking flights. In 1909 Louis Blériot of France won a prize for crossing the Channel and in 1927 Charles Lindbergh flew solo non-stop from New York to Paris. During World War I metal monoplanes had begun to replace the early fabric-covered biplanes.

Until the 1940s all aeroplanes had piston engines turning propellers. But propellers do not work well at great heights or at speeds above 800 km/h (497 mph). The first

Below: Military aviation developed rapidly in the late 1930s and during World War II (1939–45) aircraft played a vital part. The Germans used the Junkers Stuka dive-bomber to support 'blitzkrieg' advances by their armies. The British Spitfire was a fast fighter plane. It fought in the Battle of Britain (1940). The Lancaster heavy bomber carried a large bomb load and took part in the Allied bombing raids which devastated many German cities.

British Spitfire fighter

Junkers Ju 87

British Avro Lancaster

Bell X-1

Right: Concorde, the world's only commercial supersonic airliner.

Left: The first plane to fly supersonically in level flight was the US Bell X-1 in 1947. This experimental aircraft was powered by a rocket.

Below: Two modern warplanes – the European Tornado and the US A-10 Thunderbolt. The Tornado has swing wings and can fly at more than twice the speed of sound. It is built in fighter and bomber versions. The heavily armed Thunderbolt is slower but is capable of destroying a tank.

jet aircraft was the German Heinkel 178 (1939). In the 1950s jets swiftly replaced piston propeller aircraft. Radar was first used during World War II, and the helicopter (1936) became a 'work horse' of the air. Helicopters became increasingly useful, for war and peacetime rescue, from the 1950s.

The first plane to fly faster than sound in level flight was the rocket-powered Bell X-1 (1947). In the 1950s the first jet airliners (the British Comet and the US Boeing 707) came into service. Supersonic airliners such as the Anglo-French Concorde have cut travelling time on long-distance flights, while the huge 'wide-bodied' jets such as the Boeing 747 and the Airbus have brought air travel within everyone's reach.

Tornado multi-role warplane

American A-10 Thunderbolt

THE JET ENGINE

Jet engines suck air in at one end of a tube and force it out of the other end at a much greater speed. As a result, the engine – and with it the plane – is thrust in the opposite direction. To speed up the air passing through the tube, jet engines have powerful fans (or turbines) inside to compress the air. Modern turbofan engines are quieter and burn less fuel than earlier jets.

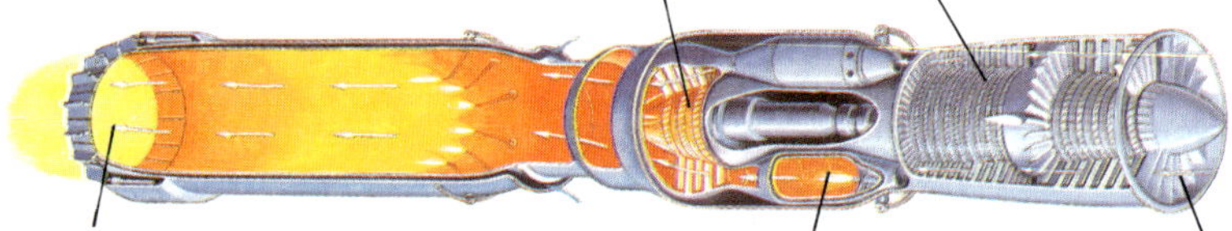

Below: The main features and cabin layout of an Airbus A300B airliner.

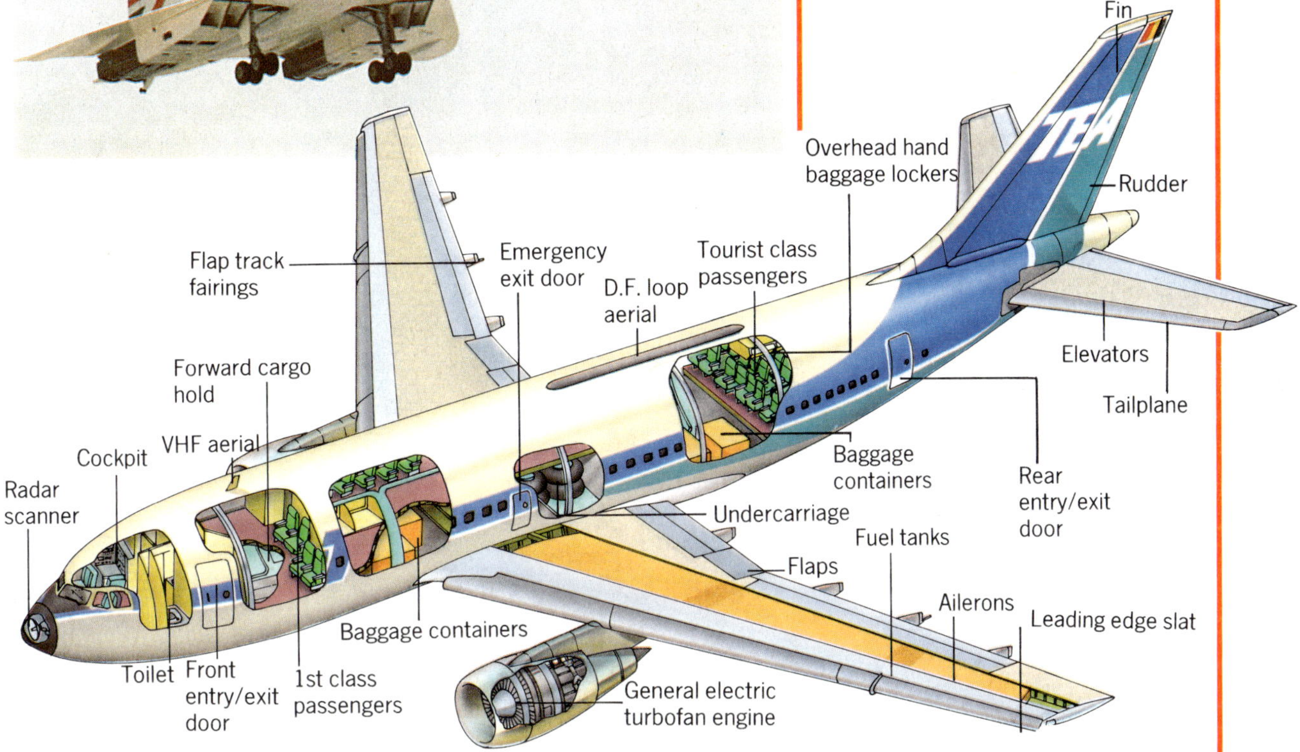

HOW A HELICOPTER FLIES

Helicopters are used for many tasks. They carry out rescue missions, ferry soldiers into action and hunt for enemy submarines. They are not very fast, but they are more manoeuvrable than fixed-wing aircraft. A helicopter's rotor blades act as wings and propellers. To fly upwards all the rotor blades are kept at the same angle, or pitch. To fly forwards the rotor tilts forward and the blades bite the air towards the tail. To move sideways the rotor head simply has to be tilted in the desired direction.

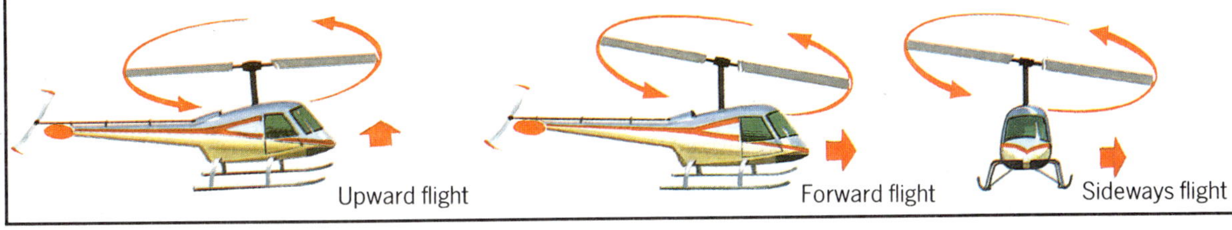

Above: A woodblock print made in 1483. This simple form of printing was invented in China more than 1000 years ago. A flat wooden block was carved to form a raised letter or design and covered with ink. A piece of paper pressed down on the block became printed with the block's design. The art of woodblock printing later spread to Europe.

Paper and Printing

Paper was invented in China, and the secret of paper-making reached Europe in the Middle Ages. In the 15th century, Johannes Gutenberg invented the first mechanical printing press. He also devised a method of making individual letters from small pieces of metal. Each letter – 'type' – was a raised surface on a metal block and could be arranged – 'set' – by hand to form words and sentences. This moveable type could be used over and over again after printing had been completed. This basic principle is called 'letterpress' printing.

Today, type is no longer set by hand – typesetting machines are used instead. Someone types the 'copy' (the words to be printed) into a keyboard like that on a typewriter. Letters are automatically produced in the form of metal or, more commonly, film.

Sentences have to be made up into whole pages, ready to be printed. (Some systems allow the printer to design and assemble each page by typing instructions into a computer that shows the page layout on a small screen.) Pages are printed from metal plates. Some have the page's contents as a raised surface pattern in the metal. Usually, the plate has a light-sensitive covering that reacts by harden-

HOW PAPER IS MADE

Logs from softwood trees (pines, firs and spruces) are sawn into small pieces. Then they are either ground or cooked with chemicals. This separates the wood fibres and makes wood-pulp. The wood-pulp is mixed with water and beaten until it is mushy. The pulp is then poured into a moving wire-mesh belt. The water drains away and leaves a damp web of fibres. This web is then rolled hard and dried. It emerges as a continuous paper sheet. The whole paper-making machine may be up to 100 metres (328 feet) long.

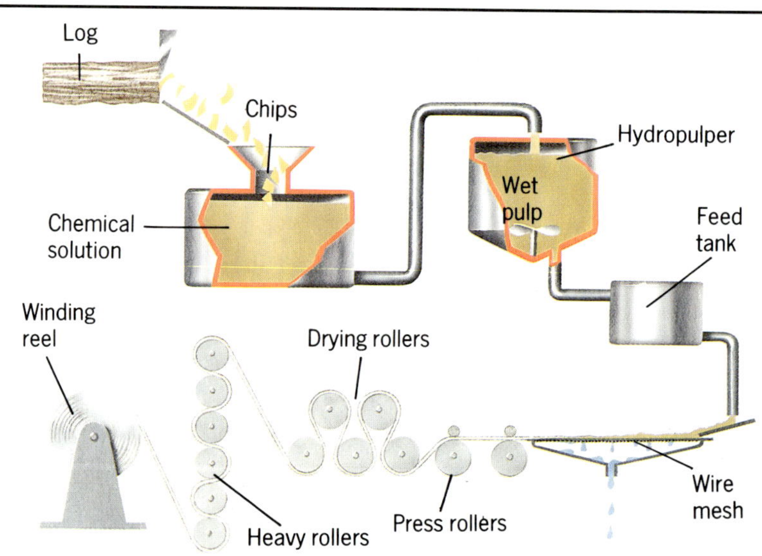

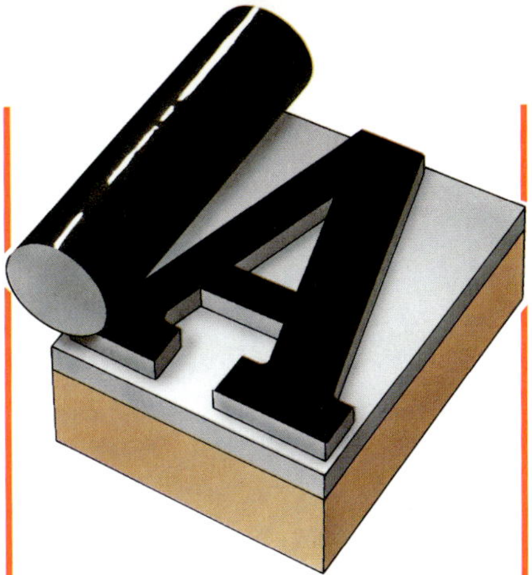

Above: 'Letterpress' printing using an inked, raised surface.

Left: Eight pages of a book are run simultaneously off a press.

Below: A modern offset lithography printing press uses a system of inked rollers to transfer ink to the large cylinder that holds the printing plate. Then ink is transferred or 'offset' from the plate to a rubber blanket and onto the paper. A printing plate is made for each colour, and each colour is printed on top of the other, to produce the final image.

ing when a photographic image of the page is shone onto it. Areas that are unaffected wash away, while the hard areas are left as a raised image that takes the ink. A huge amount of modern printing is done with totally flat plates. This is called 'photolithography' and the plates are also prepared photographically.

Once plates have been prepared, printing can begin. There are two main types of printing press – 'rotary' and 'offset lithography'. Some hold the plates flat, while others bend the plates around large cylinders. 'Sheet-fed' presses feed paper in to be printed one sheet at a time, while 'web-fed' presses use continuous rolls of paper that are cut into pages after printing.

OFFSET COLOUR PRINTING PRESS

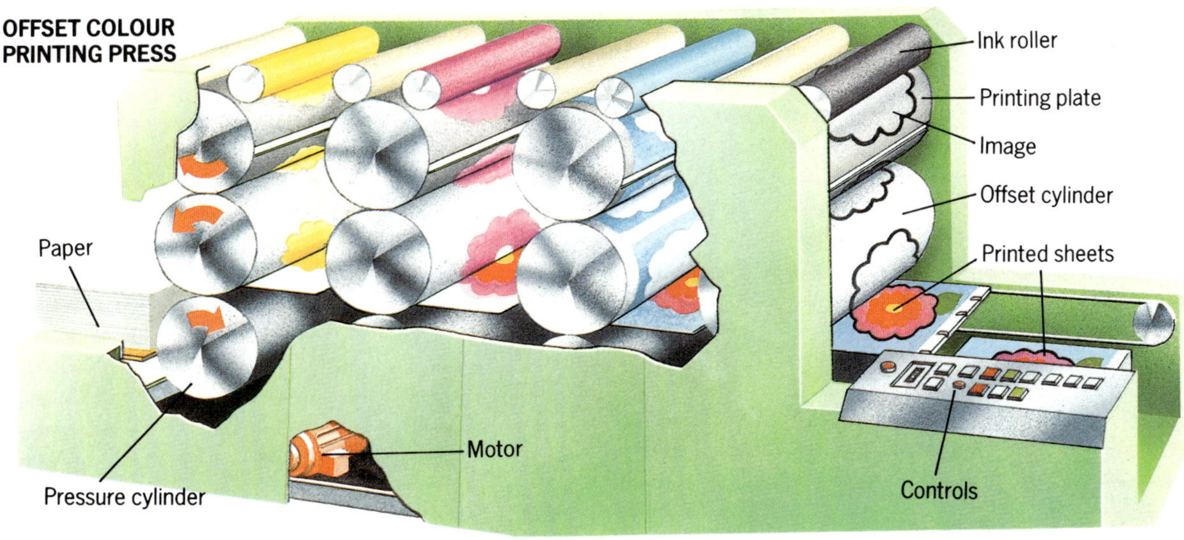

Right: This sequence of pictures of a galloping horse was photographed in 1887 by Eadweard Muybridge. It is one of the earliest examples of stroboscopic or multiple-flash exposed photography. With the use of a series of flashes, the progressive stages of objects in motion can be recorded.

Photography

Before photography, the only way to record people and places was by sketching or painting. Louis Daguerre and Joseph Niepce produced the first photograph in 1826, on a copper plate treated with light-sensitive chemicals. Plates like this became known as 'daguerreotypes'. But, in 1835, Fox Talbot produced prints from small negatives, and by 1888 George Eastman had made the first modern camera – the Kodak – and the first rolls of film.

Early cameras were simply boxes that let no light in, with light-sensitive paper at the back and a lens at the front. Instead of an automatic shutter letting in a certain amount of light, a lens cap had to be removed by hand, for up to several minutes. The subjects had to keep very still all this time so that the final image was not blurred!

Cameras today still work on the same principles. As you

Below: An early hand-cranked movie camera. The first movies were jerky and silent; soundtracks did not appear until the late 1920s.

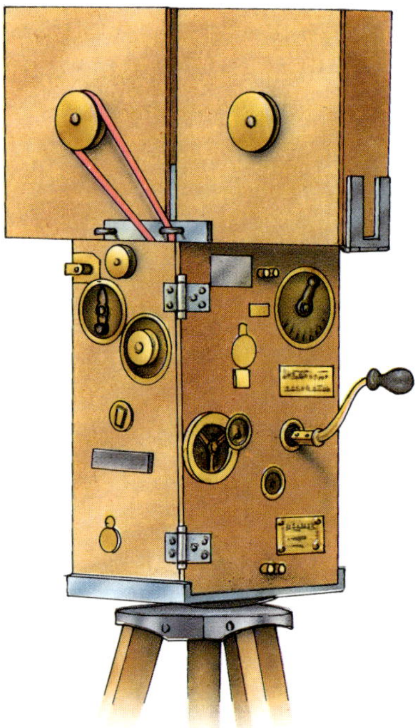

Right: Sharp, detailed action shots are taken by using a very fast shutter speed. This is the amount of time the shutter remains open to let light expose the film. Modern cameras have shutter speeds of up to 1/1000 of a second.

Left: The paper used for making colour prints has three layers of emulsions, each of which is sensitive to one of the primary colours of light: blue, green or red light. During printing the dyes on the negative hold back one of the primary colours. When the paper is developed, dyes are formed in the emulsion that reproduce the colour of the subject of the original photograph.

press the shutter-release, you allow light through the lens onto the film at the back. The image made on film is 'negative' – the dark areas of the subject appear light and the light areas dark – but when the film has been processed, the image is seen correctly. To adjust the amount of light that falls on the film, the lens may have an aperture (opening) that can be made larger or smaller – in dim conditions it can be opened further to let in more light and in bright conditions it can be opened less.

Photography is possible because light makes certain silver compounds – in particular silver bromide – turn black when treated with the appropriate chemicals. Film is made of plastic, with a light-sensitive emulsion on one side. Black and white film has one layer, while colour film has three – one sensitive to red, one to blue and one to yellow.

Below: The camera works on the same principle as the human eye. Light enters our eyes through a small hole, called the pupil. In a camera this is the aperture, which can be open or shut to let light onto the film. The wider the aperture (or the pupil in the eye), the more light is let in. The amount of light let into a camera is known as the exposure.

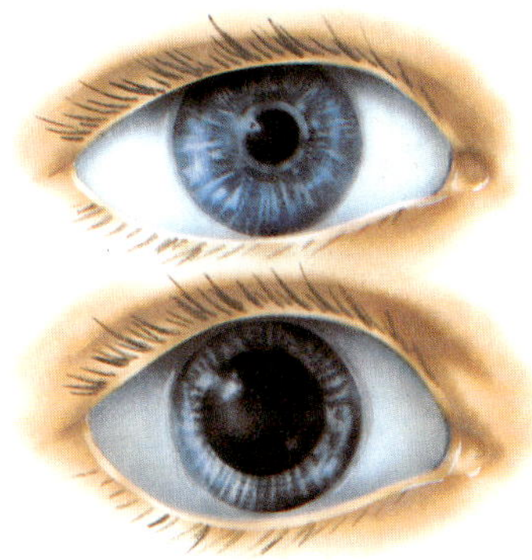

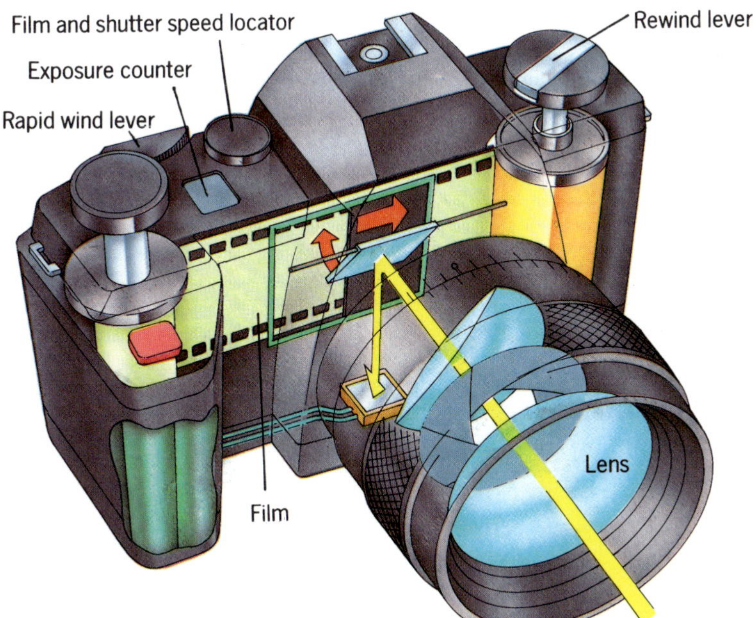

Left: A modern single lens reflex camera has automatic control of exposure and focusing so the photographer can concentrate on the arrangement of the subject.

 INTERNATIONAL SIGNAL FLAGS

Signals and Flags

A flag may represent a country, an organization or a person. Every country has its own national flag. Organizations such as the United Nations and the Red Cross have flags, and kings and queens have their own personal flags. Often flags are flown on special occasions, public holidays and to show respect during times of mourning.

The first flags were ornamental streamers. In battle, flags or standards raised high on poles, were a rallying point for the soldiers. The emblems of the Roman legions were eagle standards.

In the Middle Ages there were several flags of different shapes, called gonfanons, banners and pennons. Often flags showed family crests or heraldic devices, such as animals. The flags were passed on from one generation to another and many of the same emblems are still used.

Above: Some early emblems showing allegiance.

Below: Trades unions often display elaborate banners expressing their ideals in symbolical form.

Above: Warships during the 1500s flew large colourful battle flags.

Flags have been used as a means of identification and communication at sea for as long as there have been ships. They might declare the purpose of the vessel, whether it was bound for war or on a trading venture, the port from which it sailed and the owner. The small coloured flags of the International Code of Signals (shown on page 208) are used to send messages at sea.

Some flags are symbols of the ideology and way of life of a nation or group of people. In the second half of the 18th century rebels against English rule in America had a famous flag portraying a rattlesnake and the words 'Don't tread on me'. Dating from the same period, the star came to be seen as a symbol of liberty and independence. This emblem is now used on many national flags. The flag of the Soviet Union shows a gold five-pointed star above a crossed hammer and sickle. These tools symbolize the power of the manual worker.

SOME MODERN NAVAL FLAGS

UNION JACK DESIGN

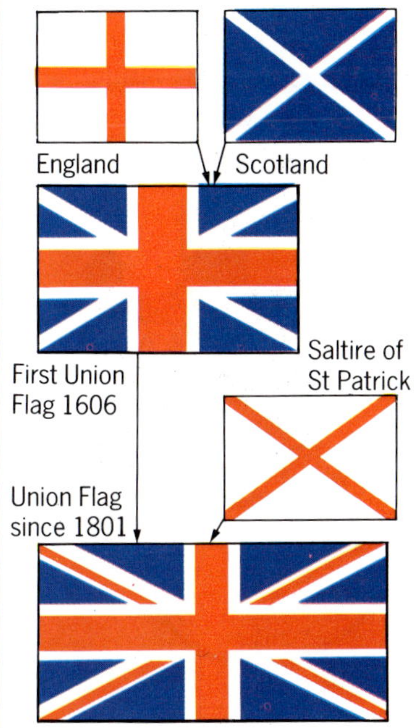

The British Union Jack combines the different crosses of St George, St Andrew and St Patrick. The evolution of the flag began in 1603 when Scotland and England were united under King James. The cross of St Patrick was added in 1801.

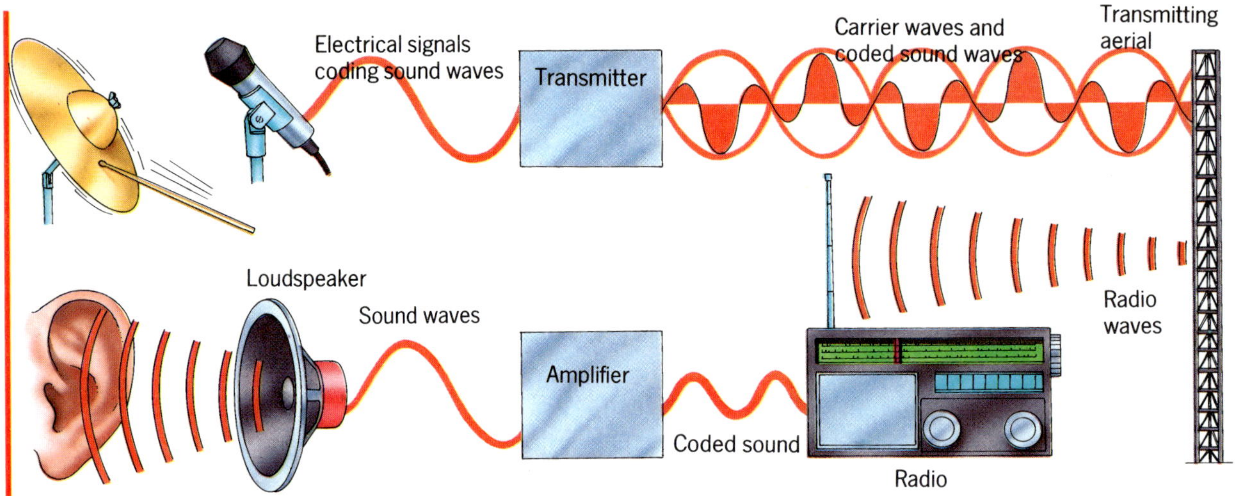

Above: In broadcasting the vibrations that we hear as sounds are picked up by microphones, transmitted as electronic signals from aerials, and reproduced as vibrations by a loudspeaker.

Above: An early telephone. Since Alexander Graham Bell's first message in 1876, much has been done to improve the telephone. By 1923 it was possible to speak from London to New York, and now no business could be run without a telephone.

Telecommunications

The last 500 years have produced two communications explosions. The printing revolution made books available to all. And in the last 100 years science has given us amazing new ways of message-sending and message-storing. Inventions such as photography, the telephone, sound recording, radio, television and computers, are the 'keys' to the modern world. They give us instant communication. Information can be stored and 'called for' at the touch of a switch. And people's faces and voices can be recorded and preserved for ever.

In the 1790s Claude Chappe invented the semaphore, a kind of mechanical 'arm waver'. Semaphores could send messages from hilltop to hilltop far faster than a horse could gallop. Despite this, the 'Pony Express' operated between Missouri and California from 1860 to 1861. Relays of riders galloped the 3000 km (1800 miles) in about 10 days carrying the mail.

But even this was not fast enough for governments and businessmen who needed to send urgent messages before the development of the railway network. The solution was the electric telegraph, which came into use in 1838. A signal could be sent by passing an electric current along a wire connected to a receiver which clicked each time the current was switched on or off. Samuel Morse invented a telegraph code, replacing the letters of the alphabet with dots and dashes. Before long telegraph wires were spanning the continents.

The next step was to transmit speech along the wire. Alexander Graham Bell proved that sound waves made by a voice could be changed into electric current, sent along a wire, and then changed back into sounds. He demonstrated the first telephone in 1876. It was an instant success. For the first time people could talk to someone who was far beyond earshot.

Was it possible to send sound messages without wires? James Clerk Maxwell and, later, Heinrich Hertz had shown that it was possible to produce electromagnetic waves or 'radiation'. These waves travelled at the speed of light. Several engineers wondered if these 'Hertzian waves' could be made to carry sounds.

These ideas were used by the pioneer of the radio, the Italian Guglielmo Marconi. Marconi had his first success in 1895, and in 1901 he sent the first wireless telegraphy message – the Morse code for the letter S – across the Atlantic. Ships fitted the new system, and soon radio telephony made it possible to transmit voices and even music. The impact of radio was enormous. News could be flashed round the world in minutes. And a new form of entertain-

MORSE CODE

A	·–	M	––	Y	–·––
B	–···	N	–·	Z	––··
C	–·–·	O	–––	1	·––––
D	–··	P	·––·	2	··–––
E	·	Q	––·–	3	···––
F	··–·	R	·–·	4	····–
G	––·	S	···	5	·····
H	····	T	–	6	–····
I	··	U	··–	7	––···
J	·–––	V	···–	8	–––··
K	–·–	W	·––	9	––––·
L	·–··	X	–··–	0	–––––

Samuel Morse, who developed the first successful electric telegraph, also invented the Morse code. This code is a system of sending messages along a wire in the form of dots, dashes and spaces.

Below: Today, communications satellites can relay thousands of phone calls instantaneously around the world.

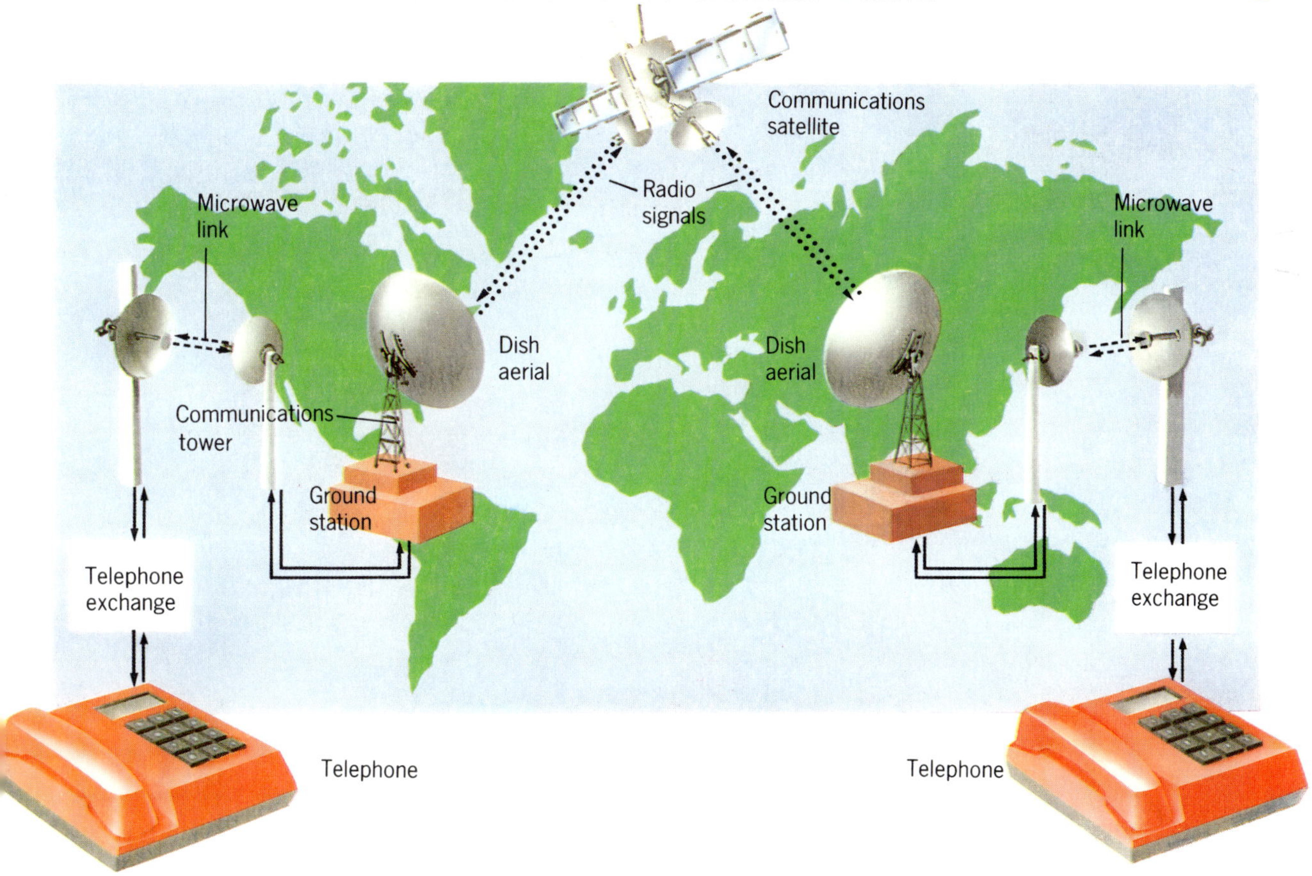

Below: When a scene is filmed for television, cameras and microphones change the image and sound into video and audio electronic signals. From these signals a transmitting coder produces a TV signal which is taken by wire to the transmitting antenna. The antenna is normally positioned on a mast so the signal can travel as far as possible. The signal is picked up by aerials on roofs and televisions. It is decoded (see page 150) so we can see and hear the programme in our homes.

ment developed from the first radio broadcast transmitted by Reginald Fessenden in December 1906.

John Logie Baird demonstrated a mechanical television system, using rotating discs, in 1926. But the rival electronic system of Marconi-EMI, based on the cathode ray tube (invented in the 1920s by Vladimir Zworykin) was finally chosen for transmitting broadcasts. The world's first public television service began in Britain in 1936.

Colour television began replacing black-and-white in the 1950s. In 1956 videotape recording gave the viewer an 'instant replay', and in 1962 the Telstar communications satellite relayed the first television pictures across the Atlantic. Early Bird (1965) and the Intelsat series (1971–1980s) have made round-the-world television a reality.

The first sound recordings were made only 100 years ago by Thomas Edison. In the time since then, the world has become used to instant communications: radio, television, movies and now satellite broadcasting. Television's

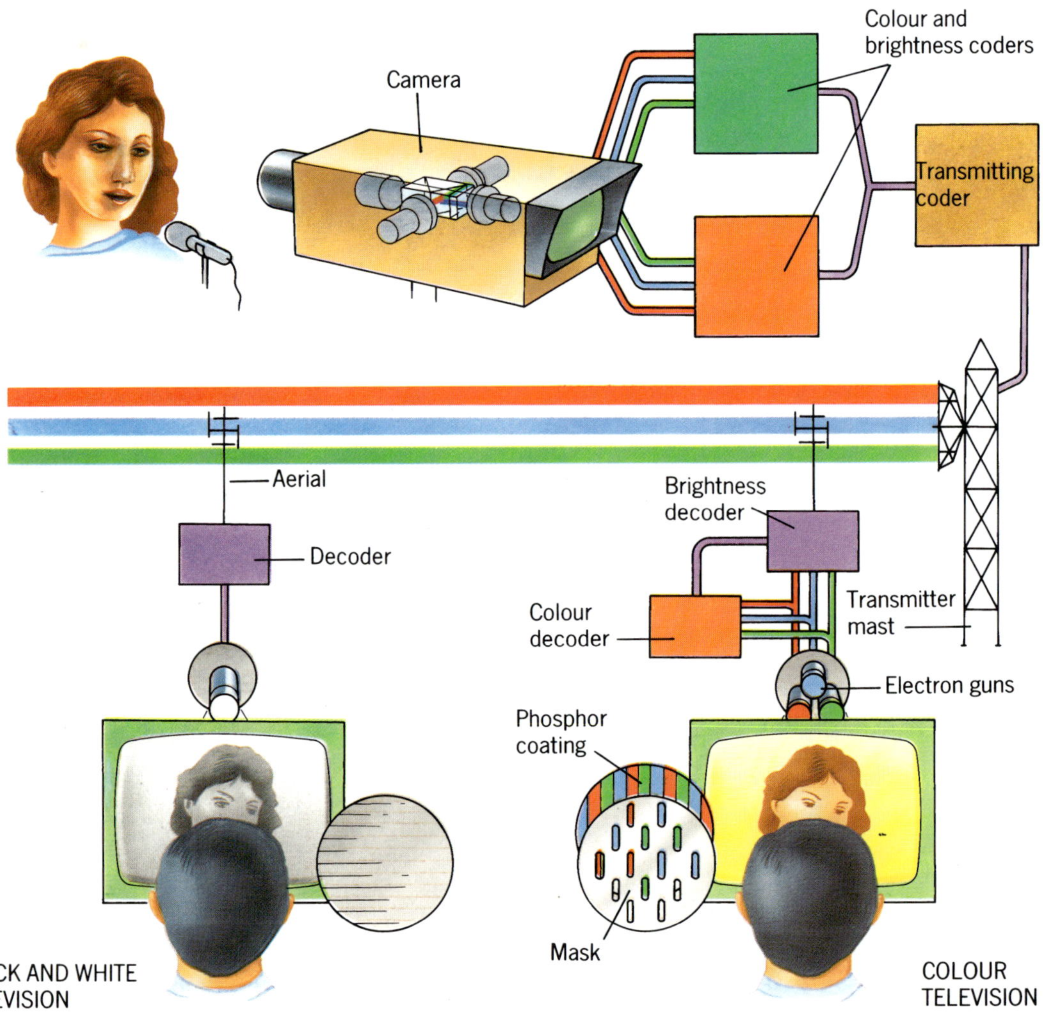

main use in communications is in bringing into people's homes news and pictures of events as they happen. It is also used for surveillance purposes by police and shopkeepers. Both radio and television play an important role in education, beaming learning material to schools, colleges and people's homes.

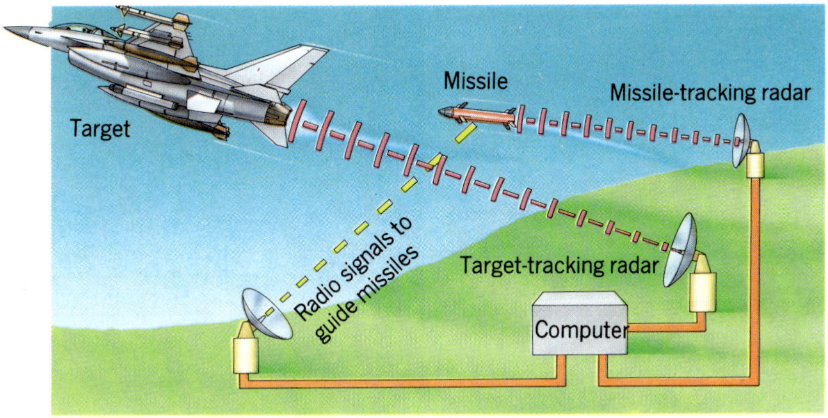

Above: Radar is essential equipment for the army, navy and air force. Radar can guide and control rocket-powered missiles from devices on Earth or from within the missile itself. This enables the missile to hit its target accurately.

Below: Developments in micro-chip technology have led to the miniaturization of many pieces of electronic equipment. This television and video system can be operated by batteries and is small enough to be easily carried in a briefcase.

HOW RADAR WORKS

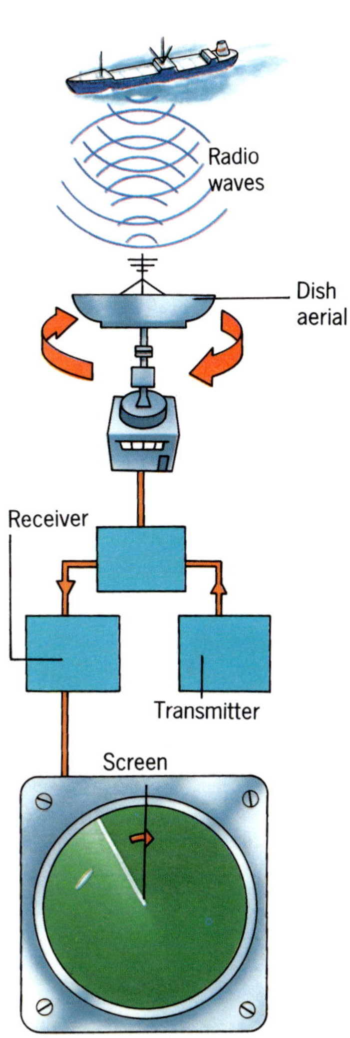

Above: Radar (**ra**dio **d**etection **a**nd **r**anging) locates objects by using very short radio waves. The rotating dish aerial sends out signals from the transmitter that bounce back off objects in their path. The returning signals are decoded by a receiver that shows the direction and distance of the objects as 'blips' on a screen. Radar can be used for air traffic control. It can also be used for navigation on ships and to direct anti-aircraft missiles to their targets.

Right: Early computers contained thousands of transistors wired together. One computer filled an entire room – there were so many parts. All this changed with the coming of the silicon chip which made possible 'miniaturization'. Computers got much smaller, leading to the desk-top computer.

Below: The data (information) the computer needs can be stored on a cassette or a floppy disk (which works much faster). Data is stored on magnetic disks in concentric tracks. Each track is divided into sectors so data can be found quickly. The computer displays its work or 'output' either on a screen or as a paper printout. Since the 1960s computers have changed the way we work and learn.

Computers and Robots

The first working electronic computer was built at the University of Pennsylvania in 1945. It was called ENIAC (Electronic Numeral Integrator And Calculator). It weighed 30 tonnes and occupied a large hall of 140 square metres (1,500 square feet) and contained more than 18,000 valves. Such have been the developments in computer technology and miniaturization that today's personal computers occupy just a small amount of desk space, and have as much power as ENIAC.

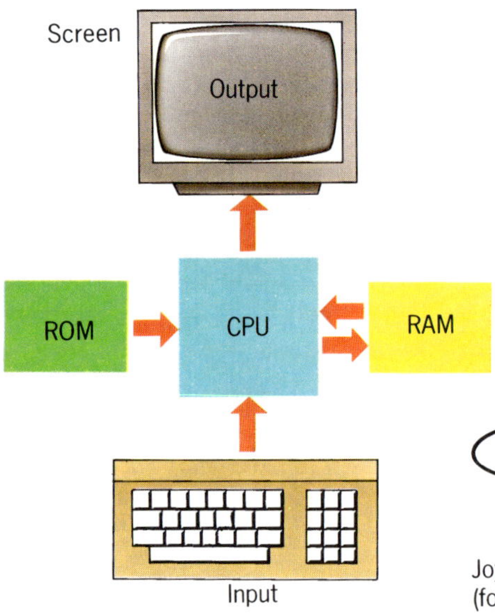

All computers work in more or less the same way. They have four basic parts – the 'input', the 'memory', 'central processing unit' (CPU) and the 'output'. The input is usually a keyboard, like that on a typewriter. It is used to feed a program of instructions into the computer and also data (information) such as numbers or words. The data and instructions go to a part of the computer's memory called the RAM. Here they are stored until they are ready to be used by the central processing unit. There is another part of the computer's memory called the ROM. This memory unit contains instructions that operate the central processing unit.

The CPU takes the instructions and data from the memory and carries out a calculation. The result is sent back to the memory to wait until it is needed. When required, the CPU orders the results to be sent to the output unit – a screen or a printer.

A robot is a computer on the move. It is a machine that can be taught to do the same job over and over again. Computers control factory robots that can do jobs which are either too dangerous for people or which are dull and repetitive. The most advanced robots have sensors to enable them to gather information and alter their own programs if necessary.

ROBOTS ON SCREEN
The robots we see on films and television are not real robots at all. Most, like the Daleks from the television series *Dr Who* (above), are models worked by people. Making real computerized robots would be too expensive.

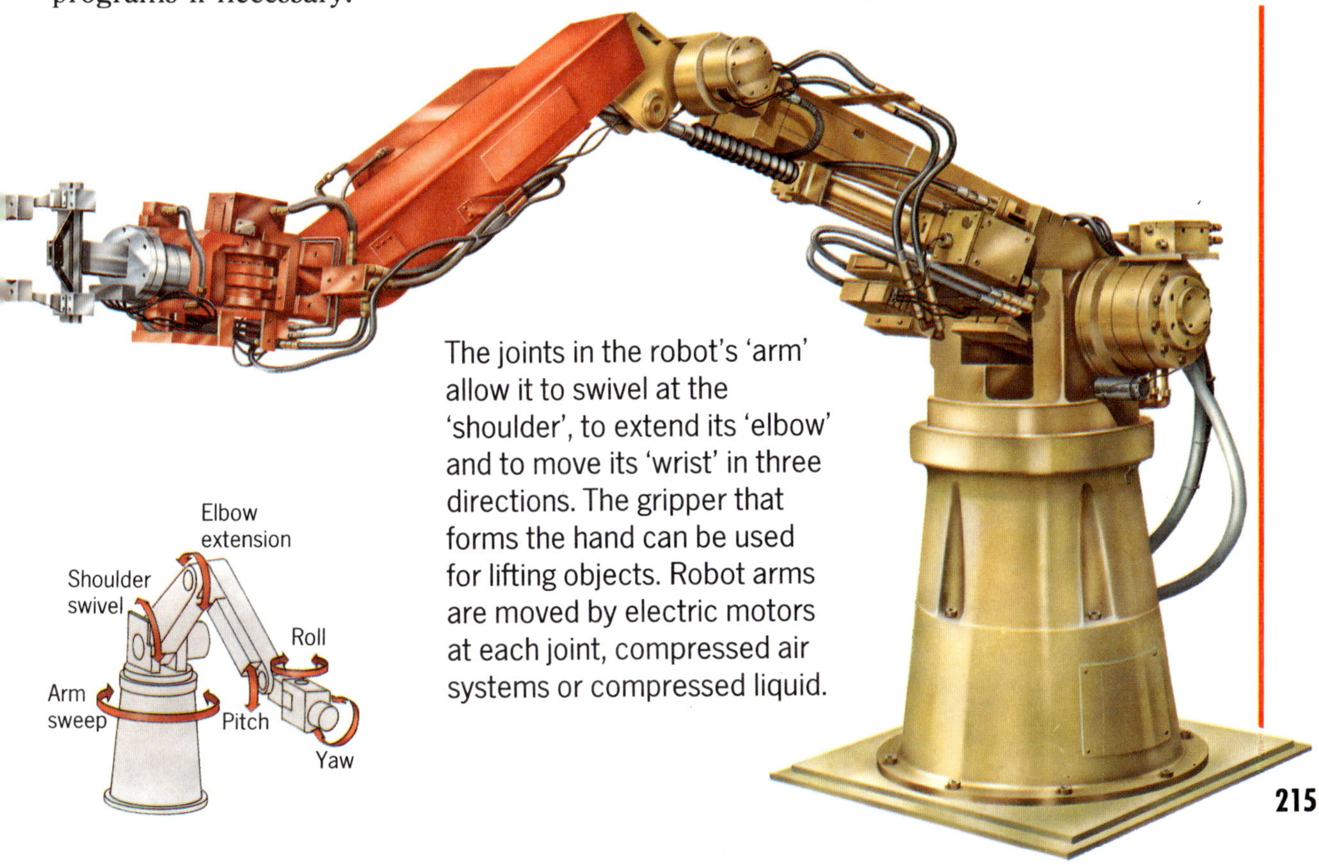

The joints in the robot's 'arm' allow it to swivel at the 'shoulder', to extend its 'elbow' and to move its 'wrist' in three directions. The gripper that forms the hand can be used for lifting objects. Robot arms are moved by electric motors at each joint, compressed air systems or compressed liquid.

HUMAN BIOLOGY

HUMAN BODY
How do the body's systems – nerves, blood, digestion, glands and so on – keep the body working properly? (See page 218.)

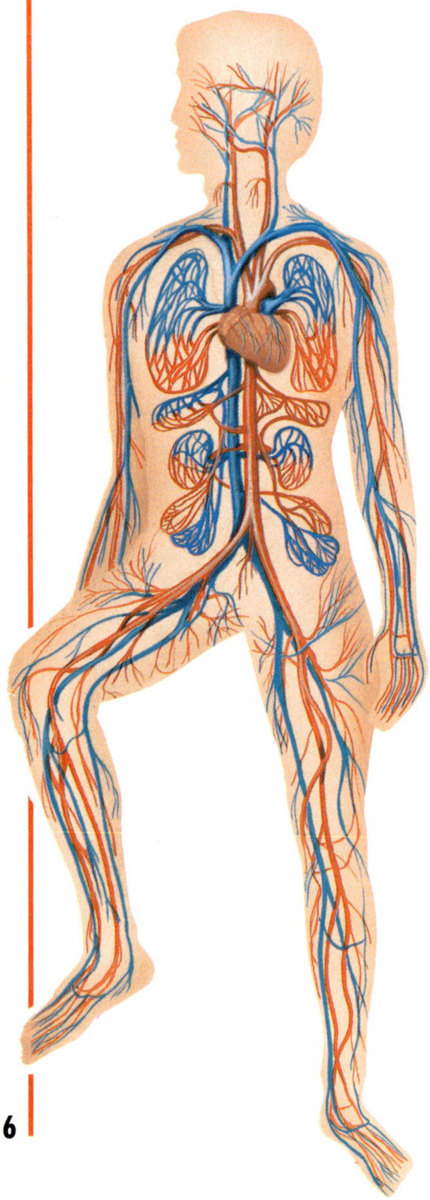

REPRODUCTION
How does a human baby develop and grow from a tiny fertilized egg cell? The reproduction of life is a miracle. (See page 222.)

DISEASES
The body may be attacked by many different diseases. How does it fight the microscopic carriers of disease? (See page 226.)

HEALTH AND FITNESS
What we eat, how we live, what exercise we take – good health depends on living sensibly. (See page 224.)

MEDICINE
Doctors have conquered many once-feared diseases, thanks to the medical revolution. (See page 228.)

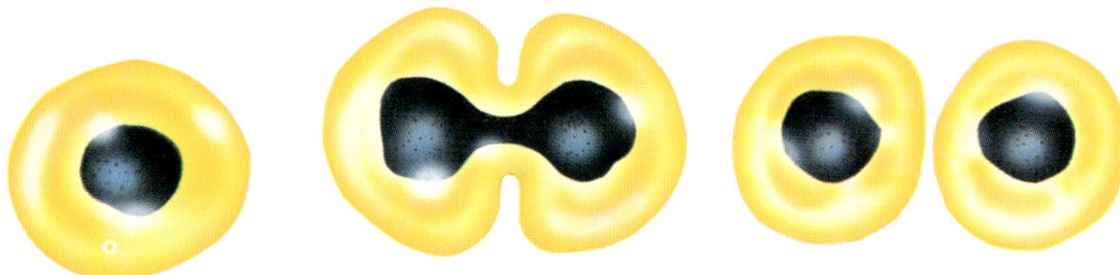

Cell division

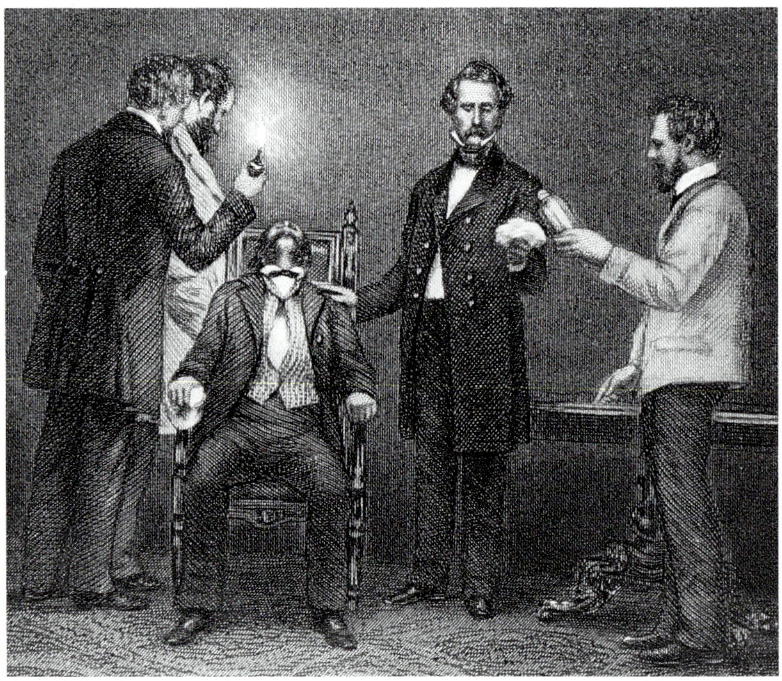

Your body is made up of millions of tiny living units called cells. Cells come in different shapes and sizes. Some are round, others are flat. But all cells have the same basic structure. Each kind of cell has its own job to do within your body. Some of the smallest are brain cells which are only 0.005 mm across.

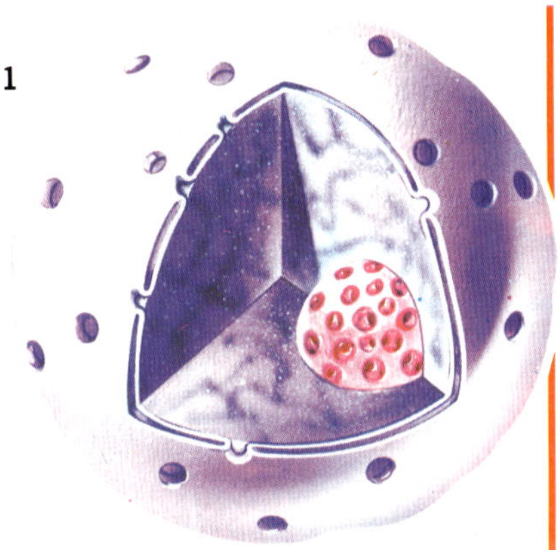

Some cells live only a few days, while others last for weeks, months or years. The control centre of the cell is the nucleus (*left*). It contains the coded instructions the cell needs, in the form of genes. Genes are made of a chemical called DNA. Our cells' genetic instructions determine what each of us looks like.

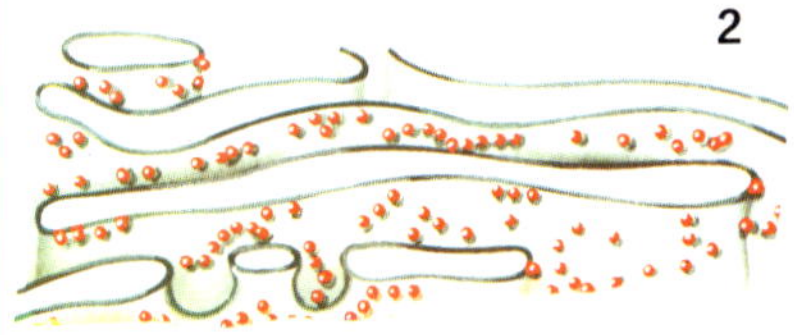

The cell's parts float in liquid *cytoplasm*, containing the *endoplasmic reticulum* (*above*) a system which carries substances throughout the cell.

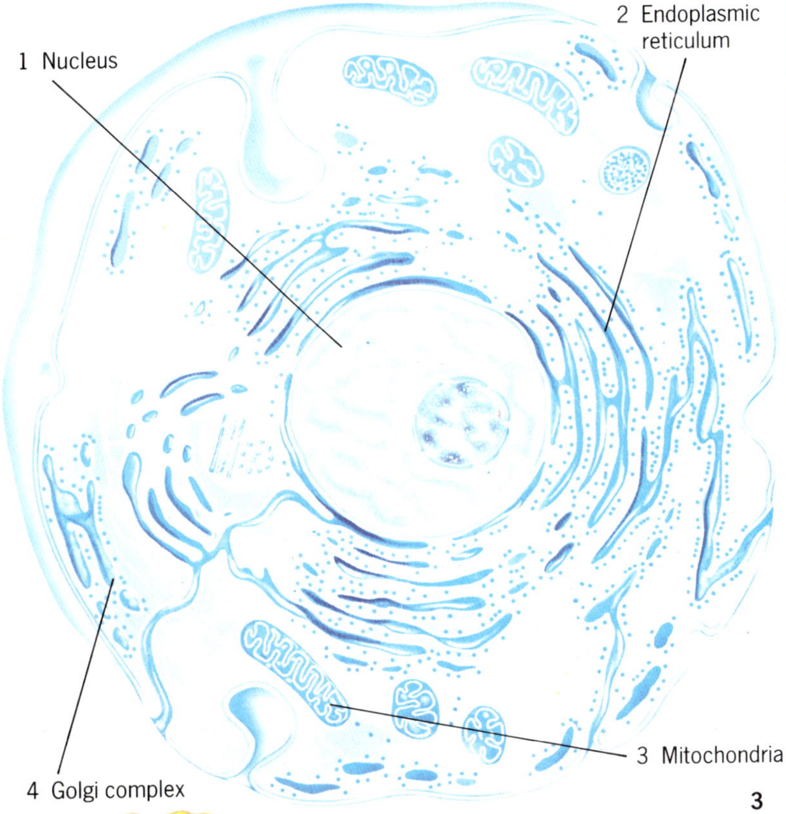

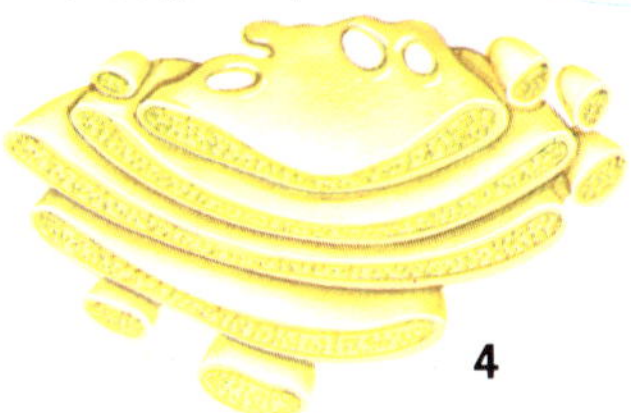

The golgi complex (*above*) is the part of the cell where substances the body needs are stored or prepared. It looks like a flat arrangement of pockets.

Above: Mitochondria are the cell's powerhouses. They release energy from the food and oxygen we take into our bodies. The cell uses this energy to keep working.

BODY MAKE-UP

The diagram below shows the most abundant chemical elements in the human body. About a fifth is carbon. Oxygen and hydrogen are found combined as water. About 70 per cent of your body is water.

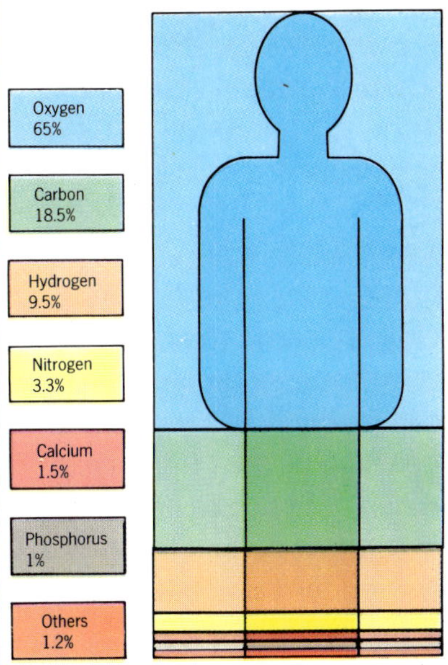

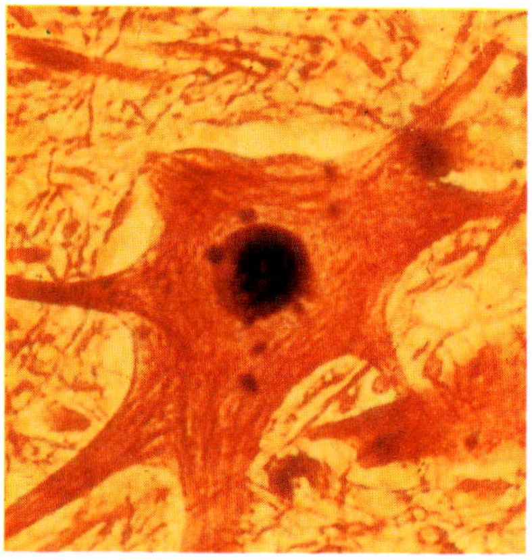

Above: A nerve cell seen through a microscope. The black spot is the nucleus, which contains all the instructions a cell needs to do its job.

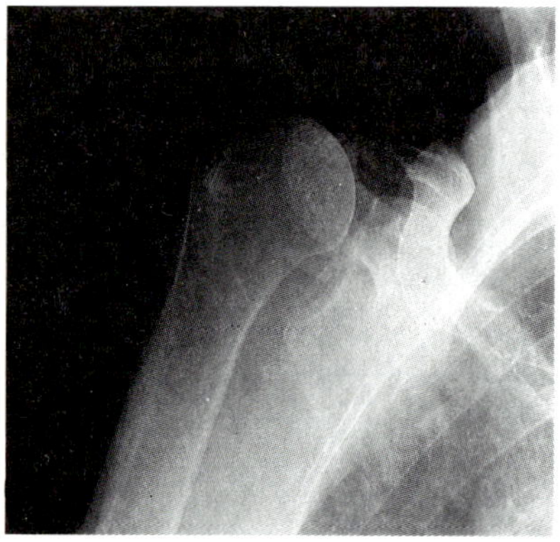

Above: This X-ray photograph shows a dislocated shoulder, where the upper bone of the arm – the humerus – has been pulled out of its socket.

Right: Adults have about 206 bones in their skeleton. The largest bone in the body is the thigh bone, or femur. Bones cannot bend, but where two bones meet they form a joint, which allows us to bend, twist or turn our bodies. If a joint is twisted too far, it may be pulled out of place, or dislocated.

Human Body

Our bodies are made of millions of tiny cells which are grouped together into separate tissues and organs. On the outside of our body is skin. This protects us from heat, cold, injury and germs. Inside we have a skeleton. Without our skeleton, our bodies would be quite floppy. Our bones give us our shape and allow us, with the help of our muscles, to move about. Bones also protect the soft parts inside us. The skull protects the brain, the ribs protect the lungs and the spine (backbone) protects the rope of nerves that runs down our backs and is linked to all parts of the body. The brain controls almost all we do. Some nerves bring it signals from the senses. Other nerves send signals from the brain to the muscles.

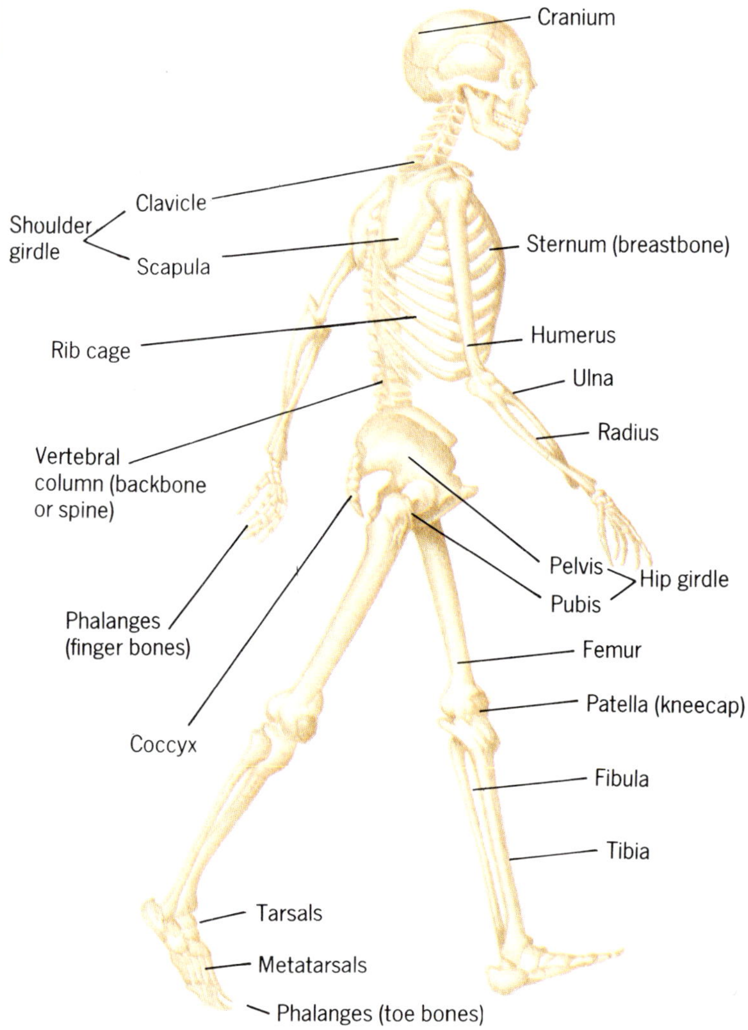

Bones are held together by *ligaments*, which are rather like elastic bands. Some bones are fastened so tightly that they cannot move. Others are connected by *joints*, which can open and shut like hinges. Muscles attached to the bones by *tendons* make the body move.

When muscles contract, they pull your bones and you can move your body. Muscles contract when they receive messages from your nerves.

Most muscles are long and thin and made up of many fibres – muscle cells – arranged in bundles. Usually one end of a muscle is attached to one side of a joint and the other end to the other side. Muscles can only pull, they cannot push. That is why most muscles come in pairs and work together. As one contracts, the other extends.

As well as being arranged in different shapes, there are different kinds of muscle tissue. One kind of muscle moves food along the digestive system, as well as doing other jobs in the body. Another type of muscle keeps the heart beating. Some muscles work automatically, others are controlled by messages from the brain.

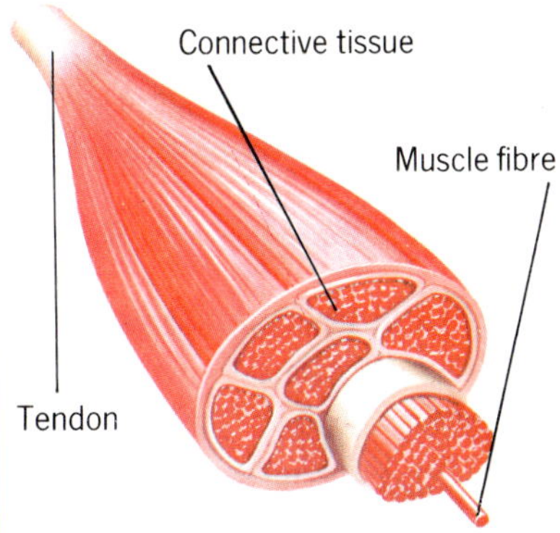

Above: A cross-section through a skeletal or voluntary muscle which moves in response to messages from the brain. The muscles are made up of fibres, each in contact with a nerve. The contraction of each tiny filament or fibre causes the whole muscle to contract.

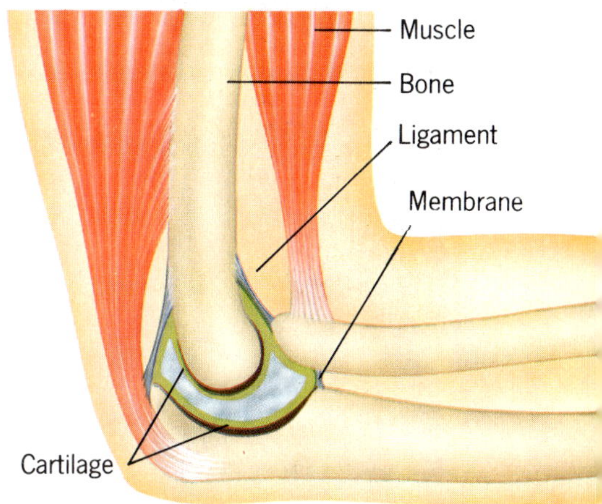

Different kinds of joint allow bones to move in different ways. Hinge joints, like the elbow (*above*) and knee can only move in one direction. The bones are held together by ligaments and by muscles; their ends are covered with soft, tough cartilage, to prevent them from grinding against each other. Liquid called synovial fluid lubricates them, as oil does a hinge.

SOME OF THE MAIN HUMAN MUSCLES

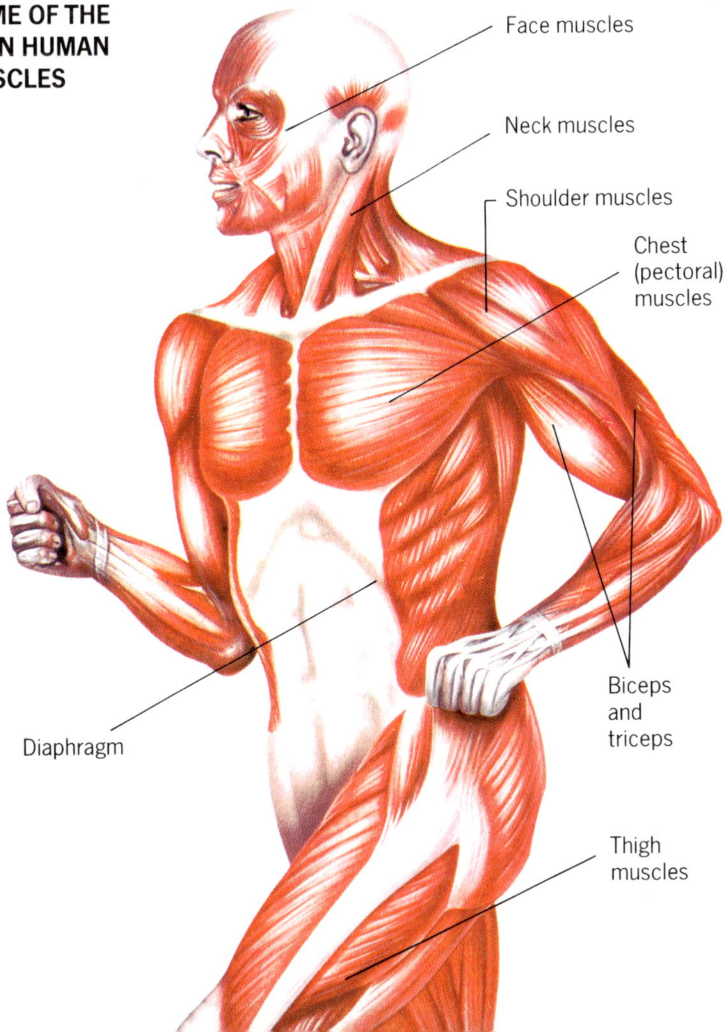

Below: The main vessels of the blood or circulatory system. Arteries (shown in red) take blood containing food and oxygen from the heart to the cells of the body. Veins (shown in blue) carry blood back to the heart. The heart is the pump which powers the whole blood system.

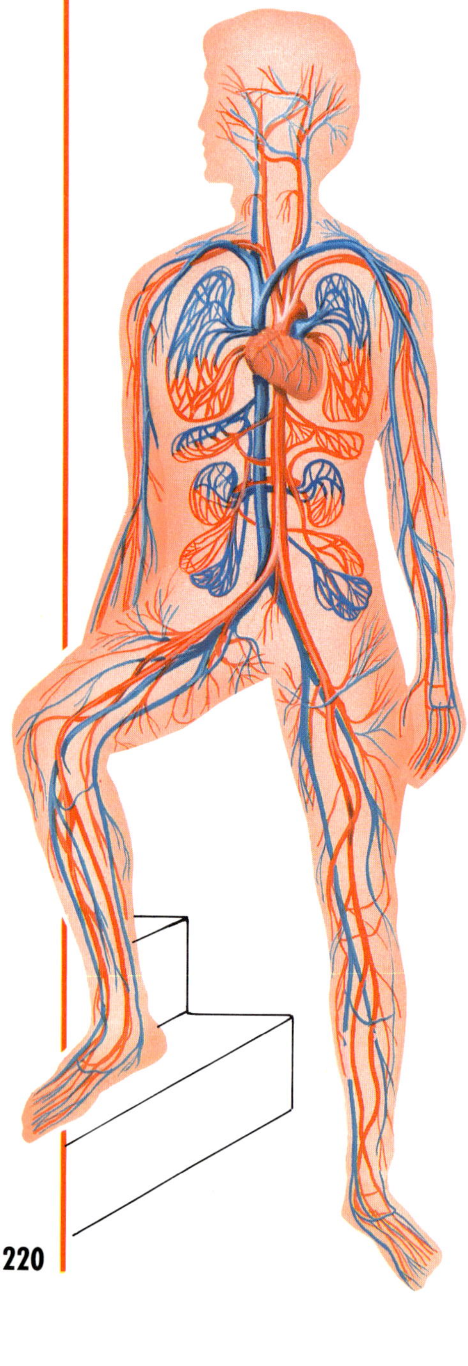

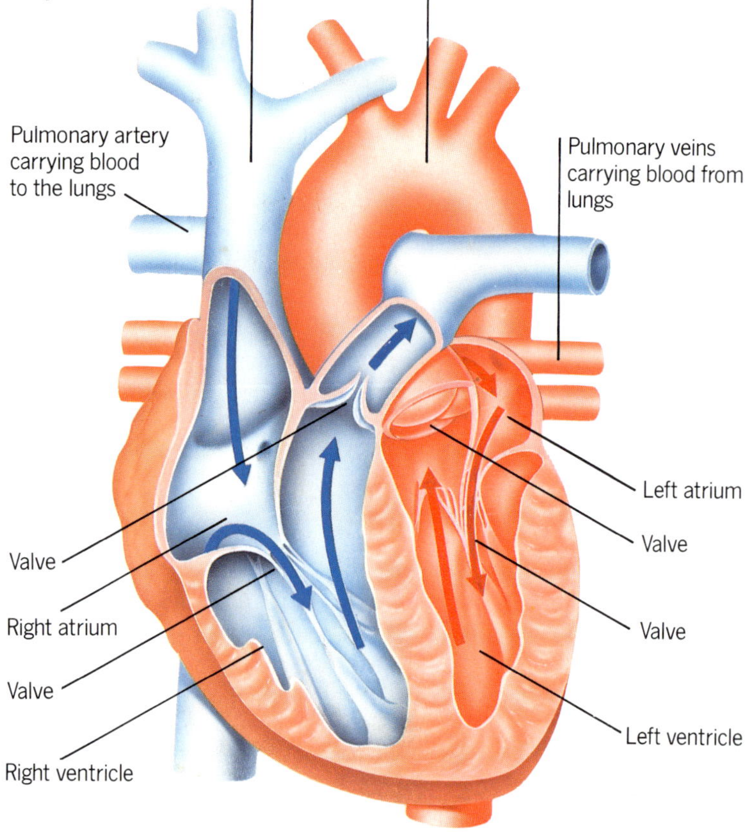

Above: Arrows show how blood is pumped through the heart.

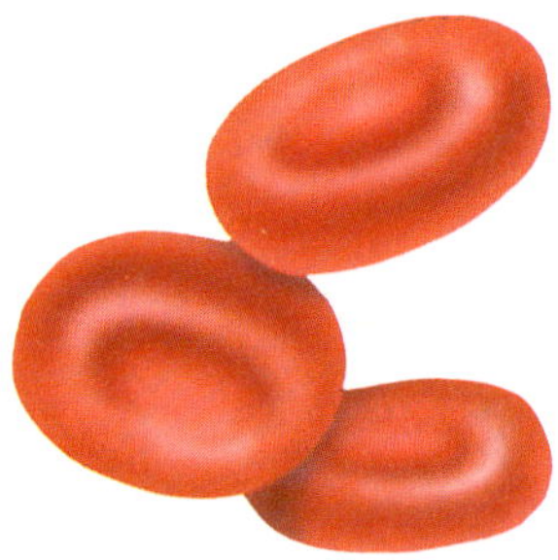

Blood contains red cells (*left*), white cells and tiny platelets, all floating in liquid called plasma. The red blood cells are the oxygen-carriers.

The heart is a bag of extra strong muscle that pumps blood around the body. It is divided into four parts, a left and right atrium above a left and right ventricle. Blood fresh from the lungs enters the left atrium and is forced down through a valve into the left ventricle. From there it is forced into the body's main artery, the aorta, and out of the heart ready to flow around the body. On the other side 'stale' blood from the body enters the right atrium, passes into the right ventricle and is forced out towards the lungs where it will dump its carbon dioxide and at the same time pick up vital oxygen.

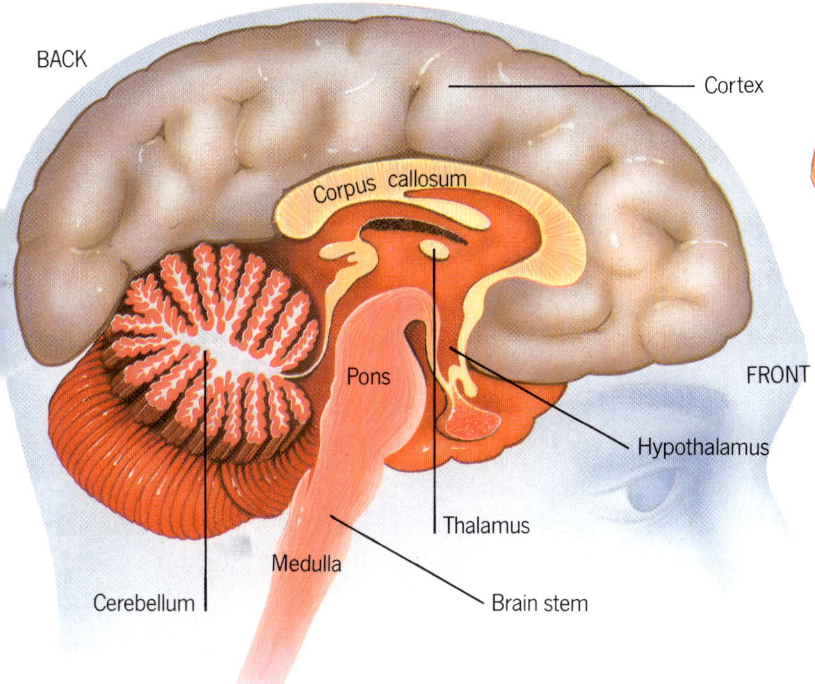

Above: Different parts of the brain control various activities of our bodies. The cortex, the largest area, controls intelligence, personality and our senses.

Below: Hormones or chemical messages reinforce the nervous system. Adrenalin, for example, raises the level of sugar in the blood allowing this athlete to run faster.

Above: The brain, spinal cord and nerves form the nervous system, which keeps the body working properly. Nerves carry messages to and from the brain where data is processed and some is stored. The parts of the body have differing amounts of nerves. If the number of nerves corresponded to the size of the organ, our bodies would look something like this.

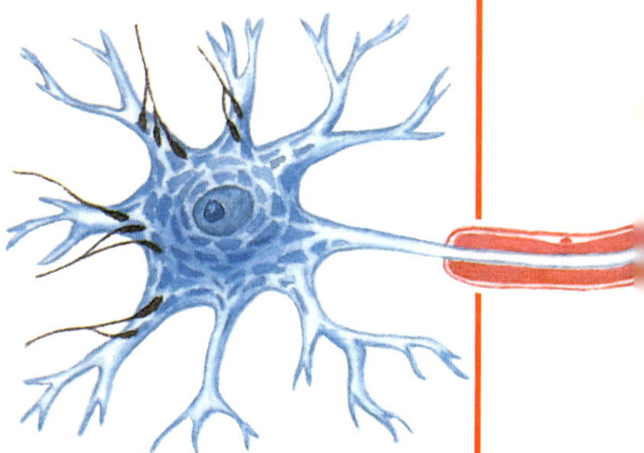

Above: A nerve cell, or neurone, is part of the body's messenger network. Much of the brain and spinal cord are made of neurones.

Reproduction

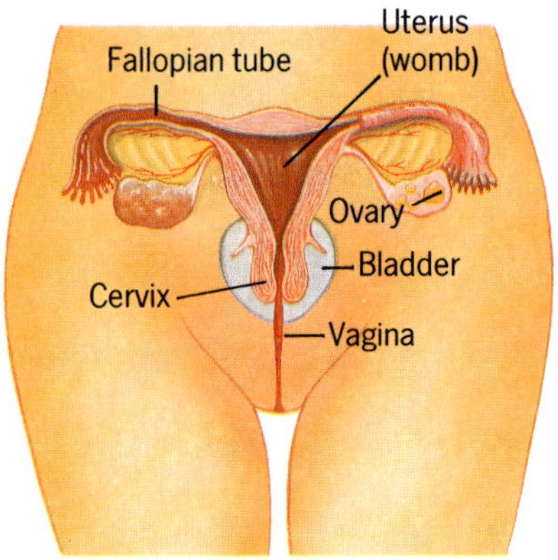

A cross-section through the lower part of the body of a woman (*above*) and a man (*below*) to show the reproductive organs.

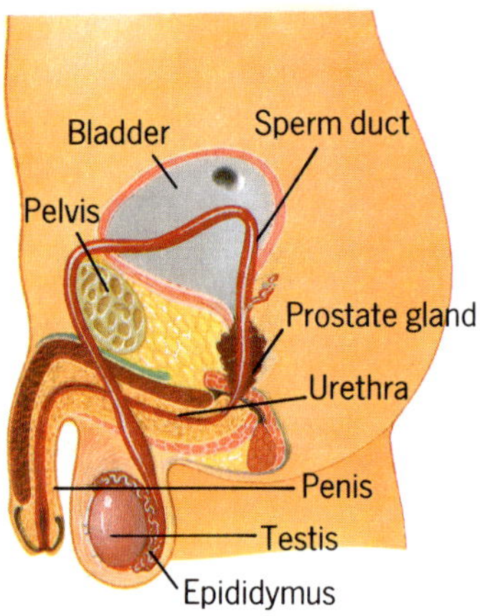

All animals and plants can reproduce, that is, they can make other living things like themselves. All but the simplest animals reproduce sexually, by producing special sex cells. When a male cell joins with and fertilizes a female cell, this grows into a new individual. In animals the male cells are called sperms and the female cells are called eggs.

A human baby begins life when a sperm cell from its father meets an egg cell (or ovum) from its mother inside the mother's body. Once a single sperm cell has penetrated an egg cell, no more sperm can enter. The nuclei of the two cells merge (fertilization) and the fertilized egg travels down the Fallopian tube towards the uterus, or womb. On the way down, it divides first into two cells, then into four, then eight and so on until a ball of at least 64 cells has been formed.

The ball of cells embeds itself in the uterus lining, which has thickened in preparation. The baby develops very quickly. After four weeks its heart begins to beat. Some cells form the umbilical cord, which joins the baby to its mother through a special organ in the uterus called the placenta. Other cells form the amnion – a 'bag' filled with fluid which protects the baby. After 12 weeks the foetus has all its essential features and it grows for the remaining six months, after which it will be born.

THE MENSTRUAL CYCLE

Each month, the uterus lining thickens as it prepares to receive a fertilized ovum. If it is not fertilized, the lining is not needed so it passes out of the woman's body through the vagina, along with the egg and some blood. This loss is called menstruation, or a 'period'. After menstruation, a new uterus lining starts to form, ready to receive the next possible fertilized egg. The menstruation cycle takes about four weeks although the precise length of the cycle varies slightly from woman to woman.

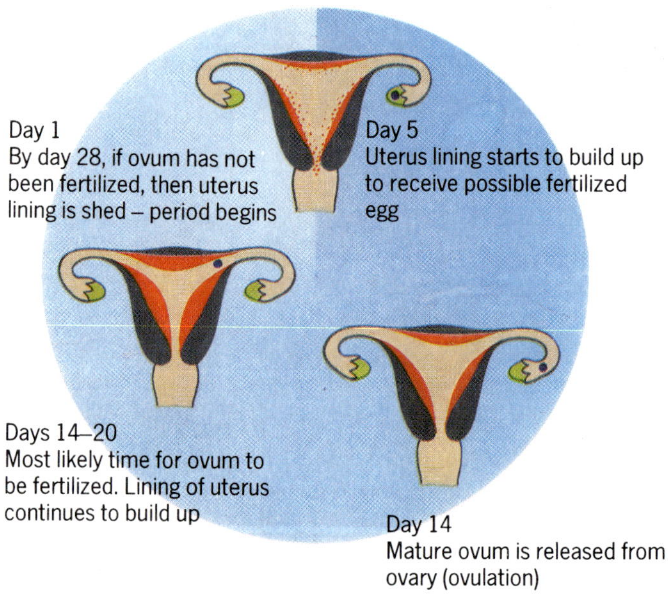

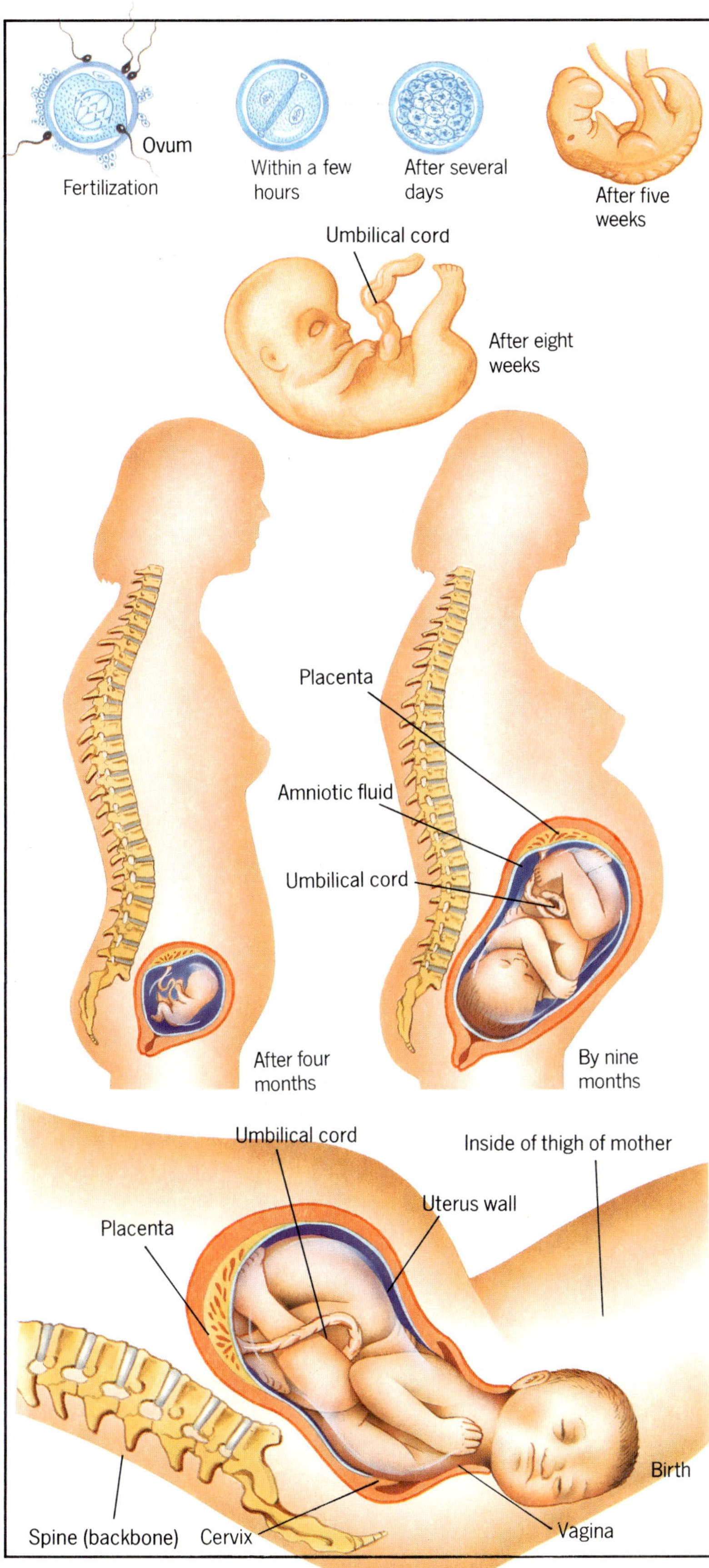

DEVELOPMENT OF A PREGNANCY

After 8 weeks, the embryo is about 2·5 cm (1 in) long and is called a foetus. After about 12 weeks, it has all its organs. During the next 6 months, it grows larger and develops 'details' such as fingernails and hair. At about the fifth month of development the foetus begins to move its limbs and can be felt to kick. At this stage the baby can hear, tell light from dark, swallow and suck its thumb. Some unborn babies even get hiccups. At about 6 months the baby turns itself around in the uterus so that its head is pointing downwards – the position in which it is ready to be born. Birth normally takes place about 9 months after the baby began its development as a fertilized cell.

REPRODUCTION MARVELS

- An ovum measures about 0·1–0·2 mm across.
- Each sperm cell consists of a 'head', which contains its nucleus, and a 'tail'. A sperm is about 0·05 mm long.
- The uterus is only about the size and shape of a pear, but during pregnancy it can stretch to about 30 cm (12 in) in length.
- It is through the umbilical cord that food and oxygen pass to the baby from the mother's bloodstream. Waste products from the growing baby pass back to be disposed of by the mother's body.
- Sperm 'swim' by thrashing their tails. It takes them about 2 hours to reach the Fallopian tubes. As many as 300 million sperm may start the journey, but only a few hundred reach the Fallopian tubes and only one sperm fertilizes the egg.
- The testes are outside the body in the scrotum because the cooler temperature helps the production of sperm.

Right: To stay healthy, you need a balanced diet, enough sleep, fresh air and exercise. Cycling is good for promoting strong muscles, good breathing and general staying power.

BODY FACTS

About 70% of your body is water. You could live for 2 to 3 weeks without food, but without water, you could die in 2 or 3 days. An adult loses 2 to 3 litres of water (about half a gallon) every day in sweat, urine and through breathing. About half of this is replaced by drinking, and the rest comes from foods – for example, melon, marrow and lettuce are about 90% water.

Muscles account for 40% of your total body weight. Muscles produce heat when they use energy, which is why you get hot when you exercise. The harder the muscles work, the more energy they need. This is why you pant and your heart beats faster as you exercise – your body is working to supply muscles with extra food and oxygen.

Children need about 3 or 4 grams of protein for every kilogram (about 2 pounds) of their body's weight because they are growing. Teenagers need even more than this.

The energy produced from different foods is measured in kilocalories (Calories) or kilojoules. (1 Calorie = 4·2 kilojoules.) A glass of milk contains 150 Cal while a boiled egg has 80 Cal. The number of calories a person needs depends on how active they are. For example, swimming uses about 600 Cal an hour, but sleeping uses only 70 Cal an hour. On average, a man needs about 3000 calories each day; a woman needs 2200 calories and a child of 4 years old needs about 1600.

Health and Fitness

Just as a car cannot work without fuel, the body cannot work without food. It gets the energy it needs to drive itself from a well-balanced diet. Different types of food contain different nutrients which are used for particular jobs in your body, so everybody needs a good balance of each type. Your diet must include proteins, carbohydrates, fats, mineral salts, vitamins and water.

More than 10 per cent of your body tissue is made of protein – a body-building substance found in fish, meat, cheese, nuts, eggs and milk. You need proteins to grow and also to repair and replace damaged cells. Protein is important for muscles too, providing them with energy.

Carbohydrates also supply us with energy. The main types of carbohydrate are sugars and starch. Bread and potatoes contain starch; fruit and jam contain sugar called glucose. Only glucose can be used by the body for energy, so all other forms of carbohydrates have to be turned into glucose inside the body by the digestive process.

VITAMIN	FOUND IN . . .	NEEDED FOR . . .
A	Milk, butter, eggs, green vegetables, fish oil, liver (and carotene in carrots)	Fighting disease and seeing in dim light
B_1 (thiamine)	Yeast and wheatgerm (whole wheat bread)	All 'B' vitamins needed for healthy appetite, energy production in cells and healthy nerves and skin
B_2	Yeast	
9 other 'B' vitamins	Milk, meat and green vegetables	
C	Oranges, lemons, tomatoes, black-currants, strawberries and fresh vegetables	Healthy blood and gums, healing wounds and possibly protection against colds
D	Cod-liver oil, cream, egg yolks (and with sunlight, fat below the skin forms vitamin D)	Strong bones and teeth
E	Whole wheat bread, brown rice and butter	Not fully understood
K	Green vegetables, liver	Clotting blood

If you eat more carbohydrates than your body needs, the extra amount is stored as fat. The body can later convert this fat store into energy, but eating too much carbohydrate for too long can make you put on weight.

To keep all your muscles fit and strong you need exercise. To keep the chemical processes in your body going you need small amounts of 15 different vitamins. A summary of vitamins and their uses is shown above.

Monday				
Tuesday				
Wednesday				
Thursday				
Friday				
Saturday				
Sunday				

1
2
3

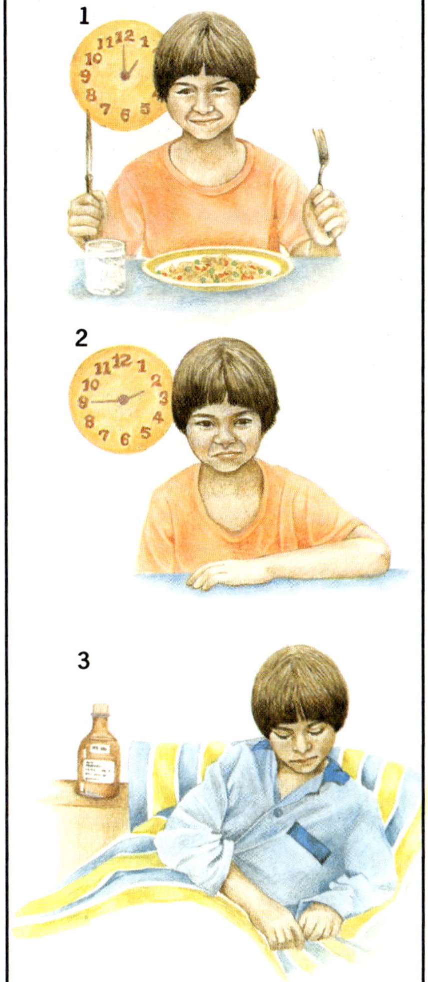

FOOD POISONING

Food poisoning results from eating or drinking contaminated food or water (1). Various bacteria can cause this, for example salmonella. Food poisoning develops quickly – between 30 minutes and 2 days; symptoms are sickness, diarrhoea and stomach ache (2). Do not eat too much while you are suffering from it; avoid drinking milk, but drink plenty of water. If food poisoning lasts for more than 2 days, you should see a doctor (3).

Left: Everyone needs a balanced diet containing different vitamins. Keeping a diet diary is a good way to check your intake.

Diseases

Our bodies do not work perfectly all the time. Sometimes we feel ill as the body fights back against disease. Most common illnesses are caused either by bacteria or by viruses – tiny organisms which invade our bodies. Our defence or immune system is used to fight the illnesses these cause, such as influenza, food poisoning or measles.

Bacteria and viruses can enter the body in several ways. They may be in the air you breathe or the food and water you eat and drink. They reproduce inside your body and many make you feel ill as they damage your tissues, or

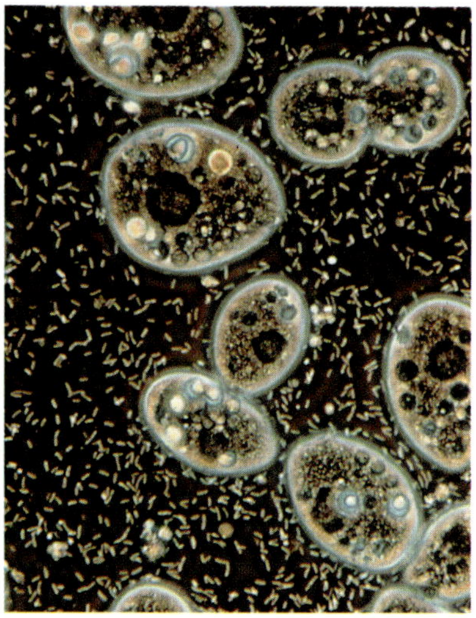

Above: Bacteria are tiny organisms that can measure just 0·001 mm across. They exist all around us and most are harmless. When harmful bacteria reproduce in your body they cause illness as they damage tissue or produce poisons. Bacteria cause both tonsillitis and pneumonia.

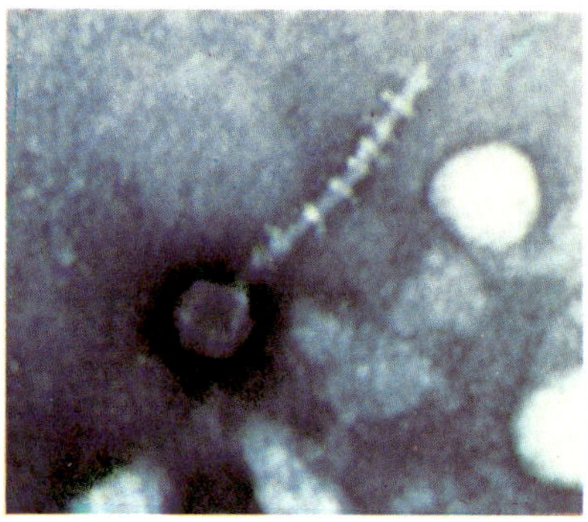

Above: Viruses are much smaller than bacteria. They can only grow inside living body cells, which they destroy as they grow. Then, signs or symptoms of a disease develop. These may be spots, a rash or pains. Influenza, measles, chickenpox and polio are caused by viruses.

THE LYMPH SYSTEM

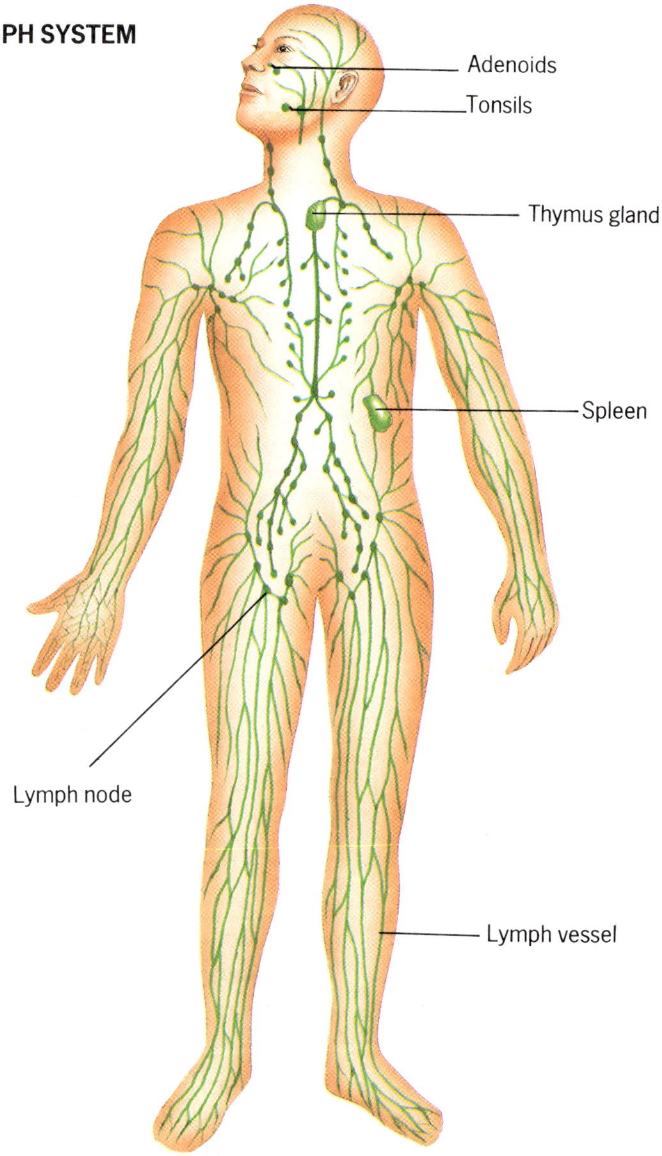

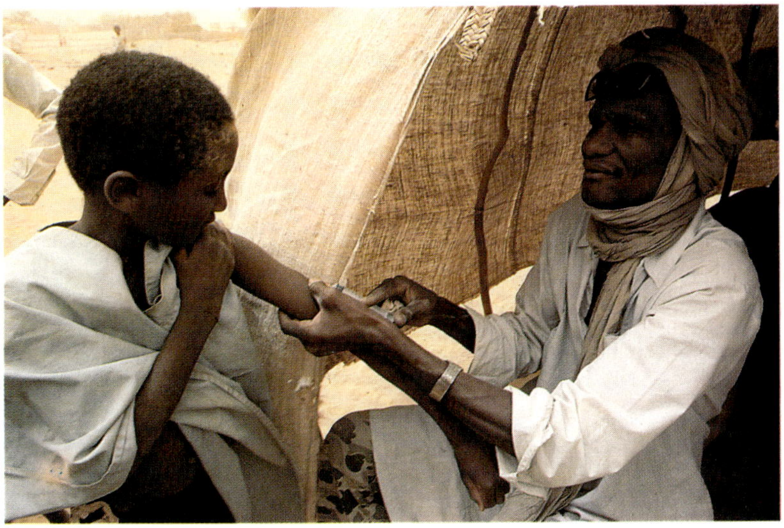

Left: The lymph system runs throughout the body. Lymph nodes may swell when they fight an infection.

Above: Vaccines make the body produce antibodies. The body is then prepared to fight real disease should it strike.

produce poisons. They can enter your body through the skin if you cut yourself. To guard your body openings, you have eyelids and tears protecting the eyes, wax in your ears and hairs in your nose. If these defences are overcome, the body has ways of fighting viruses and bacteria.

In your bloodstream are white blood cells. Some destroy bacteria by eating them. When you have an illness, extra white blood cells are made and are rushed to the trouble spot. These white blood cells are made in the bone marrow. Other white blood cells called antibodies are made in the lymph system, which is also called the immune system. When you are ill, antibodies are released into the blood-stream. They prevent the bacteria and viruses from reproducing, and capture them so that they can be eaten by other white blood cells. The lymph or immune system is a powerful defence organizer. It can make thousands of different antibodies. Each type of bacterium or virus is tackled by a particular type of antibody.

Doctors have developed drugs and other kinds of treatment to fight many diseases. Some, like smallpox, have been wiped out completely. Others, including the common cold and influenza, and more serious diseases, still remain to be tackled. The most common serious illnesses in richer countries are those affecting the heart and blood circulation. They are usually caused by things such as stress, smoking, too much food and too little exercise.

Above: Simple precautions can stop disease spreading. Cover your mouth if you sneeze or cough; wash your hands before touching food; keep food from flies and mice; don't share food or drink; don't leave food uncovered in a warm place, otherwise bacteria and viruses can pass on and thrive.

Medicine

Above: The Chinese practice of acupuncture is based on inserting needles into precise points on the body.

Above: Andreas Vesalius (1514–64), a Flemish doctor, made the first accurate drawings of the human body.

Right: Louis Pasteur treated a child with his vaccination against rabies in 1885.

When you are ill, the doctor may prescribe medicines to relieve the symptoms of the illness. For example, aspirin can help to get rid of a headache and lozenges may soothe a sore throat. From very early times people have searched for medicines to heal wounds and cure diseases. The first drugs came from berries and herbs which had healing powers. Magic was also thought to be important.

The Greek doctor Hippocrates, who lived about 2500 years ago, is often called the 'Father of Medicine'. The ancient Greeks and Romans knew what the inside of the human body looked like. But they did not know how the different parts worked, or what made them go wrong. Until the Middle Ages doctors thought that there were four liquids called 'humours' inside the body, and that if these liquids were not mixed properly, people became ill. They also believed disease was caused by 'bad air'.

Medicine made little progress until the 1600s, when doctors began studying anatomy (the parts of the body). By cutting up dead bodies, they began to find out how the body works. Since no one knew about germs, doctors did not bother very much about cleanliness. Many patients died because hospitals were dirty and unhygienic places.

Over the next 200 years progress in medicine was slow. But in the 1700s vaccination was discovered as a way of preventing disease, and later antiseptics were developed to kill harmful germs. Anaesthetics were used to stop people feeling pain during operations. In the 1900s the discovery of X-rays meant that doctors could examine the insides of their patients to find out what was wrong. Powerful new drugs called antibiotics, which attack bacteria without harming body cells, were also discovered.

These and other discoveries help to make the modern hospital very different from the hospitals of 100 years ago. Equipment such as 'heart and lung' machines is available to help doctors. Surgeons can 'transplant' kidneys and other organs from one person to another. Today doctors study diseases of the mind as well as diseases of the body.

There have been many amazing advances, such as the first heart transplant (1967), the invention of the CAT scanner (1973), the first 'test tube' baby (1978), and the first artificial heart transplant (1982). However, there are still many challenges facing doctors, and diseases for which there is as yet no cure, such as AIDS (Acquired Immune Deficiency Syndrome).

Below: Operations today are carried out in scrupulously hygienic conditions, using modern machinery and drugs.

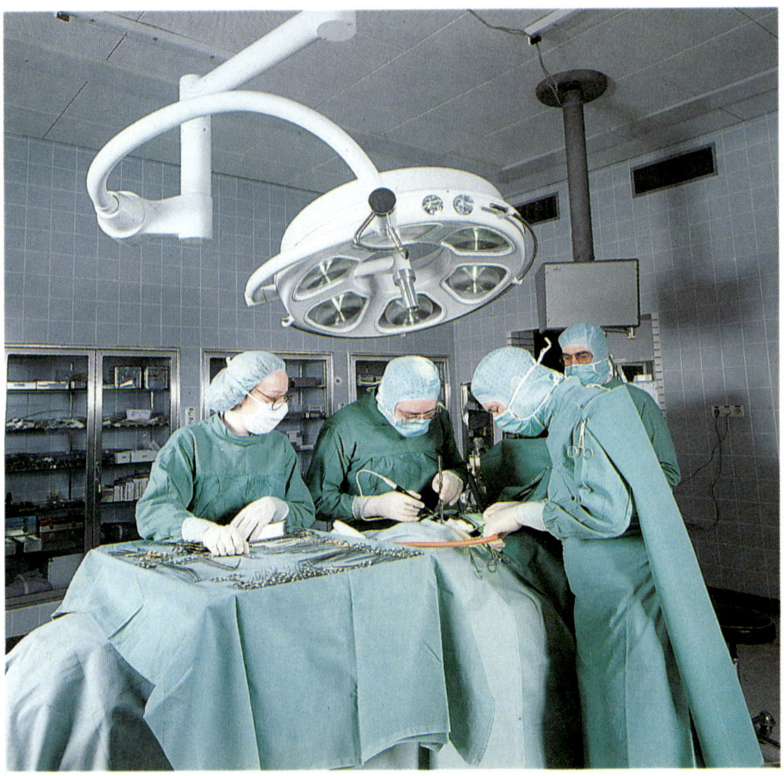

Below: The surgeon Joseph Lister developed a carbolic spray (1875) to kill harmful organisms in the air.

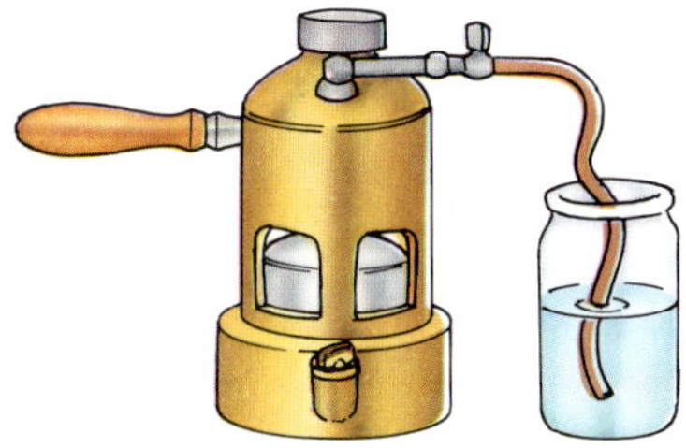

Below: A person whose own kidneys have stopped working may be treated by a machine that acts as an artificial kidney. This process of cleansing the blood is called renal dialysis.

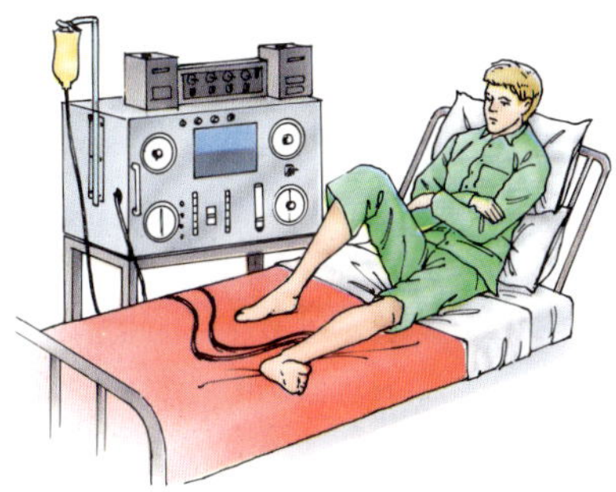

Below: The iron hooks and wooden stumps once used in place of lost limbs were replaced by flexible artificial limbs, forerunners of the lightweight plastic types fitted today.

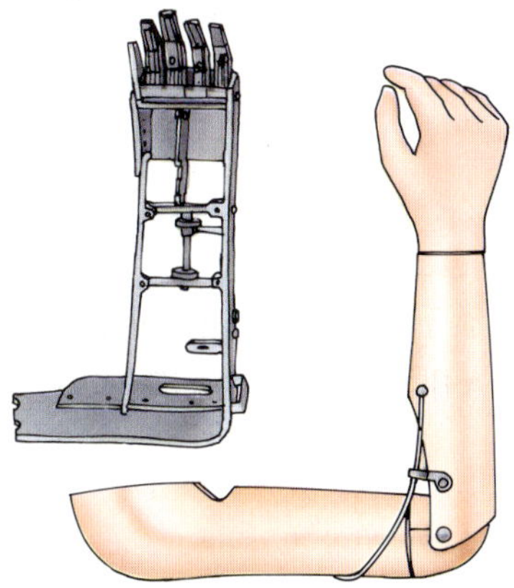

THE WORLD AND ITS PEOPLE

LAND AND SEA

How are mountains and volcanoes made? What causes ocean currents and waves? The face of Earth is always changing, as the planet ages. (See page 232.)

WEATHER

The weather affects how people live, how plants and animals behave. How is weather made? Why does it rain? What are clouds? (See page 236.)

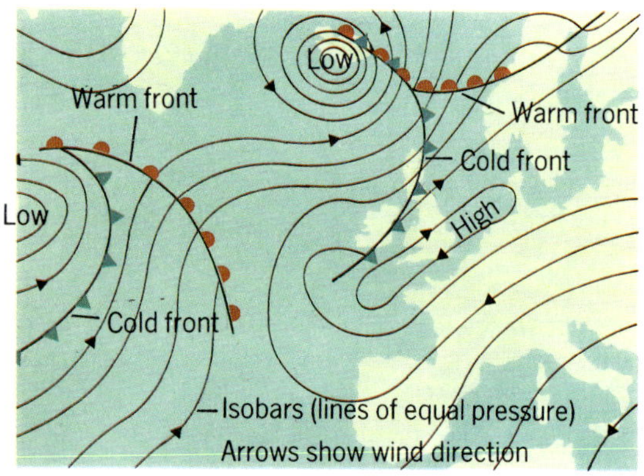

ENVIRONMENT

Each of the Earth's environments has its own climate, vegetation and animal life. Looking after the environment is our responsibility. (See page 238.)

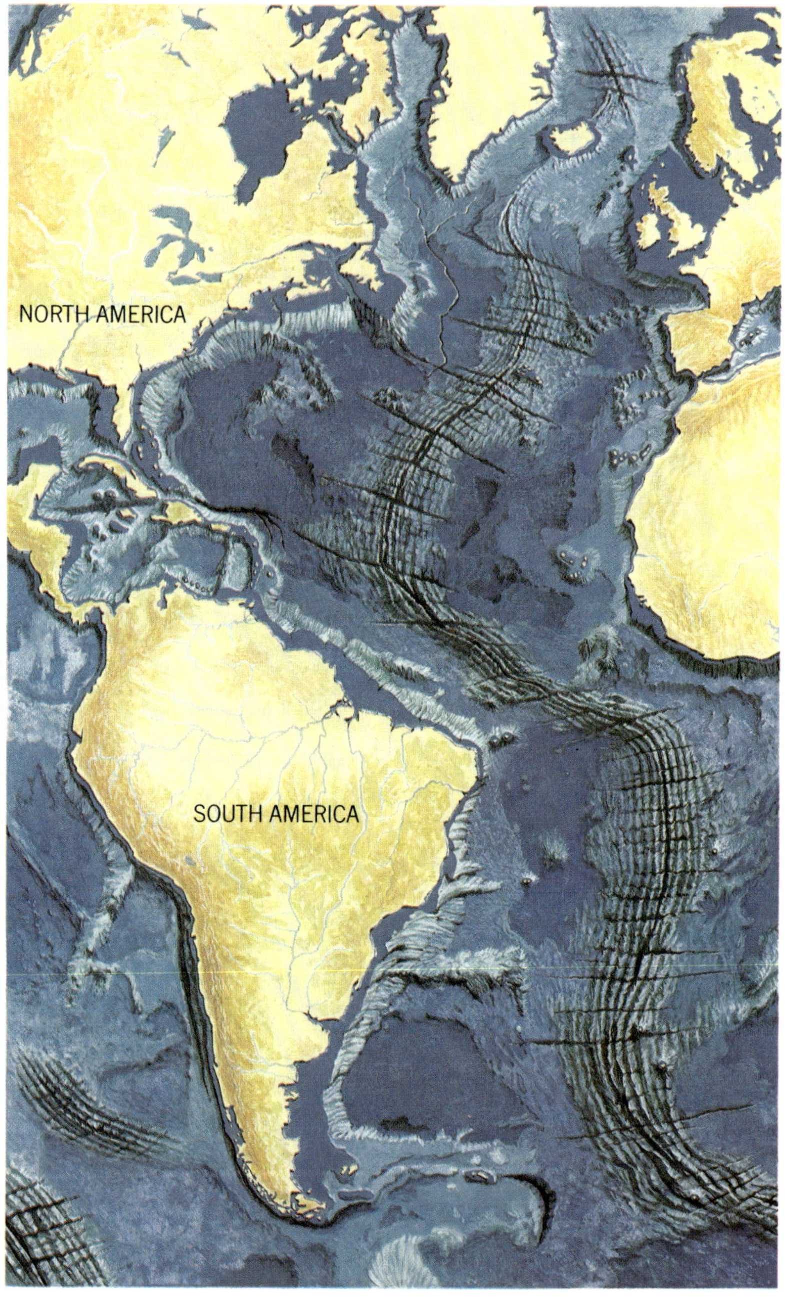

PEOPLES
Humans are the most widespread species. There are more than five billion people on our planet. (See page 242.)

BELIEFS
Religious beliefs and many different customs have influenced human society. (See page 244.)

SPORT
In the past few people had time for leisure. Now sports and pastimes are enjoyed worldwide. (See page 246.)

LAWS AND GOVERNMENT
We live by laws. Who makes the laws, and how did governments and parliaments come about? (See page 248.)

TRADE
People in many countries earn their living making, buying and selling goods. The Industrial Revolution is still going on all over the world. (See page 250.)

Land and Sea

Geologists and geophysicists, the scientists who study the Earth, believe that it is made of several layers. The crust or outer layer is comparatively thin. It is thicker beneath the continents, which are made of lighter rocks than the ocean floors. Beneath the crust is the mantle, which is probably slightly liquid and moves very slowly. This movement is gradually shifting the continents and the ocean floors. The evidence of this today is in earthquakes and volcanic eruptions. Geologists believe that millions of years ago the continents were joined together, and have drifted apart.

The core of the Earth is thought to be partly molten and partly solid. It is probably mainly made of iron and nickel. Like the mantle, the core is almost certainly moving – and its movement may make the Earth act like a magnet, causing a compass needle to point north.

Two hundred million years ago, all the continents lay jammed close together to form one mighty mass of land. Geographers call it Pangaea, meaning 'all Earth'. By 100 million years ago Pangaea had begun to break up as conti-

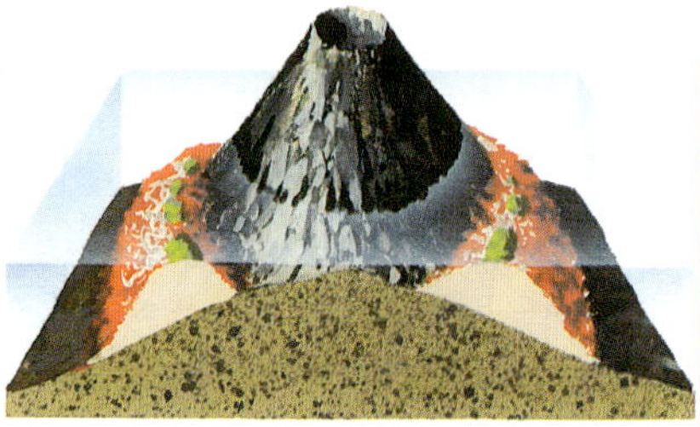

1. Volcanic islands are shaped like cones.

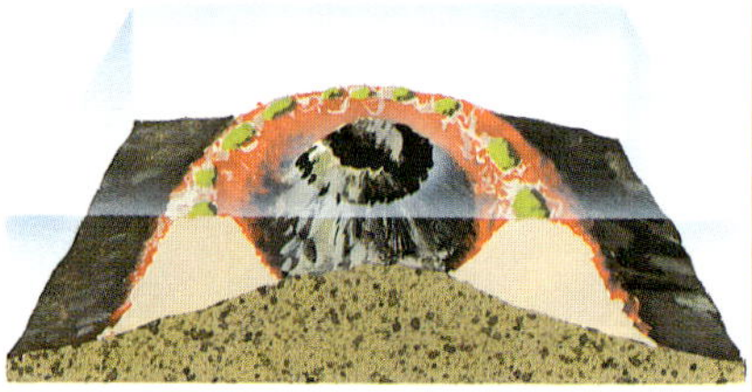

2. In time the volcanic island may sink below the water.

3. Only a coral reef, or atoll, remains above the water.

Below: Inside a volcano molten rock or magma is forced up through the Earth's crust. Cones of ash and lava (hot, liquid rock), domes or batholiths and geysers may result.

Key: 1 Volcanic cone. **2** Volcano's vent. **3** Magma. **4** Lava flow. Magma may penetrate the rock strata to form **5** a dyke, **6** a sill, **7** a batholith. **8** Extinct volcano. **9** Geyser.

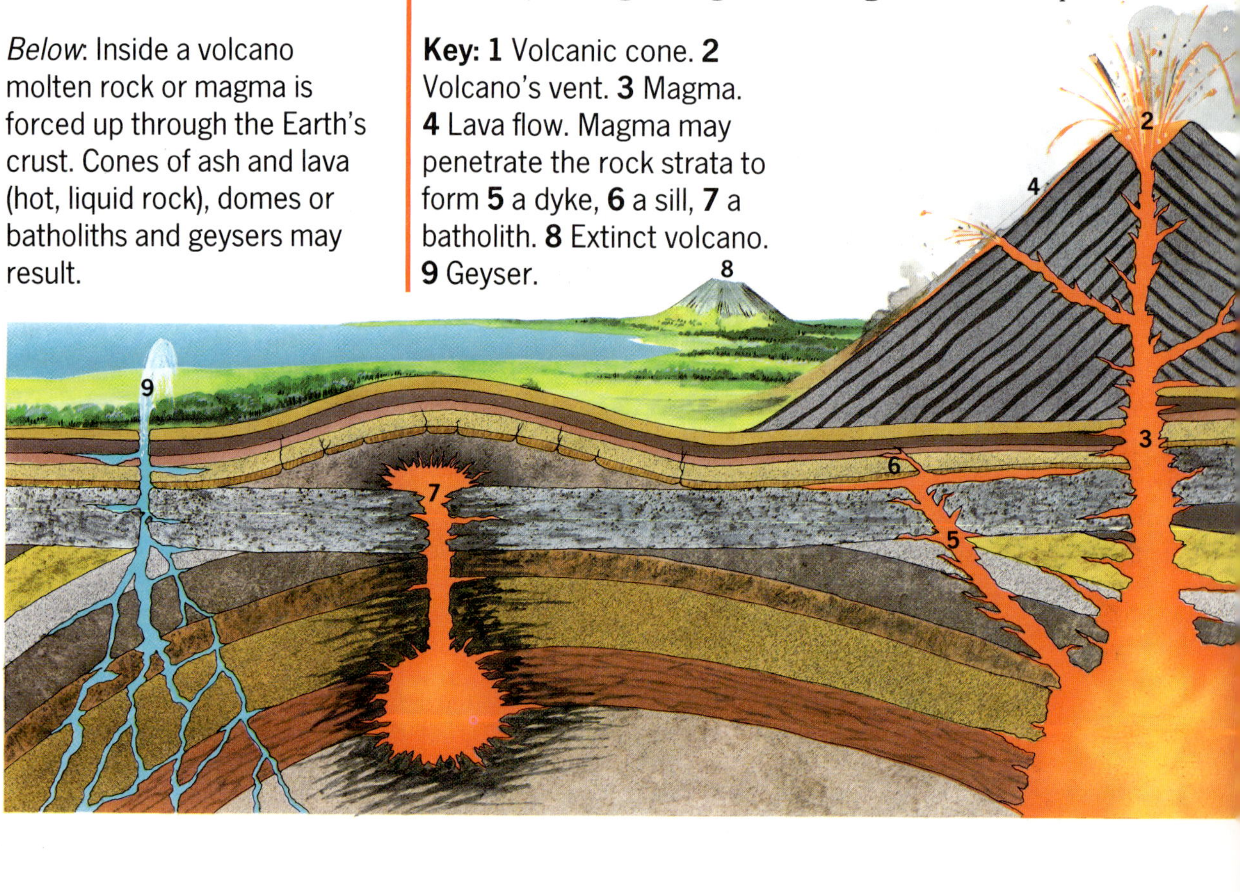

nents drifted apart. For a while there may have been two super-continents. North America, Europe and most of Asia formed one northern continent called Laurasia. South America, Africa, India, Antarctica and Australia formed a southern continent: Gondwanaland.

By 50 million years ago South America became a giant island. India was drifting north towards Asia. Today, a corridor of land joins North and South America. India has collided with Asia (pushing up the Himalayan mountains).

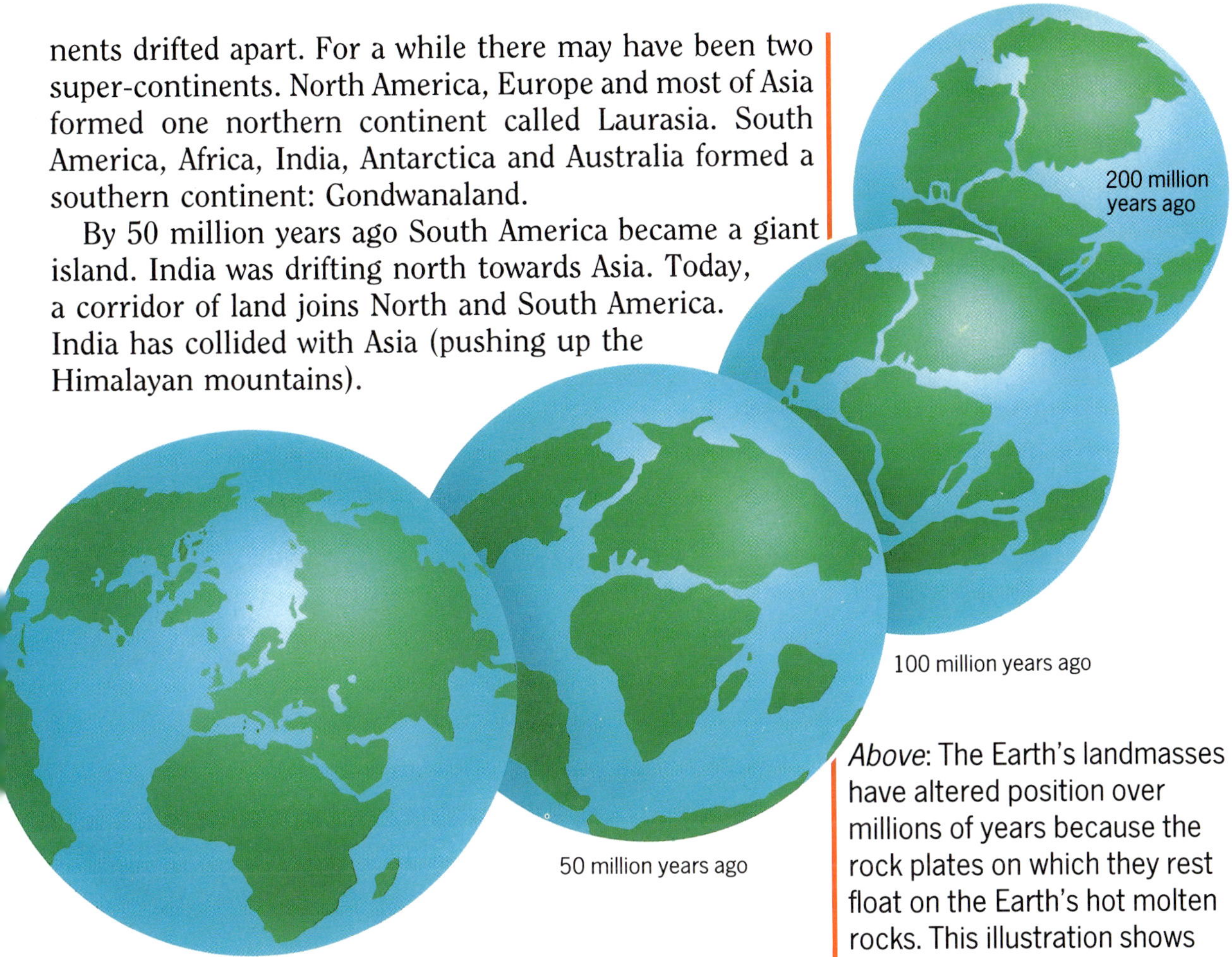

Above: The Earth's landmasses have altered position over millions of years because the rock plates on which they rest float on the Earth's hot molten rocks. This illustration shows how the continents we know today have taken shape gradually over the past 200 million years.

Right: Caves are formed by the wearing away of rock by water. Caverns form in limestone because underground streams flow through the rock and slowly dissolve away the limestone. Stalactites and stalagmites form as water drips slowly from the cave roof, leaving tiny deposits of mineral behind. This section through a limestone cave system shows numerous caves and tunnels, with **1** stalactites, **2** a stalagmite, **3** a natural rock column, **4** a stream entering from the surface of the rock, **5** a stream re-emerging at the base of the limestone.

Right: Around the continents is an area of shallow water, called the continental shelf. It is about 180 metres (590 feet) deep. Beyond the shelf, the ocean floor slopes away into deeper water. It flattens out at about 3650 metres (11,975 feet). The bottom of the ocean is a flat plain, crossed by ridges and trenches. Rising from it are mountains and volcanoes. A bathyscaphe has descended 11,033 metres (36,198 feet) into the Mariana Trench in the Pacific Ocean.

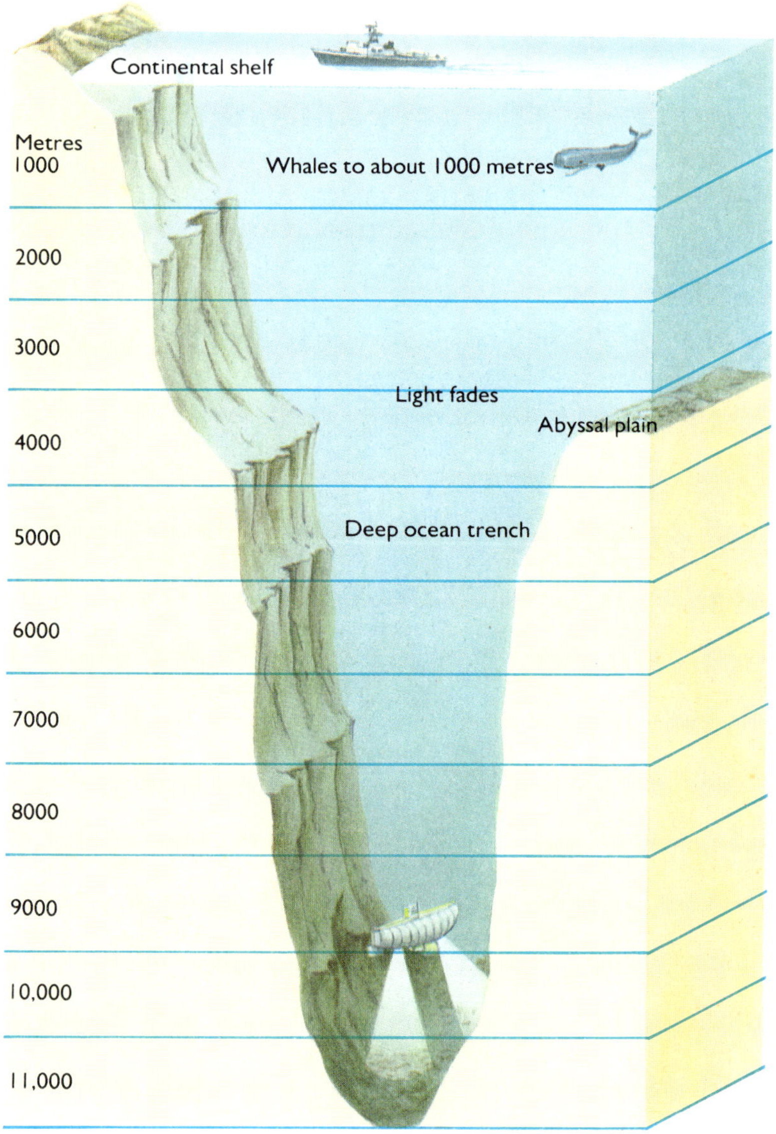

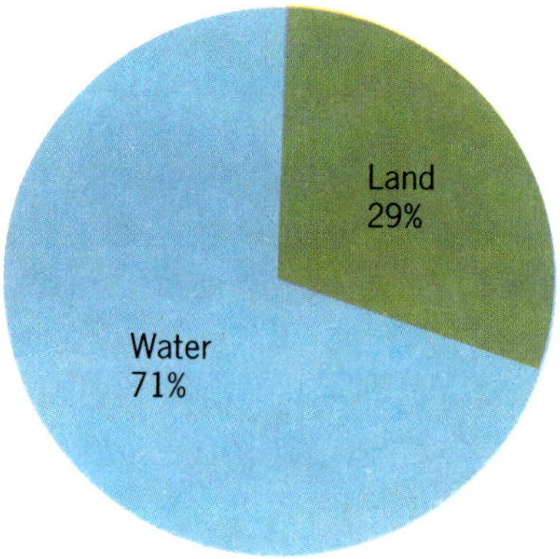

Above: Water covers 71 per cent of the Earth's surface.

Below: The chief minerals in sea water.

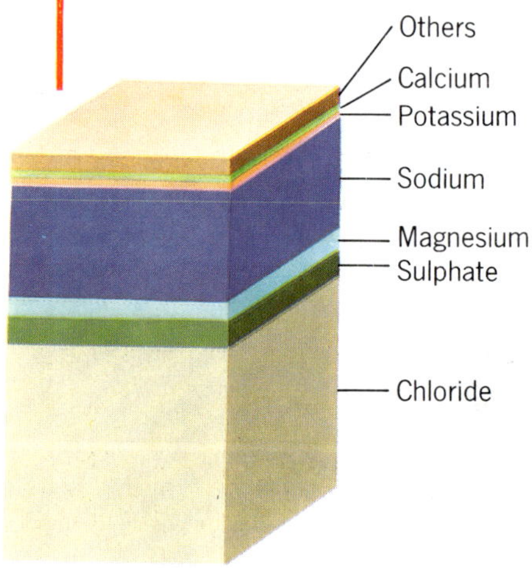

Almost three-quarters of the Earth's surface is covered by sea. Beneath the water is a landscape quite like that of the dry land. There are mountains and valleys, plateaus and plains. Around the edges of the great continents runs a sloping platform. The shallow water on this continental shelf is rich in plant and animal life.

The oceanic crust is made up of a series of curved plates, constantly grinding together to form ridges and trenches. The deepest parts of the sea lie in the Pacific Ocean. Here the crust disappears into trenches delving deep into the Earth's interior. The deepest of the ocean trenches is the Mariana Trench in the eastern Pacific Ocean. It is 11,033 metres (36,198 feet) deep. The deepest point in the Atlantic Ocean is 8,648 metres (28,373 feet) in the Puerto Rico Trench. Because of all this movement, the oldest rocks found on the seabed are only 200 million years old – much younger than rocks found on land.

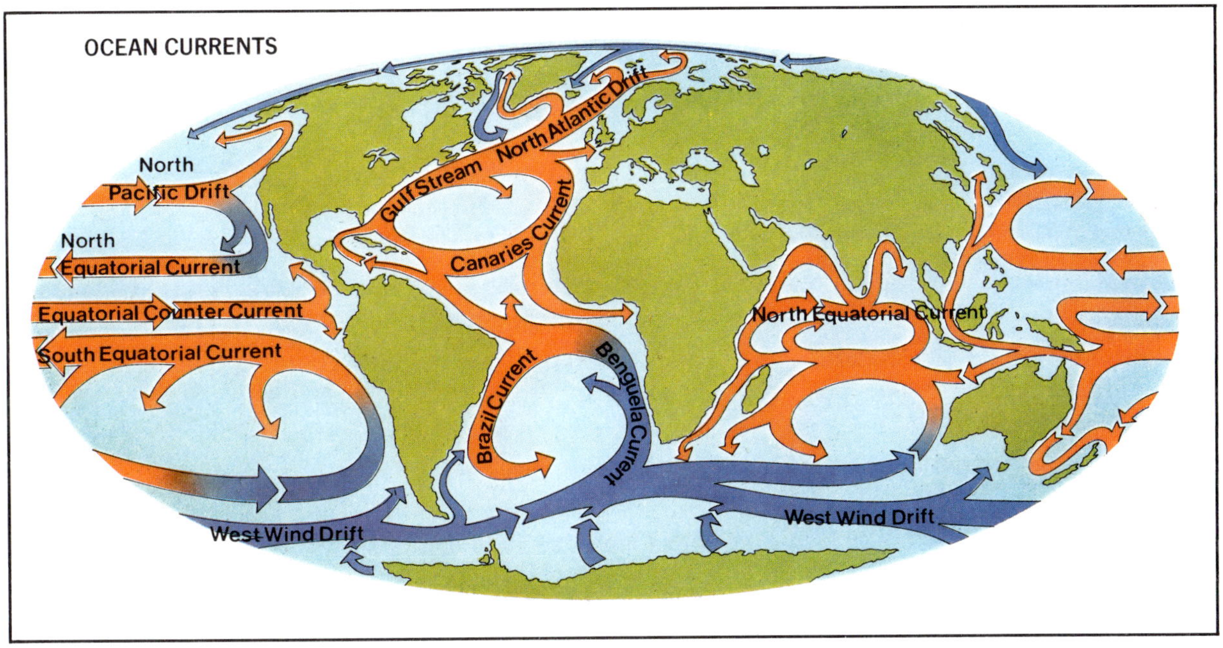

Ocean currents are caused by the movement of warm and cold water. Currents flow in regular patterns. The warm waters of the North Atlantic Drift, which flows from the Gulf of Mexico across the Atlantic, keep winters in Britain mild. The wind causes waves. A wave breaks when the water at its crest starts moving quicker than the rest of the wave, toppling over on itself. Wave action can erode, or wear away, the coastline.

Above: A map showing the chief ocean currents. Red arrows indicate warm currents and blue arrows, cold currents.

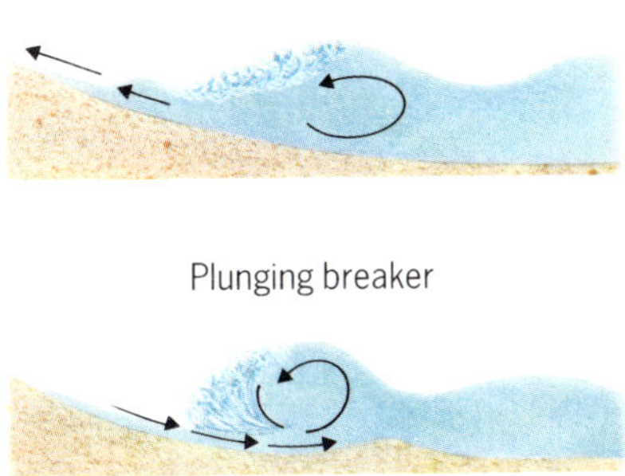

Below: Although waves move, the water does not travel forwards, but circles.

Right: Spilling waves build up beaches, but plunging waves are destructive.

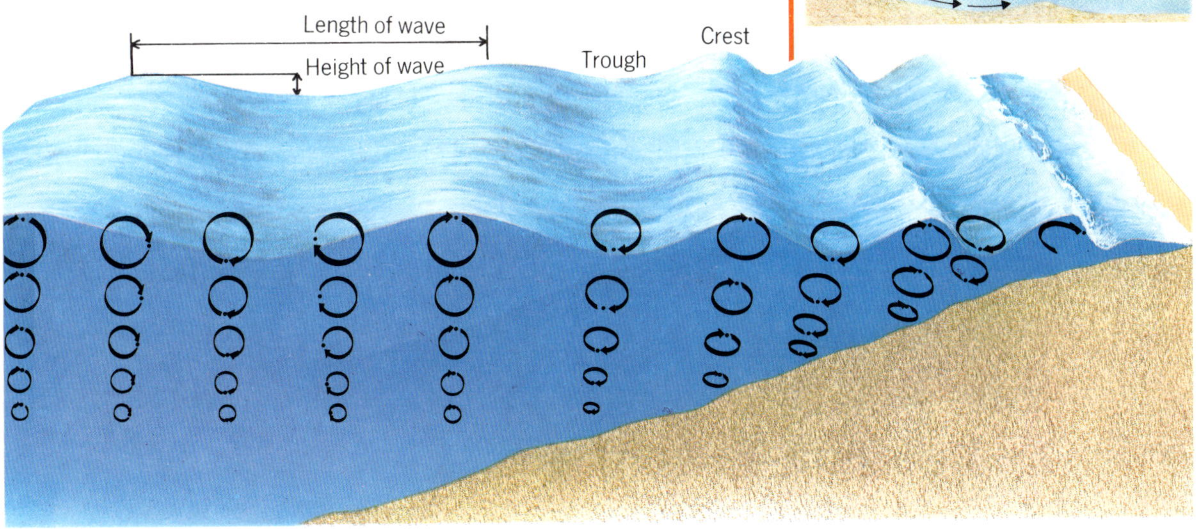

Weather

The weather of a particular part of the Earth over a long period is called its climate. The weather at any place depends on conditions in the Earth's atmosphere. The most important cause of weather is wind. Hot air rises and cool air moves in underneath it. Huge masses of air, some hot and some cool, are always moving over the Earth's surface as wind.

At the Equator and at the North and South Poles the weather changes very little. It is hot most of the time at the Equator and cold most of the time at the Poles. Between the Equator and the Poles there are areas known as the temperate zones. Here the weather is generally mild but changes a good deal. Hot air and cold air are constantly meeting to form regions of low pressure called depressions, which bring unsettled weather.

Weather forecasters show what is happening on charts showing winds, temperatures and pressures. Weather ships at sea, balloons, and satellites in space collect information about the changing weather.

THE BEAUFORT SCALE

The Beaufort Scale is used to classify wind strength.

0	Smoke rises straight up
1	Smoke drifts gently
2	Wind felt on face
3	Leaves and twigs move
4	Small branches sway; dust blows
5	Small trees sway; waves break on lakes
6	Large branches move
7	Whole trees move; walking difficult
8	Twigs break off
9	Chimneys may be blown off houses
10	Trees are uprooted
11	Widespread damage
12	Violent destruction

Above left: When storms have wind speeds over 120 kilometres per hour they are called hurricanes. This is the eye or centre of a hurricane.

Below: This map shows the amount of water falling in one year in different places. Most falls as rain, but some falls as hail, sleet or snow.

WORLD RAINFALL

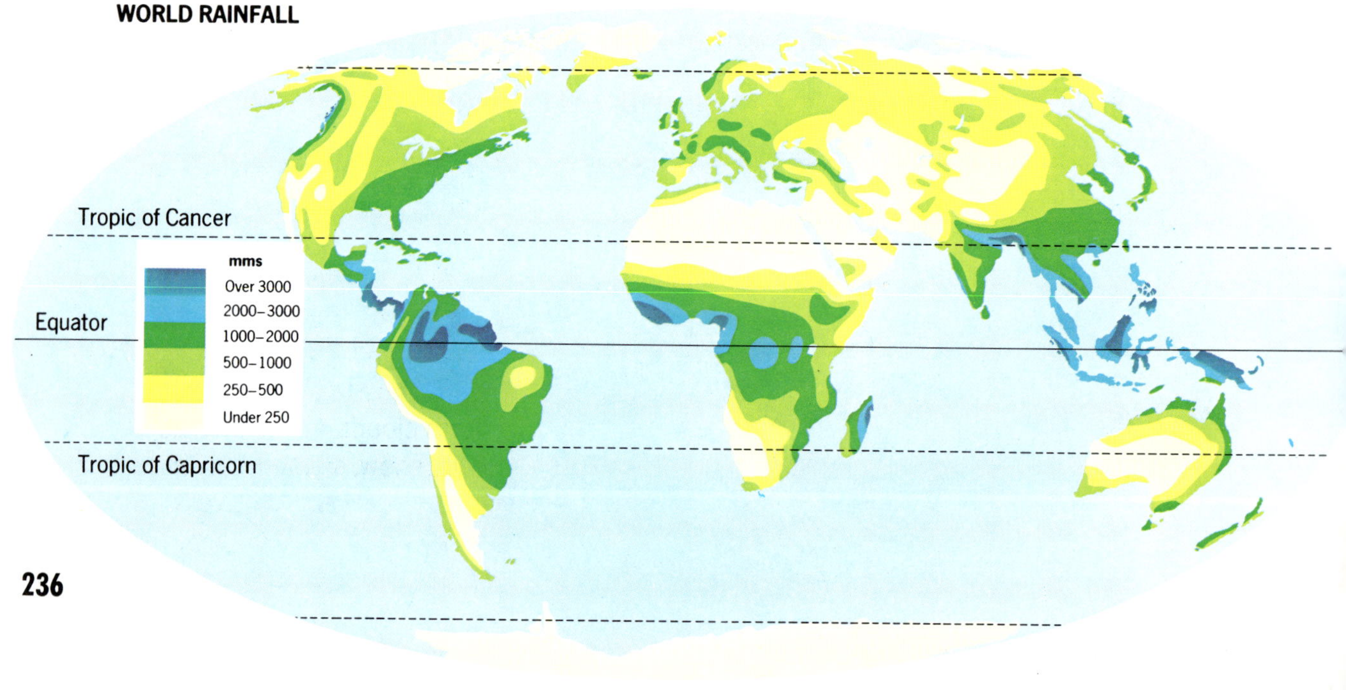

TYPES OF CLOUD

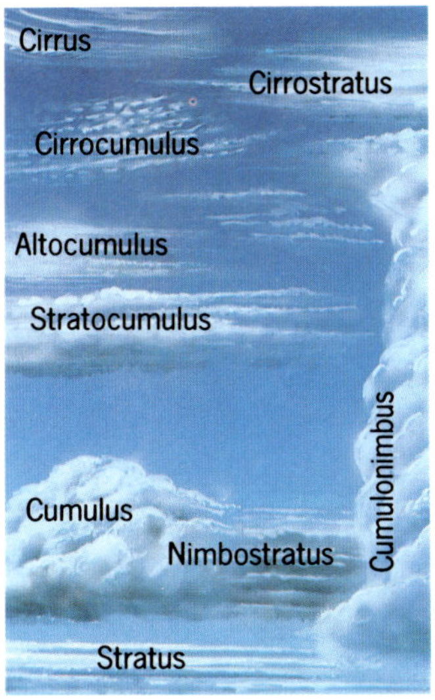

Cirrus: High, wispy ice clouds.
Cirrostratus: Milky, thin, high cloud producing a halo round the Sun.
Cirrocumulus: Thin high lines of cloud with rippled edges.
Altostratus: A greyish sheet of cloud with a hazy Sun above.
Altocumulus: Fleecy bands of cloud with blue sky between.
Stratocumulus: Like a low, dark heavy kind of altocumulus.
Cumulus: A white, heaped-up cloud usually seen in fair weather.
Nimbostratus: Low, grey, sheet-like cloud producing steady rain.
Stratus: Low grey sheet-like cloud.
Cumulonimbus: A towering cloud that may give heavy rain showers.

Above: A depression, or circling mass of low pressure, often brings rain at both the cold and warm fronts.

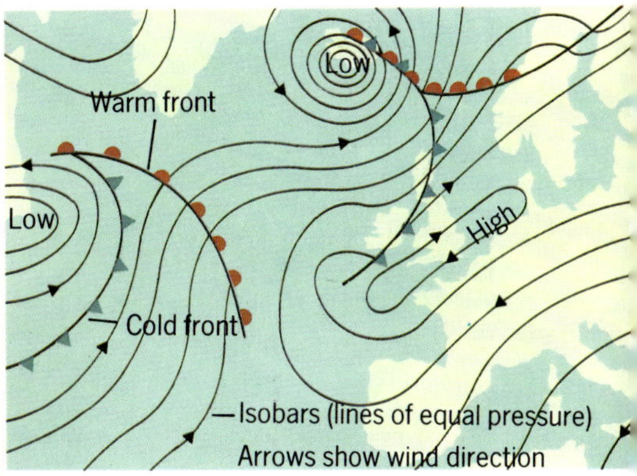

Above: Weather maps show what conditions to expect.

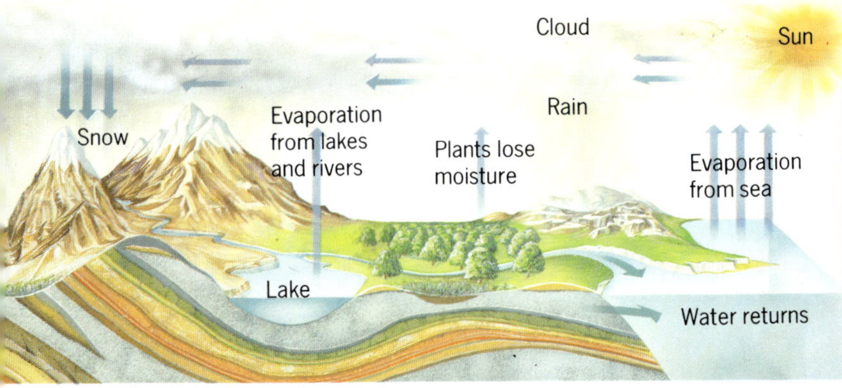

Left: The water cycle. The Sun's heat evaporates sea water. Rising vapour cools and condenses into droplets that form clouds. Water falls as rain, snow, sleet or hail and runs into rivers or the soil. Both surface and underground water flows back to the sea.

Above: A huge sand dune. Sand dunes are shaped by the wind and, as their tops are blown, they move across the desert.

Above: A glacier is a river of ice moving very slowly down a mountainside.

Right: Savanna consists mainly of grassland with a few widely scattered trees such as acacia and baobab. Many savanna regions suffer periods of drought – in some regions for up to five months. A wide variety of animals has become adapted to these environmental conditions. Giraffes, for example, get most of their food and moisture from leaves, and can go for over a month without drinking.

Environment

Animal and plant communities live in particular habitats, or environments. These are classified according to vegetation, which in turn depends on the climate.

Some of the world's wettest areas are near the Equator. It is always hot. The natural vegetation is luxuriant rain forest, with tall trees and dangling creepers.

The world's driest places are hot deserts in the tropics, a zone either side of the Equator. Years may pass with little or no rain, but when storms do come, plants can spring up overnight from dormant seeds.

Between the rain forest and the deserts are areas where it rains only at certain times of the year. In Asia, heavy rain falls during the monsoon. In Africa and South America, the savanna vegetation is well suited to these climatic conditions. The savanna is mainly grass, dotted with trees that can withstand the long dry season.

Away from the tropics, the climate gets steadily colder towards the Poles. Near the tropical deserts it is still warm in the winter, as it is around the Mediterranean Sea. The centres of the continents, far from the coast, are dry and have very cold winters. In some parts the vegetation is true desert, other areas have grasslands which are sometimes called steppes or prairies. Places facing winds blowing from the oceans, such as the Atlantic coast of Western Europe, are milder and wetter. In this part of the world the natural vegetation is deciduous forest.

Vast areas of coniferous forest stretch across the cold northern lands. In the far north the vegetation is tundra – mosses, lichens and low plants which can survive the cold. It snows rather than rains, but there is plenty of water in the summer when the snow melts. Near the Arctic and Antarctic Poles, permanent snow and ice take over. There is hardly any vegetation, and few animals can survive the harsh conditions.

Above: Mexico has a wide variety of landscapes and climates within relatively short distances of one another: from mountains and plateaus, which cover two thirds of the land, to tropical forests, deserts and fertile valleys.

Left: In temperate climates, spring and summer are the main growing seasons.

Below: A tropical rain forest has four main levels. Shrubs, climbing plants and mosses cover the forest floor above which grow small trees and seedlings. Above, a mass of touching tree tops forms a dense canopy, shutting out sunlight. The tallest trees break through the canopy in places to form the top layer.

Below: All over the world, endangered animals and plants will face extinction unless more is done to protect them. This map shows just some of the animal species that are in danger.

The Earth is constantly changing. Underground forces can shift continents, raise mountains, and cause earthquakes and volcanic eruptions. Waves, winds, rivers and rainfall alter the surface shape of the land. This is a natural change to the environment.

Human beings too can alter the Earth's environment. Humans have cut down much of the natural forest that once covered vast areas. Huge tracts of rain forest are

being felled each year, both for timber and to make room for ranchers and farmers. Without the trees, the soil quickly becomes infertile and barren. Chemical pollution from our factories and cities fouls the air, the soil, and the rivers and lakes. Wildlife loses its habitat and many species face extinction. These problems must be tackled and solved if we are to protect the planet. Looking after the environment is something we must all do.

Peoples

Below: People speak many different languages and dialects (local versions of a language). The most widely spoken languages belong to a group called Indo-European. The diagram shows how these languages are grouped in related families, even though they sound different. Indo-European languages originated in Europe, central and southwest Asia, and India. They include English (the world's most widely spoken language) which belongs to the Germanic group. The Romance languages include French, Spanish, Portuguese and Italian. Russian belongs to the Balto-Slavic group; Bengali to the Indo-Iranian group. Chinese, which is spoken by a fifth of the world's people, belongs to a separate family.

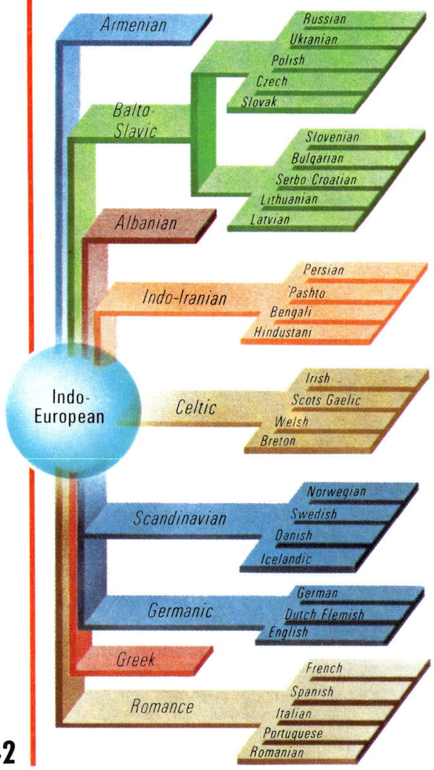

There are more than 5000 million people in the world. This means that there are only about 30 people to every square kilometre of land. But 20 per cent of the Earth's surface is too dry to support many people; another 20 per cent is too cold; 20 per cent is too rugged and mountainous; and nearly 20 per cent is dense tropical forest. That leaves only 20 per cent of the Earth's surface to support the vast majority of the world's people.

There are three main racial groups making up the Earth's people. They are known as the Caucasoid, Negroid and Mongoloid groups. These people speak an amazing number of languages and dialects, which are related to each other in language families.

Through most of history the world's population has increased steadily but slowly. Population increases when there are more births than deaths. In the last 200 years, the population of the world has leapt from 800 million to over 5000 million. This is because medical science has been able to conquer many killer diseases, such as smallpox, tuberculosis and cholera. So, although parents are actually producing fewer babies now than in the past, more

European

Indian

Aborigine

Arabic

Chinese

North American Indian

Negroid

Caribbean

Left, below left: We all belong to one species, *Homo sapiens*. However, scientists divide humankind into Caucasoids, Mongoloids and Negroids. The Caucasoid peoples include Europeans, Iranians, Afghans, northern and eastern Africans, and most of the peoples of India. Australian Aboriginals are also Caucasoids. The Chinese are Mongoloid people. So are the Japanese and the Koreans, and the Indians of North and South America. Negroid people include the Papuans of New Guinea, Negritos of Australasia, and certain groups of African people.

of them live to grow up and have children of their own.

The populations of Africa, Asia, and Central and South America are increasing rapidly. Many countries in these continents have a 'young' population, with nearly half of their people under 15 years of age. The growth of population is much slower in the richer developed nations of North America, Europe, the USSR and most of Australasia. In these nations, people have smaller families and the trend is for the population to become 'older'.

Below: The world is divided: North-South, East-West, rich and poor. Rivalry has also divided the world. Since 1989 Eastern Europe has been in a state of flux. With changes in the governments of many countries, communist borders have been pushed back.

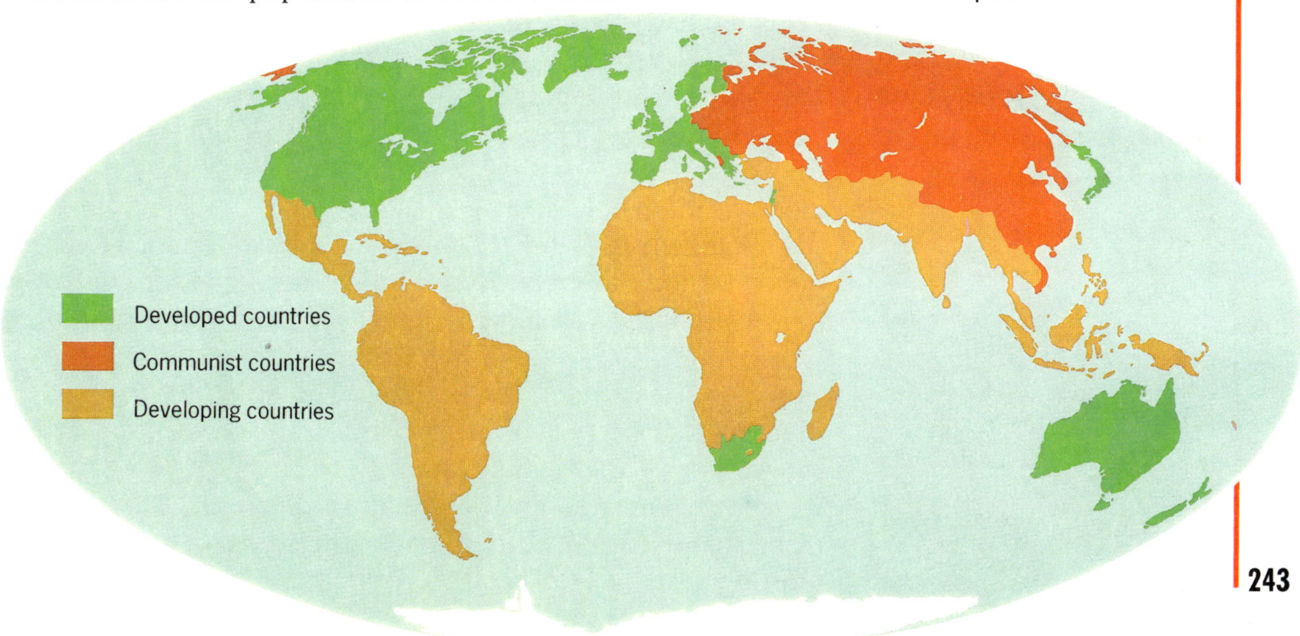

Above: The Sphinx and the Pyramids of Egypt were built by a people who believed in many gods. The Egyptians buried their kings in huge tombs, along with treasure, and other worldly possessions they thought necessary for the afterlife.

Below: The Hindu god Ganesh, son of Shiva and Parvati, is the teacher and the remover of obstacles. Hindus pray to Ganesh before major projects, as he is thought to bring success.

Beliefs

Since earliest times, people have believed in gods or spirits from another world. Many customs and ways of life developed as a result of these beliefs. The peoples of the ancient world – the Egyptians, Greeks and Romans for instance – had complex religious beliefs, with many gods.

All the world's great religions began in Asia. The oldest religion to teach that there is only one God is Judaism, the religion of the Jews. Its history is told in the Hebrew Bible, which Christians call the Old Testament. Islam was founded by the prophet Muhammad. Its followers are called Muslims. They believe in Allah, the one God. Muslims pray in a mosque and obey the teachings of the Koran, their holy book.

Hinduism is the chief religion of India. Hindus believe people's souls are reborn many times until good enough to join Brahman, a supreme power. Their gods include Vishnu and Shiva. Buddhism is another important Eastern religion. Its founder, the Buddha ('The Enlightened One'), taught that people have many lives, and move gradually towards perfection and peace.

People who follow the teachings of Jesus Christ are Christians. Not all Christians belong to one Church, but most share certain basic beliefs; they believe that God

Left: A mosque is the place of worship for Muslims, followers of the religion of Islam. From the tall minarets, the muezzins call the faithful to prayers. This mosque, Hagia Sophia, is in Istanbul in Turkey where many people are Muslims.

made the world, that Jesus was His Son and that through faith in His death and resurrection people can be forgiven their sins and can gain eternal life.

Other important world religions are Confucianism, Taoism, Zoroastrianism, Shintoism and Sikhism.

People who believe in no god and have no religion are called atheists. An agnostic is someone who does not know whether or not there is a god.

Below: Statues of Buddha are found in temples throughout Asia, where Buddhism thrives. Here, he is portrayed in a characteristic pose with his legs folded. The Buddha was Siddhartha Gautama. He was born about 563 BC in northern India and was the founder of Buddhism.

Above: A Jewish boy studies the scriptures for the bar mitzvah ceremony. The most important sacred books of Judaism are the Torah and Talmud.

Left: Christian churches often have beautiful stained glass windows with illustrations from Bible stories and the lives of the saints. This window is found in the 13th-century cathedral at Chartres, France. Churches with elaborate decoration are built to glorify God, and as places in which Christians can worship Him together.

Above: Competitors from many nations gather every four years for the Olympic Games.

Below: A downhill skier. Skiers also compete in jumping and cross-country races.

Right: Gymnasts performing on the rings and the bar. Both exercises call for strength and timing.

Sport

People enjoy many recreations – games as different as chess and football; outdoor activities such as sailing, riding, climbing and walking; indoor leisure pursuits such as squash, table tennis, judo or country dancing.

Today, people have more leisure time than ever before. To keep healthy and active, your body needs exercise. Taking part in sport is an excellent way of keeping fit, meeting new friends and having fun. People are most active between adolescence and around the age of 30. Our bodies

are then at their strongest. However, many people continue to enjoy sports and hobbies into old age.

Organized sport has a long history. The Olympic Games were first held in Greece in 776 BC. Competitors took part in sports such as athletics, boxing and wrestling, and also in poetry and arts competitions. The modern Olympic Games, inspired by those of Ancient Greece, were begun in 1896 and are held every four years. Thousands of athletes gather to take part in a variety of sports. There are separate Games for winter sports, such as skiing and skating. Several sports (archery, for example) began as military exercises for soldiers. The popular games of today such as soccer, tennis, baseball and rugby were 'organized' in the 19th century. Ruling bodies were formed, and the laws of each sport were clearly drawn up. In the 20th century contests have become international, and spectator sport has become both an entertainment and a business.

Above: A cricket bat, wicket (stumps with bails on top), pads and a ball. Cricket began in England in the 1700s.

Above left: American 'gridiron' football is now watched and played in other countries as well as in the USA.

Above: Fencing developed from sword-fighting and military training.

Left: Sumo wrestlers *(far left)* are giants, but bouts are soon over. Martial arts such as judo require lengthy training to perfect the various moves.

Above: Martin Luther King Jr led black Americans in the struggle for civil rights. He was murdered in 1968.

Below: England's King John agreeing to Magna Carta in 1215. The document stated that the people, as well as the king, had rights.

Laws and Government

Laws, or rules, and government (a system for making laws) were needed as soon as people began living in groups. In a primitive tribe the best hunter or strongest warrior might become the ruler or chief. At first the ruler was chosen by the members of the tribe. But then it became the custom that the ruler's son always took his place. This is known as 'hereditary rule'.

To help make sensible laws, good kings took advice from councils of wise people. In time, these councils grew almost as powerful as the king. The Ancient Greeks were the first to try a form of government called democracy or 'rule by the people'. The people met to discuss new laws and to decide what taxes should be paid. This was the beginning of the modern parliament.

Democracy took a long time to grow, and until the 1600s monarchs (kings and queens) remained powerful. A

challenge to their power came when the English parliament fought a war against the king. After this Civil War (1642–49), the English king or queen had to rule according to the laws of Parliament. When the Americans broke away from British rule (1776), they chose to be a republic. The US head of state is not a king, but an elected president. Most countries today are republics. In some republics, the president has a great deal of power. In others, the presidency is more ceremonial. Power lies with the government, headed by a prime minister.

In a democracy, people vote in elections to choose the law-makers. As well as voting for the country's government, we also vote in local government elections.

Above: The trial of King Charles I in 1649. Parliament challenged the king's right to rule without its consent, and this led to the Civil War. Charles was executed. His son eventually regained the throne, but power had shifted permanently away from the monarch and into the hands of Parliament.

Left: A law court in America. A country's laws are enforced by the courts, where cases are decided by a judge and jury.

Above: British ships in China in 1835. By the 19th century world trade was flourishing.

Above: Advertising seeks to increase public awareness about a product or company.

Trade

In ancient times and in the Middle Ages there was some trade between different parts of the world. Chinese silks and porcelain, precious stones from India and spices from South-East Asia reached Europe, but trade was in luxury goods only and on a small scale. After the discovery of North and South America, and the setting up of colonies there, precious metals came to Europe from Mexico and Peru. Spices and other goods were brought from Asia. Gold and silver helped the growth of international trade, linking Asia, America, Europe and Africa. A world economy was beginning to take shape.

The Industrial Revolution of the 1700s and 1800s gave another boost to world trade. Factories in western Europe could not get enough local raw materials and so traders went looking for them throughout the world. Britain imported raw cotton for the mills of Lancashire from the United States and Egypt. Tin for the plating and canning industries, and rubber for the transport and chemical industries were brought from Malaya. Australia and Canada became producers of wool, grain, timber and fruit.

Japan and West Germany rebuilt their industries after World War II with astonishing speed. By 1958 West Germany had overtaken Britain as an exporter of manufactured goods. Japan became the leading producer of electronic goods, and also a major exporter of cars and machinery. Other Asian nations, such as Taiwan and

Two different forms of trade – (*left*) bartering for goods at a street market, (*above*) trade on the stock exchange using sophisticated technology.

South Korea, have become important manufacturing centres, while China and India are fast building up their own industries. The countries of Eastern Europe have turned recently from rigid, state control of industry towards a free 'market economy'.

The effects of the Industrial Revolution and of the Technology Revolution of the 20th century are rapidly creating a world civilization. Different ways of life, customs and dress are becoming fewer. Many Asian and African teenagers wear jeans, watch television and listen to pop music just like young people in Europe and the United States.

Below: An oil refinery. Oil is the world's most important fuel. Countries which have oil have become rich by selling it to countries which need oil for their industries. A rise in the price of oil can affect people in countries all over the world, putting up the prices of goods in the shops.

COUNTRIES

AFRICA
Africa is the second largest continent and has the fastest-growing population in the world. (See page 254.)

THE AMERICAS
The Americas are made up of North America (including Central America and the West Indies) and South America. (See page 260.)

ASIA
Asia is the world's largest continent and has more people (over 2500 million) than any other continent. (See page 266.)

AUSTRALASIA
Australasia consists of Australia, New Zealand and many islands in the Pacific Ocean. (See page 272.)

EUROPE
Europe is the sixth largest continent, but the most densely populated. Only Asia, which is four times bigger, has more people. (See page 276.)

POLAR REGIONS
The Polar Regions of the Arctic and the Antarctic are cold and desolate and hardly anyone lives there. (See page 284.)

Below: A multicoloured display of national flags. Flags are symbols which stand for a country's people, land and its government.

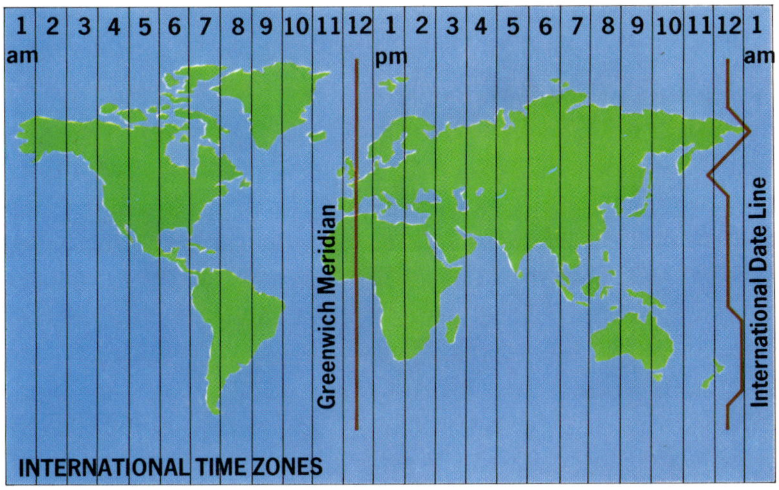

Left: Because the Earth rotates through 360° in 24 hours, there is one hour's time difference for every 15° of longitude. When it is midday in London (0°), it is 6 pm in the evening in Calcutta (90°E), but it is only sunrise and 6 am in Chicago (90°W). Each Time Zone covers about 15° of longitude, but the boundaries follow national or state borders.

Newspaper reports often divide the world into East and West. 'The East' usually refers to the Communist countries – which since the 1940s have been chiefly those of Eastern Europe, the USSR and China. The 'West' refers to Western Europe, USA, Canada, Australia and their allies.

Equally important is the 'North-South' divide. In the north are the developed countries of the world. Most of the rest of the world, south of the equator, is poor. Most southern countries are still struggling to develop. Some have huge debts, owed to foreign banks. Poverty, disease and hunger are serious problems. These developing countries are sometimes referred to as the Third World. Most of Central and South America, Africa and southern Asia belongs to the Third World.

Below: Lines of latitude and longitude on maps and globes are labelled in degrees. This is because they are measured by using angles at the centre of the Earth. 1° (degree) is divided into 60′ (minutes). The lines drawn parallel to the Equator are called lines of latitude. The Equator is 0°, and latitude is measured North and South of the Equator. Lines of longitude are drawn from Pole to Pole.

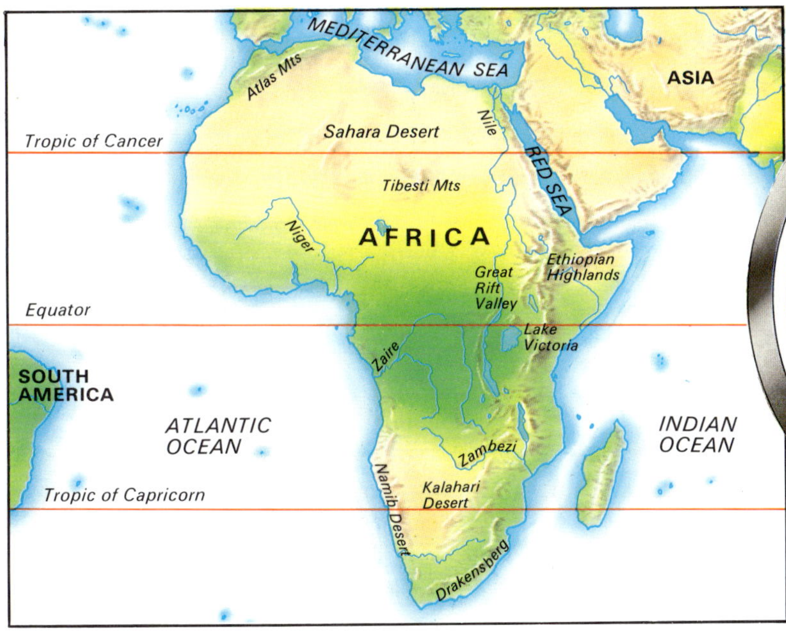

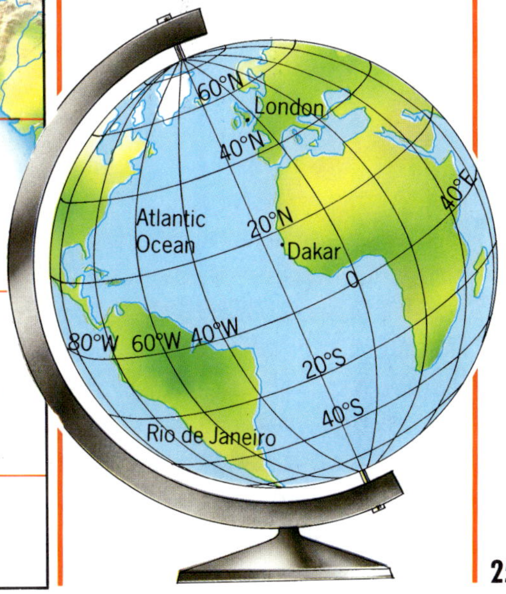

Above: Traditional shield and spears of the Masai, a nomadic group in Kenya. The Masai people are cattle herders and are well known for their skills in the use of weapons. More powerful in the 19th century, the Masai were weakened by the political changes and new diseases brought by the British colonists.

The symbol of the shield and spears is used in Kenya's national flag to represent the defence of freedom.

Right: European explorers such as Burton, Speke, Livingstone and Stanley journeyed across Africa in the 1800s. Livingstone made several expeditions into the African interior where he learned much about African customs, geography and the slave trade. His discoveries led to great competition among European nations for control of Africa.

Africa

Most of Africa is in the Tropics, but there are great differences in climate and vegetation. In North Africa there are mountains and a huge expanse of sand and rock called the Sahara Desert. It is hot and dry, with only scattered waterholes or oases. The equator runs through Central Africa. Here are hot and wet lowlands. There are thick rain forests, where the trees blot out the sunlight.

Elsewhere in Africa there are high rolling plains called *savannas*. It is cooler on the plains, but in the dry season no rain falls for months. When the rains come, plants grow very quickly. In the east are Africa's highest mountains: Kilimanjaro, which is 5895 metres above sea level, and Mount Kenya, which is 5200 metres above sea level.

Africa has some of the oldest rocks in the world, going back 3000 million years. In East Africa is a great crack, or fault, in the Earth's crust called the Great Rift Valley. In this area are Africa's largest lakes, Victoria, Nyasa and Tanganyika. Some of the world's longest rivers are in Africa. Longest of all is the Nile, followed by the Zaïre (Congo), the Niger and the Zambezi.

On the high plains of Africa lives a great variety of wild animals. Many have been killed by hunters and poachers. However, in game reserves visitors can see various kinds of antelopes, giraffes, zebras, elephants, leopards, lions and many other animals.

Much of Africa is thinly populated. The Sahara and other desert regions have no people at all. The tropical forests and grasslands are also thinly populated. Parts of

Nigeria are very densely populated and the Nile River valley is one of the world's most heavily populated regions. In the north of Africa the people are mainly Muslim Arabs or Berbers. South of the Sahara most of the people are black Africans. They are Christians or follow their own religions.

Below: There are 52 countries in Africa today. Sudan is the largest country with an area of 2,506,000 sq km (968,000 sq miles).

Right: Hungry children in a relief camp. Parts of Africa, such as Ethiopia, have been ravaged by famine. Some countries are torn by civil war; in others crops fail because of drought. Severe drought has been the cause of famine in Ethiopia several times in recent years. International aid has helped some of the starving, but many have died.

Below: The face of Africa is changing as modern cities grow larger and more crowded. Thirty per cent of Africans now live in towns. Cities with tall buildings, busy traffic and a network of roads can be found in virtually every African country.

They belong to many different tribes and speak many different languages. In Nigeria, in West Africa, there are about 250 languages. English, French and Portuguese are widely spoken. There are small groups of Bushmen and Pygmies, and people of Asian and European descent.

Most Africans are farmers. To feed themselves they grow crops of maize, yams, sweet potatoes, beans and fruit. Large farms called plantations grow crops such as cocoa-beans, coffee, oil palm, tea, tobacco, cotton and sugar.

Africa is rich in minerals. It produces gold, diamonds,

Above: Flags of some African nations. Most of these countries became self-governing in the 1950s and 1960s after being ruled as colonies by Europeans.

Above: A French mission station in Chad. By 1900, much of western Africa had come under French rule.

Below: In the 19th century each of the European powers established colonies for itself in Africa. Only Ethiopia managed to remain independent.

THE PARTITION OF AFRICA

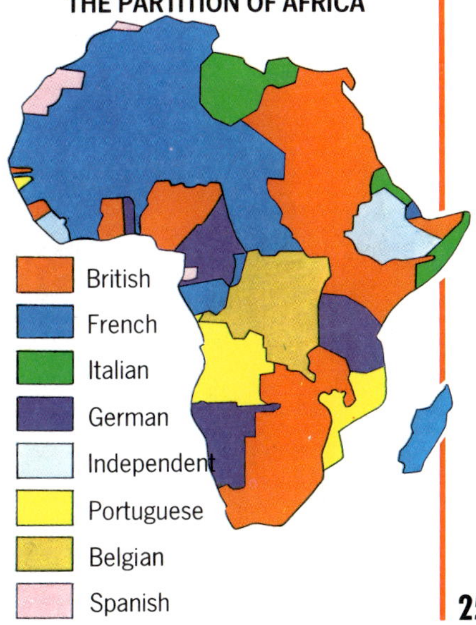

Above: Africans must grow more food to feed a fast-growing population. Most African farmers, however, still use traditional methods, such as this donkey and camel plough. Few farmers use sophisticated machinery. Where modern methods are used, in parts of South Africa, Zimbabwe and Kenya, they help to increase much needed crop yields.

oil, copper, cobalt, bauxite and uranium. Rivers and lakes are being dammed to make hydro-electricity, and industries are being developed.

Most of Africa's manufacturing industries are centred in South Africa. Industries such as metal producing, machine making and transport manufacturing are located there. There are also large industrial centres in Zimbabwe, Egypt and Algeria. Throughout the rest of Africa, most manufacturing is limited to assembling or making products such as shoes, bicycles and textiles.

Transport systems in much of Africa are poor. Most roads are no more than mud tracks, which become impossible to use during the rainy seasons. Very few people own cars. The majority of rail, shipping and road systems

Left: The Kariba Dam, which lies on the Zambezi River, supplies hydroelectric power to both the industrial centres of Zimbabwe and the copper towns of Zambia. The dam was completed in 1959. The resulting lake flooded an area of about 5200 sq km (2000 sq miles) behind it.

are concentrated in South Africa where they serve the major industrial and business centres.

Fossil remains of the earliest human beings have been found in Africa. In the Nile valley the Ancient Egyptians built one of the greatest early civilizations. But for hundreds of years people in Europe called Africa the 'Dark Continent', because it was so mysterious.

In the 1800s European governments divided Africa into colonies. New ideas and ways of life came to Africa. In time, Africans sought self-government and by the 1960s most colonies had become independent countries.

Many African countries are poor. There are not enough schools and hospitals, and there is not enough food to feed the fast-growing population. There are 12 million new Africans every year. Another problem is the continuation of white-dominated government in South Africa, with its racist *apartheid* laws, though these are being eased.

Africa's rich wildlife astonished the first European explorers. Today lions (*above*) and other game such as zebras, ostriches, wildebeest, buffalo, kudu and crocodiles (*below*) are found in greatly reduced numbers. Game parks are the best hope for their survival.

Above: Flags of the Americas. The two largest nations of North America are the USA and Canada (top).

Right: New York City, with its skyscraping skyline, is the leading business and financial city of North America. Although not the capital of the USA (that is Washington DC), New Yorkers think their city is number one – the 'Big Apple'.

The Americas

North America

North America is the third largest of the Earth's continents. It stretches from the cold wastes of Alaska in the north to the hot deserts of Mexico and the tropical forests of Central America in the south. Canada and the United States of America cover most of North America.

A narrow isthmus, or neck of land, in Central America joins North America to South America. Down the western side of North America run the rugged Rocky Mountains, and there are lower mountain chains in the east. In the centre of the continent are wide grasslands called prairies which occupy vast expanses of land.

The longest river in North America is the Mississippi, which is joined by another long river, the Missouri. The Great Lakes are the largest fresh water lakes in the world. The thundering Niagara Falls plunge 50 metres (164 feet) between two of the Great Lakes.

North America has a wide range of climates. In most of the Arctic lands of the north it is too cold for trees to grow. Farther south are huge forests, first of conifers and then of broad-leaved trees. The central plains have less rainfall, so instead of forests, there are grasslands. In the southwest there are hot deserts, and in the hot, moist isthmus of Panama there are tropical forests.

North America is a continent of great contrasts. It has some of the world's largest cities, but there are also huge areas with hardly any people at all. The United States is the most powerful country in North America.

NORTH AND CENTRAL AMERICA
Capital Cities
0 500 1000 miles
0 500 1000 1500 kilometres
Greenland
Baffin Is
Hudson Bay
CANADA
USA
MEXICO
Alaska
PACIFIC OCEAN
ATLANTIC OCEAN
Gulf of Mexico
G. of California
Caribbean Sea
Mackenzie
Great Bear L.
Great Slave L.
Rocky Mountains
L. Winnipeg
St. Lawrence
Missouri
L. Superior
L. Michigan
L. Huron
L. Erie
L. Ontario
Colorado
Red
Mississippi
Rio Grande
Sierra Madre
Nome
Fairbanks
Anchorage
Whitehorse
Juneau
Churchill
Edmonton
Vancouver
Calgary
Seattle
Regina
Winnipeg
Portland
Quebec
Halifax
Montreal
Ottawa
Toronto
Boston
Minneapolis
St Paul
Milwaukee
Detroit
Cleveland
New York
San Francisco
Salt Lake City
Chicago
Pittsburg
Philadelphia
Indianapolis
Baltimore
Columbus
Washington DC
Denver
Kansas City
St Louis
Las Vegas
Los Angeles
Santa Fe
San Diego
Phoenix
Albuquerque
Memphis
Tucson
El Paso
Atlanta
Dallas
Jacksonville
San Antonio
Houston
New Orleans
BERMUDA
Miami
Nassau
BAHAMAS
Monterrey
Havana
CUBA
DOMINICAN REP
San Juan
HAITI
Port-au-Prince
Santo Domingo
PUERTO RICO
BARBADOS
JAMAICA
Kingston
Guadalajara
Mexico City
BELIZE
Belmopan
TRINIDAD & TOBAGO
Port-of-Spain
GUATEMALA
Guatemala City
HONDURAS
Tegucigalpa
San Salvador
EL SALVADOR
NICARAGUA
Managua
Panama Canal Zone
San Jose
COSTA RICA
Panama
PANAMA

Right: Various sources are used to generate the vast amounts of power consumed in the United States each year. This industrial complex is an oil refinery. It is located at Kenai in Central Alaska where there are major oil deposits. Oil is a major source of fuel for domestic heating and industrial power.

Above: Two of the American Indian leaders who fought for their tribal lands.

Below: A wagon train of pioneers. During the 1800s thousands of settlers travelled westwards to make their homes in the new lands.

The United States is the most industrialized nation in the world; it makes a quarter of the world's steel, for example. It has rich deposits of minerals including copper, natural gas, uranium, iron ore and coal. Farmland covers nearly half the country and US farmers produce enough grain and other crops to export large quantities to other countries. The capital of the United States is Washington DC, but New York is the largest city. Other important cities are Chicago and Los Angeles.

The United States' northern neighbour is Canada, which is slightly larger but has only about a tenth as many people. Canadians include people of British and French ancestry, and both English and French are official languages. Canada is rich in minerals and has large oil deposits. Its farmers grow cereals and fruit, and rear cattle. Timber comes from Canada's huge forests.

Central America and the West Indies

The people living in Central America and the islands of the West Indies are descendants either of the American Indians or of Europeans and Africans. Most of them speak Spanish, English, French or American Indian languages. In 1492, when Christopher Columbus reached the islands in the Caribbean Sea, he thought he had reached the Indies (Asia), so the islands were named the West Indies.

Central America and the thousands of West Indian islands are mostly hot and mountainous. The climate is ideal for growing fruit, coffee, cotton, tobacco and sugarcane. Central America's main source of income is from its large plantations, forests and mines. About 10 percent of the world's bananas are produced in the lowland plantations. Cuba is the largest of the West Indian islands and it is the third largest producer of sugar in the world.

The countries of Central America include Guatemala, El Salvador, Nicaragua, Panama and Mexico. Mexico was once the home of the Aztecs, and from 1521 to 1822 was ruled by the Spaniards.

The plant and animal life of Central America is similar to that of South America. The lowland rainforests, mountains, and the pine and oak forests provide homes for a wide variety of different animal species including the opossum, jaguar, puma, sloth and deer.

Mineral deposits are rich in Central America. Gold and silver, lead and zinc, copper and nickel are found in Nicaragua and Honduras. There are deposits of natural gas offshore in the Pacific Ocean.

Above: People enjoying a colourful West Indian carnival. This traditional form of outdoor entertainment features music, dance, bright costumes and floats. Carnivals developed from traditional, usually religious, festivals.

The West Indies are divided into two groups of islands. Tobago, along with the Windward and Leeward islands and Trinidad, is part of the Lesser Antilles. The large islands of Cuba, Jamaica, Hispaniola and Puerto Rico make up the Greater Antilles. All the islands are located in an archipelago which lies between North and South America. The climate is tropical, and the vegetation is rich and varied. Much of the land is covered in forest but sugar cane, meat and exotic fruit and vegetables are the main products processed in the manufacturing industries.

SOUTH AMERICA
ATLANTIC OCEAN
PACIFIC OCEAN
ATLANTIC OCEAN
Barranquilla
Maracaibo
Caracas
Orinoco
VENEZUELA
Llanos
Medellin
Bogotá
Cali
COLOMBIA
Georgetown
GUYANA
SURINAM
Paramaribo
Cayenne
FRENCH GUIANA
Quito
ECUADOR
Guayaquil
GALAPAGOS IS.
Manáus
Amazon
Belém
Fortaleza
Selvas
PERU
Chiclayo
Trujillo
Recife
BRAZIL
Callão
Lima
Cuzco
Salvador
BOLIVIA
ANDES
La Paz
Cochabamba
Oruro
Sucre
Brasilia
Brazilian Highlands
Paraná
ATACAMA DESERT
MOUNTAINS
PARAGUAY
Gran Chaco
Asunción
Rio de Janeiro
São Paulo
Córdoba
Mt Aconcagua
Pôrto Alegre
Valparaiso
Santiago
Rosario
URUGUAY
Buenos Aires
Montevideo
La Plata
ARGENTINA
CHILE
PAMPAS
Colorado
Bahia Blanca
Chubut
Patagonia
FALKLAND IS.
Tierra del Fuego
Cape Horn
Venezuela
Colombia
Ecuador
Peru
Bolivia
Chile
Guyana
Paraguay
French Guiana
Surinam
Brazil
Uruguay
Argentina
■ Capital Cities
0 500 1000 miles
0 500 1000 1500 kilometres

South America

The continent of South America is the fourth largest in the world. There are 13 countries in South America. The largest, Brazil, covers nearly half the continent. The people are descended from the original Indians, or from Europeans and Africans. Most speak Portuguese or Spanish.

The Andes Mountains, the highest in South America, stretch for over 7000 kilometres (4350 miles) down the western side, overlooking the Pacific Ocean. In the Andes is Lake Titicaca, the highest large lake in the world. From the mountains several great rivers flow east across the continent to the Atlantic Ocean. The most important river is the mighty Amazon. Other rivers are the Orinoco, the Sâo Francisco and the River Plate system.

In the centre of the continent are vast plains. They include the rain forests of the Amazon basin, the swamps and lakes of the Gran Chaco, and the grassy pampas of Argentina where gauchos (South American cowboys) herd cattle and horses.

Because it has a variety of climates and soils, South America can produce many kinds of crops. In the hot regions coffee, cocoa, sugar and bananas are grown.

South America is rich in minerals, such as copper, tin, iron, platinum, manganese, nitrates, bauxite, diamonds and emeralds. Mining is an important industry, and there are also large oilfields. South America has some of the largest and fastest-growing cities in the world.

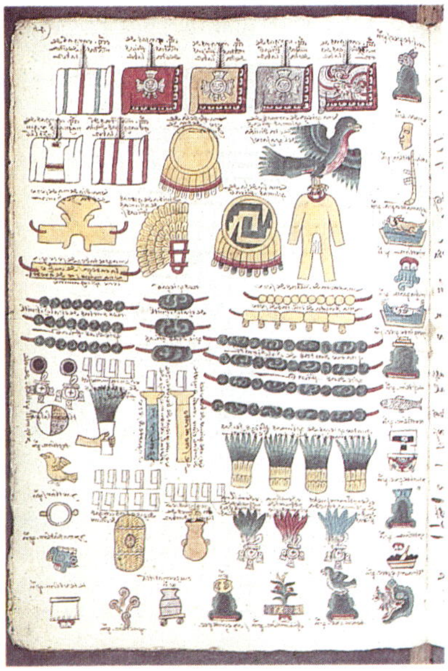

Above: Much of what is known about some of the ancient civilizations of America comes from a type of pictographic writing. It consists of a series of small pictures and was used mainly for making business and historical records. The Incas of Peru, however, had no writing, and sent messages by word of mouth, and by fires and smoke signals. Numerical records were kept using coloured and knotted strings.

Left: South America has several great cities. Brazil has three of the most important: São Paulo, Rio de Janeiro (shown here) and Brasilia, the national capital. Rio de Janeiro on the Atlantic coast, with its spectacular setting, was the capital of Brazil until 1960 when the new city of Brasília, designed by Lucia Costa and Oscar Niemeyer, was made the capital.

Below: China is the world's third largest country. It has many different landscapes. About 43 per cent of the land area is covered by mountains. Other types of land-forms include tropical rain forests, grasslands and deserts. These diverse habitats support a wide range of plants and animals. Here, lotus plants are growing on the lower land, while mountains rise steeply in the background.

More than one fifth of the world's total population lives in China. The population is mainly Han Chinese and is of Mongoloid stock. China is a mainly rural, agricultural nation, although many of its major cities have gained great importance as industrially productive centres. There are more than 30 cities in China with populations of more than one million people.

Asia

Asia is the largest continent, stretching from the Arctic to the Equator. It covers nearly a third of the Earth's land surface. With a population of over 2500 million, Asia has more than half of the world's people.

There are many different types of land and climate in Asia. In the north are evergreen forests, flat grasslands called steppes and cold tundra plains. Most of this area is called Siberia and is part of the Soviet Union. In central Asia are the world's highest mountains, including the mighty Himalaya Mountains. The high plains of Tibet are known as 'the roof of the world'. From these mountains many great rivers flow into the rest of Asia. Asia has some of the world's longest rivers. They include the Ob, Lena and Yenisey in the north; the Euphrates in the west; the Indus, Ganges, Brahmaputra, Salween, Irrawaddy and Mekong in the south; and the Huang He and Chang Jiang (Yangtze) in the east.

Some parts of Asia are very dry. There are wide deserts, such as the cold Gobi Desert of Mongolia and the hot deserts of India and Arabia. There the land is dry and barren. In other places there is heavy rainfall, but only once a year during the monsoon season. The rain is brought by the monsoon winds blowing onto the land from the sea.

Left: The city palace is one of the most spectacular buildings in Jaipur, India. Jaipur is often called the 'pink city' because of the colour of many of its buildings, and is one of the most beautiful cities in India. Founded in November 1727 by Maharaja Sawai Jai Singh II, Jaipur became the capital city of the state of Rajasthan in northern India in 1949. It is a busy and prosperous commercial centre and is famous for stone, marble and ivory carving, brass, textiles, jewellery and fine enamel work.

Few people live in the mountains, plains and deserts. Those who do are mostly nomads (wanderers), grazing flocks of sheep, goats, horses and camels. Almost all Asia's people live either in the fertile river valleys, or on the coastal plains. Most of them are peasant farmers, scraping a living out of a small patch of land. But more and more people are going to live in the cities.

In the warm, wet monsoon lands of southern Asia, rice is the chief crop. Rice and fish are the main foods of many Asians. Other crops are tea, sugar, cotton, coffee and spices. In countries like Bangladesh many of the people are very poor. There are too many people for the land to support, so they cannot grow enough food. If the crops fail because of flood or drought, many people may starve.

Asia has few large industries, but valuable raw materials. The forests provide timber and rubber. There are minerals such as coal, iron, copper and tin. In southwest Asia some countries (such as Saudi Arabia and Kuwait) have become rich because there is oil beneath the desert. The countries of the Middle East, where Europe and Asia meet, include Israel, Lebanon, Syria and Turkey.

The most important industrial country of Asia is Japan, which manufactures many products to sell in other countries. China and India are gradually developing their industries, as well as improving their agriculture.

China has a history going back 3500 years and it has more people than any other country. It was once an

Below: A Japanese temple. Buddhism and Shinto are the main religions in Japan. In the late 1900s Shinto was made a state religion. It emphasized the worship of the emperor as a divinity. All Japanese, regardless of their religion were, at that time, forced to worship at Shinto shrines. The country has many shrines and temples. The Japanese often make pilgrimages to these places of worship with offerings of fruit and flowers.

ASIA

Area: 44,418,500 sq km
Population: 3,000,000,000
Highest mountain: Everest 8848 m
Principal lakes: Caspian Sea, Aral Sea, Baikal
Principal rivers: Yangtze, Tigris, Euphrates, Indus, Ganges
Countries: 41 and part of the USSR, part of Turkey, part of Egypt
Most populous country: China

SEA OF OKHOTSK
Amur
Hokkaido
Sapporo
Harbin
Vladivostok
SEA OF JAPAN
JAPAN
NORTH KOREA
Tokyo
Honshu
Yokohama
Pyongyang
Dalian
Kyoto
Seoul
Osaka
SOUTH KOREA
Pusan
Kobe
Kitakyushu
Nagasaki
Kyushu
PACIFIC OCEAN
Shanghai
Nanjing
EAST CHINA SEA
Wuhan
Taipei
TAIWAN
HONG KONG
MACAO
Luzon
Manila
Quezon City
PHILIPPINES
Mindanao
Bandar Seri Begawan
Sulawesi
West Irian
Borneo
INDONESIA
Surabaya
Timor

Iran
China
India
Brunei
Iraq
Mongolia
Nepal
Laos
Israel
South Korea
Sri Lanka
Thailand
Jordan
North Korea
Bangladesh
Indonesia
Kuwait
Afghanistan
Myanmar (Burma)
Pakistan
Lebanon
Bhutan
Vietnam
Singapore
UAE
Oman
Saudi Arabia
Malaysia
Philippines
Yemen AR
Syria
Bahrain
Japan
Maldives
Yemen
Turkey
Cyprus

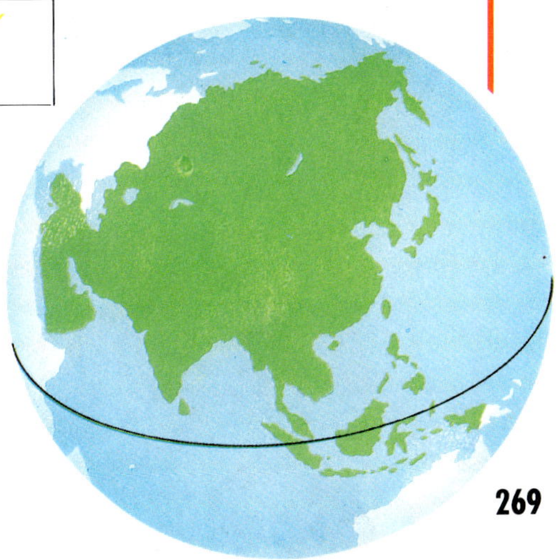

Above: An Indian farmer ploughing. Farming, particularly wheat and rice-growing, is important in India. About seven out of ten of its people earn their living by farming. Most farms are small, and the farmers still use traditional methods. There are also millions of cattle and water buffalo; these animals are sacred to the Hindus.

empire, but is now a republic. Japan too has a long history. Though it lacks natural resources such as coal and oil, it is one of the world's wealthiest industrial nations. Ten Japanese cities have populations of over a million. India, Bangladesh and Pakistan are three of the most densely populated countries in the world. India has the second largest population, after China, and (like China) India has an ancient history. It is the world's largest democracy.

The great religions of Christianity, Islam, Hinduism and Buddhism all began in Asia. The Asian peoples reached high levels of progress in the arts and sciences long before Europeans did so. But the deserts and mountains kept the

Below: In southeast Asia rice is grown in flooded paddy fields. Hillsides are planted in terraces with mudbrick banks.

Left: Hong Kong is a prosperous commercial centre located on the southeast coast of China. It is currently a British dependency but will be returned to China in 1997.

peoples of Asia apart, for only camel caravans could cross the dangerous lands between them. So each part of Asia developed its own languages, customs and ways of life.

European explorers came to Asia in search of riches and spices. They set up trading stations, and later founded colonies. Some parts of Asia were ruled by Europeans until modern times. But now all the countries of Asia are independent. The people of southeast Asia, notably in Vietnam and Cambodia, have suffered from wars in modern times. There have been political problems in Burma, Indonesia and the Philippines, and hostility between communist North Korea and non-communist South Korea.

Below: Indonesian schoolgirls attend lessons given outside at a typical elementary school in Bali.

Right: Some Asian wild animals. Many of their habitats are threatened by human activities

ANIMALS OF ASIA

Australasia

Above: An Australian Aborigine. These people probably came from Asia and drove out the native inhabitants of Australia. In the late 1700s, when the first Europeans settled in Australia, there were about 300,000 Aborigines. There were more than 500 tribes, each with its own language. Today there are fewer than 100,000, which is less than one percent of the country's population. Few Aborigines continue to follow traditional ways but some have returned to traditional homelands in northern and central Australia.

The greater part of Australasia is Australia, much of which is empty desert. The next two countries in order of size are Papua New Guinea and New Zealand. Both have more people per square kilometre than Australia, though neither is densely populated. There are also about 30,000 Pacific Ocean islands. Some, like Fiji and Western Samoa, are fairly densely populated. Others are uninhabited.

The islands in the Pacific Ocean are grouped according to their original inhabitants. These groups are Melanesia, Micronesia and Polynesia. Melanesia means 'black islands' and the people on these islands have dark skin and frizzy hair. This group includes Papua New Guinea, the Solomon Islands and Fiji. Micronesia means 'little islands'. The Micronesian islands are north of Melanesia, and include Nauru and Wake, the Caroline, Kiribati, Mariana and Marshall islands. The people have straight hair and copper-coloured skin. Polynesia, which means 'many islands', spreads over a wide area. It is bounded by New Zealand in the southwest, Easter Island in the southeast and Hawaii in the north. The Polynesians are taller than the other Pacific Islanders and have light brown skin. They include the Maoris of New Zealand.

Two large islands, the North and South Islands, and several smaller islands make up New Zealand. Probably the Maoris settled there about 1000 years ago. Later Europeans came. About 70 per cent of New Zealanders live in the North Island, many of them on the fertile plains by the coast. Wellington, the capital, is on North Island, as is the largest city, Auckland.

Right: Captain Cook and his men were met by the warlike Maoris when they explored New Zealand in 1769. Although Cook took possession of the islands, colonization did not begin for several decades.

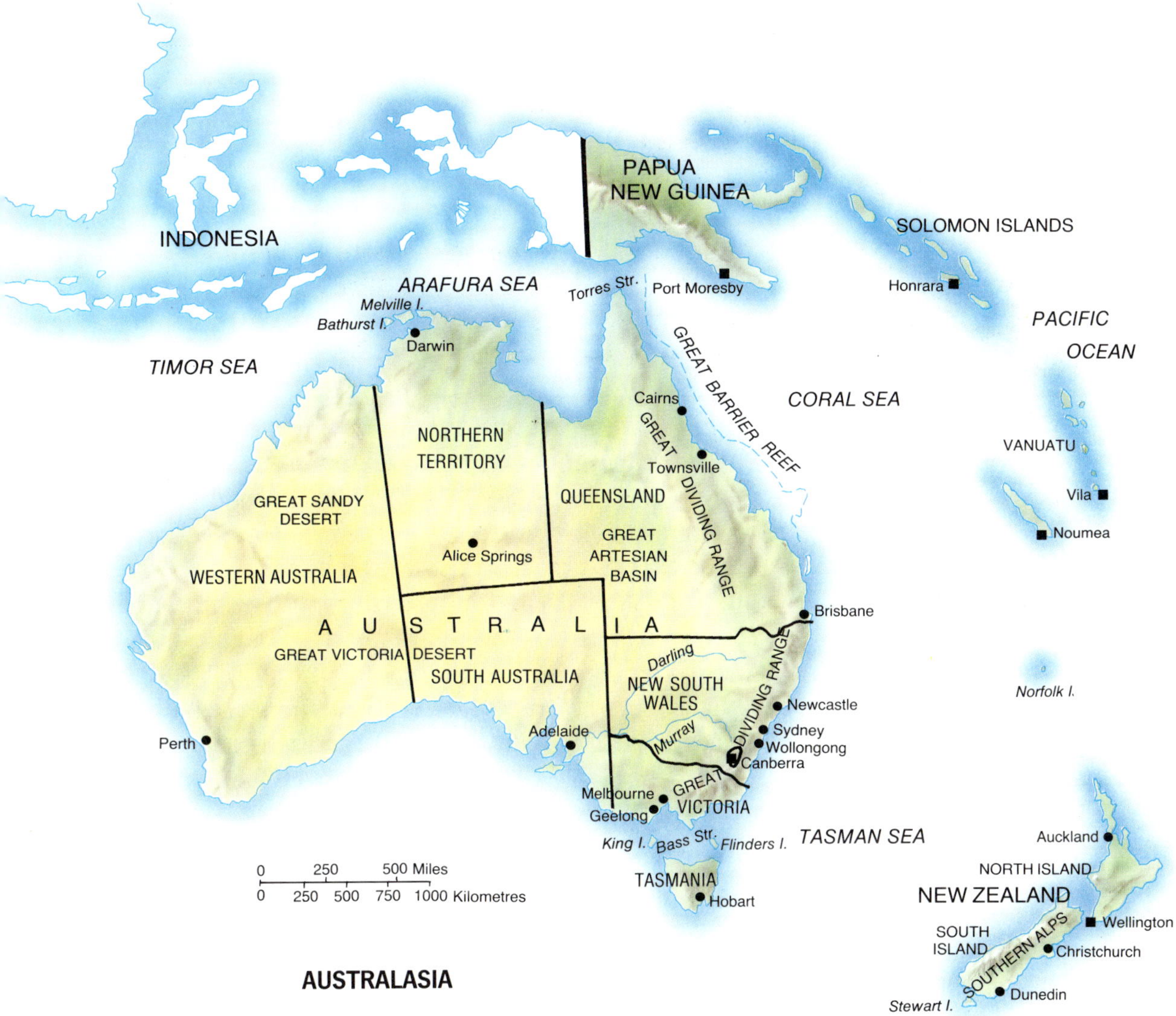

AUSTRALASIA

Below: The harsh, yet beautiful landscape of the Australian wilderness, or outback. The red rock outcrops are typical features of the Australian desert. The sparse vegetation consists mainly of coarse grass and dry bushes.

Australia

New Zealand

Nauru

Solomon Islands

Tuvalu

Western Samoa

Fiji

Kiribati

Papua-New Guinea

Tonga

Vanuatu

The climate is mild. Two-thirds of the people live in towns, but farming is the main activity. Leading exports are wool, beef, lamb, mutton and dairy products. Most of New Zealand's electricity comes from hydro-electric power stations situated in both the North and South Islands.

Australia is a very flat empty country. To the west there are plateaus, most of which are desert. There are vast, dry plains in the centre, and highlands in the east and south-east. The famous Great Barrier Reef, the largest coral reef in the world, runs along the northeastern coast. More than half the people live in the four largest cities (Sydney, Melbourne, Brisbane and Adelaide).

The first people in Australia were probably the Tasmanian Aborigines. They were driven south to the island of Tasmania by the Australian Aborigines who probably originated in Asia. In 1788 Britain set up a convict settlement in Sydney. The first free settlers arrived in 1793, and the numbers of British immigrants soon increased. After the Second World War (1939–45), settlers began to arrive from other European countries, such as Greece and Yugo-

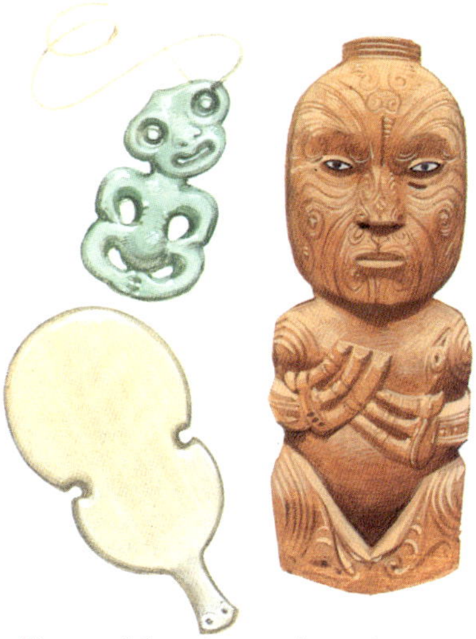

Above: Maori woodcarvings. Maoris were New Zealand's first people. Today, there are about 290,000 Maoris living in New Zealand making up the largest minority group.

Right: Mount Cook, in South Island, is the highest peak in New Zealand. It rises from the main range of mountains, the Southern Alps, to a height of 3764 metres (12,349 feet). The mountain is rugged, and glaciers lie in its upper valleys, high above the thick forests.

Above: The Fijian people make good use of the palm trees for traditional crafts and buildings.

Right: Some of Australasia's native animals. The kiwi is the only known bird that has nostrils at the end of its bill.

Above: Bora Bora is one of the Pacific Islands. It belongs to France. The island was made by volcanoes.

slavia. There are also people of Asian origin who have settled in Australia.

Australia is a leading producer of bauxite, iron ore and lead, while other metals, coal and oil are also mined. Australia's 150 million sheep produce wool which, along with wheat, beef and dairy products, is one of Australia's chief agricultural exports. The many climates in Australia (from the tropical north to temperate Tasmania) enable a variety of crops, including sugarcane, barley, rice and potatoes, to be grown. Industry is also becoming important, chiefly in the south and east.

AUSTRALASIAN ANIMALS

Above: During the late 1980s almost one million East Germans, dissatisfied with their lives under communist control, fled through the open borders of Czechoslovakia and Austria to political freedom in the West. As a result of this exodus, the East German government was forced to promise reforms and in November 1989 it relaxed travel restrictions and opened East Germany's borders. Almost immediately the people of East and West Berlin began to pull down the Berlin Wall, which had for almost 29 years divided the city into two: the east of the city belonging to communist East Germany and the west to democratic West Germany.

Europe

In order of size among the world's continents, Europe comes sixth. However, in order of population, Europe comes second. One-sixth of the world's people lives in Europe. Only Asia, which is four times the size of Europe, has a higher population.

Most of Europe has a mild and pleasant climate, neither very cold in winter nor too hot in summer. There are some inhospitable regions. The Arctic regions of northern Europe are very cold, but the northwestern shores are warmed by the waters of the North Atlantic Drift. The countries by the Mediterranean Sea in the south are very warm. Europe has a wide variety of plant life, with many different kinds of flowers, shrubs and trees. The scenery often changes rapidly as the traveller moves from mountains to valleys, from flat plains to neatly ploughed fields. There are wide fertile grasslands, especially in the east, and some thick forests of conifers and broad-leaved trees, although much of the ancient forest has been cleared to make way for cities, factories and farms.

Europe has high mountains, such as the Alps and Pyrenees in the west, and the Urals and Caucasus in the east which divide Europe from Asia. The highest mountain is Mount Elbruz in the Caucasus Mountains of the USSR. It is 5633 metres (18,480 feet) high. Europe's biggest lake is also in the USSR. It is the Caspian Sea. Much of northern

Right: Europe is famous for wine-making. The main European wine producing countries are West Germany, Spain, Greece, Italy and France. In the wine-making process, ripe grapes are harvested when they contain the maximum amount of sugar (this is tested using special equipment). Bunches of grapes are harvested with a sharp knife and taken to the crusher or wine-press. The resulting mixture of grape skins, pips and juice is then put into the fermenting vats. After fermentation the wine is run into barrels. It is refined several times, stored for a while, and later bottled.

Below: The Leaning Tower of Pisa has been sinking sideways since it was completed in 1350. The lean of the tower has increased about 30 cm during the past 100 years. It is one of Italy's most famous tourist attractions.

Europe consists of lowlands or rolling hills and river valleys. Some land is very flat and low-lying. About 40 per cent of the Netherlands is below sea level. Much of the continent has rich soil that produces high crop yields. Today, there are few parts of Europe that remain undeveloped.

Eastern Europe has only a few big rivers, but they can be navigated by river craft for long distances. Chief among these eastern rivers are the Volga and Danube. Western European rivers include the Rhine. The west coast of Europe is washed by the Atlantic Ocean. Europe has good rainfall, and there are no deserts. Much of the land is very fertile. Cereals, fruit and vegetables can be grown well, and there is good pasture for cattle and sheep. There are also a number of valuable minerals, such as coal and iron ore.

Throughout its long history, Europe has been settled by many different peoples. The Ancient Greeks and Romans were the two most influential European civilizations. Since that time Europe has been a centre of art and learning. It is often called the birthplace of Western civilization. Europe is a continent of great cities, such as London, Paris, Moscow, Rome, Athens and Vienna. Many European cities are hundreds of years old, and their castles, churches and museums are full of fascinating history. But there are also tiny villages, sometimes even older and full of interest

for the visitor. Millions of tourists journey around Europe each year to look at its historical treasures.

The people of Europe are made up of many different nationalities. There are 34 independent countries, including Turkey and the USSR (which are partly in Asia). The biggest country is the USSR. The smallest European country is the Vatican City. The people of Europe speak many languages. There are three main language groups: the Romance languages (such as Italian, French and Spanish); the Balto-Slavic languages (such as Russian and Polish); and the Germanic and Scandinavian languages (which include German, Swedish and Danish). But there are other smaller languages, such as Scottish Gaelic which belongs to the Celtic group. A number of people living in Europe are of African, Caribbean, or Asian origin.

This variety of peoples accounts for the richness of Europe's culture. In the past, differences between nations often led to quarrels and to war. European wars often affected the rest of the world, because some of the countries of Europe were very powerful. The strongest countries, such as Britain and France, built up large empires overseas from the 1600s. Today, Europeans no longer rule overseas empires. Since World War II (1939–45), which left much of Europe in ruins, the countries of Europe have

Prague (*above*), capital of Czechoslovakia,and Moscow (*below*), capital of the USSR, are rich cultural centres with many art galleries, museums and beautiful historic buildings.

Right: Switzerland has now become a popular destination for winter as well as summer holidays. Every year from late December to April, towns and villages in the Alps become full of skiers looking for excitement on the slopes, and traditional food and hospitality in the evenings. In the past few years, however, mild winters have caused a severe lack of snow in the early part of the season. Some resorts have installed machines to create snow artificially.

Above: The historic island of Sardinia attracts many thousands of tourists every year. It is popular for its beautiful beaches and hot summers. An Italian island, Sardinia keeps up many of its ancient customs and traditions. It lies in the Mediterranean Sea about 160 km (100 miles) from the Italian mainland. Sardinia is the second largest of the Mediterranean islands.

tried to live in peace. Divisions between the communist countries of the east and the free nations of the west have begun to break down, with the ending of the 'cold war'.

Twelve countries of western Europe belong to an economic and trading association called the European Community, sometimes known as the Common Market. Its aim is to remove trade barriers between members, and to make Europe as powerful in international trade as Japan and the United States.

Europe lives by trade. Although it has some of the most modern and efficient farms in the world, Europe cannot grow enough food to feed its population of more than 700 million people. Ever since the Industrial Revolution of the 1700s and 1800s, which began in Europe, the countries of

Above: Flags of most of the European nations.

Below: A beautiful and colourful way of preserving old traditions – the Swedish national costume.

Europe have relied more and more on industry. There are many factories, making all kinds of goods. European workers make aircraft, vehicles, machinery, electrical goods, textiles, clothing, processed food and other manufactured goods for sale all over the world. Europe is also a centre for banking and finance. Most of Europe's people live and work in towns and cities.

Europe has good roads, railways, airports and canals. Ships carry goods across the Baltic Sea, the North Sea and the Mediterranean Sea, and Europe has some of the world's busiest ports, such as Rotterdam in the Netherlands. In the 1400s and 1500s the search for new trade links encouraged European merchants to explore Africa, Asia and America. Later, European countries started colonies in these areas, and in the 1800s millions of poor people left Europe to begin new lives as settlers in the

Right: The fishing industry is very important to Europe as it provides jobs and food for millions of people. Limits are fixed to protect species such as haddock and cod from being overfished. Although all the coastal waters are fished, the chief fishing grounds include the North Sea, the Baltic Sea and the polar waters of the Arctic Ocean.

Below: Friesian cows are bred on Europe's farms mainly for dairy foods. They are characterized by their black and white markings. The two colours are defined in two distinct patches. They have horns and a large body, and develop and mature within two years.

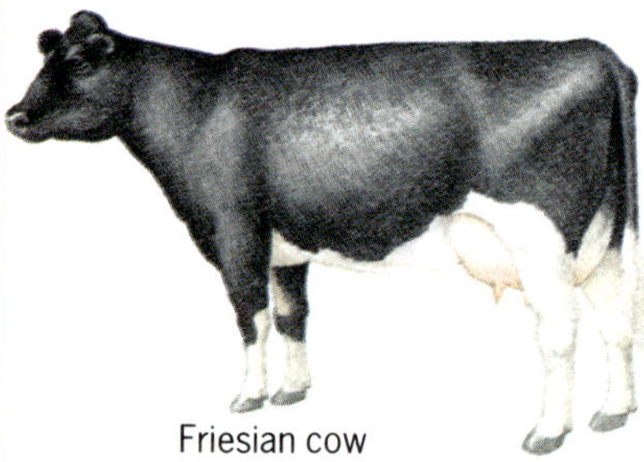

Friesian cow

Right: Much of the Netherlands is low lying and flat. About two thirds of the land is farm land. Dairy farming is a major industry. There are almost five and a half million cattle in the Netherlands, most of them are Friesians.

United States, Canada and Australia. European ideas, languages and discoveries spread throughout the world.

Today, the different nations of Europe are coming closer together. Travel and television have helped break down old national barriers. People visit each other's countries, eat similar foods, and enjoy the same entertainment – such as soccer. National costume is worn nowadays only on special or ceremonial occasions, and the people shopping in a city street in Birmingham (England), Dusseldorf (West Germany) or Milan (Italy) look much the same. Yet this small continent, with about 70 people to every square kilometre of land, still reveals amazing variety.

Left and above: Animals commonly found in Europe. Much of Europe now has few large animals. Wolves and bears, for instance, are almost extinct. Reindeer are kept in herds by the people of Lapland for their hides and meat.

Because Europe is such a crowded continent, there is little room now for the large wild animals such as bison, bears, deer and wolves that were once common. Their habitats have been destroyed in most areas to provide land for building or cultivation. Smaller mammals and birds are still plentiful, and there are fish in the rivers, lakes and seas. In parts of Europe, homes and factories threaten to engulf the countryside. Pesticides and fertilizers used in intensive farming also harm the ecological system. Pollution of soil, air and water is a serious problem in some areas. Europeans must work hard to protect the environment which they share with animals.

Below: Nocturnal (night-time) animals found in the fields and woodlands of northern Europe. In order to survive through the cold weather of winter, hedgehogs and bats hibernate or go into a deep sleep. Their heartbeats and breathing are slowed down and they live off stored fat until the spring. Foxes grow thicker coats during these months.

Right: Within the Arctic Circle is the 'land of the midnight Sun'. In midsummer, the Sun never sets. It sinks close to the horizon at midnight, but never actually sets. So there is daylight for 24 hours. In midwinter, the Sun never rises and there is day-long darkness.

Below: Polar bears live in the Arctic. Their white fur camouflages them against the snow, and they have hair on the soles of their feet to help them grip on slippery ice.

Polar Regions

The Earth has two polar regions, both cold and mostly snow-covered. The area around the North Pole is called the Arctic. Most of it consists of the Arctic Ocean, which is frozen for much of the year. Winters are long and bitterly cold, and for months the Sun never rises. However, in the short, mild summer, the Sun never sets and the warm south winds blow. As the ice melts, brightly coloured flowers, moss, and small bushes grow. Eskimo and Lapp people live in the Arctic.

The Antarctic is a vast ice-covered continent, one and a half times as big as the United States of America. It is the coldest continent in the world. Plant life grows only near the coast where ice and snow melt in summer. But the seas are rich in life, including fish, whales, seals and penguins. There are many sea birds in the Antarctic, some of which fly north to warmer lands when winter comes. The only people who live there work at weather stations and research bases. However, tourists now fly in to visit Antarctica, and in future minerals may be mined there.

Below: The wilderness of Antarctica is surprisingly rich in animal life. Birds and seals feed on fish which are plentiful in the cold plankton-rich ocean.

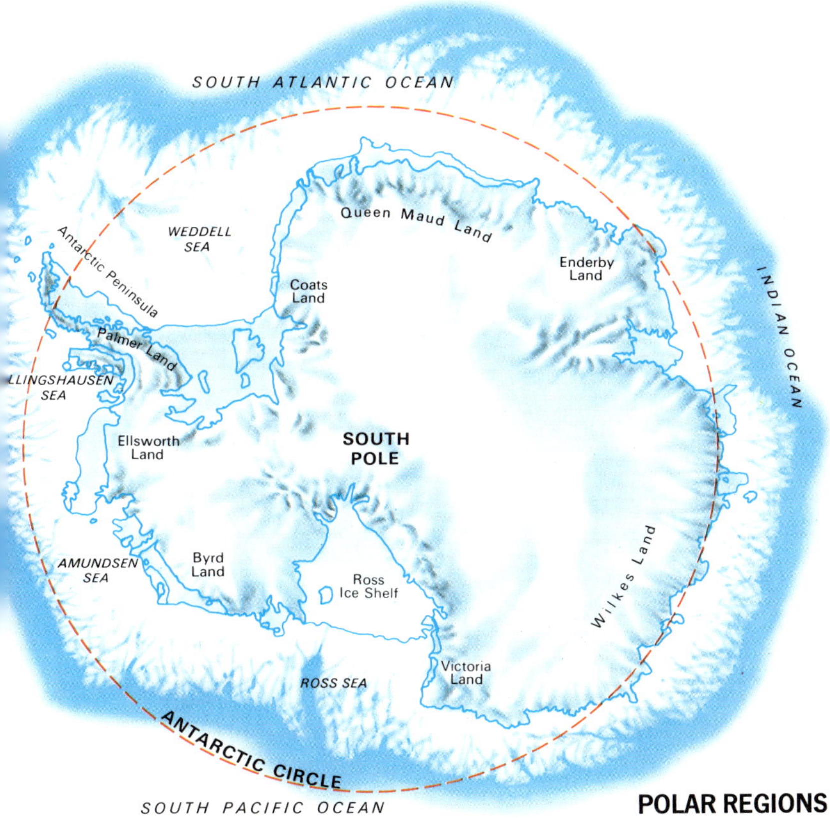

POLAR REGIONS

Above: A Polar Eskimo on a hunting expedition. Snowmobiles are often used now, instead of the traditional dog teams.

Above: The Arctic tern could be considered to be the world's migration champion. It breeds on seacoasts along the Arctic Ocean, and in August each year migrates to the Antarctic, at the other end of the world.

FACTS AND FIGURES

AFRICA

ALGERIA Republic of North Africa.
Area: 2,382,000 sq. km (919,600 sq. mi.).
Population: 25,000,000.
Capital: Algiers.

ANGOLA Republic of west-central Africa.
Area: 1,247,000 sq. km (481,000 sq. mi.).
Population: 8,970,000.
Capital: Luanda.

ASCENSION Island in the South Atlantic, 800 km (500 miles) south of the Equator, a dependency of St Helena.
Area: 88 sq. km (34 sq. mi).
Population: 1000.
Capital: Georgetown.

BENIN Republic on the Gulf of Guinea, West Africa.
Area: 112,600 sq. km (43,480 sq. mi.).
Population: 4,550,000.
Capital: Porto Novo.

BOTSWANA Republic of Southern Africa, a member of the Commonwealth.
Area: 600,400 sq. km (232,000 sq. mi.).
Population: 1,200,000.
Capital: Gaborone.

BURKINA FASO Republic of West Africa formerly called Upper Volta.
Area: 274,200 sq. km (105,900 sq. mi.).
Population: 7,700,000.
Capital: Ouagadougou.

BURUNDI Republic of Central Africa.
Area: 27,800 sq. km (10,750 sq. mi.).
Population: 5,200,000.
Capital: Bujumbura.

CAMEROON Republic of West Africa.
Area: 475,450 sq. km (183,580 sq. mi.).
Population: 10,870,000.
Capital: Yaoundé.

CAPE VERDE Republic, a number of islands in the North Atlantic.
Area: 4030 sq. km (1560 sq. mi.).
Population: 318,000.
Capital: Praia.

CENTRAL AFRICAN REPUBLIC Republic of Equatorial Africa within the French Community.
Area: 622,984 sq. km (240,550 sq. mi.).
Population: 3,000,000.
Capital: Bangui.

CHAD Republic of Equatorial Africa within the French Community.
Area: 1,284,000 sq. km (496,000 sq. mi).
Population: 5,700,000.
Capital: N'djamena.

COMOROS Island republic in Indian Ocean off Mozambique, Africa.
Area: 2170 sq. km (838 sq. mi.).
Population: 460,000.
Capital: Moroni.

CONGO Republic of Equatorial Africa within the French Community.
Area: 342,000 sq. km (132,000 sq. mi.).
Population: 2,030,000.
Capital: Brazzaville.

DJIBOUTI Republic of north-east Africa within the French Community, on the Red Sea.
Area: 22,000 sq. km (8500 sq. mi.).
Population: 330,000.
Capital: Djibouti.

EGYPT Arab republic of north-east Africa.
Area: 1,000,000 sq. km (387,000 sq. mi.).
Population: 54,800,000.
Capital: Cairo.

EQUATORIAL GUINEA Republic of West Africa.
Area: 28,000 sq. km (10,800 sq. mi.).
Population: 390,000.
Capital: Malabo.

ETHIOPIA Republic of north-east Africa.
Area: 1,222,000 sq. km (472,000 sq. mi.).
Population: 43,900,000.
Capital: Addis Ababa.

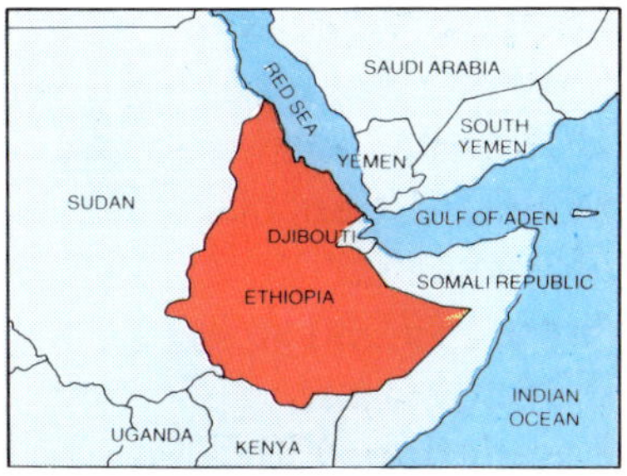

GABON Republic of Equatorial Africa within the French Community.
Area: 268,000 sq. km (103,000 sq. mi.).
Population: 1,100,000.
Capital: Libreville.

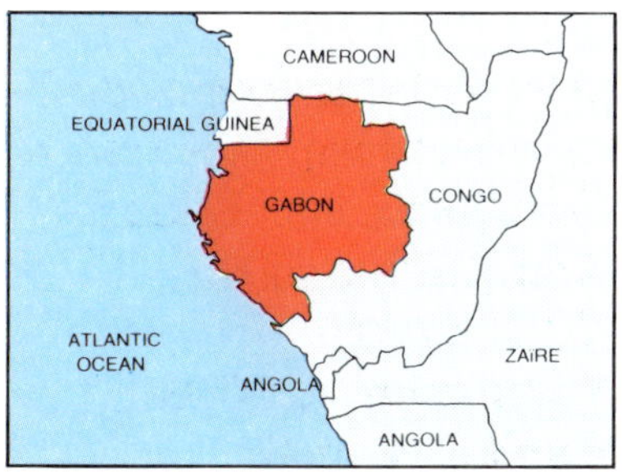

GAMBIA Republic within the Commonwealth in West Africa.
Area: 11,300 sq. km (4300 sq. mi.).
Population: 840,000.
Capital: Banjul.

GHANA Republic of West Africa, a member of the Commonwealth.
Area: 239,000 sq. km (92,000 sq. mi.).
Population: 13,700,000.
Capital: Accra.

GUINEA Republic of West Africa.
Area: 246,000 sq. km (95,000 sq. mi.).
Population: 6,150,000.
Capital: Conakry.

GUINEA-BISSAU Republic of West Africa which includes the Bijagós Islands.
Area: 36,000 sq. km (14,000 sq. mi.).
Population: 930,000.
Capital: Bissau.

IVORY COAST Republic of West Africa.
Area: 322,500 sq. km (124,000 sq. mi.).
Population: 11,800,000.
Capital: Abidjan.

KENYA Republic of East Africa, a member of the Commonwealth.
Area: 582,700 sq. km (225,000 sq. mi.).
Population: 23,700,000.
Capital: Nairobi.

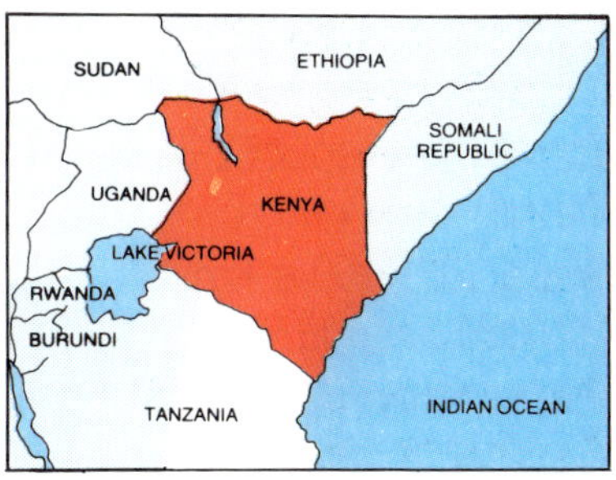

LESOTHO Kingdom of Southern Africa surrounded by the country of South Africa.
Area: 30,360 sq. km (11,700 sq. mi.).
Population: 1,700,000.
Capital: Maseru.

LIBERIA Republic of West Africa.
Area: 98,938 sq. km (38,200 sq. mi.).
Population: 2,500,000.
Capital: Monrovia.

LIBYA Republic of North Africa.
Area: 1,760,000 sq. km (680,000 sq. mi.).
Population: 4,300,000.
Capital: Tripoli.

MADAGASCAR An island republic in Indian Ocean about 400 km (250 miles) east of Africa.
Area: 587,000 sq. km (226,700 sq. mi.).
Population: 11,100,000.
Capital: Antananarivo.

MALAWI Republic of Southern Africa lying on the western shore of Lake Nyasa.
Area: 118,500 sq. km (45,800 sq. mi.).
Population: 8,000,000.
Capital: Lilongwe.

MALI Republic of north-west Africa.
Area: 1,240,000 sq. km (479,000 sq. mi.).
Population: 7,900,000.
Capital: Bamako.

MAURITANIA Republic of north-west Africa.
Area: 1,030,700 sq. km (400,000 sq. mi.).
Population: 1,800,000.
Capital: Nouakchott.

MAURITIUS An independent state in the Indian Ocean, made up of two main islands. A member of the Commonwealth.
Area: 2050 sq. km (790 sq. mi.).
Population: 1,000,000.
Capital: Port Louis.

MAYOTTE A French territory, an island in the Comoro Archipelago.
Area: 374 sq. km (145 sq. mi.).
Population: 77,000.
Capital: Dzaoudzi.

MOROCCO A monarchy of north-west Africa.
Area: 446,500 sq. km (172,400 sq. mi.).
Population: 25,400,000.
Capital: Rabat.

MOZAMBIQUE Republic of south-east Africa.
Area: 800,310 sq. km (309,000 sq. mi.).
Population: 15,300,000.
Capital: Maputo.

NAMIBIA Republic in south-west Africa which became independent in 1990. Prior to this, Namibia's status had been in dispute. South Africa claimed control as it had been granted a mandate to govern the country after World War I by the League of Nations. However, the United Nations voted to end the mandate in 1966.
Area: 824,000 sq. km (318,000 sq. mi.).
Population: 1,200,000.
Capital: Windhoek.

NIGER Republic of West Africa.
Area: 1,267,000 sq. km (489,000 sq. mi.).
Population: 7,400,000.
Capital: Niamey.

NIGERIA Republic of West Africa.
Area: 923,000 sq. km (356,700 sq. mi.).
Population: 115,200,000.
Capital: Lagos (Abuja).

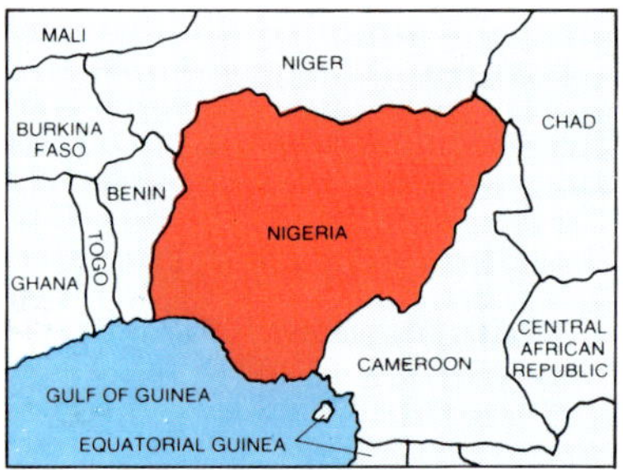

RÉUNION A French overseas department in the Indian Ocean.
Area: 2500 sq. km (969 sq. mi.).
Population: 575,000.
Capital: St Denis.

RWANDA Republic of Central Africa.
Area: 26,400 sq. km. (10,000 sq. mi.).
Population: 7,300,000.
Capital: Kigali.

ST HELENA British colony, including the island of Ascension and the four islands of Tristan da Cunha, in the South Atlantic.
St Helena **area:** 122 sq. km (47 sq. mi.).
Population: 5,200.
Capital: Jamestown.

SÃO TOMÉ AND PRINCIPE Island republic off the west coast of Africa.
Area: 964 sq. km (372 sq. mi.).
Population: 114,000.
Capital: São Tomé.

SENEGAL Republic of West Africa.
Area: 196,000 sq. km (76,000 sq. mi.).
Population: 7,700,000.
Capital: Dakar.

SEYCHELLES Island republic of the Indian Ocean, a member of the Commonwealth.
Area: 443 sq. km (171 sq. mi.).
Population: 70,000.
Capital: Victoria.

SIERRA LEONE Republic of West Africa, an independent member of the Commonwealth.
Area: 71,700 sq. km (27,700 sq. mi.).
Population: 4,300,000.
Capital: Freetown.

SOMALI REPUBLIC Republic of Africa, facing Aden.
Area: 637,700 sq. km (246,000 sq. mi.).
Population: 8,600,000.
Capital: Mogadishu.

SOUTH AFRICA Republic of Southern Africa.
Area: 1,221,000 sq. km (471,500 sq. mi.).
Population: 35,600,000.
Capital: Cape Town (seat of Legislature or law-making assembly); Pretoria (seat of Government); Bloemfontein (judicial capital).

SUDAN Republic of north-east Africa.
Area: 2,506,000 sq. km (967,500 sq. mi.).
Population: 25,000,000.
Capital: Khartoum.

SWAZILAND Kingdom of Southern Africa, a member of the Commonwealth.
Area: 17,400 sq. km (6,700 sq. mi.).
Population: 760,000.
Capital: Mbabane.

TANZANIA Republic of East Africa, a member of the Commonwealth.
Area: 945,000 sq. km (365,000 sq. mi.).
Population: 24,700,000.
Capital: Dodoma.

TOGO Republic of West Africa.
Area: 56,000 sq. km (21,600 sq. mi.).
Population: 3,400,000.
Capital: Lomé.

TRISTAN DA CUNHA Island in the South Atlantic Ocean, a dependency of St Helena.
Area: 98 sq. km (38 sq. mi.).
Population: 320.
Capital: Edinburgh.

TUNISIA Republic of North Africa.
Area: 163,000 sq. km (63,000 sq. mi.).
Population: 7,900,000.
Capital: Tunis.

UGANDA Republic of east-central Africa. A member of the Commonwealth.
Area: 236,000 sq. km (91,000 sq. mi.).
Population: 16,800,000.
Capital: Kampala.

WESTERN SAHARA A North African territory claimed by Morocco and local nationalists.
Area: 266,000 sq. km (102,700 sq. mi.).
Population: 76,000.
Capital: El Aiun.

ZAIRE Republic of west-central Africa.
Area: 2,345,400 sq. km (905,600 sq. mi.).
Population: 34,000,000.
Capital: Kinshasa.

ZAMBIA Republic in south-central Africa. A member of the Commonwealth.
Area: 752,600 sq. km (290,600 sq. mi.).
Population: 7,800,000.
Capital: Lusaka.

ZIMBABWE Republic of Southern Africa. A member of the Commonwealth.
Area: 390,600 sq. km (150,800 sq. mi.).
Population: 10,000,000.
Capital: Harare.

ASIA

AFGHANISTAN Republic of south-western Asia.
Area: 650,000 sq. km (250,000 sq. mi.).
Population: 16,600,000.
Capital: Kabul.

BAHRAIN Island group off Saudi Arabia forming a state.
Area: 622 sq. km (240 sq. mi.).
Population: 480,000.
Capital: Manama.

BANGLADESH Republic in south-east Asia. A member of the Commonwealth.
Area: 144,000 sq. km (55,600 sq. mi.).
Population: 113,000,000.
Capital: Dacca.

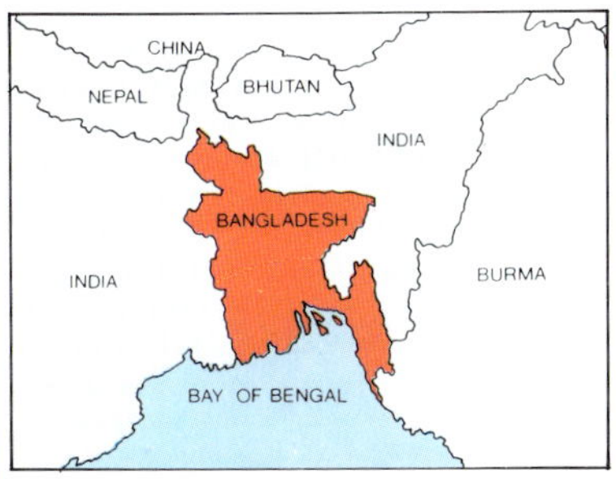

BHUTAN Kingdom of the Himalayas.
Area: 47,000 sq. km (18,000 sq. mi.).
Population: 1,500,000.
Capital: Thimphu.

BRUNEI Sultanate of Borneo. Commonwealth member.
Area: 5,760 sq. km (2,230 sq. mi.).
Population: 240,000.
Capital: Bandar Seri Begawan.

CAMBODIA (Kampuchea) Republic of south-east Asia.
Area: 181,000 sq. km (70,000 sq. mi.).
Population: 6,900,000.
Capital: Phnom Penh.

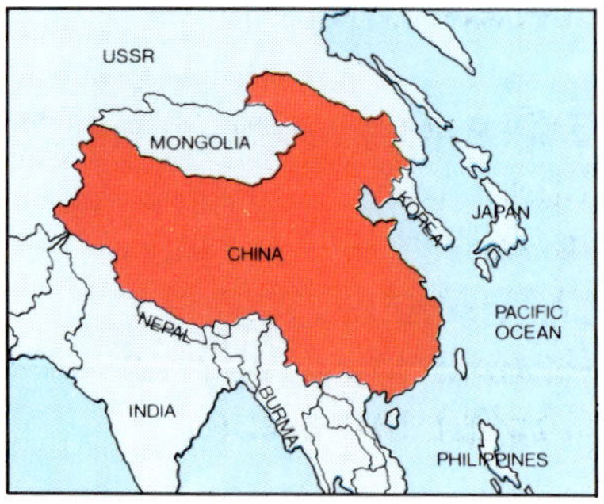

CHINA Republic of east Asia.
Area: 9,597,000 sq. km (3,706,000 sq. mi.).
Population: 1,070,600,000.
Capital: Beijing (Peking).

HONG KONG British dependency on the south coast of China.
Area: 1061 sq. km (410 sq. mi.).
Population: 5,423,000.
Capital: Victoria, usually called Hong Kong.

INDIA Republic of Asia. A member of the Commonwealth.
Area: 3,287,590 sq. km (1,269,345 sq. mi.).
Population: 833,400,000.
Capital: New Delhi.

INDONESIA Republic of south-east Asia.
Area: 1,903,650 sq. km (735,003 sq. mi.).
Population: 187,700,000.
Capital: Djakarta.

IRAN Islamic Republic of south-west Asia. It is one of the Gulf States.
Area: 1,648,000 sq. km. (636,296 sq. mi.).
Population: 51,000,000.
Capital: Tehran.

IRAQ Republic of south-west Asia.
Area: 435,000 sq. km (168,000 sq. mi.).
Population: 17,600,000.
Capital: Baghdad.

ISRAEL Republic of the Middle East.
Area: 20,700 sq. km (8000 sq. mi.).
Population: 4,500,000.
Capital: Jerusalem.

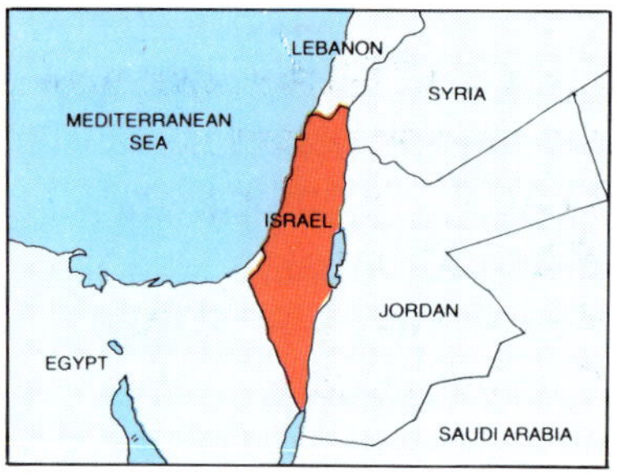

JAPAN Constitutional monarchy of the Far East.
Area: 372,300 sq. km (143,800 sq. mi.).
Population: 123,200,000.
Capital: Tokyo.

JORDAN Kingdom of the Middle East.
Area: 97,740 sq. km (37,700 sq. mi.).
Population: 3,000,000.
Capital: Amman.

KOREA, NORTH Republic of the Far East bordering on north-east China.
Area: 120,500 sq. km (46,500 sq. mi.).
Population: 22,000,000.
Capital: Pyongyang.

KOREA, SOUTH Republic of the Far East.
Area: 98,000 sq. km (38,000 sq. mi.).
Population: 45,200,000.
Capital: Seoul.

KUWAIT An Emirate on the Persian Gulf in south-west Asia.
Area: 17,800 sq. km (6900 sq. mi.).
Population: 2,000,000.
Capital: Kuwait.

LAOS Republic of south-east Asia lying in the Mekong Basin.
Area: 236,800 sq. km (91,400 sq. mi.).
Population: 3,900,000.
Capital: Vientiane.

LEBANON Republic of the Middle East at the eastern end of the Mediterranean Sea.
Area: 10,400 sq. km (4000 sq. mi.).
Population: 2,900,000.
Capital: Beirut.

MACÃO An overseas territory of Portugal on the south-east coast of China.
Area: 16 sq. km (6 sq. mi.).
Population: 430,000.
Capital: Macão.

MALAYSIA A state of south-east Asia. A member of the Commonwealth.
Area: 330,000 sq. km (127,300 sq. mi.).
Population: 16,900,000.
Capital: Kuala Lumpur.

MALDIVES An island republic of the Indian Ocean southwest of India, with about 2000 islands. A member of the Commonwealth.
Area: 300 sq. km (115 sq. mi.).
Population: 200,000.
Capital: Malé.

MONGOLIA Republic of central Asia.
Area: 1,565,000 sq. km (604,300 sq. mi.).
Population: 2,000,000.
Capital: Ulan Bator.

MYANMAR (Burma) Republic of south-east Asia.
Area: 676,500 sq. km (261,230 sq. mi.).
Population: 40,000,000.
Capital: Yangon (Rangoon).

NEPAL A monarchy of the Himalayas between China and India.
Area: 140,800 sq. km (54,000 sq. mi.).
Population: 18,800,000.
Capital: Katmandu.

OMAN A sultanate at the eastern end of the Arabian peninsula, bordering the Arabian Sea.
Area: 212,400 sq. km (82,000 sq. mi.).
Population: 1,400,000.
Capital: Muscat.

PAKISTAN Republic of southern Asia. Member of the Commonwealth.
Area: 804,000 sq. km (310,400 sq. mi.).
Population: 110,400,000.
Capital: Islamabad.

PHILIPPINES Republic of many islands in south-east Asia.
Area: 330,000 sq. km (116,000 sq. mi.).
Population: 62,000,000.
Capital: Manila.

QATAR An Emirate, a peninsula in the Persian Gulf.
Area: 11,000 sq. km (4000 sq. mi.).
Population: 340,000.
Capital: Doha.

SAUDI ARABIA Kingdom of the Arabian peninsula.
Area: 2,175,600 sq. km (840,000 sq. mi.).
Population: 12,700,000.
Capital: Riyadh.

SINGAPORE Island republic at tip of the Malaya peninsula, a member of the Commonwealth.
Area: 580 sq. km (224 sq. mi.).
Population: 2,700,000.
Capital: Singapore.

SRI LANKA Island republic of south Asia in the Indian Ocean, a member of the Commonwealth.
Area: 65,600 sq. km (25,000 sq. mi.).
Population: 17,500,000.
Capital: Colombo.

SYRIA Republic of the Middle East.
Area: 185,000 sq. km (71,500 sq. mi.).
Population: 12,200,000.
Capital: Damascus.

TAIWAN (Republic of China). Republic about 140 km (90 miles) off mainland China.
Area: 36,000 sq. km (14,000 sq. mi.).
Population: 20,300,000.
Capital: Taipei.

THAILAND Kingdom of south-east Asia.
Area: 514,000 sq. km (198,000 sq. mi.).
Population: 55,000,000.
Capital: Bangkok.

TURKEY Republic partly in Europe, partly in Asia.
Area: 780,000 sq. km. (301,400 sq. mi.).
Population: 55,400,000.
Capital: Ankara.

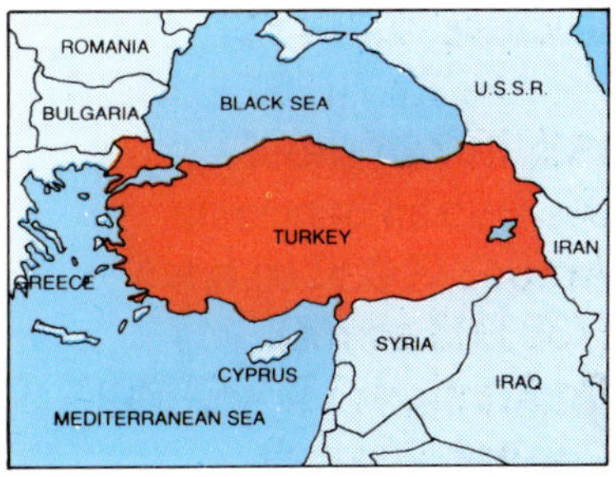

UNITED ARAB EMIRATES A federation of seven independent emirates in the Persian Gulf. They are: Abu Dhabi, Ajman, Dubai, Fujairah, Ras al Khaimah, Sharjah and Umm al Qaiwain.
Area: 83,600 sq. km (32,300 sq. mi.).
Population: 1,500,000.
Capital: Abu Dhabi.

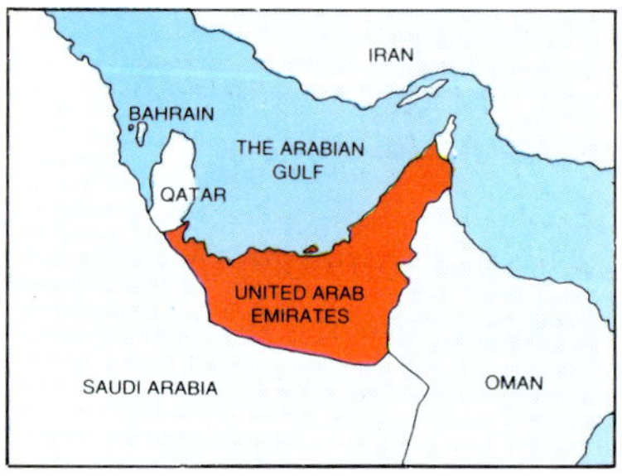

VIETNAM Republic of south-east Asia bordering on south China.
Area: 330,000 sq. km (127,250 sq. mi.).
Population: 66,700,000.
Capital: Hanoi.

YEMEN ARAB REPUBLIC (North Yemen). Republic in the southwest of the Arabian peninsula.
Area: 195,000 sq. km (75,300 sq. mi.).
Population: 7,000,000.
Capital: San'a.

YEMEN PEOPLE'S DEMOCRATIC REPUBLIC (South Yemen). Republic in the Arabian peninsula.
Area: 333,000 sq. km (128,600 sq. mi.).
Population: 2,500,000.
Capital: Aden.

EUROPE

ALBANIA Republic of Europe in the Balkans.
Area: 28,700 sq. km (11,100 sq. mi.).
Population: 3,200,000.
Capital: Tirana.

ANDORRA Tiny landlocked country of the Pyrenees: sovereignty divided between France and the Spanish Bishop of Urgel.
Area: 453 sq. km (175 sq. mi.).
Population: 56,000.
Capital: Andorra la Vella.

AUSTRIA Republic of central Europe.
Area: 83,850 sq. km (32,376 sq. mi.).
Population: 7,500,000.
Capital: Vienna.

BELGIUM Kingdom of northern Europe.
Area: 30,500 sq. km (11,800 sq. mi.).
Population: 9,900,000.
Capital: Brussels.

BULGARIA Republic of Europe in the Balkans.
Area: 111,000 sq. km (42,855 sq. mi.).
Population: 9,000,000.
Capital: Sofia.

CYPRUS Island republic in the Mediterranean, divided since Turkish forces occupied the North in 1974. A member of the Commonwealth.
Area: 9,250 sq. km (3600 sq. mi.).
Population: 700,000.
Capital: Nicosia.

CZECHOSLOVAKIA Republic of central Europe.
Area: 128,000 sq. km (50,000 sq. mi.).
Population: 15,500,000.
Capital: Prague.

DENMARK Kingdom of northern Europe.
Area: 45,000 sq. km (17,400 sq. mi.).
Population: 5,100,000.
Capital: Copenhagen.

FINLAND Republic of north-east Europe
Area: 337,000 sq. km (130,000 sq. mi.).
Population: 5,000,000.
Capital: Helsinki.

FRANCE Republic of western Europe.
Area: 547,000 sq. km (213,000 sq. mi.).
Population: 55,800,000.
Capital: Paris.

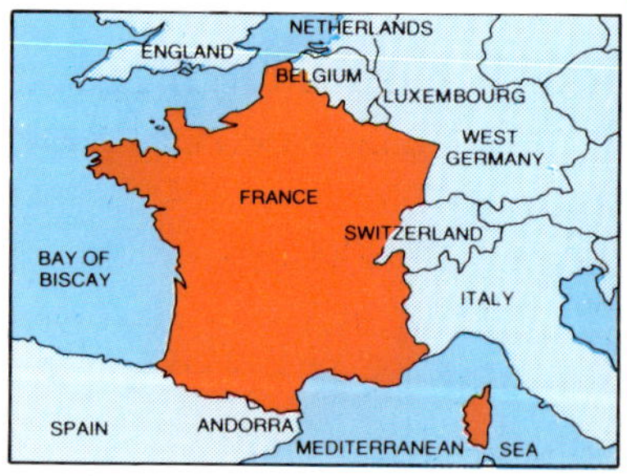

GERMAN DEMOCRATIC REPUBLIC (East Germany) Republic of eastern Europe.
Area: 108,000 sq. km (41,800 sq. mi.).
Population: 16,700,000.
Capital: East Berlin.

GERMANY, FEDERAL REPUBLIC OF (West Germany) Republic of western Europe.
Area: 248,000 sq. km (96,000 sq. mi.).
Population: 61,000,000.
Capital: Bonn.

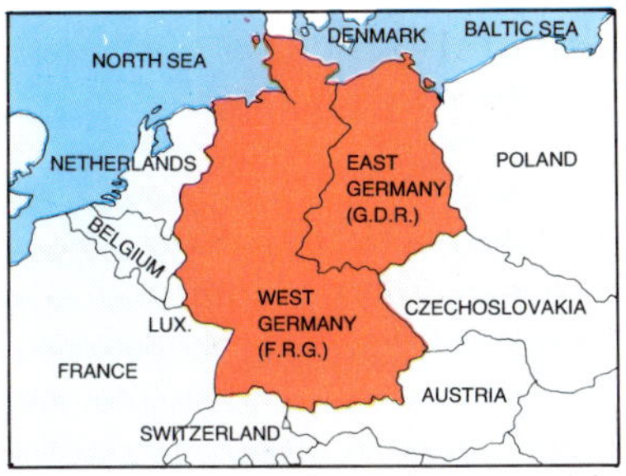

GIBRALTAR British colony at tip of Spain.
Area: 6.5 sq. km ($2\frac{1}{2}$ sq. mi.).
Population: 31,000.
Capital: Gibraltar.

GREECE Republic of south-east Europe which includes many islands.
Area: 132,000 sq. km (51,000 sq. mi.).
Population: 10,100,000.
Capital: Athens.

GREENLAND Self-governing part of Denmark in the North Atlantic.
Area: 2,176,000 sq. km (840,000 sq. mi.).
Population: 54,000.
Capital: Godthaab.

HUNGARY Republic of central Europe.
Area: 93,000 sq. km (36,000 sq. mi.).
Population: 10,500,000.
Capital: Budapest.

ICELAND Island republic of the northern Atlantic.
Area: 103,000 sq. km (40,000 sq. mi.).
Population: 244,000.
Capital: Reykjavik.

IRELAND, REPUBLIC OF Republic of northern Europe.
Area: 70,200 sq. km (27,000 sq. mi.).
Population: 3,700,000.
Capital: Dublin.

ITALY Republic of southern Europe.
Area: 301,000 sq. km (116,000 sq. mi.).
Population: 57,400,000.
Capital: Rome.

LIECHTENSTEIN A principality of western Europe.
Area: 157 sq. km (62 sq. mi.).
Population: 28,000.
Capital: Vaduz.

LUXEMBOURG A Grand Duchy of western Europe.
Area: 2600 sq. km (1000 sq. mi.).
Population: 400,000.
Capital: Luxembourg City.

MALTA An island republic of the Mediterranean, a member of the Commonwealth.
Area: 316 sq. km (122 sq. mi.).
Population: 400,000.
Capital: Valetta.

MONACO A principality on the Mediterranean coast, in south-east France.
Area: 1.9 sq. km (467 acres).
Population: 28,000.
Capital: Monaco.

NETHERLANDS Kingdom of north-west Europe.
Area: 40,844 sq. km (15,770 sq. mi.).
Population: 14,700,000.
Capital: Amsterdam.

NORWAY Kingdom of northern Europe.
Area: 324,219 sq. km (125,182 sq. mi.).
Population: 4,200,000.
Capital: Oslo.

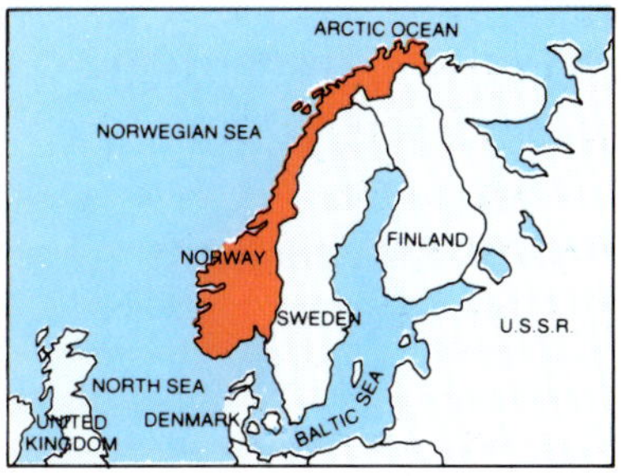

POLAND Republic of eastern Europe.
Area: 312,677 sq. km (120,725 sq. mi.).
Population: 38,400,000.
Capital: Warsaw.

PORTUGAL Republic in south-west Europe.
Area: 92,082 sq. km (35,553 sq. mi.).
Population: 10,240,000.
Capital: Lisbon.

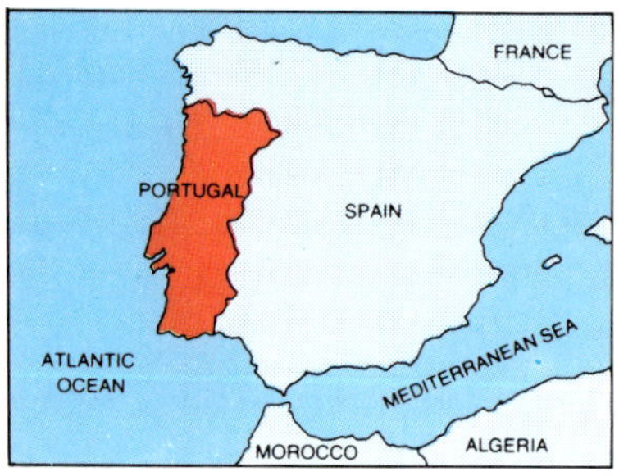

ROMANIA Republic in eastern Europe.
Area: 237,500 sq. km (91,699 sq. mi.).
Population: 22,316,000.
Capital: Bucharest.

SAN MARINO Republic in the Apennines, Italy.
Area: 61 sq. km (24 sq. mi.).
Population: 23,000.
Capital: San Marino.

SPAIN Kingdom of Europe.
Area: 504,700 sq. km (195,000 sq. mi.).
Population: 39,800,000.
Capital: Madrid.

SWEDEN Kingdom of northern Europe.
Area: 450,000 sq. km (173,700 sq. mi.).
Population: 8,300,000.
Capital: Stockholm.

SWITZERLAND Republic of western Europe.
Area: 41,000 sq. km (16,000 sq. mi.).
Population: 6,500,000.
Capital: Bern.

UNION OF SOVIET SOCIALIST REPUBLICS The world's largest nation spanning Europe and Asia.
Total Area: 22,402,200 sq. km (8,650,000 sq. mi.).
Population: 287,015,000.
Capital: Moscow.
Republics of the USSR: Armenia; Azerbaijan; Belorussia; Estonia; Georgia; Kazakhstan; Kirgizia; Latvia; Lithuania; Moldavia; Russian SFSR; Tadzhikistan; Turkmenistan; Ukraine; and Uzbekistan.

UNITED KINGDOM Kingdom of north-west Europe.
Area: 244,046 sq. km (94,232 sq. mi.).
Population: 56,800,000.
Capital: London.
The United Kingdom consists of the following:

England
Area: 130,363 sq. km (50,336 sq. mi.).
Population: 47,250,000.
Capital: London.

Scotland
Area: 78,772 sq. km (30,416 sq. mi.).
Population: 5,120,000.
Capital: Edinburgh.

Wales
Area: 20,763 sq. km (8017 sq. mi.).
Population: 2,820,000.
Capital: Cardiff.

Northern Ireland
Area: 14,148 sq. km (5463 sq. mi.).
Population: 1,600,000.
Capital: Belfast.

Isle of Man
Area: 588 sq. km (227 sq. mi.).
Population: 62,000.
Capital: Douglas.

Channel Islands Group of islands off north-west coast of France.
Area: 195 sq. km (75 sq. mi.).
Jersey
Area: 116 sq. km (45 sq. mi.).
Population: 73,000.
Capital: St. Helier.
Guernsey
Area: 63 sq. km ($24\frac{1}{2}$ sq. mi.).
Dependencies: Alderney 8 sq. km (3 sq. mi.), Sark 5 sq. km (2 sq. mi.), Herm 130 hectares (320 acres), Brechou 30 hectares (74 acres), Jethou 18 hectares (44 acres), Lithou 15 hectares (38 acres).
Total population: 131,000.
Capital: St. Peter Port.

VATICAN CITY State in north-west Rome, Italy, in which is located the government of the Roman Catholic Church.
Area: 44 hectares (108.7 acres).
Population: 1000.

YUGOSLAVIA A federal republic on the Adriatic.
Area: 255,800 sq. km (98,800 sq. mi.).
Population: 23,753,000.
Capital: Belgrade.

NORTH AND CENTRAL AMERICA

ANGUILLA British colony of the Leeward Islands, West Indies.
Area: 90 sq. km (35 sq. mi.).
Population: 6,500.
Capital: The Valley.

ANTIGUA and BARBUDA State of the West Indies within the Commonwealth.
Area: 440 sq. km (170 sq. mi.).
Population: 82,000.
Capital: St. John's.

BAHAMAS An independent Commonwealth member in the West Atlantic.
Area: 14,000 sq. km (5,380 sq. mi.).
Population: 240,000.
Capital: Nassau.

BARBADOS Independent Commonwealth member in the West Indies.
Area: 430 sq. km (166 sq. mi.).
Population: 250,000.
Capital: Bridgetown.

BELIZE State on the east coast of Central America, a member of the Commonwealth.
Area: 22,960 sq. km (8860 sq. mi.).
Population: 180,000.
Capital: Belmopan.

BERMUDA British dependent territory in the West Atlantic.
Area: 53 sq. km (20 sq. mi.).
Population: 62,000.
Capital: Hamilton.

CANADA Independent member of the Commonwealth in the north of North America.
Area: 9,976,000 sq. km (3,852,000 sq. mi.).
Population: 25,600,000.
Capital: Ottawa.
Canada has 12 provinces listed below:

Canada

Province	**Capital**
Alberta	Edmonton
British Columbia	Victoria
Manitoba	Winnipeg
New Brunswick	Fredericton
Newfoundland	St. John's
Northwest Terr.	Yellowknife
Nova Scotia	Halifax
Ontario	Toronto
Prince Edward Is.	Charlottetown
Quebec	Quebec
Saskatchewan	Regina
Yukon Territory	Whitehorse

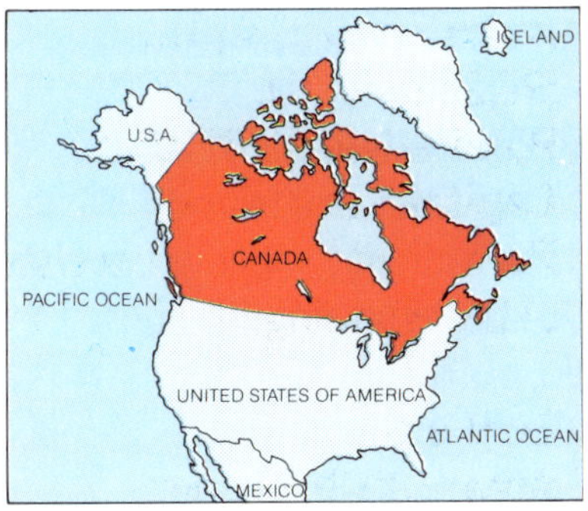

CAYMAN ISLANDS British colony, a number of islands in the West Indies.
Area: 260 sq. km (100 sq. mi.).
Population: 23,000.
Capital: George Town.

COSTA RICA Republic of Central America.
Area: 50,700 sq. km (19,600 sq. mi.).
Population: 2,900,000.
Capital: San José.

CUBA West Indian republic.
Area: 114,500 sq. km (44,220 sq. mi.).
Population: 10,600,000.
Capital: Havana.

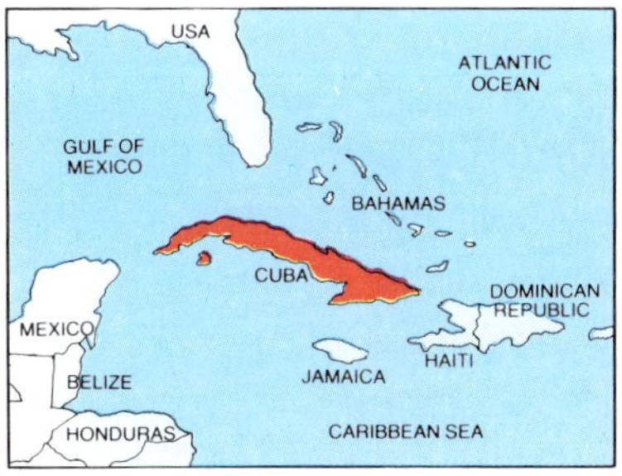

DOMINICA Republic within the Commonwealth in the Windward Islands, West Indies
Area: 751 sq. km (290 sq. mi.).
Population: 74,000.
Capital: Roseau.

DOMINICAN REPUBLIC Republic of the West Indies, occupying two-thirds of the island of Hispaniola.
Area: 49,000 sq. km (18,800 sq. mi.).
Population: 7,300,000.
Capital: Santo Domingo.

EL SALVADOR Republic of Central America.
Area: 21,000 sq. km (8000 sq. mi.).
Population: 5,550,000.
Capital: San Salvador.

GRENADA An independent country within the Commonwealth, one of the Windward Islands.
Area: 344 sq. km (133 sq. mi.).
Population: 86,000.
Capital: St. George's.

GUADELOUPE A French overseas department in the West Indies.
Area: 1780 sq. km (688 sq. mi.).
Population: 332,000.
Capital: Basse-Terre.

GUATEMALA Republic of Central America.
Area: 108,900 sq. km (42,000 sq. mi.).
Population: 9,400,000.
Capital: Guatemala City.

HAITI Republic of the West Indies, occupying one third of the island of Hispaniola.
Area: 28,000 sq. km (10,700 sq. mi.).
Population: 6,200,000.
Capital: Port-au-Prince.

HONDURAS Republic of Central America.
Area: 112,000 sq. km. (43,000 sq. mi.).
Population: 5,100,000.
Capital: Tegucigalpa.

JAMAICA An independent member of the Commonwealth in the West Indies.
Area: 11,000 sq. km (4,200 sq. mi.).
Population: 2,400,000.
Capital: Kingston.

MARTINIQUE A French overseas department in the West Indies.
Area: 1,100 sq. km (426 sq. mi.).
Population: 117,000.
Capital: Fort-de-France.

MEXICO Republic of North America.
Area: 1,970,000 sq. km (761,000 sq. mi.).
Population: 88,000,000.
Capital: Mexico City.

MONTSERRAT British colony in the Leeward Islands, West Indies.
Area: 98 sq. km (38 sq. mi.).
Population: 12,000.
Capital: Plymouth.

NETHERLANDS ANTILLES (Dutch West Indies) Two groups of Dutch islands in the Caribbean, with full internal autonomy.
Area: 960 sq. km (370 sq. mi.).
Population: 187,000.
Capital: Willemstad.

NICARAGUA Republic of Central America.
Area: 130,000 sq. km (50,000 sq. mi.).
Population: 3,700,000.
Capital: Managua.

PANAMA Republic of Central America.
Area: 75,700 sq. km (29,000 sq. mi.).
Population: 2,400,000.
Capital: Panama.

PUERTO RICO A United States self-governing Commonwealth in the West Indies.
Area: 8900 sq. km (3435 sq. mi.).
Population: 3,666,000.
Capital: San Juan.

ST KITTS-NEVIS A state in the Leeward Islands of the West Indies within the Commonwealth.
Area: 260 sq. km (100 sq. mi.).
Population: 40,000.
Capital: Basseterre.

ST LUCIA An independent state within the Commonwealth; one of the Windward Islands.
Area: 616 sq. km (238 sq. mi.).
Population: 120,000.
Capital: Castries.

ST PIERRE AND MIQUELON A French overseas department; eight islands off Newfoundland, Canada.
Area: 242 sq. km (93 sq. mi.).
Population: 6000.
Capital: St. Pierre.

ST VINCENT AND THE GRENADINES An independent member of the Commonwealth in the Windward Islands, West Indies.
Area: 388 sq. km (150 sq. mi.).

Population: 100,000.
Capital: Kingstown.

TRINIDAD AND TOBAGO Island Republic of the West Indies within the Commonwealth.
Area: 5000 sq. km (2000 sq. mi.).
Population: 1,300,000.
Capital: Port-of-Spain.

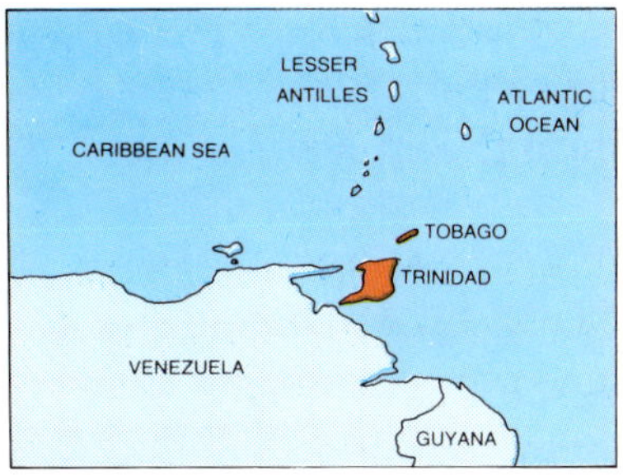

TURKS AND CAICOS ISLANDS British colony in the Caribbean.
Area: 430 sq. km (166 sq. mi.).
Population: 7,200.
Capital: Cockburn Town.

UNITED STATES OF AMERICA Federal republic of North America.
Area: 9,363,123 sq. km (3,615,319 sq. mi.).
Population: 249,800,000.
Capital: Washington, District of Columbia. The United States is made up of 50 states. These are listed below:

State	Capital
Alabama	Montgomery
Alaska	Juneau
Arizona	Phoenix
Arkansas	Little Rock
California	Sacramento
Colorado	Denver
Connecticut	Hartford
Delaware	Dover
Florida	Tallahassee
Georgia	Atlanta
Hawaii	Honolulu
Idaho	Boise
Illinois	Springfield
Indiana	Indianapolis
Iowa	Des Moines
Kansas	Topeka
Kentucky	Frankfort
Louisiana	Baton Rouge
Maine	Augusta
Maryland	Annapolis
Massachusetts	Boston
Michigan	Lansing
Minnesota	St. Paul
Mississippi	Jackson
Missouri	Jefferson City
Montana	Helena
Nebraska	Lincoln
Nevada	Carson City
New Hampshire	Concord
New Jersey	Trenton
New Mexico	Santa Fé
New York	Albany
North Carolina	Raleigh
North Dakota	Bismarck
Ohio	Columbus
Oklahoma	Oklahoma City
Oregon	Salem
Pennsylvania	Harrisburg
Rhode Island	Providence
South Carolina	Columbia
South Dakota	Pierre
Tennessee	Nashville
Texas	Austin
Utah	Salt Lake City
Vermont	Montpelier
Virginia	Richmond
Washington	Olympia
West Virginia	Charlestown
Wisconsin	Madison
Wyoming	Cheyenne

VIRGIN ISLANDS (British) Group of 36, West Indies.
Area: 153 sq. km (59 sq. mi.).
Population: 11,500.
Capital: Road Town.

VIRGIN ISLANDS (US) A territory near Puerto Rico in the West Indies.
Area: 344 sq. km (133 sq. mi.).
Population: 119,000.
Capital: Charlotte Amalie.

SOUTH AMERICA

ARGENTINA Republic lying on the east coast of South America.
Area: 2,766,890 sq. km (1,068,360 sq. mi.).
Population: 32,600,000.
Capital: Buenos Aires.

BOLIVIA Landlocked republic at the centre of South America.
Area: 1,093,500 sq. km (424,000 sq. mi.).
Population: 6,900,000.
Capital: La Paz (seat of government); Sucre (legal capital).

BRAZIL Republic, largest country of South America in both area and population.
Area: 8,512,000 sq. km (3,286,670 sq. mi.).
Population: 154,000,000.
Capital: Brasilia.

CHILE Republic lying on the western coast of South America.
Area: 757,000 sq. km (292,274, sq. mi.).
Population: 12,900,000.
Capital: Santiago.

COLOMBIA Republic of South America.
Area: 1,139,000 sq. km (440,000 sq. mi.).
Population: 31,800,000.
Capital: Bogota.

ECUADOR Republic of South America.
Area: 283,600 sq. km (109,500 sq. mi.).
Population: 10,500,000.
Capital: Quito.

FALKLAND ISLANDS British colony in the South Atlantic.
Area: 12,200 sq. km (4700 sq. mi.).
Population: 2000.
Capital: Stanley.

FRENCH GUIANA A French overseas department in north-east South America.
Area: 91,000 sq. km (35,000 sq. mi.).
Population: 92,000.
Capital: Cayenne.

GUYANA Republic of north-east South America, a member of the Commonwealth.
Area: 215,000 sq. km (83,000 sq. mi.).
Population: 770,000.
Capital: Georgetown.

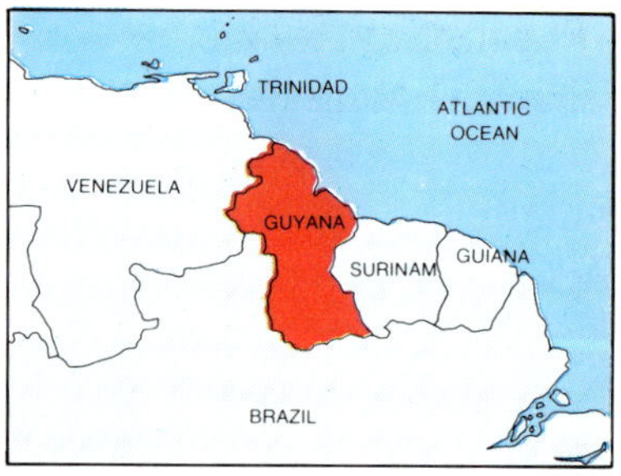

PARAGUAY Landlocked republic at the centre of South America.
Area: 406,700 sq. km (157,000 sq. mi.).
Population: 4,500,000.
Capital: Asunción.

PERU Republic lying on the western coast of South America.
Area: 1,285,000 sq. km (496,000 sq. mi.).
Population: 21,800,000.
Capital: Lima.

SURINAM Small republic of the north-east coast of South America.
Area: 163,300 sq. km (63,000 sq. mi.).
Population: 380,000.
Capital: Paramaribo.

URUGUAY Republic of South America.
Area: 176,200 sq. km (68,000 sq. mi.).
Population: 3,000,000.
Capital: Montevideo.

VENEZUELA Republic of South America.
Area: 912,000 sq. km (352,000 sq. mi.).
Population: 19,200,000.
Capital: Caracas.

OCEANIA

AUSTRALIA An independent Commonwealth member, occupying the continent of Australia and outlying islands.
Area: 7,686,800 sq. km (2,968,000 sq. mi.).
Population: 16,100,000.
Capital: Canberra.
States and territories include:

Australian Capital Territory
New South Wales
Northern Territory
South Australia
Western Australia
Queensland
Tasmania
Victoria.

COOK ISLANDS Self-governing territory of New Zealand in the South Pacific.
Area: 234 sq. mi (90 sq. mi.).
Population: 18,000.
Capital: Avarua.

FIJI Republic in south-west Pacific.
Area: 18,300 sq. km (7050 sq. mi.).
Population: 700,000.
Capital: Suva.

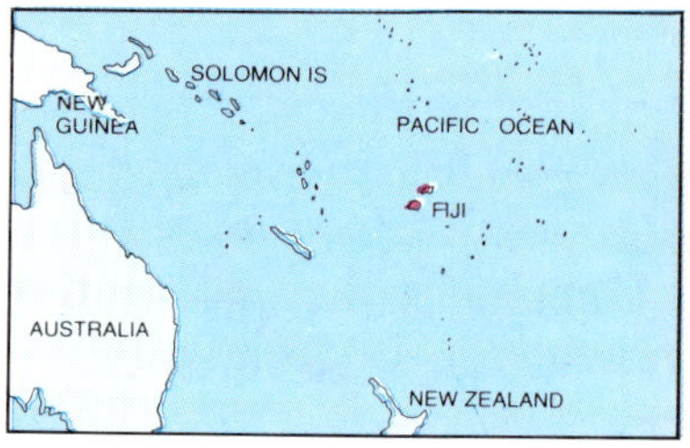

FRENCH POLYNESIA A French overseas department in the Eastern Pacific.
Area: 4000 sq. km (1550 sq. mi.).
Population: 166,000.
Capital: Papeete.

GUAM A territory of the United States in the Marianas archipelago in the North Pacific.
Area: 549 sq. km (212 sq. mi.).
Population: 99,000.
Capital: Agana.

KIRIBATI Island republic of the Central Pacific, a member of the Commonwealth.
Area: 930 sq. km (360 sq. mi.).
Population: 63,000.
Capital: Tarawa.

NAURU An island republic in the Western Pacific, with special status within the Commonwealth.
Area: 21 sq. km (8 sq. mi.).
Population: 8000.
Capital: Nauru.

NEW ZEALAND An independent member of the Commonwealth in the south-west Pacific.
Area: 268,000 sq. km (103,700 sq. mi.).
Population: 3,400,000.
Capital: Wellington.

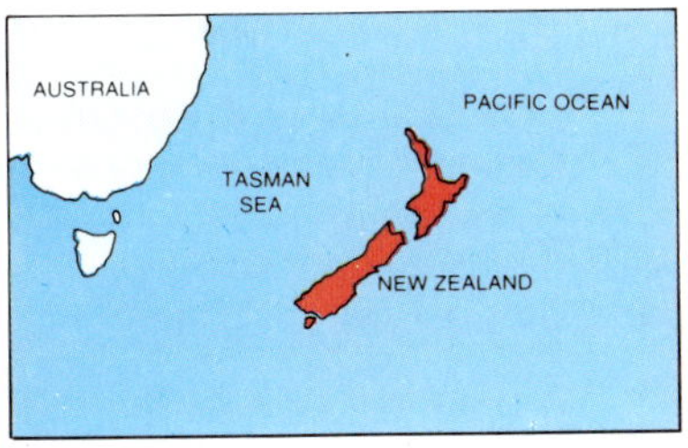

NIUE A self-governing territory of New Zealand in the Cook Islands, South Pacific.
Area: 260 sq. km (100 sq. mi.).
Population: 4000.
Capital: Alofi.

NORFOLK ISLAND An Australian territory in the south-west Pacific.
Area: 36 sq. km (14 sq. mi.).
Population: 2000.
Capital: Kingstown.

PACIFIC ISLANDS TRUST TERRITORY Group of islands, including the Marianas, Caroline and Marshall Islands, governed by the United States.
Area: 1780 sq. km (687 sq. mi.).
Population: 149,000.
Capital: Saipan.

PAPUA NEW GUINEA An independent Commonwealth state in the south-west Pacific.
Area: 461,700 sq. km (178,200 sq. mi.).
Population: 3,600,000.
Capital: Port Moresby.

PITCAIRN ISLAND British colony in the South Pacific.
Area: 5 sq. km (2 sq. mi.).
Population: 63.
Capital: Adamstown.

SAMOA, AMERICAN Group of eight islands in the South Pacific, governed by the United States.
Area: 197 sq. km (76 sq. mi.).
Population: 35,000.
Capital: Pago Pago.

SAMOA, WESTERN An independent Commonwealth member in the Pacific.
Area: 2900 sq. km (1090 sq. mi.).
Population: 200,000.
Capital: Apia.

SOLOMON ISLANDS An independent state, a member of the Commonwealth, in the south-west Pacific.
Area: 28,500 sq. km (11,000 sq. mi.).
Population: 300,000.
Capital: Honiara.

TONGA Island kingdom in the South Pacific within the Commonwealth.
Area: 700 sq. km (270 sq. mi.).
Population: 100,000.
Capital: Nuku'alofa.

TUVALU An independent member of the Commonwealth, a group of islands in the South Pacific.
Area: 8 sq. km (3 sq. mi.).
Population: 8,500.
Capital: Fongafale.

VANUATU Island republic in the south-west Pacific, a member of the Commonwealth.
Area: 14,800 sq. km (5700 sq. mi.).
Population: 136,000.
Capital: Port Vila.

WALLIS AND FUTUNA ISLANDS A French overseas territory in the south-west Pacific.
Area: 200 sq. km (77 sq. mi.).
Population: 9000.
Capital: Mata-Uta.

MAJOR WARS

Name	Date	Won by	Against
Abyssinian War	1935–1936	Italy	Abyssinia (Ethiopia)
American War of Independence	1775–1783	Thirteen Colonies	Britain
Austrian Succession, War of the	1740–1748	Austria, Hungary, Britain, Holland	Bavaria, France, Poland, Prussia, Sardinia, Saxony, Spain
Boer (South African) War	1899–1902	Britain	Boer Republics
Chinese-Japanese Wars	1894–1895	Japan	China
	1931–1933	Japan	China
	1937–1945	China	Japan
Civil War, American	1861–1865	23 Northern States (the Union)	11 Southern States (the Confederacy)
Civil War, English	1642–1646	Parliament	Charles I
Civil War, Nigerian	1967–1970	Federal government	Biafra
Civil War, Pakistan	1971	East Pakistan (Bangladesh) and India	West Pakistan
Civil War, Spanish	1936–1939	Junta de Defensa Nacional (Fascists)	Republican government
Crimean War	1853–1856	Britain, France, Sardinia, Turkey	Russia
Franco-Prussian War	1870–1871	Prussia and other German states	France
Hundred Years War	1337–1453	France	England
Iran-Iraq War	1980–1988	Neither side	—
Korean War	1950–1953	South Korea and United Nations forces	North Korea and Chinese forces
Mexican-American War	1846–1848	United States	Mexico
Napoleonic Wars	1792–1815	Austria, Britain, Prussia, Russia, Spain, Sweden	France
October War	1973	Ceasefire arranged by UN; fought by Israel against the Arab States of Egypt, Syria, Iraq, Sudan, Saudi Arabi, Lebanon	
Peloponnesian War	431–404 BC	Peloponnesian League – Sparta and allies	Athens
Punic Wars	264–146 BC	Rome	Carthage
Russo-Japanese War	1904–1905	Japan	Russia
Seven Years' War	1756–1763	Britain, Prussia, Hanover	Austria, France, Russia, Sweden
Seven Weeks' War	1866	Prussia, Italy	Austria, German states
Six-Day War	1967	Israel	Egypt, Syria, Jordan, Iraq
Spanish-American War	1898	United States	Spain
Spanish Succession, War of the	1701–1713	England, Austria, Prussia, the Netherlands	France, Bavaria, Cologne
Thirty Years War	1618–1648	France, Sweden, the German Protestant states	The Holy Roman Empire, Spain
Vietnam War	1957–1975	North Vietnam	South Vietnam, United States
War of 1812	1812–1814	United States	Britain
Wars of the Roses	1455–1485	House of Lancaster	House of York
World War I	1914–1918	Belgium, Britain and Empire, France, Italy, Japan, Russia, Serbia, United States	Austria-Hungary, Bulgaria, Germany, Ottoman Empire
World War II	1939–1945	Australia, Belgium, Britain, Canada, China, Denmark, France, Greece, Netherlands, New Zealand, Norway, Poland, Russia, South Africa, United States, Yugoslavia	Bulgaria, Finland, Germany, Hungary, Italy, Japan, Romania
Yom Kippur	1973	Israel	Egypt, Syria

THE UNITED NATIONS

The United Nations (UN) is an international organization that works for world peace and security, and for the betterment of mankind. More than 140 independent nations belong to the UN. Member countries send representatives to the UN headquarters in New York City. There are six major organs of the UN, which carry on the work of the organization at the headquarters. There are also a number of self-governing specialized agencies, such as the World Health Organization and the International Monetary Fund, that have a special relationship with the UN.

Principal Organs of the UN

General Assembly consists of all members, each having one vote. Most of work done in committees: (1) Political Security, (2) Economic and Financial, (3) Social, Humanitarian, and Cultural, (4) Trust and Non-Self-Governing Territories, (5) Administrative and Budgetary, (6) Legal.

Security Council consists of 15 members each with one vote. There are five permanent members – China, France, UK, USA, and USSR – the others being elected for two-year terms. Main object: maintenance of peace and security.

Economic and Social Council is responsible under General Assembly for carrying out functions of the UN with regard to international economic, social, cultural, educational, health, and related matters.

Trusteeship Council administers Trust Territories.

International Court of Justice composed of 15 judges (all different nationalities) elected by UN. Meets at The Hague.

The Secretariat is composed of the Secretary-General who is chief administrative officer of the UN and is appointed by the General Assembly, and an international staff.

Above: The symbol of the United Nations – a map of the world inside olive branches – signifies peace. It is shown here on the UN flag.

Left: The United Nations General Assembly has a huge auditorium where representatives from all the member countries can take part in the debates.

UNITED NATIONS MEMBER COUNTRIES

Country	Joined
Afghanistan	1946
Albania	1955
Algeria	1962
Angola	1976
Antigua and Barbuda	1981
Argentina	1945
Australia	1945
Austria	1955
Bahamas	1973
Bahrain	1971
Bangladesh	1974
Barbados	1966
Belgium	1945
Belize	1981
Benin	1969
Bhutan	1971
Bolivia	1945
Botswana	1966
Brazil	1945
Brunei	1984
Bulgaria	1955
Burkina Faso	1960
Burundi	1962
Byelorussian SSR	1945
Cambodia	1955
Cameroon	1960
Canada	1945
Cape Verde	1975
Central African Republic	1960
Chad	1960
Chile	1945
China	1945
Colombia	1945
Comoros	1975
Congo	1960
Costa Rica	1945
Cuba	1945
Cyprus	1960
Czechoslovakia	1945
Denmark	1945
Djibouti	1977
Dominica	1978
Dominican Republic	1945
Ecuador	1945
Egypt	1945
El Salvador	1945
Equatorial Guinea	1968
Ethiopia	1945
Fiji	1970
Finland	1955
France	1945
Gabon	1960
Gambia	1965

Country	Joined
Germany, East	1973
Germany, West	1973
Ghana	1957
Greece	1945
Grenada	1974
Guatemala	1945
Guinea	1958
Guinea-Bissau	1974
Guyana	1966
Haiti	1945
Honduras	1945
Hungary	1955
Iceland	1946
India	1945
Indonesia	1950
Iran	1945
Iraq	1945
Ireland, Rep. of	1955
Israel	1949
Italy	1955
Ivory Coast	1960
Jamaica	1962
Japan	1956
Jordan	1955
Kenya	1963
Kuwait	1963
Laos	1955
Lebanon	1945
Lesotho	1966
Liberia	1945
Libya	1955
Luxembourg	1945
Madagascar	1960
Malawi	1964
Malaysia	1957
Maldives, Rep. of	1965
Mali	1960
Malta	1964
Mauritania	1961
Mauritius	1968
Mexico	1945
Mongolian PR	1961
Morocco	1956
Mozambique	1975
Myanmar	1948
Nepal	1955
Netherlands	1945
New Zealand	1945
Nicaragua	1945
Niger	1960
Nigeria	1960
Norway	1945
Oman	1971
Pakistan	1947

Country	Joined
Panama	1945
Papua New Guinea	1975
Paraguay	1945
Peru	1945
Philippines	1945
Poland	1945
Portugal	1955
Qatar	1971
Romania	1955
Rwanda	1962
St Kitts–Nevis	1983
St Lucia	1979
St Vincent & the Grenadines	1980
São Tomé & Principe	1975
Saudi Arabia	1945
Senegal	1960
Seychelles	1976
Sierra Leone	1961
Singapore	1965
Solomon Islands	1978
Somali Republic	1960
South Africa	1945
Spain	1955
Sri Lanka	1955
Sudan	1956
Surinam	1975
Swaziland	1968
Sweden	1946
Syria	1945
Tanzania	1961
Thailand	1946
Togo	1960
Trinidad & Tobago	1962
Tunisia	1956
Turkey	1945
Uganda	1962
Ukrainian SSR	1945
USSR	1945
United Arab Emirates	1971
United Kingdom	1945
United States	1945
Uruguay	1945
Vanuatu	1981
Venezuela	1945
Vietnam	1976
Western Samoa	1976
Yemen Arab Republic	1947
Yemen PDR	1967
Yugoslavia	1945
Zaire	1960
Zambia	1964
Zimbabwe	1980

THE COMMONWEALTH OF NATIONS

This is a voluntary association of independent states. The Head of the Commonwealth is HM Queen Elizabeth II. Present members of the Commonwealth (with date of independence from British rule in brackets) are:

Antigua & Barbuda (1981), Australia (1901), Bahamas (1973), Bangladesh (from Pakistan, 1971), Barbados (1966), Belize (1981), Botswana (1966), Brunei (1984), Canada (1931), Cyprus (1960), Dominica (1978), *Fiji (1970), The Gambia (1965), Ghana (1957), Great Britain, Grenada (1974), Guyana (1966), India (1947), Jamaica (1962), Kenya (1963), Kiribati (1979), Lesotho (1966), Malawi (1964), Malaysia (1957), Maldives (1965), Malta (1964), Mauritius (1968), Nauru (1968), New Zealand (1907), Nigeria (1960), **Pakistan (1947), Papua New Guinea (1975), St Kitts-Nevis (1983), St Lucia (1979), St Vincent (1979), Seychelles (1976), Sierra Leone (1961), Singapore (1965), Solomon Islands (1978), Sri Lanka (1948), Swaziland (1968), Tanzania (1961), Tonga (1970), Trinidad & Tobago (1962), Tuvalu (1978), Uganda (1962), Vanuatu (1980), Western Samoa (1962), Zambia (1964), Zimbabwe (1980).

**Fiji's membership was suspended after the overthrow of the government in 1987 and the declaration of a republic.*
*** Pakistan left the Commonwealth in 1972, but rejoined in 1989.*

Above: Jefferson, author of the Declaration of Independence.

Above: Eisenhower, leader of the Allied Forces in World War II.

AMERICAN PRESIDENTS

President (party)	Term	President (party)	Term
1 George Washington (F)	1789–97	23 Benjamin Harrison (R)	1889–93
2 John Adams (F)	1797–1801	24 Grover Cleveland (D)	1893–97
3 Thomas Jefferson (DR)	1801–09	25 William McKinley† (R)	1897–1901
4 James Madison (DR)	1809–17	26 Theodore Roosevelt (R)	1901–09
5 James Monroe (DR)	1817–25	27 William H. Taft (R)	1909–13
6 John Quincy Adams (DR)	1825–29	28 Woodrow Wilson (D)	1913–21
7 Andrew Jackson (D)	1829–37	29 Warren G. Harding* (R)	1921–23
8 Martin Van Buren (D)	1837–41	30 Calvin Coolidge (R)	1923–29
9 William H. Harrison* (W)	1841	31 Herbert C. Hoover (R)	1929–33
10 John Tyler (W)	1841–45	32 Franklin D. Roosevelt* (D)	1933–45
11 James K. Polk (D)	1845–49	33 Harry S. Truman (D)	1945–53
12 Zachary Taylor* (W)	1849–50	34 Dwight D. Eisenhower (R)	1953–61
13 Millard Fillmore (W)	1850–53	35 John F. Kennedy† (D)	1961–63
14 Franklin Pierce (D)	1853–57	36 Lyndon B. Johnson (D)	1963–69
15 James Buchanan (D)	1857–61	37 Richard M. Nixon (R)	1969–74
16 Abraham Lincoln† (R)	1861–65	38 Gerald R. Ford (R)	1974–77
17 Andrew Johnson (U)	1865–69	39 James E. Carter (D)	1977–80
18 Ulysses S. Grant (R)	1869–77	40 Ronald Reagan (R)	1980–89
19 Rutherford B. Hayes (R)	1877–81	41 George Bush (R)	1989–
20 James A. Garfield† (R)	1881		
21 Chester A. Arthur (R)	1881–85		
22 Grover Cleveland (D)	1885–89		

*Died in office †Assassinated in office
F = Federalist. DR = Democratic–Republican.
D = Democratic. W = Whig. R = Republican. U = Union.

RULERS OF ENGLAND

Saxons	
Egbert	827–839
Ethelwulf	839–858
Ethelbald	858–860
Ethelbert	860–866
Ethelred I	866–871
Alfred the Great	871–899
Edward the Elder	899–924
Athelstan	924–939
Edmund	939–946
Edred	946–955
Edwy	955–959
Edgar	959–975
Edward the Martyr	975–978
Ethelred I the Unready	978–1016
Edmund Ironside	1016
Danes	
Canute	1016–1035
Harold I Harefoot	1035–1040
Hardicanute	1040–1042
Saxons	
Edward the Confessor	1042–1066
Harold II	1066
House of Normandy	
William I the Conqueror	1066–1087
William II	1087–1100
Henry I	1100–1135
Stephen	1135–1154
House of Plantagenet	
Henry II	1154–1189
Richard I	1189–1199
John	1199–1216
Henry III	1216–1272
Edward I	1272–1307
Edward II	1307–1327
Edward III	1327–1377
Richard II	1377–1399
House of Lancaster	
Henry IV	1399–1413
Henry V	1413–1422
Henry VI	1422–1461
House of York	
Edward IV	1461–1483
Edward V	1483
Richard III	1483–1485
House of Tudor	
Henry VII	1485–1509
Henry VIII	1509–1547
Edward VI	1547–1553
Mary I	1553–1558
Elizabeth I	1558–1603

RULERS OF SCOTLAND

Malcolm II	1005–1034
Duncan I	1034–1040
Macbeth (usurper)	1040–1057
Malcolm III Canmore	1057–1093
Donald Bane	1093–1094
Duncan II	1094
Donald Bane (restored)	1094–1097
Edgar	1097–1107
Alexander I	1107–1124
David I	1124–1153
Malcolm IV	1153–1165
William the Lion	1165–1214
Alexander II	1214–1249
Alexander III	1249–1286
Margaret of Norway	1286–1290
(*Interregnum* 1290–1292)	
John Balliol	1292–1296
(*Interregnum* 1296–1306)	
Robert I (Bruce)	1306–1329
David II	1329–1371
House of Stuart	
Robert II	1371–1390
Robert III	1390–1406
James I	1406–1437
James II	1437–1460
James III	1460–1488
James IV	1488–1513
James V	1513–1542
Mary	1542–1567
James VI (I of Great Britain)	1567–1625

RULERS OF BRITAIN

House of Stuart	
James I	1603–1625
Charles I	1625–1649
(*Commonwealth* 1649–1659)	
Charles II	1660–1685
James II	1685–1688
William III } jointly	1689–1702
Mary II } jointly	1689–1694
Anne	1702–1714
House of Hanover	
George I	1714–1727
George II	1727–1760
George III	1760–1820
George IV	1820–1830
William IV	1830–1837
Victoria	1837–1901
House of Saxe-Coburg	
Edward VII	1901–1910
House of Windsor	
George V	1910–1936
Edward VIII	1936
George VI	1936–1952
Elizabeth II	1952–

BRITISH PRIME MINISTERS

Sir Robert Walpole (W)	1721–1742
Earl of Wilmington (W)	1742–1743
Henry Pelham (W)	1743–1754
Duke of Newcastle (W)	1754–1756
Duke of Devonshire (W)	1756–1757
Duke of Newcastle (W)	1757–1762
Earl of Bute (T)	1762–1763
George Grenville (W)	1763–1765
Marquess of Rockingham (W)	1765–1766
Earl of Chatham (W)	1766–1767
Duke of Grafton (W)	1767–1770
Lord North (T)	1770–1782
Marquess of Rockingham (W)	1782
Earl of Shelbourne (W)	1782–1783
Duke of Portland (Cln)	1783
William Pitt (T)	1783–1801
Henry Addington (T)	1801–1804
William Pitt (T)	1804–1806
Lord Grenville (W)	1806–1807
Duke of Portland (T)	1807–1809
Spencer Perceval (T)	1809–1812
Earl of Liverpool (T)	1812–1827
George Canning (T)	1827
Viscount Goderich (T)	1827–1828
Duke of Wellington (T)	1828–1830
Earl Grey (W)	1830–1834
Viscount Melbourne (W)	1834
Sir Robert Peel (T)	1834–1835
Viscount Melbourne (W)	1835–1841
Sir Robert Peel (T)	1841–1846
Lord John Russell (W)	1846–1852
Earl of Derby (T)	1852
Earl of Aberdeen (P)	1852–1855
Viscount Palmerston (L)	1855–1858
Earl of Derby (C)	1858–1859
Viscount Palmerston (L)	1859–1865
Earl Russell (L)	1865–1866
Earl of Derby (C)	1866–1868
Benjamin Disraeli (C)	1868
William Gladstone (L)	1868–1874
Benjamin Disraeli (C)	1874–1880
William Gladstone (L)	1880–1885
Marquess of Salisbury (C)	1885–1886
William Gladstone (L)	1886
Marquess of Salisbury (C)	1886–1892
William Gladstone (L)	1892–1894
Earl of Rosebery (L)	1894–1895
Marquess of Salisbury (C)	1895–1902
Arthur Balfour (C)	1902–1905
Sir Henry Campbell-Bannerman (L)	1905–1908
Herbert Asquith (L)	1908–1915
Herbert Asquith (Cln)	1915–1916
David Lloyd-George (Cln)	1916–1922
Andrew Bonar Law (C)	1922–1923
Stanley Baldwin (C)	1923–1924
James Ramsay MacDonald (Lab)	1924
Stanley Baldwin (C)	1924–1929
James Ramsay MacDonald (Lab)	1929–1931
James Ramsay MacDonald (Cln)	1931–1935
Stanley Baldwin (Cln)	1935–1937
Neville Chamberlain (Cln)	1937–1940
Winston Churchill (Cln)	1940–1945
Winston Churchill (C)	1945
Clement Attlee (Lab)	1945–1951
Sir Winston Churchill (C)	1951–1955
Sir Anthony Eden (C)	1955–1957
Harold Macmillan (C)	1957–1963
Sir Alec Douglas-Home (C)	1963–1964
Harold Wilson (Lab)	1964–1970
Edward Heath (C)	1970–1974
Harold Wilson (Lab)	1974–1976
James Callaghan (Lab)	1976–1979
Margaret Thatcher (C)	1979–

W = Whig. T = Tory. Cln = Coalition. P = Peelite.
L = Liberal. C = Conservative. Lab = Labour.

TSARS OF RUSSIA

Ivan III the Great	1462–1505
Basil III	1505–1533
Ivan IV the Terrible	1533–1584
Fëdor I	1584–1598
Boris Godunov	1598–1605
Fëdor II	1605
Demetrius	1605–1606
Basil (IV) Shuiski	1606–1610
[Interregnum, 1610–1613]	
Michael Romanov	1613–1645
Alexis	1645–1676
Fëdor III	1676–1682
Ivan V and Peter the Great	1682–1689
Peter the Great	1689–1725
Catherine I	1725–1727
Peter II	1727–1730
Anna	1730–1740
Ivan VI	1740–1741
Elizabeth	1741–1762
Peter III	1762
Catherine II the Great	1762–1796
Paul I	1796–1801
Alexander I	1801–1825
Nicholas I	1825–1855
Alexander II	1855–1881
Alexander III	1881–1894
Nicholas II	1894–1917

ANIMAL SPEED RECORDS

	km/h	mph
Spine-tailed swift	170	106
Sailfish	109	68
Cheetah	105	65
Pronghorn antelope	97	60
Racing pigeon	97	60
Lion	80	50
Gazelle	80	50
Hare	72	45
Zebra	64	40
Racehorse	64	40
Shark	64	40
Greyhound	63	39
Rabbit	56	35
Giraffe	51	32
Grizzly bear	48	30
Cat	48	30
Elephant	40	25
Sealion	40	25
Human	32	20
Black mamba	32	20
Bee	18	11
Pig	18	11
Chicken	14	9
Spider	1·88	1·17
Tortoise	0·8	0·5
Snail	0·05	0·03

TRADITIONAL ANNIVERSARY NAMES

It is sometimes the custom to give married couples gifts on their wedding anniversary that correspond to the traditional anniversary name.

Year	Name
1	paper
2	cotton
3	leather
4	fruit, flowers
5	wood
6	iron, sugar
7	wool, copper
8	bronze
9	pottery
10	tin, aluminium
11	steel
12	silk, fine linen
13	lace
14	ivory
15	crystal
20	china
25	silver
30	pearl
35	coral
40	ruby
45	sapphire
50	golden
55	emerald
60	diamond
75	platinum

SI UNITS

Basic units	Symbol	Measurement
metre	m	length
kilogram	kg	mass
second	s	time
ampere	A	electric current
kelvin	K	thermodynamic temperature
mole	mol	amount of substance
candela	cd	luminous intensity
Derived units*		
hertz	Hz	frequency
newton	N	force
pascal	Pa	pressure, stress
joule	J	energy, work, quantity of heat
watt	W	power, radiant flux
coulomb	C	electric charge, quantity of electricity
volt	V	electric potential, potential difference, emf
farad	F	capacitance
ohm	Ω	electric resistance
siemens	S	conductance
weber	Wb	magnetic flux
tesla	T	magnetic flux density
henry	H	inductance
lumen	lm	luminous flux
lux	lx	illuminance
Supplementary units		
radian	rad	plane angle
steradian	sr	solid angle

*These have special names; there are other derived units such as m^2 (area), mol/m^3 (concentration), m^3/l_2 (specific volume), etc.

PRINCIPAL LANGUAGES OF THE WORLD

Language	Speakers (millions)	Where spoken
Mandarin	575	China (north and east central)
English	360	UK and Commonwealth, Ireland, South Africa, USA
Hindi	170	India (north central)
Great Russian	170	USSR
Spanish	140	Spain, Central and South America (not Brazil)
German	100	Germany, Austria, Switzerland
Japanese	100	Japan
Bengali	90	Bangladesh, India (east)
Arabic	80	Middle East, North Africa
French	80	France and French Community, Canada
Malay/Indonesian*	80	Malaysia, Indonesia
Portuguese	80	Portugal, Brazil
Urdu	80	Pakistan
Italian	60	Italy
Cantonese	50	China (south)
Min	50	China (south and east)
Wu	50	China (east)
Javanese	45	Java
Telugu	45	India (south-east)
Ukrainian	41	USSR
Bihar	40	India (north-east)
Marathi	40	India (west)
Tamil	40	India (south-east), Sri Lanka
Korean	37	Korea
Punjabi	35	India (north)
Polish	33	Poland
Turkish	28	Turkey

*Officially called *Bahasa Indonesia* in Indonesia.

EARTH EXTREMES

Hottest shade temperature recorded: 57·7°C (136·4°F) at Al 'Aziziyah, Libya, on 13.9.22

Coldest temperature recorded: −88·3°C (−126·9°F) at Vostok, Antarctica, on 24.8.60

Highest annual average rainfall: 11,680 mm (460 in) at Mt Waialeale, Hawaii

Most rain in one month: 9300 mm (366.14 in) at Cherrapunji, India, in July 1861

Driest place on earth: Arica, Chile, averages 0·76 mm (0·03 in) of rain per year

Most snow in one year: 31,102 mm (1224·5 in) on Mt Rainier, Washington State, USA, 1971–2

Greatest ocean depth: 11,033 m (36,198 ft) Mariana Trench, Pacific Ocean

Greatest tides: 16·3 m (53·5 ft) Bay of Fundy, Nova Scotia, Canada

Strongest surface wind recorded: 372 km/h (231 mph) at Mt Washington, N.H., USA, in 1934

Deepest gorge: 2400 m (7874 ft) Hells Canyon, Idaho, USA

Longest gorge: 349 km (217 mi) Grand Canyon, Arizona, USA

Highest navigated lake: Titicaca, Peru/Bolivia, 3810 m (12,500 ft) above sea level

Deepest lake: Baikal, Siberia, USSR, 1940 m (6365 ft)

DAYS AND MONTHS

Day/Month	Named after
Sunday	the Sun
Monday	the Moon
Tuesday	Tiu, Norse god of war
Wednesday	Woden, Anglo-Saxon chief of gods
Thursday	Thor, Norse god of thunder
Friday	Frigg, Norse goddess
Saturday	Saturn, Roman god of harvests
January	Janus, Roman god of doors and gates
February	Februa, Roman period of purification
March	Mars, Roman god of war
April	aperire, Latin 'to open'
May	Maia, Roman goddess of spring and growth
June	Juno, Roman goddess of marriage
July	Julius Caesar
August	Augustus, first emperor of Rome
September	septem, Latin 'seven'
October	octo, Latin 'eight'
November	novem, Latin 'nine'
December	decem, latin 'ten'

BIRTHSTONES

Month	Hebrew	Present day
January	garnet	garnet
February	amethyst	amethyst
March	jasper	acquamarine bloodstone
April	sapphire	diamond
May	chalcedony carnelian agate	emerald chrysoprase
June	emerald	pearl moonstone alexandrite
July	onyx	ruby carnelian
August	carnelian	peridot sardonyx
September	chrysolite	sapphire lapis lazuli
October	aquamarine beryl	opal tourmaline
November	topaz	topaz
December	ruby	turquoise zircon

Above: Mackenzie discovered the largest river system in Canada.

Above: Pizzaro conquered the Inca empire in Peru.

Above: Balboa first sighted the Pacific Ocean in 1513.

EXPLORATION AND DISCOVERY

Place	Achievement	Explorer or discoverer	Date
World	circumnavigated	Ferdinand Magellan (Port. for Sp.)	1519–21
Pacific Ocean	discovered	Vasco Núñez de Balboa (Sp.)	1513
Africa			
River Congo (mouth)	discovered	Diogo Cão (Port.)	c. 1483
Cape of Good Hope	sailed round	Bartolomeu Diaz (Port.)	1488
River Niger	explored	Mungo Park (GB)	1795
River Zambezi	discovered	David Livingstone (GB)	1851
Sudan	explored	Heinrich Barth (Germ. for GB)	1852–5
Victoria Falls	discovered	Livingstone	1855
Lake Tanganyika	discovered	Richard Burton & John Speke (GB)	1858
River Congo	traced	Sir Henry Stanley (GB)	1877
Asia			
China	visited	Marco Polo (Ital.)	c. 1272
India (Cape route)	visited	Vasco da Gama (Port.)	1498
Japan	visited	St Francis-Xavier (Sp.)	1549
China	explored	Ferdinand Richthofen (Germ.)	1868
North America			
North America	discovered	Leif Ericsson (Norse)	c. 1000
West Indies	discovered	Christopher Columbus (Ital. for Sp.)	1492
Newfoundland	discovered	John Cabot (Ital. for Eng.)	1497
Mexico	conquered	Hernando Cortés (Sp.)	1519–21
St Lawrence River	explored	Jacques Cartier (Fr.)	1534–6
Mississippi River	discovered	Hernando de Soto (Sp.)	1541
Canadian interior	explored	Samuel de Champlain (Fr.)	1603–9
Hudson Bay	discovered	Henry Hudson (Eng.)	1610
Alaska	discovered	Vitus Bering (Dan. for Russ.)	1728
South America			
South America	visited	Columbus	1498
Venezuela	explored	Alonso de Ojeda (Sp.)	1499
Brazil	discovered	Pedro Alvares Cabral (Port.)	1500
Tierra del Fuego	discovered	Magellan	1520
Peru	explored	Francisco Pizarro (Sp.)	1530–8
River Amazon	explored	Francisco de Orellana (Sp.)	1541
Cape Horn	discovered	Willem Schouten (Dut.)	1616
Australasia, Polar regions, etc			
Greenland	visited	Eric the Red (Norse)	c. 982
Spitsbergen	discovered	Willem Barents (Dut.)	1596
Australia	visited	Abel Tasman (Dut.)	1642
New Zealand	sighted	Tasman	1642
New Zealand	visited	James Cook (GB)	1769
Antarctica	sighted	Nathaniel Palmer (US)	1820
Antarctica	circumnavigated	Fabian von Bellingshausen (Russ.)	1819–21
Australian interior	explored	Charles Sturt (GB)	1828
Antarctica	explored	Charles Wilkes (US)	1838–42
Australia	crossed (S–N)	Robert Burke (Ir.) & William Wills (GB)	1860–1
Greenland	explored	Fridtjof Nansen (Nor.)	1888
North Pole	reached	Robert Peary (US)	1909
South Pole	reached	Roald Amundsen (Nor.)	1911
Antarctica	crossed	Sir Vivian Fuchs (GB)	1957–8

GEOLOGICAL TIME SCALE

Eras	Periods	Epochs	Millions of years ago	Lifeforms
CENOZOIC	Quaternary	Holocene (recent)	0·01	(End of ice age)
		Pleistocene	2	(Ice ages) Mammoths, woolly rhinoceroses. Development of modern human beings
	Tertiary	Pliocene	7	Mammals spread; earliest human creatures
		Miocene	26	Whales and apes
		Oligocene	38	Modern types of mammals
		Eocene	54	First horses and elephants
		Palaeocene	64	Early mammals
MESOZOIC	Cretaceous		136	End of dinosaurs; flowering plants spread
	Jurassic		195	Giant dinosaurs; first birds
	Triassic			Small dinosaurs; first mammals
PALAEOZOIC	Permian		280	Rapid increase in reptiles
	Carboniferous (Pennsylvanian and Mississippian)		345	Forests formed coal; first reptiles; first insects
	Devonian		410	First forests and land animals, amphibians. Age of fishes.
	Silurian		440	First land plants. First jawed fishes
	Ordovician		530	First vertebrates – armoured fish – appear in the sea
	Cambrian		570	Fossils abundant in rocks. All major groups of invertebrates represented
PRE-CAMBRIAN	Proterozoic		1,850	Sea animals without backbones; seaweeds
	Archaeozoic			First primitive plants and animals
	Azoic		4,000 about 4,500	(Earliest known rocks) (Earth formed)

LONGEST RIVERS

	km	mi
Nile (Africa)	6670	4145
Amazon (S America)	6437	4000
Chang Jiang (China)	6380	3964
Mississippi–Missouri–Red Rock (N America)	6231	3872
Ob-Irtysh (USSR)	5150	3200
Huang He (China)	4672	2903
Zaire* (Africa)	4828	3000
Lena (USSR)	4828	3000
Amur (Asia)	4506	2800
Yenisey (USSR)	4506	2800
Mekong (SE Asia)	4184	2600
Niger (Africa)	4000	2486

*Formerly Congo River

LARGEST ISLANDS

	sq km	sq mi
Greenland (N Atlantic)	2,175,000	840,050
New Guinea (SW Pacific)	794,090	306,600
Borneo (SW Pacific)	751,078	289,993
Madagascar (Indian Ocean)	587,041	226,670
Baffin I. (Canadian Arctic)	476,066	183,810
Sumatra (Indian Ocean)	431,982	166,789
Great Britain (N Atlantic)	229,522	88,619
Honshu (NW Pacific)	226,087	87,293
Ellesmere (Canadian Arctic)	198,393	76,600
Victoria I. (Canadian Arctic)	192,695	74,400

LARGEST LAKES

	sq km	sq mi
Caspian Sea (USSR/Iran)	438,695	169,390
Superior (USA/Canada)	82,409	31,820
Victoria (Africa)	69,484	26,828
Aral (USSR)	67,770	26,166
Huron (USA/Canada)	59,570	23,000
Michigan (USA)	58,016	22,400
Tanganyika (Africa)	31,999	12,355
Great Bear (Canada)	31,598	12,200
Baikal (USSR)	31,499	12,162
Malawi* (Africa)	28,490	11,000

*Also called Lake Nyasa

MAJOR WATERFALLS

Highest	m	ft
Angel Falls (Venezuela)	979	3212
Yosemite Falls (California)	739	2425
Mardals Fossen (Norway)	655	2149
Greatest Volume	**m^3/sec**	**ft^3/sec**
Guaira (Brazil/Paraguay)	13,300	470,000
Niagara (N America)	6000	212,200

HIGHEST MOUNTAINS

Asia	m	ft
Everest (Himalaya–Nepal/Tibet)	8848	29,028
K2 Godwin Austen (Pakistan/India)	8611	28,250
Kanchenjunga (Himalaya–Nepal/Sikkim)	8579	28,146
Makalu (Himalaya–Nepal/Tibet)	8470	27,790
Dhaulagiri (Himalaya–Nepal)	8172	26,810
Nanga Parbat (Himalaya–India)	8126	26,660
Annapurna (Himalaya–Nepal)	8075	26,492
Gasherbrum (Karakoram–India)	8068	26,470
Gosainthan (Himalaya–Tibet)	8013	26,291
Nanda Devi (Himalaya–India)	7817	25,645
South America		
Aconcagua (Andes–Argentina)	6960	22,835
North America		
McKinley (Alaska–USA)	6194	20,322
Africa		
Kilimanjaro (volcanic–Tanzania)	5895	19,341
Europe		
Elbruz (Caucasus–USSR)	5633	18,481
Mont Blanc (Alps–France)	4810	15,781
Antarctica		
Vinson Massif	5139	16,860
Australasia		
Jaya (New Guinea)	5029	16,500

OCEANS

	sq km	sq mi
Pacific	181,000,000	70,000,000
Atlantic	106,000,000	41,000,000
Indian	73,490,000	28,375,000
Arctic	14,350,000	5,541,000

Above: Large waterfalls are awesome sights.

SEVEN WONDERS OF THE WORLD*

*Originally compiled by Antipater of Sidon, a Greek poet, in the 100s BC.

Pyramids of Egypt Oldest and only surviving 'wonder'. Built in the 2000s BC as royal tombs, about 80 are still standing. The largest, the Great Pyramid of Cheops, at el-Gizeh, was 147 metres (482 feet) high when new.

Hanging Gardens of Babylon Terraced gardens adjoining Nebuchadnezzar's palace said to rise from 23 to over 90 metres (75 to 295 feet). Supposedly built by the king about 600 BC to please his wife, a princess from the mountains, but they are also associated with the Assyrian Queen Semiramis.

Statue of Zeus at Olympia Carved by Phidias, the 12-metre (39-foot) statue marked the site of the original Olympic Games in the 400s BC. It was constructed of ivory and gold, and showed Zeus (Jupiter) on his throne.

Temple of Artemis (Diana) at Ephesus Constructed of Parian marble and more than 122 metres (400 feet) long with over 100 columns 18 metres (59 feet) high, it was begun about 350 BC and took some 120 years to build. Destroyed by the Goths in AD 262.

Mausoleum at Halicarnassus Erected by Queen Artemisia in memory of her husband King Mausolus of Caria (in Asia Minor), who died 353 BC. It stood 43 metres (141 feet) high. The only remains are a few pieces in the British Museum and the word 'mausoleum' in the English language.

Colossus of Rhodes Gigantic bronze statue of sun-god Helios (or Apollo); stood about 36 metres (118 feet) high, dominating the harbour entrance at Rhodes. The sculptor Chares supposedly laboured for 12 years before he completed it in 280 BC. It was destroyed by an earthquake in 244 BC.

Pharos of Alexandria Marble lighthouse and watchtower built about 270 BC on the island of Pharos in Alexandria's harbour. Possibly standing 122 metres (400 feet) high, it was destroyed by an earthquake in 1375.

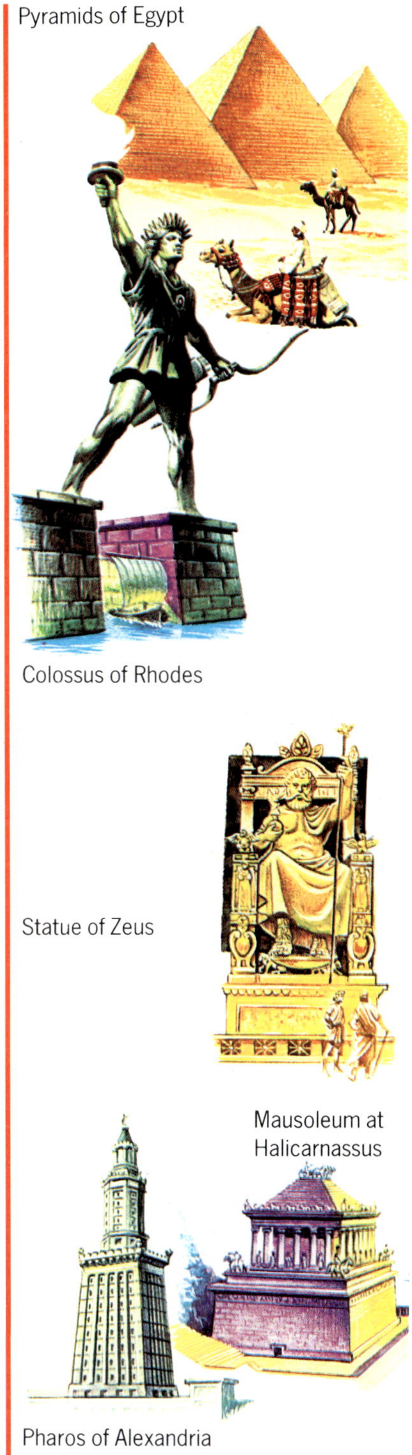

Above: Some of the Seven Wonders of the World as they may have looked. Only the Egyptian pyramids have survived.

INDEX

Figures in *italics* indicate pictures or information in picture captions

T

U

ACKNOWLEDGEMENTS

The publishers wish to thank the following for supplying photographs for this book:

Page 6 National Optical Astronomy; 9 Royal Observatory, Edinburgh; 14 NASA; 16 NASA; 17 NASA; 18 NASA; 21 Science Museum (top left) Max Planck Institute of Radio Astronomy (bottom left) Ian Ridpath (bottom right); 25 NHPA/S.Dalton; 27 NHPA/J.Shaw; 30 NHPA/J.Shaw; 44 Zefa; 49 Terence Lambert; 57 Bruce Coleman; 54 IMITOR; 61 French National Tourist Board; 62 Michael Holford; 63 Associated Press; 64 British Museum; 66 ZEFA; 69 British Museum; 70 Bridgeman Art Library; 73 Michael Holford; 74 British Museum (left) Michael Holford (right); 75 National Maritime Museum (left) Michael Holford (right); 79 Mary Evans Picture Library (top) Bridgeman Art Library (bottom); 80 National Army Museum; 82 Camera Press (top) Hulton-Deutsch Collection (bottom); 84 Camera Press; 85 ZEFA (top) British Red Cross (bottom); 86 Associated Press; 87 M.A.R.S.; 91 Peter Newark's Pictures (top) The Mansell Collection (bottom); 93 Popperfoto; 95 ZEFA (left) Press Association (right); 97 The Mansell Collection; 98 Hulton-Deutsch Collection (left) Novosti Press Agency (right); 100 National Portrait Gallery; 101 National Portrait Gallery; 102 Narodni Gallerie, Prague (top) ZEFA (bottom); 105 Stedelyk Museum (top) Courtesy Petersburg Press (bottom); 106 Bulloz/Petit Palais, Paris (left) A.C.Cooper/Victoria & Albert Museum; 107 Bridgeman Art Library; 108 Rijksmuseum-Stichting, Amsterdam (right) Michael Holford (left); 109 Michael Holford (top) Institute of Chicago (left) Tate Gallery (right); 110 Sonia Halliday Photographs (top) SCALA (bottom left) ZEFA (right); 111 ZEFA (top) Collection of the Art Institute of Chicago for the Civic Centre (bottom); 112 Lally St. Muir; 113 Michael Holford; 114 National Trust (left) ZEFA (right); 115 ZEFA; 116 SCALA; 117 Mary Evans Picture Library (left) National Portrait Gallery (right); 119 French Institute; 121 Japanese Tourist Office; 122 Michael Holford (left) Italian Tourist Board (right); 123 Bildarchiv Preussischer Kulturbesitz; 125 Popperfoto; 126 Zoe Dominic; 127 EMI; 128 ZEFA; 129 Frank Spooner; 130 Science Museum (left) Mary Evans Picture Library (right); 131 National Film Archive (top) ZEFA (bottom); 132 National Film Archive (left) Kobal (right); 133 Supersport Photos; 134 Turkish Tourist Board; 135 ZEFA (top) British Museum (middle); 136 ZEFA; 140 Darlington Glass; 151 Casio (top) Ferranti (bottom); 152 Hughes Aircraft Co (top) ZEFA (bottom); 159 ZEFA; 160 Derby Museum & Art Gallery; 161 ZEFA; 166 P.&G.Bowater; 168 Design Council; 169 Pat Morris (left) Louisiana Tourist Office (right); 171 JCB; 176 ZEFA; 177 Rowntree Mackintosh; 189 National Maritime Museum; 190 Ministry of Defence; 195 Science Museum (middle) ZEFA (bottom); 199 V.W. Press Office; 204 British Museum; 206 Mary Evans Picture Library (top) Supersport Photos (bottom); 207 Ilford; 208 Transport & General Workers Union; 209 National Maritime Museum; 213 Sony (UK) Ltd; 216 The Mansell Collection; 218 Gene Cox (top) Middlesex Hospital (middle); 221 ZEFA; 226 Gene Cox; 227 Panos Pictures; 228 Mary Evans Picture Library; 229 Siemens Ltd; 231 Mary Evans Picture Library (middle) ZEFA (bottom); 236 NASA; 238 ZEFA (top) R.I.Lewis Smith (middle) Satour (bottom); 239 ZEFA (top) U.S. Travel (bottom); 240 Bruce Coleman; 244 ZEFA; 245 ZEFA (top) Sonia Halliday Photographs (bottom); 246 Supersport Photos; 247 ZEFA; 248 Popperfoto (top) Mary Evans Picture Library (bottom); 249 ZEFA; 250 Mary Evans Picture Library; 251 ZEFA (top) Vision International (bottom); 254 Mary Evans Picture Library; 256 British Red Cross (top) ZEFA (bottom); 257 Mary Evans Picture Library; 258 ZEFA; 259 Zimbabwe Tourist Office; 260 ZEFA; 262 ZEFA; 263 Trinidad Tourist Board; 265 ZEFA; 266 ZEFA; 267 India Tourist Office; 271 ZEFA; 273 ZEFA; 274 ZEFA; 275 Louise Wright (top) ZEFA (middle); 276 Camera Press; 278 ZEFA; 279 ZEFA; 280 B. J. Cruickshank (left) Swiss National Tourist Office (right); 282 Dennis Gilbert (top) Bart Hofteester (bottom); 285 Vidocq Photo Library; 301 United Nations; 308 The Mansell Collection; 310 U.S. Travel.

Illustrators include: Graham Allen, Sue Barclay, Russell Barnett, Owain Bell, Mark Bergin, Jim Channel, Peter Chesterton, Jeane Colville, Gill Elsbury, Chris Forsey, John Francis, Jeremy Gower, Richard Hook, Ian Jackson, Ron Jonson, Chris Lyon, Andrew Macdonald, Kevin Maddison, Alan Male, Janos Marffy, Ralph Orme, Roger Payne, Mike Saunders, John Scorey, Sue Sharpes, Phil Weare and David Wright.